CRYPTOCURRENCIES AND CRYPTOASSETS

REGULATORY AND LEGAL ISSUES

CRYPTOCURRENCIES AND CRYPTOASSETS

REGULATORY AND LEGAL ISSUES

ANDREW HAYNES AND PETER YEOH

informa law
from Routledge

First published 2020
by Informa Law from Routledge
2 Park Square, Milton Park, Abingdon, Oxon OX14 4RN

and by Informa Law from Routledge
52 Vanderbilt Avenue, New York, NY 10017

Informa Law from Routledge is an imprint of the Taylor & Francis Group, an informa business

© 2020 Andrew Haynes and Peter Yeoh

The right of Andrew Haynes and Peter Yeoh to be identified as authors of this work has been asserted by them in accordance with sections 77 and 78 of the Copyright, Designs and Patents Act 1988.

All rights reserved. No part of this book may be reprinted or reproduced or utilised in any form or by any electronic, mechanical, or other means, now known or hereafter invented, including photocopying and recording, or in any information storage or retrieval system, without permission in writing from the publishers.

Trademark notice: Product or corporate names may be trademarks or registered trademarks, and are used only for identification and explanation without intent to infringe.

British Library Cataloguing in Publication Data
A catalogue record for this book is available from the British Library

Library of Congress Cataloging-in-Publication Data
Names: Haynes, Andrew, 1953– author. | Yeoh, Peter, author.
Title: Cryptocurrencies and cryptoassets : regulatory and legal issues /
    Andrew Haynes and Peter Yeoh.
Description: Abingdon, Oxon ; New York, NY : Informa Law from Routledge, 2020. |
    Includes bibliographical references and index.
Identifiers: LCCN 2019059794 (print) | LCCN 2019059795 (ebook) | ISBN 9780367472740
    (hardback) | ISBN 9780367486365 (paperback) | ISBN 9781003034599 (ebook)
Subjects: LCSH: Cryptocurrencies—Law and legislation.
Classification: LCC K4433 . H39 2020 (print) | LCC K4433 (ebook) | DDC 343/.032—dc23
LC record available at https://lccn.loc.gov/2019059794
LC ebook record available at https://lccn.loc.gov/2019059795

ISBN: 978-0-367-47274-0 (hbk)
ISBN: 978-0-367-48636-5 (pbk)
ISBN: 978-1-003-03459-9 (ebk)

Typeset in Times New Roman
by Swales & Willis, Exeter, Devon, UK

CONTENTS

Table of Cases	ix
Table of Statutes	xi
Table of Regulations	xiv
List of Abbreviations	xvi

CHAPTER 1	INTRODUCTION AND OVERVIEW	1
CHAPTER 2	CRYPTOCURRENCIES AND ASSETS, OPPORTUNITIES AND RISKS	7

2.1 Introduction 7
2.2 Cryptocurrencies and blockchain 10
2.3 Price variations relative to other geographic areas 16
2.4 Price variations relative to fiat currencies 17
2.5 Black-Scholes 17
2.6 Cryptoassets 18
2.7 Relevant risks 21
    2.7.1 Regulatory risk 21
    2.7.2 Security risk 21
    2.7.3 Insurance risk 22
    2.7.4 Fraud risk 23
    2.7.5 Market risk 23
    2.7.6 Tax risk 24
    2.7.7 Legal risk 25
    2.7.8 Scale risk 26

CHAPTER 3	A DIGITAL GLOBAL CURRENCY	27

3.1 Introduction 27
3.2 The case against 27
3.3 The evolution of Bitcoin 29
3.4 Beyond currency functions 35
3.5 The multi-coin world 37
3.6 Digital fiat currencies 38
3.7 Different types of cryptoassets 41

	3.7.1	Altcoins	41
	3.7.2	Asset-backed tokens	41
	3.7.3	Blockchain native tokens	42
	3.7.4	Commodity tokens	42
	3.7.5	Crypto fiat currencies	42
	3.7.6	dApp tokens	43
	3.7.7	Hybrid tokens	44
	3.7.8	Internal tokens	44
	3.7.9	Security token offerings (STOs)	44
	3.7.10	Network tokens	44
	3.7.11	Network value tokens	44
	3.7.12	Non-native protocol tokens	44
	3.7.13	Pure cryptocurrencies	45
	3.7.14	Usage tokens	45
	3.7.15	Utility tokens	45
	3.7.16	Work tokens	45

CHAPTER 4   WHY ARE THE REGULATORS WATCHING?   47

4.1 Introduction   47
4.2 Practical issues with cryptoassets   49
4.3 Countries with weak currencies and weak democracies   54
4.4 Offshore countries positioning as global currency hubs   54
4.5 Countries with a tendency towards freedom and innovation   55
4.6 Superpowers that may set the de facto standards for regulation   56
4.7 Countries that have competing agendas   58
4.8 Government worries   59

CHAPTER 5   GLOBAL CRYPTOASSET HUBS   67

5.1 Introduction   67
5.2 Western advanced economies   71

	5.2.1	The United States	71
	5.2.2	The United Kingdom	71
	5.2.3	Canada	74
	5.2.4	Australia	74
	5.2.5	Germany	76
	5.2.6	The Netherlands	77
	5.2.7	Finland	78
	5.2.8	Denmark	78
	5.2.9	Sweden	79
	5.2.10	Estonia	80

5.3 Asian advanced economies   81

	5.3.1	Japan	81
	5.3.2	South Korea	83
	5.3.3	Singapore	85

	5.3.4 China and India	87
5.4	Offshore financial centres (OFCs)	90
5.5	Comparative note	94

CHAPTER 6 CRYPTOASSET POLICIES OF INTERNATIONAL BODIES 96

6.1	Introduction	96
6.2	G20 economies	96
6.3	The Organisation for Economic Co-operation and Development (OECD)	98
6.4	The International Monetary Fund (IMF)	105
6.5	The Financial Stability Board (FSB)	115
6.6	The Bank for International Settlements (BIS)	119
6.7	The International Organisation of Securities Commissions (IOSCO)	123
6.8	Financial Action Task Force (FATF)	128
6.9	The challenge of Facebook's Libra	128
6.10	A brief comparative note regarding multilateral cryptoasset regulators	131

CHAPTER 7 CRYPTOASSET REGULATORY POLICIES IN SELECTED ADVANCED WESTERN ECONOMIES 134

7.1	Introduction	134
7.2	Historical background	135
7.3	The US cryptoasset regulatory policy	137
7.4	Potential cryptoasset regulation in the US	152
7.5	The EU's cryptoasset regulatory policy	162
7.6	The UK's cryptoassets regulatory policy	175
7.7	Australia's cryptoassets regulatory policy	186
7.8	Canada's cryptoassets regulatory policy	189
7.9	Switzerland's cryptoassets regulatory policy	191
7.10	The Cayman Islands' cryptoasset regulatory policy	193
7.11	Malta's cryptoasset regulatory policy	195
7.12	A comparative note	197

CHAPTER 8 CRYPTOASSET REGULATORY POLICIES IN SELECTED ASIAN ECONOMIES 200

8.1	Introduction	200
8.2	China's cryptoasset regulatory policy	201
8.3	India's cryptoasset regulatory policy	211
8.4	Japan's cryptoasset regulatory policy	213
8.5	Singapore's cryptoasset regulatory policy	220
8.6	South Korea's cryptoasset regulatory policy	225
8.7	A comparative note	231

CHAPTER 9 DISTRIBUTED LEDGER TECHNOLOGY	235
9.1 Introduction	235
9.2 Encryption	236
9.3 Overheads	237
9.4 Security offerings	239
9.5 Criminal factors	240
9.6 Downsides	243
9.7 The current situation	243
CHAPTER 10 CONCLUSIONS	248
10.1 Introduction	248
10.2 Cryptocurrency regulatory issues	249
10.3 General regulatory issues	251
10.4 Public opinion	253
10.5 Regulation – historical issues	254
10.6 Global co-operation	255
10.7 The essentials of good regulation	256
Index	*261*

TABLE OF CASES

Canada
Pacific Coast Coin Exchange v Ontario Securities Commission, [1978] 2 S.C.R. 112 (Pacific Coast) 190n210

EU
Skatteverket v. David Hedqvist, 22 October 2015. C-264/14 172

South Korea
Coinis Exchange v. Nongyup Bank (2018) Central District Court's 50th Civil Affairs Division 231

UK
Balfour Beatty Civil Engineering Ltd v Technical and General Guarantee Co Ltd [2000] 68 Con. L.R. 108 .... 238n13
Goodwin v Robarts (1876) 1 App. Cas. 476 .... 25n103, 30n11
Kvaerner John Brown Ltd v Lear Siegler Services Ltd [2006] EWCA Civ 1130 .... 238n13
Moss v Hancock [1899] 2 Q.B. 111 39
United City Merchants v Royal Bank of Canada [1983] 1 A.C. 168 (HL) 238n13

US
Dunn v. Commodity Futures Trading Commission, 519 U.S. 465 (1997) 159
Florida v Espinoza (22 July 2016) 31
Reeves v. Ernst & Young 494 U.S. 56,57 (1990) 159
SEC v Trenton T Shavers and Bitcoin Savings and Trust Co (2014) 4:13-CU-416 160
Securities & Exchange Commission v. W.J. Howey Co. 328 U.S. 293 (1946) 32n26, 159n87
Shawmut Worcester County Bank v. First American Bank & Trust, 731 F. Supp. 57, 61 (D. Mass. 1990) 157
Spain v. Union Trust, 674 F. Supp. 1496, 1500 (D. Conn. 1987) 157

TABLE OF CASES

Tcherepnin v. Knight, 389 U.S. 332, 336 (1967) 159n85
United Hous. Found., Inc. v. Forman, 412 U.S. 837, 838 (1975) 159n86
United States v Lord, No CR 15-00240-01/02, 2017 WL
 1,424,806 (W.D. La. 20/4/2017) 31n24
United States v Murgio, 209 F.Supp. 3d 698, 707
 (SDNY , 19/11/2016) 31n23
United States v Petix, No 15-CR -227A, 2016 WL 7,017,919 .... 31n22
United States v Ulbricht, 858 F. 3d 71, 82–83 (2nd Cir. 2017) 31n24
US v Failella (2014) 39 F Supp 3d 544 160
US v Petrix (2016) No 15-CR-227A 160

TABLE OF STATUTES

Australia

Anti-Money Laundering and Counter-Terrorism Financing
  Act 2006, No. 169, 2006 and amendments up to 2018 186
ASIC Act (AA) 75, 188
Corporations Act (CA) 75–6, 188
Double Taxation Relief legislation 75

Brazil

Law No.2 12,865, Article 6-VI 249

Canada

Proceeds of Crime (Money Laundering) and Terrorist Financing Act 190

Cayman Islands

2015 (Revised) Securities Investment Business Law 90–1
Anti-Money Laundering Laws and Regulations (2017) 91
Data Protection Law 194
Money Services Law 194
Mutual Funds Law 194
Proceeds of Crime Law (PCL) 194
Revised 2003 Electronic Transactions Law 91
Revised 2010 Money Services Law 91
Securities Investment Business Law 194
Stock Exchange Companies Law 194

China

Securities Law: Article 20 210

Estonia

Money Laundering Act 62
Terrorism Financing Prevention Act 62

EU

4th Anti-Money Laundering Directive 2015/849 .... 167, 169, 171, 173
5th Anti-Money Laundering Directive (5AMLD)
  (EU) 2018/43 .... 166–7, 169, 171, 173, 175–6, 181, 183, 185
Alternative Investment Fund Managers Directive 169
Anti-laundering Directive.. 104
EBA (Regulation (EU) No. 1093/2010) Article 9 .... 165, 167
EBA (Regulation (EU) No. 1093/2010) Article 9(2) 167
EBA (Regulation (EU) No. 1093/2010) Article 34(1)................................. 167
EBA (Regulation (EU) No. 1093/2010) Article 56 167
ESA Article 9(3).. 169–70
Markets in Financial Instruments Directive (MiFID) 1 and 2 169
Payment Services Directive (Directive (EU) 2015/2366 (PSDS2)...... 167, 168
Prospectus Directive 169, 184
VAT Directive 172

France

Action Plan for Business Growth and Transformation (PACTE) bill 64

Germany

Payment Supervision Act... 172

Iceland

Exchange Act 248

Isle of Man

Online Gambling (Amendments) Regulations 2016............................. 91n130
Proceeds of Crime Act 2015 91

Japan

Act on Settlement of Funds... 219
Banking Act 126
Consumer Protection Act...217
Crypto Regulation Bill... 82–3
Financial Instruments and Exchange Act (FIEA) 216, 217, 219
Law Controlling Contributions Money Deposits and Interest 214–15
Payment Services Act 81, 126, 213, 214, 216, 217, 218–19
Specified Commercial Transaction Act...217

Malta

Digital Innovation Authority Act (MDIA) 195
Financial Institutions Act... 196

TABLE OF STATUTES

Innovative Technology Arrangements and Services Act (ITAS) 195
Investment Services Act 196
Virtual Financial Assets Act (VFAA) 62, 195, 196

Mexico

Law to Regulate Financial Technology 62

Singapore

Financial Advisers Act (FAA) 222n85, 223
Payment Services Act 224
Payments Services Bill (PSB) 86
Securities and Futures Act 221, 223

South Korea

Electronic Financial Transactions Act 226
Foreign Exchange Transactions Act 226

Switzerland

Banking Act 193

UK

Bank of England Act 1833 39–40
Financial Services and Markets Act 2000 .... 176, 177, 179n177

US

12 C.F.R. S. 205.2(i) (2010) 158n80
12 U.S.C. S. 24 .... 155n68
15 U.S.C. S. 1693a 158n78, 158n79
Bank Secrecy Act 34, 141–2, 156
Coinage Act 39–40
Commodity Exchange Act (CEA) 32, 139, 149, 150, 159
Dodd-Frank Act 2010 147
Electronic Fund Transfer Act of 1978 (EFTA) 157–8
Florida. Statutes Section 560.125 (29) 31
Foreign Account Tax Complaint Act (FATCA) 194
Patriot Act 156
Regulation of Virtual Currency Businesses Act 140–1
Securities Exchange Act 1934 .... 159, 160

TABLE OF REGULATIONS

Australia
Information Sheet (INFO 225) 62, 188–9

Cayman Islands
Beneficial Ownership regime 194

CFTC (Commodities Futures Trading Commission)
Regulations part 32 139

China
PBOC Circular 2013 210
PBOC Circular 2017 210

OECD (Organisation for Economic Co-operation and Development)
CRS 194

Singapore
Payment Services Regulation 221

Switzerland
FINMA Guidelines Section 1.2(b) 193n220

UK
Electronic Money Regulations 2011 (EMRs) 184
Financial Promotions Order 2005 SI 2005/1529 179
Financial Services and Markets Act 2000 (Regulated
  Activities) Order 2001 177
Financial Services (Regulated Activities) Order 2001 SI 2001/544 176

US
Federal Reserve Regulation E. 155
IRS 2014 Virtual Currency Guidance 140

TABLE OF REGULATIONS

Munchee Inc., Release No. 10,445/December 11, 2017,
    Administrative Proceeding File No. 3–18,304 153
Regulation A+ 139
Regulation E 158
Uniform Commercial Code (UCC) 158

ABBREVIATIONS

5AMLD	5th Anti-Money Laundering Directive
PACTE	Action Plan for Business Growth and Transformation
AMLCTF	Anti-Money Laundering and Counter-Terrorism Financing Amendment Bill 2017 (Australia)
AML	anti-money laundering procedures
AA	ASIC Act
AFS	Australian financial services
AUSTRAC	Australian financial and intelligence agency
AFSL	Australian Financial Services Licence
ASIC	Australian Securities and Investments Commission
ATO	The Australian Taxation Office
BIS	Bank for International Settlements
BoE	Bank of England
BEPS	Base Erosion and Profit Shifting
CSA	Canadian Securities Administrators
CGT	capital gains tax
CIMA	Cayman Islands Monetary Authority
CBDC	Central Bank Digital Currency
CBOE	Chicago Board Options Exchange
CME	Chicago Mercantile Exchange Inc.
CBIRC	China Banking and Insurance Regulatory Commission
CIS	Collective investment scheme
CFPB	Consumer Finance Protection Bureau
CPMI	Committee on Payments and Market Infrastructures
CFTC	Commodities Futures Trading Commission
CEA	Commodity Exchange Act
CRS	Common Reporting Standard
CA	Corporations Act
CTF	counter-terrorism financing
CAT	Cryptoassets Taskforce (UK)
CTP	cryptoasset trading platforms
DCEP	Digital Currency Electronic Payment (China)

ABBREVIATIONS

DDR	digital depository receipts
DIA	Digital Innovation Authority Act (Malta)
DLT	distributed ledger technology
DOJ	US Department of Justice
EFTA	Electronic Fund Transfer Act of 1978
EMRs	Electronic Money Regulations 2011
EDD	enhanced due diligence
EBA	European Banking Authority
ECB	European Central Bank
ECBCTF	ECB Crypto-Assets Task Force
EC	European Commission
EIOPA	European Insurance and Occupational Pensions
EP	European Parliament
ESMA	European Securities and Markets Authority
ESAs	European Supervising Authorities
ETF	Exchange traded funds
BaFin	Federal Financial Supervisory Authority (Germany)
FAA	Financial Advisers Act (Cap.110) (Singapore)
FATF	Financial Action Task Force
FCA	Financial Conduct Authority
FinCEN	Financial Crimes Enforcement Network
FINRA	Financial Industry Regulatory Authority
FIEA	Financial Instruments and Exchange Act (Japan)
FIT	financial instrument test
FINMA	Financial Market Supervisory Authority (Switzerland)
FSAP	Financial Sector Assessment Programmes
FSC	Financial Services Commission (Korea)
FSB	Financial Stability Board
FATCA	Foreign Account Tax Complaint Act (US)
GST	goods and services tax
HMRC	HM Revenue and Customs
HMT	HM Treasury
ICO	Initial coin offerings
IIROC	Investment Industry Regulatory Organization of Canada
ITO	initial token offerings
IVFAOs	initial virtual financial assets offerings (Malta)
IRS	Inland Revenue Service
IMF	International Monetary Fund
IOSCO	International Organization of Securities Commissions
IAMAI	Internet and Mobile Association of India
ICT	Investment Contract Test (Canada)

ABBREVIATIONS

JBA	The Japanese Blockchain Association
JFSA	Japan Financial Services Agency
JVCEA	Japanese Virtual Currency Exchange Association
KYC	know your customer procedures
KYT	know your transaction
LOLR	lender of last resort
LA	Libra Association
LETS	Local Exchange Trading System
MFSA	Malta Financial Services Authority
MGA	Malta Gaming Authority
MIS	managed investment scheme
MiFID	Markets in Financial Instruments Directive
MAS	Monetary Authority of Singapore
MROS	Money Laundering Reporting Office Switzerland
ML/TF	money laundering/terrorism funding
NCAs	national competent authorities
NYSDFS	New York State Department of Financial Services
NIFA	National Internet Finance Association (China)
NASAA	North American Securities Administrators Association
OECD GBPF	OECD 2019 Global Blockchain Policy Forum
OCEO	Office of Consumer Education and Outreach (part of CFTC)
OECD	Organisation for Economic Co-operation and Development
PSA	Payment Services Act (Japan)
PSB	Payments Services Bill
PBOC	People's Bank of China
PCL	Proceeds of Crime Law (Cayman Islands)
PRA	Prudential Regulation Authority
RFBs	relevant financial businesses
IIROC	Regulatory Organisation of Canada
RS	Regulatory sandbox
RBI	Reserve Bank of India
SFA	Securities and Futures Act (Japan or Singapore))
SEC	Securities Exchange Commission
SAR	South Korea, Taiwan, Singapore, and Hong Kong
SCAV	Standing Committee on the Assessment of Vulnerabilities
SIF	State Secretariat for International Finance
SARs	suspicious activity reports
SIFI	systemically important financial institutions
FCA	UK Financial Conduct Authority
UCC	Uniform Commercial Code
UNODC	UN Office on Drugs and Crime
SEC	US Securities Exchange Commission
VAT	value added tax

ABBREVIATIONS

VC	venture capital
VASP	virtual asset service providers
V20	Virtual Asset Service Providers Summit
VFAs	virtual financial assets
VFAA	Virtual Financial Assets Act (Malta)
WTO	World Trade Organisation

CHAPTER 1

Introduction and overview

The spectacular price changes that have taken place with regard to cryptocurrencies in 2017, 2018 and 2019 have attracted a great deal of public and professional attention. The price crash of 2018 also highlighted the risk involved for those investing money in them, which in turn has attracted the attention of banking and financial services regulators and central banks.[1] It has also expanded to the blockchain based system that they operate on and some of the other types of instrument that are now issued and traded on a similar basis.

Aside from this financial or "market" risk there are those who unwittingly lost their highly valued Bitcoins and other cryptocurrencies due of a lack of care. These include one man who accidentally lost his computer, together with the Bitcoins stored in it, in a UK council landfill because of complaints by his then girlfriend of the endless computer whirring in the mining process,[2] and others who could no longer retrieve their Bitcoins because of forgotten passwords. Altogether, around 2.78 million Bitcoins have been lost.[3] Some of those who lost their Bitcoins took to retrieving them from toxic landfill sites and hacking their own Bitcoin vaults.[4] These and other similar cases narrate the loss of a small fortune when measured at the price operating in early 2018. Tales are also told of those who bought cheaply in the early days and who were sitting comfortably on very large apparent profits, with monetary gains exceeding 1,000%, before the rapid decline in price over the course of 2018.[5] The initial price surge

---

1 Morris, C. (2017), "Winklevoss Twins Used Facebook Payout to Become Bitcoin billionaires", *Fortune*, 04/12/17, https://fortune.com/2017/12/04/winklevoss-twins-bitcoin-billionaires/, accessed 21/01/18.

2 Smith, A. (2017), "Man threw away laptop with bitcoin that is now worth £74 million", *Metro*, 09/12/17, https://metro.co.uk/2017/12/09/man-threw-away-laptop-with-bitcoin-that-is-now-worth-74-million-7145361/, accessed 21/01/18.

3 Sider, A. & Yang, S. (2017), "Good news! You Are a Bitcoin Millionaire. Bad News! You Forgot Your Password", *The Wall Street Journal*, 19/12/17, https://www.wsj.com/articles/good-news-you-are-a-bitcoin-millionaire-bad-news-you-forgot-your-password-1513701480, accessed 21/01/18.

4 Umoh, R. (2017), "3 of the craziest things people are doing to recover their lost bitcoins", *CNBC*, 21/12/17, https://www.cnbc.com/2017/12/21/3-crazy-things-people-are-doing-to-recover-lost-bitcoin.html, *CNBC*, 21/12/17, accessed 21/01/18.

5 Blatchford, E. (2017), "Is It Too Late To Invest In Bitcoin? For those wondering if they've missed the money-making boat", The Huffington Post Australia, 25/08/17, www.huffingtonpost.com.au/2017/08/22/is-it-too-late-to-invest-in-bitcoin_a_23156491/?guccounter=1, accessed 21/01/18.

contributed to a surge in the fear of missing out syndrome thereby propelling more to use their savings and even borrowings to participate so as not to miss out on the illusion of easy gain.[6] This may re-emerge if another price surge takes place, and indeed it did albeit relatively modestly in July 2019 compared to previous stratospheric hikes.

Bad news comes in other forms than price reductions, for example, the sporadic occasional hacks and thefts[7] associations with money-laundering and other illicit activities.[8] One example was a South Korean college student who started to suffer from depression and subsequently committed suicide after losing money as a result of trading in Bitcoins.[9] Also, more than £108,000 in Bitcoins were paid by victims of the WannaCry ransomware attack that crippled parts of the NHS including businesses in 150 countries worldwide.[10]

Investors, whether sophisticated or not are attracted by the possibility of rapid and extremely high returns from cryptocurrencies. As for businesses, with the excitement and hype around Bitcoin and blockchain there is the associated emotional element which has affected the share prices in crypto companies, which is reminiscent of the dot.com boom. One such example was the surging share price of LongFin, which specialises in trade finance and which went public on 13 December 2017 on Nasdaq. When LongFin announced that it was buying a blockchain related venture called Ziddu.com, its share price shot up by more than 1,000%, causing its own founder to call the price surge unwarranted.[11] According to Jordan Rochester, a Nomura analyst, the level of speculative mania had reached a point in 2017 where share prices had been boosted by businesses simply inserting "blockchain" on to the end of their names.[12] Blockchain is the technology underpinning Bitcoin and other cryptocurrencies.

This text arises because the extensive writings on the topic of cryptocurrencies and cryptoassets do not include a comprehensive breakdown of these instruments coupled with an explanation of the current and proposed legal and regulatory situation.

---

6 Bosotti, A. (2017), "Bitcoin craze: 'Fear of missing out' trade will lead to 'DRAMATIC' falls in Bitcoin value", *Express*, 31/12/17, www.express.co.uk/finance/city/898512/Bitcoin-news-price-update-value-fall-cryptocurrency-fomo-market-prices-finance-business, accessed 21/01/18.

7 Roberts, J. J. (2017), "How Bitcoin Is Stolen: 5 Common Threats", *Fortune*, 08/12/17, https://fortune.com/2017/12/08/bitcoin-theft/, accessed 21/01/18.

8 Bloomberg, J. (2017), "Using Bitcoin Or Other Cryptocurrency To Commit Crimes? Law Enforcement Is Onto You", *Forbes*, 28/12/17, www.forbes.com/sites/jasonbloomberg/2017/12/28/using-bitcoin-or-other-cryptocurrency-to-commit-crimes-law-enforcement-is-onto-you/, accessed 21/01/18.

9 Kwak, Y-S. (2018), "Man commits suicide after loss on cryptocurrency", *The Korea Times*, 01/02/18, www.koreatimes.co.kr/www/nation/2018/02/121_243438.html, accessed 03/02/18.

10 Gibbs, S. (2017), "WannaCry: Hackers withdraw £108, 000 of bitcoin ransom", *The Guardian*, 03/08/17, www.theguardian.com/technology/2017/aug/03/wannacry-hackers-withdraw-108000-pounds-bitcoin-ransom, accessed 21/01/18.

11 Bullock, N. & Wigglesworth, R. (2017), "Blockchain fervour evokes memories of dotcom bubble", *Financial Times*, 19/12/17, www.ft.com/content/40ec964a-e429-11e7-8b99-0191e45377ec, accessed 21/01/18.

12 Supra, note [11], Bullock & Wigglesworth (2017).

INTRODUCTION AND OVERVIEW

As is explained in Chapter 2, cryptocurrencies and assets have come to capture the imaginations of individuals, businesses, and more recently regulators across the world. It has fired the dreams and ambitions of many others looking for quick wealth. There were huge gains, running beyond 1,000%, from Bitcoin punting resulted in the spectacular run of Bitcoin from less than US$1,000 to an all-time high of US$19,500 by 1 January 2017; a hefty surge of 1,824% before the later 80% decline; and then in turn relative price stability followed by mid-2019.[13] Bitcoin prices received a further boost from Wall Street regulated futures trading including the imminent implementation of the Lighting Network.[14] The Chicago Board Options Exchange (CBOE) and the Chicago Mercantile Exchange Inc.(CME) launched their respective futures product respectively on 10 and 18 December 2017. New all-time highs appeared to come and go in the blink of an eye, such that new price predictions are now hard to form, with regular commentators instead advising new investors to learn more about cryptocurrencies before committing. Such then is their price volatility.[15]

Bitcoin's stellar price movement is accompanied by an even greater switchback ride by thirteen other main cryptocurrencies. For example for 2018 and 2019, Ripple gained 36,018% then dropped by 59.3% of the previous total; Dash up 9,265% then down 70.18% of that, Ethereum up 9,162% then down 85.84% of that amount, Litecoin up 5,056% before losing 70.53% of that and OmiseGo up 3,315% before dropping 90.49% of that, compared to Bitcoin's gain of 1,318% at the end of 2017 before losing 59.3% of its highest amount.[16] These other cryptocurrencies joined the Bitcoin bandwagon with wider oscillations because of their prior much smaller capital base.

The common denominator tying the different crypto-systems is the public ledger or blockchain shared between network participants and the employment of native tokens to incentivise participants for manning the network in lieu of a central authority. They differ in the level of innovation.[17] The majority are mainly clones of bitcoin, while other cryptocurrencies feature different block time, currency supply and issuance themes, reflecting little to no innovation. These are commonly referred to as "altcoins" as exemplified by Dogecoin and Ethereum Classic. Others, while drawing on some Bitcoin concepts, offer novel

---

13 Morris, D. Z. (2017), "Bitcoin Hits a New Record High, But Stops Short of US$20,000", *Fortune*, 17/12/17, https://fortune.com/2017/12/17/bitcoin-record-high-short-of-20000/, accessed 12/02/18.

14 Suberg, W. (2017), "Bitcoin Hits $20,000 Per Coin, Capping Year of Enormous Growth" *Coin Telegraph*, 17/12/17, https://cointelegraph.com/news/bitcoin-hits-20000-per-coin-capping-year-of-enormous-growth, accessed 12/02/18.

15 Suberg, W. (2017), "Another Day, Another Thousand Dollars: Bitcoin Hits $15k", *Coin Telegraph*, 07/12/17, www.cointelegraph.com/news/another-day-another-thousand-dollars-bitcoin-hits-15k, accessed 12/02/18.

16 Wong, J. I. (2018), "Here are the top 10 cryptoassets of 2017 (and bitcoin's 1,000% rise doesn't even make the list", *Quartz*, 01/01/18, www.qz.com/1169000/ripple-was-the-best-performing-cryptocurrency-of-2017-beating-bitcoin/, accessed 02/02/18.

17 Hileman, G. & Rauchs, M. (2017), *Global cryptocurrency benchmarking study*, Cambridge, Cambridge Centre for Alternative Finance.

and innovative features with substantive differences, and comprise two main species, namely: those that exist on additional layers built on top of existing blockchain systems, and those offering new public blockchain systems.

As of 2015 Bitcoin accounted up to about 86% of the total cryptocurrency market capitalisation but this fell to less than 80% in 2016,[18] and to around 35% of market capitalisation or about US$713 billion by the end of 2017,[19] The major growth in overall market cap in 2017 has been driven by altcoins like Ripple, Ether, Stellar and little-known Tron. The extreme Bitcoin price volatility that occurred shows that those who committed financially close to its peak just before Christmas 2017 suffered significant losses in 2018. Hence, while there are opportunities for speculative gains, equally there are risks attached to Bitcoin investing. Many people buy cryptocurrencies for their value rather than as a medium of exchange. Their lack of guaranteed value and digital nature implies that transacting in cryptocurrency involves several inherent unique risks extending from regulatory to security, insurance, fraud, market and tax.[20]

Chapter 3 discusses the controversies surrounding Bitcoin and its later imitators intended to function as global digital currencies and as an alternative to the existing fiat currency regime. There are those who would argue that cryptocurrencies' mission to be the future global digital currencies would eventually be realised,[21] while others, and in particular world-renowned economists, would claim otherwise.[22] The ongoing debates between the two sides as to whether cryptocurrency is money are therefore explored. Regardless of how different jurisdictions view cryptocurrencies, they have been employed for various purposes across many economies from advanced to emerging.

Chapter 4 deals with the ramifications of the current situation in various parts of the world and considers the problems that may arise in the context of cryptocurrencies and cryptoassets. The countries themselves are considered in terms of the stability of their fiat currencies and their democracies: those that are positioning themselves as crypto hubs, those that have a tradition of innovation, those that may well up setting the regulatory standards and those with competing agendas.

Chapter 5 takes a look at the more notable "hotspots" around the world and in particular the world's most cryptocurrency friendly cities to ascertain how

---

18 Supra, note [18], Hileman & Rauchs (2017).
19 Buck, J. (2018), "Total Crypto Market Cap Hits New All-Time Over $700 bln", *Coin Telegraph*, 03/01/18, https://cointelegraph.com/news/total-crypto-market-cap-hits-new-all-time-high-over-700-bln, accessed 12/02/18.
20 Investopedia (2018), "Bitcoin", *Investopedia*, www.investopedia.com/terms/b/bitcoin.asp, accessed 02/02/18.
21 Arnold, M. (2017), "Six global banks join forces to create digital currency", *Financial Times*, 31/08/17, www.ft.com/content/20c10d58-8d9c-11e7-a352-e4gf43c5825d, accessed 02/02/18.
22 Roubini, N. (2018), "Blockchain's broke promises", *Project Syndicate*, 26/01/18, www.project-syndicate.org/commentary/why-bitcoin-is-a-bubble-by-nouriel-roubini-2018-01?utm_sources=Project+Syndicate+, accessed 02/02/18.

widespread cryptocurrencies are around the world.[23] Insights drawn from these could, together with the conclusions that can be drawn from the economies that discouraged the use of cryptocurrencies, help to provide some answers as to why regulators in both advanced and emerging economies are watching. This is not altogether surprising with Nobel economics laureates[24] and others in global platforms[25] advising against widening the usage.

The regulatory perspective is expanded in Chapter 6, which considers the various international bodies which have taken positions on this issue and considers their views. It covers the G20, the OECD, the IMF, the Financial Stability Forum, the Bank for International Settlements, the International Organization of Securities Commissions and the Financial Action Task Force.

Chapters 7 and 8 respectively cover the position taken by national regulators in the advanced Western and Asian economies of the US,[26] the UK,[27] the EU[28] and Australia; and those in major Asian economies like China,[29] Japan,[30] South Korea,[31] India[32] and Singapore, amongst others.

Chapter 9 looks at the wider potential impact of blockchain and puts the rest of the work in a wider context at the start of what may well be a journey that significantly affects finance, banking and financial services, among many other areas.

---

23 Guibourg, C. (2016), "Which cities have the most businesses accepting bitcoin? London, New York, San Francisco among the world's 11 most bitcoin-friendly cities", *City AM*, 18/01/16, www.cityam.com/232552/what-cities-have-most-businesses-accepting-bitcoin-london-new-york-san-franscisco-among-the-world's, accessed 02/02/18.

24 Frank, J., Chian, K. & Ciolli, J. (2017), "PAUL KRUGMAN: Bitcoin is a more obvious bubble than housing was", *Business Insider*, 15/12/17, www.businessinsider.com/paul-krugman-says-bitcoin-is-a-bubble-2017-12?r=US&IR=T, accessed 02/02/18.

25 Kharpal, A. (2018), "Bitcoin is getting bashed at Davos but the crypto world is fighting back" *CNBC*, 26/01/18, www.cnbc.com/2018/01/26/bitcoin-criticized-at-wef-in-davos-but-cryptocurrency-world-fights-back.html, 02/02/18.

26 Price, M. & Schroeder, P. (2018), "U.S. regulators to back more oversight of virtual currencies", *Reuters*, 06/02/18, www.reuters.com/article/us-global-bitcoin-congress/u-s-regulators-to-back-more-oversight-of-virtual-currencies-idUSKBN1FP2FJ, accessed 08/02/18.

27 BBC (2017), "UK government mulls bitcoin regulation", *BBC*, 04/12/17, www.bbc.co.uk/news/technology-42223577, accessed 02/02/18.

28 Meyer, D. (2017), "Here's When Europe's New Bitcoin Rules Will Come Into Effect", *Fortune*, 04/12/17, https://fortune.com/2017/12/04/eu-bitcoin-anti-money-laundering-uk/, accessed 02/02/18.

29 Gibbs, S. (2018), "Bitcoin continues rapid slide as Russia and China stoke regulatory fears", *The Guardian*, 17/01/18, www.theguardian.com/technology/2018/jan/17/bitcoin-continues-slide-drop-russia-china-regulatory-fears-cryptocurrency, accessed 02/02/18.

30 Yagami, K. (2017), "Japan: A forward thinking bitcoin nation", Forbes, 02/11/17.

31 De, N, (2018), "Report: South Korea Eyes Joint Crypto Regulations With China, Japan", *Coin Desk*, 09/01/18, www.coindesk.com/report-south-korea-eyes-joint-crypto-regulations-with-china-japan, accessed 02/02/18.

32 De, N. (2017), "India's Supreme Court Prods Government On Bitcoin Regulation", *CoinDesk*, 16/11/17, www.coindesk.com/indias-supreme-court-calls-government-regulate-bitcoin, accessed 02/02/18.

Chapter 10 provides the concluding remarks for the book. It assesses the cryptocurrency evolutionary process; spells out its key opportunities and risks; gauges the extent of its applications across major emerging and advanced economies; deliberates on the feasibility of cryptocurrencies as global virtual currencies; examines the main regulatory approaches employed thus far; and finally reflects on what the real potential of cryptocurrencies and cryptoassets are.

CHAPTER 2

Cryptocurrencies and assets, opportunities and risks

2.1 Introduction

A cryptocurrency is a digital or virtual currency employing cryptography to provide security and verify transactions on its network and at the time of writing the dominant specie is bitcoin.[1] They all operate on the basis of cryptography which is the "practice and study of techniques for secure communication in the presence of third parties" employed in multiple places to provide security for the crypto network.[2] It primarily consists of a mathematical and computer science algorithms applied to encrypt and decrypt information and is used in crypto addresses, hash functions and the blockchain.

A cryptocurrency is not issued by a central authority, but is a peer-to-peer blockchain based system and it is therefore argued that it is immune from government interference or manipulation. That said the same arguments were put forward concerning the internet in its early days[3] and the view proved false. However, the reason that this was the case was that the internet has key points of control and operators had to be located in a physical space which brought them within the control of state governments.[4] That said this control has been of limited success with the result that child pornography and arms sales, amongst other criminal activities, still take place on the web. As De Filippi and Wright[5] have pointed out blockchain has taken us back to the start of this problem because blockchain is based on autonomous transactionally-operating code-based rules. The whole decentralised peer-to-peer basis renders the state law-making process potentially marginal and it is this rather than just the legal and regulatory issues of utilising cryptocurrencies and assets (discussed later) which is the greatest potential threat that blockchain-based systems pose.

---

1 Bitcoin (2018), "Bitcoin glossary", Bitcoin, 16/01/2018, www.Bitcoin.com/get-started/Bitcoin-glossary, accessed 12/02/2018.
2 Supra, note [1], Bitcoin (2018).
3 Post, D. G. and Johnson, D. R. (1997) "Chaos Prevailing on Every Continent: Towards a New Theory of Decentralized Decision-making in Complex Systems." *Chicago-Kent Law Review*, 73 (1997), pp. 1055–1099.
4 Goldsmith, J. and Wu, T. (2006), *Who Controls the Internet?: Illusions of a Borderless World*, Oxford University Press, pp. 142–161.
5 De Filippi, P. & Wright, A. (2018), *Blockchain and the Law: The Rule of Code*, Harvard University Press, p. 51.

Bitcoin is an electronic peer-to-peer (P2P) cash system. Bitcoin Cash (BCH) and Bitcoin Core (BTC) represent the two main versions of bitcoin. BCH is digital money offering very fast transaction times with low fees, while BTC has proved to be of limited use as money because of extremely high fees and slow transaction times.[6] A blockchain is a cryptographically secured public ledger, shared among a distributed network of validating computers, each running common software that guides them to a consensus on the legitimacy of new entries and prevents anyone from unilaterally rewriting that agreed record.[7] This is how the technology solves the double spend problem. Double spending occurs when someone tries to send a bitcoin transaction to two different recipients simultaneously. However, when bitcoin transactions are confirmed, it is nearly impossible to double spend it. This further means that the more confirmations a transaction has, the harder it is to double spend the bitcoin. Bitcoin and other cryptocurrencies are related to cryptography insofar as they employ mathematics to secure information. Within Bitcoin, cryptography generates and secures wallets, signs all transactions, and verifies each and every transaction in the blockchain. Even in the event of the blockchain becoming corrupted or part of the network failing it is possible to reconstruct it from the records kept elsewhere by others. It is thus unusually resilient.[8]

Digital currencies or cryptocurrencies represent something more than the digitisation of money. It is a way to reconstruct trust,[9] an innovative response by its designer to the erosion of trust in the banking system when the 2007 global financial crisis unfolded.[10] Some claim bitcoin to be items of inherent value, like gold or cash. They differ from fiat money such as the US dollar or the Japanese Yen in that they are decentralised, virtual stores of value and are transacted over the internet by different entities in anonymous fashion. Cryptocurrencies are therefore not controlled nor supported by any bank or central authority. Their unique features[11] enable them to achieve financial transactions with no spatial constraints or middle party interventions; transactions finality; economical transaction costs; and the capacity to publicly verify transactions on the internet.

---

6 Supra, note [1], Bitcoin (2018).

7 Casey, M. (2016), "How Bitcoin and the blockchain are challenging the global economic order", *Paper Presented at the 2016 MIT Consumer Dynamics Conference MIT Industrial Liaison Programme 07/12/2016*, http://ilp.mit.edu/images/conferences/2016/consumer/presentations/Casey.2016.CD.pdf, accessed 12/02/2018.

8 De Filippi, P. & Wright, A. (2018), *Blockchain and the Law. The Rule of Code*, Harvard University Press, p. 2.

9 Shin, L. (2016), "Why A Wall Street Journal Currency Reporter Didn't Understand Money Until He Learned About Bitcoin", *Forbes*, 20/09/2016, https://www.forbes.com/sites/laurashin/2016/09/20/why-a-wall-street-journal-currency-reporter-didnt-understand-money-until-he-learned-about-Bitcoin/, accessed 12/02/2018; Vigna, P. and Casey, M. J. (2015), *Cryptocurrency: How Bitcoin and Digital Money are Challenging the Global Economic Order*, New York, St. Martin's Press.

10 Crotty, J. (2009), "Structural causes of the global financial crisis: A critical assessment of the new 'financial architecture'", *Cambridge Journal of Economics*, 33 (4), pp. 563–580.

11 D'Alfonso, A., Langer, P. & Vandelis, Z. (2016), "The Future of Cryptocurrency: An Investor's Comparison of Bitcoin and Ethereum", *Ryerson University Working Paper*, 17/10/2016, www.econoist.com/sites/default/files/the_future_of_cryptocurrency.pdf, accessed 12/02/2018.

It is debatable as to whether they are "money". The classis definition is that of Mann who said that it must function as:

(a) "a medium of exchange;
(b) as a measure of wealth or as a standard for contractual obligations;
(c) as a store or value of wealth; and
(d) as a unit of account."[12]

However, as he went on to remark "'money' can have very different meanings in different contexts."[13] So, the classic definition of money seems to encapsulate cryptocurrencies as well as the traditional fiat currencies. The only remaining definitional issue is that the right to regulate money lies with sovereign states[14] who have the capacity to restrict the right, delegate it or transfer it.[15] The last point becomes critical in the context of the regulation of cryptocurrencies, an area examined later in the book.

This book maintains a focus on Bitcoin, the maiden, and still by far the most successful, cryptoasset for now. Bitcoin, designed by Satoshi Yakamoto, was launched into use mainly among software aficionados in 2008.[16] The attention then was largely confined to this small crypto partisan community until it broke into public consciousness in 2013. This was the year that the digital currency evolved from a subcultural phenomenon into the mainstream of business, economics and finance.[17] A wider range of goods and services could then be purchased by bitcoins as an increasing number of merchants signed up. This caused the bitcoin price to surge from US$13 per bitcoin in January 2013 to US$1,242 at the end of November 2013 and reached US$8,510 by 1 June 2019.[18] There are now 17 million bitcoins in circulation[19]; but as the rate at which new bitcoins will be created is being halved every four years, there can only be a maximum of 24 million coins issued.[20] Still, it remains enigmatic, just like its shadowy designer whose official identity remains a mystery to this day.

Increasingly, as bitcoin prices oscillate wildly, the bitcoin excitement that had earlier gained traction as a potential global digital currency began to shift focus to the blockchain technology underpinning it. This supports cryptocurrencies

---

12 Proctor C. (2005), *Mann on the Legal Aspect of Money*, Seventh edition. Oxford, Oxford University Press, p. 10.
13 Ibid, Proctor C. (2005), p. 10.
14 Carreau, D. and Juillard, P. (2003), *Droit international économique*, Dalloz-Sirey 2003.
15 Brownlie I. (1973), *Principles of International Law*, Sixth edition, Oxford, Oxford University Press, Chapter 15.
16 Supra, note [9], Vigna & Casey (2016).
17 Christensen, N. (2013), "2013: year of the Bitcoin", *Forbes*, 10/12/2013, www.forbes.com/sites/kitconews/2013/12/10/2013-year-of-the-Bitcoin, accessed 12/02/2018.
18 99 Bitcoins (2018), "Bitcoin price chart with historic events", *99 Bitcoins*, 11/12/2019, www.99Bitcoins.com/price-chart-history, accessed 12/02/2018.
19 Buchko, S. (2018), "How many Bitcoins are left?", *Coincentral*, 03/01/2018, https://coincentral.com/how-many-bitcoins-are-left/, accessed 13/02/2020.
20 Supra, note [17], Christensen (2013).

such as bitcoin and is used for verifying and recording transactions. This public online ledger is now increasingly perceived as having the potential to reshape the global financial system and possibly have a significant impact on other industries too.[21] Bitcoin has gained imitators and adherents as well,[22] although it has its critics including a Nobel economics Laurette, who called it "a bubble, a scam or Ponzi-scheme."[23] Being a relatively new technology, blockchain has to survive not only with the support of optimists, but with strong faith in its business applications[24] and despite critics who argue that despite a decade of existence its only main contribution is as a payment mechanism that is more suited for business to business (B2B) use.[25]

2.2 Cryptocurrencies and blockchain

It could be helpful to step back to see the initial agenda of Bitcoin's designer so as to provide a balanced assessment of Bitcoin's potential. On 31 October 2008 Satoshi Nakamoto emailed a Bitcoin white paper to several hundred members of an obscure mailing list comprising cryptography experts and enthusiasts with the following abstract:

> A purely peer-to-peer version of electronic cash would allow online payments to be sent directly from one party to another without going through a financial institution. Digital signatures provide part of the solution, but the main benefits are lost if a trusted third party is still required to prevent double spending. We proposed a solution to the double spending problem using a peer-to-peer network. The network timestamps transactions by hashing them into an ongoing chain of hash-based proof-of-work, forming a record that cannot be changed without redoing the proof-of-work. The longest chain not only serves as proof to the sequence of events witnessed, but proof that it came from the largest pool of CPU power. As long as a majority of CPU power is controlled by nodes that are not cooperating to attack the network, they'll generate the longest chain and outpace attackers. The network itself requires minimal structure. Messages are broadcast on a best effort basis, and nodes can leave and rejoin the network at will, accepting the longest proof-of-work chain as proof of what happened while they were gone.[26]

---

21 Tapscott, D. & Tapscott, A. (2016), *Blockchain Revolution: How the Technology Behind Bitcoin is Changing Money, Business, and the World*, New York, Penguin Random House.

22 Douma, S. (2016), "Bitcoin: The pros and cons of regulation", *Universiteit Leiden Project Paper*, 12/06/2016, https://openaccess.leidenuniv.nl/bitstream/handle/1887/42104/Bitcoin%2C%20 The%20Pros%20and%20Cons%20of%20Regulation.pdf?sequence=1, accessed 12/02/2018.

23 Frank, J., Chin, K. & Ciolli, J. (2017), "PAUL KRUGMAN: Bitcoin is a more obvious bubble than housing was", *Business Insider*, 15/12/2017, www.businessinsider.com/paul-krugman-says-Bitcoin-is-a-bubble-2017-12, accessed 12/02/2018; Deen, A. (2017), "Should You Invest in Bitcoin? Here are the Pros and Cons", *Equities*, 03/05/2017, www.equities.com/news/should-you-invest-in-Bitcoin-the-pros-and-cons, accessed 12/02/2018.

24 Supra, note [21], Tapscott & Tapscott (2016).

25 Roubini, N. (2018), "Blockchain's Broken Promises", *Project Syndicate Paper*, 26/01/2018, https://www.project-syndicate.org/commentary/why-Bitcoin-is-a-bubble-by-nouriel-roubini-2018-01?barrier=accesspaylog, accessed 28/01/2018.

26 Nakamoto, S. (2008), "Bitcoin: A Peer-to-Peer Electronic Cash System", *Bitcoin White Paper*, 31/10/2018, http://satoshinakamoto.me/whitepaper/, accessed 09/02/2020.

To this day, the identity of this emailer has not been formally established, such that most believe that it is the pseudonym used by an entity, an individual, or a group of individuals who seek anonymity for their own reasons. As has been pointed out[27] this is essentially a combination of preceding ideas by others, though the end result is certainly innovative.[28]

Blockchain seems to work effectively for Bitcoin.[29] When payments are effected with a physical coin, the party handing it over will not be able to spend it again. Preventing double spending in a digital currency like bitcoin is more complicated. In a typical bitcoin transaction, Jane uses bitcoin to buy, say, a cup of tea at Sally's internet café, using her private key to transfer ownership of the currency. Word of the transaction is sent through the Bitcoin network to "miners" with powerful computers. The miners employ trial and error computations to solve a puzzle created by combining data about recent transactions. The first to locate the unique number that unlocks the puzzle earns the right to bundle the transactions into a confirmed batch known as a block. The successful miner is rewarded with newly minted bitcoin, but only after other miners confirm that the block's transactions do not contain any attempts to spend the same funds twice. This may be Bitcoin's Achilles heel as once a certain number of bitcoins have been issued further issues of the currency will terminate. After that an alternative way will be needed to validate transactions and that will require payment by the users, something that will make the currency less attractive.

The blockchain acts as a public ledger showing all transactions, though the identities of participants are obscured. Each block has a cryptographic link to the previous one. Every addition of a new linked block to the chain makes it harder for a rogue miner to steal Sally's bitcoin by rewriting the sequence of transactions. Fink[30] defines it as "a database that is replicated across a network of computers updated through a consensus algorithm" and

> a shared and synchronized digital database that is maintained by an algorithm and stored on multiple nodes (the computers that store a local version of the distributed ledger). Blockchains can be imagined as a peer-to-peer network with the nodes serving as the different peers.[31]

Thus, the construction looks like this. The central block at the bottom is the original arrangement and each participant adds their own block as they engage in a transaction. Each transaction includes the cryptographic hash of the prior

---

27 Narayanan, A. and Clark, J. (2017), "Bitcoin's Academic Pedigree: The concept of cryptocurrencies is built from forgotten ideas in research literature", *acmqueue* vol 15, iss 4, 29/08/2017, https://queue.acm.org/detail.cfm?id=3136559. Atkinson, R. and Ezell, S. (2012), *Innovation Economics: The Race for Global Advantage*, Yale University Press, 2012.

28 Fink, M. (2019) *Blockchain, Regulation and Governance in Europe*, Cambridge, Cambridge University Press, p. 147.

29 Kharif, O. & Leising, M. (2018), "Bitcoin and Blockchain", *Bloomberg*, 2/11/2018, www.bloomberg.com/quicktake/Bitcoins, accessed 29/01/2018.

30 Fink, M. (2019) *Blockchain, Regulation and Governance in Europe*, Cambridge, Cambridge University Press, p. 1.

31 *Ibid*, p. 6.

block thus connecting them together. As shown, a separate fork can be added by someone adding a different software component, resulting in what is called a "hard fork". After that, transactions on the old software will be added to the previous structure and ones carried out on the new software will be added to the blockchain that has split off from the original construction. Either way the blockchain becomes progressively longer and safer from interference after the event with each transaction. Thus the structure looks like this:

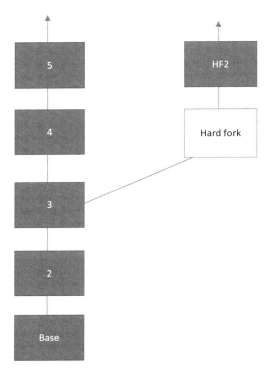

Figure 1

Hard forks are not reversible and involve all the miners in updating their clients. Once this is done those who do not implement the alteration to their part of the blockchain can no longer use it. Soft forks introduce voluntary changes to the software and can be reversed. They occur when the majority of the miners impose their approach on any dissenting minority.

These blocks are each made up of a header, a hash using standard cryptographic functions[32] (a kind of unique electronic fingerprint), a time stamp and

---

32 De Fillipi, P. & Wright, A. (2018) *Blockchain and the Law: The Rule of Code*, Harvard University Press, p. 22. Carter, J. L. & Wegman, M. N. (1979) "Universal Classes of Hash Functions." *Journal of Computer and System Sciences*, 18 (2), pp. 143–154.

a hash of the previous block. Other information may be added to it. The protocol of the relevant cryptocurrency or asset will link these together sequentially.

Bitcoin economic opportunities flow from Bitcoin and related cryptocurrency business applications. An empirical global study suggests the following[33]:

(1) Unique active numbers of cryptocurrency wallets[34] including bitcoin currently stand at 31.9 million.[35] About 1,876 people are said to be working full-time in the crypto industry, but the number probably exceeds 2,000 when large mining entities and others are included.

(2) Crypto exchanges[36] have the highest number of operating entities and employ more people than others in this industry. Of these, some 52% are small exchanges hold formal government licences compared to only 35% of large exchanges.

(3) Around 22 million wallets are estimated to be active. The lines between wallets and exchanges are increasingly blurring. Some 52% of wallets surveyed provide an integrated exchange feature, of which 80% offer a national-to-cryptocurrency exchange service. The majority of wallets in contrast do not control access to user keys.

(4) Even as 79% of payment companies enjoy existing relationships with banking institutions and payment networks, the difficulty of obtaining and maintaining these relationships is cited as the sector's biggest challenge. National-to-cryptocurrency payments on average constitutes two thirds of total company transaction volume, while national-to-national currency transfers and cryptocurrency to cryptocurrency payments accounts for 27% and 6% respectively.

(5) Some 79% of large mines rate their influence on protocol development as high to very high, compared to 51% of small miners. Publicly known mining facilities are geographically dispersed, but a significant concentration can be observed in particular Chinese provinces.

As of 14 February 2018, cryptoassets valuation stood at some US$422.33 billion, of which Bitcoin still dominates with a market cap of US$146.7 billion or 34.7% of total market capitalisation.[37] As at 17th February 2020 the top ten cryptocurrencies by market capitalization were, in declining order of size: Bitcoin,

---

33 Hileman, G. & Rauchs, M. (2017) *Global cryptocurrency benchmarking study*, Cambridge, Cambridge Centre for Alternative Finance.

34 The Bitcoin wallet replaces Bitcoin addresses with a secret number (the private key) which acts as access to a store from which the owner can retrieve the Bitcoin by using that access code. This can be held on a laptop, desktop, smartphone or for a fee they can be held by a specialist company on their software system.

35 https://www.statista.com/statistics/647374/worldwide-blockchain-wallet-users/, accessed 11/02/2019.

36 The exchanges are online markets for buying and selling the relevant cryptocurrency, in the same way that an online stock exchange enables people to buy and sell shares.

37 Coin Market Cap (2018), "Cryptocurrency market capitalizations", *Coin Market Cap*, 14/02/2018, www.coinmarketcap.com/, accessed 18/02/2018.

Etherium, XRP, Bitcoin cash, Bitcoin SV, Tether, Litecoin, EOS, Binance Coin and Tezos.[38] Given the general volatility of cryptoassets, in particular Bitcoin,[39] their respective order of ranking could change daily.

While various forces drive daily price fluctuations in equities, ultimately it is changes in the expectation of corporate earnings that has the most influence. For Bitcoin and other cryptoassets, there is no such earnings yardstick, only the waxing and waning of enthusiasm for a potentially revolutionary assets class for which at times the sky might seem to be the limit.[40] The return and volatility characteristics of bitcoin compares starkly with those of the Standard & Poor 500. The annualised volatility of Bitcoin in 2017 was double that of 2016, even as its price rose 15-fold. Bull market years in equities, such as 2013, when the S&P 500 rose 29.6% and 2017 when it gained 19.4% invariably come about when volatility is low. The S&P had a volatility rate of 11.2% in 2013, much lower than the 41% in 2008 when the benchmark dived by 38.5%. The 2008 and 2013 differences can be attributed to a marked shift in both reported and anticipated corporate profits, suggesting that dividend earnings drive equity prices.[41]

In the case of cryptocurrencies, and in particular Bitcoin, there are no interest payments or earnings and there is no consensus valuation framework.[42] There is rather a rampant enthusiasm and the powerful fear of missing out interspersed with periods of panic. Captivating tales of substantial wealth generated over a very short period inspire fresh capital into the market.[43] The rush to purchase boosts prices even higher. This leads to a frenetic and positive volatility spiral where Bitcoin emerges as the poster child for self-reinforcing price momentum and speculation. Ignoring fundamental valuation guidance, price action drives demand that further drives the price before an inevitable price correction then occurs.[44]

The "sky is the limit" syndrome has been observed over the past two decades including the dotcom era of 1998 and 1999, crude oil in 2008, and gold in 2011.[45] In each of these, the spot price implied volatility moved dramatically higher when the fear of missing out leading to a strong price surge. In the dotcom boom, for example the Nasdaq 100 Index jumped by 85% in 1998 and 102% in 1999. The volatility of the technology index was 33% in that span, a sharp

---

38 https://coinmarketcap.com. Accessed 17/02/2020
39 Burger, D. (2017), "Bitcoin Has Become So Volatile It Looks Like An ETF On Steroids", *Bloomberg*, 29/06/2017, https://www.bloomberg.com/news/articles/2017-06-29/Bitcoin-s-become-so-volatile-that-it-looks-like-a-steroidal-etf, accessed 02/02/2018.
40 Curnutt, D. (2018), "Cryptocurrencies Steal Volatility Away From Stocks", *Bloomberg*, 12/01/2018, https://www.bloomberg.com/opinion/articles/2018-01-11/cryptocurrencies-steal-volatility-away-from-stocks, accessed 02/02/2018.
41 Supra, note [41], Curnutt (2018).
42 Supra, note [41], Curnutt (2018).
43 Ambler, A., Au-Yeang, A., Chung, G., Kauflin, J., Konrad, A., Shin, L. & Vardi, N. (2018), "The richest people in cryptocurrency", *Forbes*, 07/02/2018, www.forbes.com/richest-in-cryptocurrency, accessed 18/02/2018.
44 Supra, note [41], Curnutt (2018).
45 Supra, note [41], Curnutt (2018).

increase from the prior two-year period. The impact of the 2008 crude oil and the US debt ceiling crisis suggest much of the same.

These three historical narratives appear to resemble the current risk dynamic in Bitcoin and other cryptocurrencies; a seductive path breaking narrative and the resulting price action becomes sufficiently persuasive to demand action.[46] This positive relationship between price and volatility makes it almost impossible for investors to initiate a bearish bet as the risks of being wrong are simply too great. This was the case for tech stocks in the late 1990s where earnings became irrelevant to the valuation narrative. Indeed, volatility to both the upside and downside is almost likely when fundamentals are superseded by the alluring story and the power of price momentum.[47]

Though, with a capitalisation of US$237.52 billion, bitcoin currently dominates all other cryptocurrencies,[48] it is still small in scale when compared to other conventional asset instruments. The total value of all the world's coins and banknotes is estimated at US$7.6 trillion, the world's gold estimated at US$7.7 trillion basing on US$1,275 per ounce and the total value of the world's money or broad money is estimated at US$90.4 trillion.[49] The world stock market capitalisation stands at about US$65.6 trillion,[50] and the daily foreign exchange market at about US$5.5 trillion[51] also overwhelms current Bitcoin capitalisation. As at the end of 2018 cryptocurrencies accounted for less that 1% of global assets as opposed to credit default swaps in 2008 which represented 100% of GDP.[52] The challenge for Bitcoin is to achieve higher market capitalisation, though this is not easy based on current trends. Much depends on the pace of adoption across the world, the acceleration of business application cases and the kind of regulatory initiatives forthcoming from national and international regulators.

Meanwhile, the general public became interested following media stories telling how at one point various notable personalities had become so called cryptoasset billionaires, largely because of their holdings of various cryptocurrencies, but mainly Bitcoin.[53] Based on crypto asset prices on 19 January 2018, the crypto billionaire list suggests that the average age of those on this list is 42 versus 67 for those owing conventional financial assets.[54] The average 2017 price change of cryptoassets was 14,409%, certainly overwhelming those in the

---

46 Supra, note [41], Curnutt (2018).
47 Supra, note [41], Curnutt (2018).
48 www.statista.com/statistics/377382/Bitcoin-market-capitalisation, accessed 11/02/2019.
49 Kaminska, I. (2017), "What happens when Bitcoin's market cap overtakes world GDP?", *Financial Times*, 07/12/7, https://ftalphaville.ft.com/2017/12/07/2196526/what-happens-when-Bitcoins-market-cap-overtakes-world-gdp/, accessed 18/02/2018.
50 Iskyan, K. (2016), "China's stock markets have soared by 1,479% since 2003", *Business Insider*, 06/11/2016, www.businessinsdier.com/world-stock-market-capitalizations-2016-11, accessed 18/02/2018.
51 McGeever, J. (2016), "Daily FX trading volume falls 5.5 pct to $5.1 trillion-BIS", *Reuters*, 01/09/2016, https://uk.reuters.com/article/bis-currency-idUKL8N1BC4PL, accessed 18/02/2018.
52 Noss J. at conference "The Regulation of Cryptocurrencies." City & Financial Global. London, 20/11/2018.
53 Supra, note [44], Ambler, Au-Yeang, Chung, Kauflin, Konrad, Shin & Vardi (2018).
54 Supra, note [44], Ambler, Au-Yeang, Chung, Kauflin, Konrad, Shin & Vardi (2018).

conventional asset class.[55] The average daily price volatility in January 2018 for Apple was 1.37%, Procter & Gamble 1.15%, gold 0.7%, Bitcoin 10.25%, Ether 12.62%, and XRP 16.75%.[56]

There are now some 1,500 cryptoassets in existence, valued at an aggregate US$550 billion (or over US$700 billion at its mid-December 2017 peak), up thirty-one times since commencement of 2017.[57] Bitcoin is down almost 80% from its peak and it remains to be seen to what extent they will re-emerge. It seems that the blockchain based currency is here to stay and that these virtual assets have real, albeit volatile and speculative, value. Black market transactions, tax avoidance by entities and sanctions dodging by countries like North Korea fan part of the demand, but this includes widespread excitement over the technology and the ideological aspiration for money free from interventions of whimsical nation-states.[58]

Following on from the analysis of fluctuations in cryptocurrency prices three other issues arise: variations in cryptocurrency prices relative to other geographic areas, price variations relative to fluctuations in fiat currencies and finally whether or not the same approach in fluctuations in cryptocurrencies show price variations correlating with the Black-Scholes formula,[59] which explains price changes in certain derivative contracts[60] that correlate with underlying price volatility in the commodities the derivative relates to.

2.3 Price variations relative to other geographic areas

One recent analysis[61] illustrates that there are significant price variations in cryptocurrencies between states. Indeed, the variation between them was much higher than within them. The analysis only consisted of looking at Bitcoin prices[62] but it is rational to suppose that the principle will carry over to cryptocurrencies generally. The price variations between the US and Korea varied between 15% and 40% in February 2018, and between the US and Japan it was around 10%. Between the US and the European average was only 3%. Generally speaking, prices trade at a premium above the US price elsewhere in the world.

---

55 Supra, note [44], Ambler, Au-Yeang, Chung, Kauflin, Konrad, Shin & Vardi (2018).

56 Supra, note [44], Ambler, Au-Yeang, Chung, Kauflin, Konrad, Shin & Vardi (2018).

57 Kauflin, J. (2018), "Forbes' First List Of Cryptocurrency's Richest: Meet The Secretive Freaks, Geeks And Visionaries Minting Billons From Bitcoin Mania", *Forbes*, 07/02/2018, https://www.forbes.com/sites/jeffkauflin/2018/02/07/cryptocurrency-richest-people-crypto-Bitcoin-ether-xrp/#7d8e14a372d3, accessed 18/02/2018.

58 Ibid note [58], Kauflin (2018).

59 Essentially it shows that it is possible to perfectly hedge a European style put or bought option by buying and selling the underlying commodity at the right time. Thus, the financial risk can be removed.

60 Specifically, options contracts.

61 Makarov, I. and Schoar, A. (2018), "Trading and Arbitrage in Cryptocurrency Markets", *SSRN*, 12/07/2019, https://papers.ssrn.com/sol3/papers.cfm?abstract_id=3171204, accessed 17/02/2020.

62 Some of the analysis related to Ripple and Etherium in the context of arbitrage spreads between cryptocurrencies.

The price deviations seem to have occurred most markedly when there has been a big increase in worldwide demand. Interestingly though, where there is a large arbitrage spread relative to fiat currencies, cryptocurrencies have narrower price variations between themselves. Thus, when the 20% price variation between the US and Korean price of bitcoin existed there was only a 3% price variation between bitcoin and etherium.[63]

It is rational to suppose that as data on such price variations becomes more the recipient of focus by traders, arbitrage trading will start to smooth out these price differentials. This will occur as a result of a party buying in a country with lower bitcoin prices, and this is currently normally the US, and selling where the price is higher. This will only make sense if the state where the cryptocurrency is based has no exchange controls or the profit may become trapped there. It will be interesting to see how long this takes.

2.4 Price variations relative to fiat currencies

Fiat currencies can be put into two categories: those where there are no significant exchange controls and those where there are. In the former case it would be expected that there would be a smaller price differentiation with respective cryptocurrency prices between two such currencies for the reasons discussed just above. However, in the latter case, cryptocurrencies offer the opportunity to change money from one state to another by buying the cryptocurrency inside the state with currency controls and then selling them in a state where there are none. Different cryptocurrency price levels should therefore be expected in this situation with cryptocurrency prices pulling into line between different fiat currencies. Different price relationships might be anticipated between two cryptocurrencies in separate states both having exchange controls.

2.5 Black-Scholes

The Black-Scholes formula is a mathematical model which estimates the price of options[64] traded on a European style basis (i.e. options that can only be exercised on their final date).[65] What it shows is that the option can be perfectly hedged by buying and reselling the underlying asset at the right time and thus any financial risk is removed.[66] It is therefore possible to determine

---

63 Supra, note [62], Makarov, I. and Schoar, A. (2018), p. 3.
64 An option contract is an arrangement whereby one counterparty contracts to buy, and the other to sell an asset at a future date at a price agreed now, though in practice the parties just settle up financially on the settlement date rather than trading the underlying commodity. The holder of the contract has to pay a deposit to enter into the contract and then has the right, but not the obligation, to perform. The deposit will be calculated in proportion to the risk to the other party. The holder may forfeit the contract and walk away if the price has moved against them by a greater amount than the value of the deposit, as the counterparty would then keep the deposit. The party who has received the deposit is however bound by the arrangement and is obliged to perform.
65 As opposed to American ones that can be exercised at any point up until that time.
66 Technically this is called "continuously revised delta hedging."

the right price for the option in the first place. Variations on this model have been created to cover different scenarios and its existence was the cause of a huge increase in options trading. In the context of cryptocurrencies, it will be interesting to see whether the price movements lend themselves to similar mathematical calculations predicting hedging performance. If so, the possibilities for those utilising cryptocurrency-based options as an investment or for hedging purposes will be huge.

2.6 Cryptoassets

Cryptoasset investors exist in a similar group to cryptocurrency holders, extending from anti-establishment crypto activists and electricity consuming "miners" to prescient Silicon Valley financiers and investors who got lucky, known as "hodlers".[67] Banking heir Matthew Mellon saw his US$2 million investment in Ripple (XRP) blossom into approximately US$1 billion at the peak, before tragically dying and leaving US$200 million inaccessible as his wallet key codes died with him in May 2018.[68] Others include former child actor Brock Pierce who went into Bitcoin mining and financing blockchain startups, Changpeng Zhao the owner of Binance a Bitcoin exchange, Chris Larsen, Joseph Lubin, Cameron & Tyler Winklevoss, Brian Armstrong, Matthew Roszak, Anthony Di Iorio, Michale Novogratz, Brendan Blumer, Dan Larimer, Valery Vavilov, Charles Hoskinson, Brad Garlinghouse, Barry Silbert, Vitalik Buterin, Tim Draper, Song Chi-Hyung[69] Included also in the list are various successful issuers of initial coin offerings (ICOs).[70]

The above and others would no doubt spur many on, but others could be held back from participating because of the significant risks posed by cryptoasset investments as well as from powerful cautionary statements from regulators around the world.

The International Organization of Securities Commissions (IOSCO), comprising global securities regulators, recently issued an investors' alert notice to the perceived risks connected with ICOs.[71] Its more notable members include the US Securities Exchange Commission (SEC), the UK Financial Conduct Authority (FCA), and the European Securities and Markets Authority (ESMA).

---

67 Supra, note [58], Kauflin (2018).
68 Semenova, L. (2018), "$500 Million in Ripple Lost as Billionaire Matthew Mellon Dies Suddenly", *Madeincrypto, 31/05/2018,* https://madeincrypto.com/500-million-in-ripple-lost-as-billionaire-matthew-mellon-dies-suddenly/, accessed 11/02/2019. Also Cook J, Field, M. & Chowdhury, H. (2019), "The Bitcoin fortune taken to the grave." *Daily Telegraph*, Business Section, p. 5. 06/02/2019.
69 Supra, note [44], Ambler, Au-Yeang, Chung, Kauflin, Konrad, Shin & Vardi (2018).
70 Shin, L. (2017), "The Emperor's New Coins: How Initial Coin Offerings Fueled A $100 Billion Crypto Bubble", *Forbes*, 10/07/2017, www.forbes.com/sites/laurashin/2017/07/10/the-emperors-new-coins-how-initial-coin-offerings-fueled-a-100-billion-crypto-bubble, accessed 02/02/2018.
71 IOSCO (2018), "IOSCO board communication on concerns related to initial coin offerings (ICOs)", *IOSCO Media Release,* accessed 18/01/2018.

OPPORTUNITIES AND RISKS

The IOSCO claims that these coin offerings are not standardised and their legal and regulatory status would likely depend on the merits of individual ICOs. The IOSCO regard ICOs/token sales/coin sales as highly speculative investments where investors could be putting their entire invested capital at risk. Although some operators could be providing legitimate investment opportunities to fund projects or businesses, there is a significant and growing risk coming from the increased targeting of ICOs to retail investors via online distribution channels by entities often located outside an investor's home jurisdiction. These might not be subject to regulation or could be operating illegally[72] and in violation of existing civil and regulatory laws, and in turn this raises investor protection concerns. There have also been instances of fraud,[73] and as such investors are cautioned to exercise vigilance when deciding on investing in ICOs.

So far 2018 saw ICO issues raise over US$12 billion raised and $7 billion the previous year, although two huge projects accounted for roughly half the 2018 figure.[74] Over 50% of ICO attempts failed to raise the money needed and 15% seems to have disappeared as a result of financial fraud.[75] There also appears to be a correlation between failure rates and the nature of the ICO. Kickstarter projects have a 65% failure rate, venture backed start-ups 70% and dot.com tech IPOs 85% over a period of ten years.[76] Nonetheless, such funds now hold over US$7.5 billion with a smaller sum, estimated at somewhere between US$2 and 4 billion indirectly exposed to cryptocurrencies through funds or derivatives.[77] It will be interesting to see if this period of expansion continues given that regulators are starting to treat such offerings as securities (see Chapter 4) and that as a result the legal and regulatory overheads are starting to rise. That said the sales and distribution costs should remain much lower than a traditional share or equity offer.

EOS developed a successful model by releasing its tokens over a 341-day period at a rate of 2 million a day to retain a sense of limited availability and exclusivity in the sale. The total amount raised was US$4.2 billion. Even so, its capacity to raise finance did not leave it with a trouble-free business launch. Nonetheless, the success of this approach to selling the ICOs may well result in imitators.

---

72 Wildau, G. (2017), "China central bank declares initial coin offerings illegal", *Financial Times*, 04/09/2017, https://www.ft.com/content/3fa8f60a-9156-11e7-a9e6-11d2f0ebb7f0, accessed 02/02/2018.
73 Morris, D. Z. (2017), "The SEC Filed Fraud Charges Against 2 'Initial Coin Offerings'", *Fortune*, 01/10/2017, https://fortune.com/2017/10/01/sec-ico-fraud-charges/. See also HM Treasury (2018) "Cyproassets Tasforce, final report", *HMSO*, 29/10/2018, at p. 35.
74 Telegram and EOS.
75 "#Crypto Utopia. The $20 billion Cambrian explosion of tokenized digital assets, and the emerging infrastructure being built to support them." *Autonomous Next*, 2018, https://next.autonomous.com/crypto-utopia, p. 3.
76 Ibid *Autonomous Next*, 2018, p. 4.
77 Ibid, *Autonomous Next*, 2018, p. 5.

There has been a definite change in the range of activities for which ICOs have raised money. For example:

	% in 2016	% in 2018 (Total 300% greater than 2016)
Finance and investments	73	5
Core technology	10	17
Media and social	5	17
Cloud	4	3
Gambling	3	8
Financial markets	2	12
Banking and payments	2	14
Cryptocurrency[78]	1	3
Internet of things and people	0	21

The two key issues are the obvious explosion in the utilisation of ICOs in certain areas and one element that has helped facilitate this is the utilisation of discounts in the form of "airdrops". This is the payment of a sign-up bonus to the people buying the ICOs, typically of 5–10%. It is rather like a discounted bond issue or, were they are permitted, a discounted share issue.[79] Even so, at present they are high risk investments: 34% lose more than half their original price and 60% have underperformed relative to both Bitcoin and Ether.[80]

Thus far, the IOSCO further advised that financial regulators from more than twenty-six countries have issued warnings on ICO risks. The IOSCO's investor alert in 2015 mentioned that investors should wake up quickly and get up to speed on this issue.[81] The investors' alert on the perceived risks of cryptoassets merits close scrutiny given the range of risks associated with Bitcoin despite IOSCO falling behind on the FinTech curve earlier. This is exacerbated by the absence of a clear legal framework as the systems have emerged too quickly for the legal and regulatory systems to stay in front. A state of affairs which De Filippi and Wright refer to as the *lex cryptographica*,[82] a state of affairs which is exacerbated by the fact that the peer-to-peer basis on which blockchain operates means that there is not a dominant party or intermediary to impose a code.

---

78 Adapted from Ibid, *Autonomous Next*, 2018, p. 19.

79 Shares can be issued on a partly paid basis with the balance to be paid at a later date but most states have controls on the share buy backs, so discounted shares become a more difficult area. That said a firm issuing shares has a lot of freedom to set their price and, in the case of a public issue, the underwriters will tend to put downward pressure on the launch price to reduce the risk of having to start buying them.

80 Supra, note [76], *Autonomous Next*, 2018, p. 36.

81 Zhao, W. (2018), "Global Securities Watchdog Warns Investors On ICO Risks", *Coin Desk*, 19/01/2018, https://www.coindesk.com/global-securities-watchdog-warns-investors-on-ico-risks, accessed 02/02/2018.

82 De Filippi, P. & Wright, A. (2018), *Blockchain and the Law. The Rule of Code*. Harvard University Press, p. 5.

OPPORTUNITIES AND RISKS

The risk here is to both issuers and investors. There seems to have been an assumption made in many ICO-type issues that if the issue is termed a "token" and the issuing document a "white paper" then the existing securities laws of the state of issuance do not apply. That this is not the case is apparent from the analysis of the securities laws of a number of states analysed later in the book. The attraction to the parties of assuming the issuance takes place outside the securities laws arises from the very high cost of conforming with the prospectus or information memorandum document (a type of advertising brochure which has to comply with strict securities laws and where relevant stock exchange rules). If an issue appears to be in the nature of a share or a bond or an interest in a collective investment scheme then the starting assumption should be that the home securities regulator will treat it as such.

Cryptoassets and in particular Bitcoin have unique investment risks and these are outlined as follows.[83]

2.7 Relevant risks

2.7.1 Regulatory risk

Bitcoin has been associated with black market transactions, money laundering, illicit activities and tax evasion.[84] Many governments across the world are responding with policies and measures to regulate, restrict or ban the use and sale of bitcoin, and some, like China, have already done so.[85] Others, like Japan, require bitcoin exchanges to maintain minimum capitalisation and follow general anti-money laundering (AML) and know your customer (KYC) procedures resembling those in the banking sector.[86] Yet, other countries are initiating their own regulatory approaches, but the likely lack of uniform regulations covering bitcoins and other cryptocurrencies could lead to questions over their longevity, liquidity, and universality. Regulatory aspects are discussed at length later in the book.

2.7.2 Security risk

Though until now the Bitcoin platform has not been significantly compromised, Bitcoin exchanges, which are entirely digital, are at risk from hackers, malware and operational glitches. These have occurred on various occasions, the more

---

[83] Investopedia (2018), "Bitcoin", *Investopedia*, www.investopedia.com/terms/b/Bitcoin.asp, accessed 18/02/2018.

[84] Bloomberg, J. (2017), "Using Bitcoin or Other Cryptocurrency To Commit Crimes? Law Enforcement Is Onto You", *Forbes*, 28/12/2017, www.forbes.com/sites/jasonbloomberg/2017/12/28/using-Bitcoin-or-other-cryptocurrency-to-commit-crimes-law-enforcement-is-onto-you/#4e623af93bdc, accessed 02/02/2018.

[85] Leng, S. (2017), "Why has China declared war on Bitcoin and digital currencies?", *South China Morning Post (SCMP)*, 16/09/2017, www.scmp.com/news/china/economy/article/2111456/why-has-china-declared-war-Bitcoin-and-digital-currencies, accessed 02/02/2018.

[86] Yagami, K. (2017), "Japan: A forward thinking Bitcoin nation", *Forbes*, 02/11/2017, www.forbes.com/sites/outofasia/2017/11/02/japan-a-forward-thinking-Bitcoin-nation/#6608953733a3, accessed 02/02/2018.

notable ones involve Mt. Gox, a bitcoin exchange in Japan that was the largest in the world at the time, which had to close down following the theft of millions of dollars of bitcoin.[87] There was also the 2018 Coincheck case where some US$530 million worth of coins were stolen[88] and one report suggests that US$927 million was stolen in hacking attacks in the first nine months of 2018 alone.[89] There are ways to enhance the security features of bitcoin exchanges, but equally users could opt for safer ways to store their bitcoins, such as the option of offline cold wallets. Major global insurers are beginning to offer protection against cryptocurrency theft. They appear willing to solve the daunting challenges this brings rather than miss out on this volatile and loosely regulated, but rapidly growing business.[90] Guardian Vaults, a leading Australian private vault and safety deposit box operator, now offers a custodial safety deposit box using technology such as biometric hand scanners, facial recognition protocols and so on. It is seeing a growing customer demand trend for its services.[91]

2.7.3 Insurance risk

Some investments in the US could be insured via the Securities Investor Protection Corporation, while conventional bank accounts are insured via the Federal Deposit Insurance Corporation, up to a stipulated amount depending on the jurisdiction. Bitcoin exchanges and bitcoin accounts are generally not insured by any federal or government initiative in the US and this appears to be the case in most other economies. Insurance coverage for loss or theft of bitcoin represents an opportunity and a challenge as cryptocurrencies are purely digital and hold a variable market value. So far, the insurance industry responds to cryptocurrencies rather slowly, with only a few offering insurance covers. These include XL Catlin, Chubb, and Mitsui Sumitomo Insurance. Several others are said to be looking into theft coverage for companies handling cryptocurrencies such as Bitcoin and Ether which transact between anonymous parties. The challenge for insurers is how to cover those risks for customers they know little about, who use technology few understand and a nascent industry lacking troves of data insurers usually rely on in designing and pricing coverage.

---

87 Harney, A. & Stecklow, S. (2017), "Twice burned-How Mt. Gox's Bitcoin customers could lose again", *Reuters*, 16/11/2017, www.reuters.com/investigates/special-report/Bitcoin-gox/, accessed 02/02/2018.

88 Uranaka, T. & Wilson, T. (2018), "Japan raps Coincheck, orders broader checks after $530 million cryptocurrency theft", *Reuters*, 29/01/2018, https://de.reuters.com/article/us-japan-crypto-currency-idUSKBN1FI06S, accessed 02/02/2018.

89 Chavez-Dreyfuss, G. (2018), "Cryptocurrency theft hits nearly $1 billion in first nine months: report", *Reuters*, 10/10/2018, https://uk.reuters.com/article/uk-crupto-currency-crime/cryptocurrency-theft-hits-nearly-1-billion-in-the-first-nine-months-idUKKCN1MK1JD.

90 Barlyn, S. (2018), "Insurers gingerly test Bitcoin business with heist policies", *Reuters*, 01/02/2018, www.reuters.com/article/us-markets-Bitcoin-insurance-insight/insurers-gingerly-test-Bitcoin-business-with-heist-policies-idUSKBN1FL406, accessed 18/02/2018.

91 Redman, J. (2017), "Australian Vault Provider Says Securing Bitcoin In Safety Boxes Is Trending", *Bitcoin,* 05/12/2017, https://news.Bitcoin.com/australian-vault-provider-says-securing-Bitcoin-in-safety-boxes-is-trending/, accessed 02/02/2018.

2.7.4 Fraud risk

Fraudsters profit from the selling of false coins, a situation that may become more common as Bitcoin users exercise more care when using and safeguarding the use of their private key encryptions. In the US for instance, the SEC initiated legal action against an operator of a bitcoin related Ponzi scheme in July 2013.[92] The SEC's enforcement division opened dozens of investigations involving ICOs and digital assets in 2017, of which many were ongoing at the close of 2018. The SEC mentioned that while many of its investigations have focused on fraud, it is also examining cases to ensure compliance with the registration requirements of US federal securities laws. As such, while companies raised millions of dollars through ICOs prior to mid-2017, these fundraising activities have fallen sharply subsequent to the SEC cautioning that it treats nearly all digital tokens as securities.[93]

Likewise, in the UK, Action Fraud[94] showed that there were 203 reports of cyproasset fraud in June–July 2018 alone in the UK. Total losses exceeded £2 million with an average of over £10,000 per victim.

2.7.5 Market risk

The extreme price volatility of cryptocurrencies presents a serious challenge for most investors and users. Until their applications or uses expand significantly, their price remains highly speculative and risky. For example, the Consumer Finance Protection Bureau (CFPB) reported Bitcoin prices falling as much as 61% in a single day in 2013, and as much as 80% in 2014 with a similar collapse in 2018.[95] Bitcoin's fate as a currency rests on more individuals and merchants using it for transaction purposes rather than mainly for speculation. Bitcoin price volatility surged further in 2017 and then fell back in 2018 before rising steadily in mid-2019.[96] Though Bitcoin no longer dominates the cryptocurrency market to the extent that it used to it still leads the pack, because it appears to benefit from an early mover advantage, brand recognition and venture capital backup.[97] Still, technological breakthroughs in the shape of a better digital coin could always present a threat.

---

92 SEC (2013), "SEC charges Texas man with running Bitcoin-denominated Ponzi scheme", *SEC Media Release*, 23/07/2013, www.sec.gov/news/press-release/2013-132, accessed 02/02/2018.

93 Roberts, J.J. (2018), "Cryptocurrency Scams Are Now Among the SEC's Top Enforcement Priorities", *Forbes*, 2/11/2018, https://fortune.com/2018/11/02/sec-ico-report-cryptocurrency-scams/, accessed 5/03/2019; SEC, "Annual Report 2018: Division of Enforcement", SEC, 2/11/2018, www.sec.gov/files/enforcement-annual-report-2018.pdf, accessed 5/05/2019.

94 Action Fraud (2018), "Cryptocurrency fraud leads to £2 million worth of losses this summer", *Action Fraud*, 10/08/2018. www.actionfraud.police.uk/alert/2m-lost-to-cryptocurrency-fraud.

95 Consumer Finance Protection Bureau (2014), "CFPB warns consumers about Bitcoin" *CFPB*, 11/08/2014, www.consumerfinance.gov/about-us/newsroom/cfpb-warns-consumers-about-Bitcoin/, accessed 02/02/2018.

96 Chaparro, F. (2017), "Bitcoin went bonkers in 2017-here's what happened as the cryptocurrency surged more than 1000%", *Business Insider*, 30/12/2017, www.businessinsider.com/Bitcoin-price-in-2017-review-2017-12, accessed 02/02/2018.

97 Zhao, W. (2018), "Crypto Market Sets To New High as Bitcoin Dominance Drops to Historic Low", *Coin Desk*, 02/01/2018, www.coindesk.com/crypto-market-cap-sets-time-high-Bitcoin-share-drops-historic-low, accessed 18/02/2018.

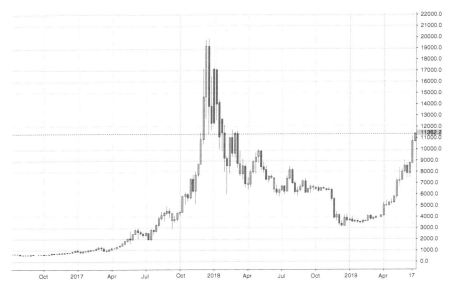

Figure 2 Bitcoin's price variations 2006–2019

2.7.6 Tax risk

Tax laws in various jurisdictions across the world are not entirely clear or explicit, implying the possibility of tax infringements for investors who fail to report on their bitcoin transactions.[98] In the US bitcoin is also ineligible from inclusion in any tax relief for retirement accounts, suggesting that in the US there are no good legal options to shield these investments from taxation. The HM Revenue and Customs in the UK (HMRC) has provided guidance targeted at individuals to provide clarity on when tax might need to be paid on Bitcoin and other cryptoassets.[99]

There are therefore periods when there is great potential for financial gain, especially from the top ten cryptocurrencies ranked in terms of market cap, which is led by Bitcoin since their inception in 2009 until now; but there are also all kinds of risks attached to the world of digital currencies. Opinions about this are not permanent as the technology underpinning them continues to evolve, as business applications expand and as regulations emerge. One prominent US bank CEO, for example, recently retracted his previous claim that

---

[98] Roberts, J.J. (2018), "Bitcoin and Taxes: What You Need To Know About Cryptocurrency and the IRS", *Fortune*, 29/01/2018, https://fortune.com/2018/01/29/Bitcoin-taxes-cryptocurrency-irs/, accessed 02/02/2018.

[99] HM Revenue & Customs (HMRC) (2018), "Cryptoassets for individuals", *HMRC Policy Paper*, 19/12/2018, www.gov.uk/government/.../tax-on-cryptoassets/cryptoassets-for-individuals, accessed 5/03/2019.

Bitcoin was a fraud and now believes in the technology behind it, but remains concerned about how government policies will impact on it in the future.[100] More interestingly, the bank's respectable Global Research Unit concludes that cryptocurrencies could one day play a role in the diversification of global bond and equity portfolios.[101] The next chapter evaluates Bitcoin's role as a global digital currency.

2.7.7 Legal risk

Perhaps surprisingly one element that has been neglected is the legal basis on which it is possible to own cryptocurrencies and crypto wallets. The closest existing basis for such legal ownership in common law countries is that of bailment, which traditionally covered leaving an item in store but retaining ownership. The owner can thus withstand a claim against it by the creditors of the warehouse or other location where the goods are stored. There is a parallel here with crypto wallets which store the cryptocurrency concerned, hopefully securely by way of a private electronic key.[102] However, it remains a legal grey area as to whether it is possible to have digital bailment of digital products. The long-standing English tradition, adopted by common law states is that the custom of the market place will be applied by the courts and it is therefore reasonable to assume that the courts would apply the principles of bailment to digital assets.[103]

The alternative possibility in common law jurisdictions is to apply the law of trusts and in civil law jurisdictions, the law of agency. In the case of applying the law of trusts the structure would be that that the custodian holds the assets for the cryptocurrency owner and holds the legal title to it. The benefits of ownership belong to the owner who has an equitable title and can claim the assets from the custodian and who also has priority over the custodian's creditors in the event of the custodian's insolvency.[104] In most civil law states the same structure can be constructed through existing legal principles of agency law.

The question which then arises is the legal status of the cryptocurrency itself. Is it digital property, with a new legal status, or alternately would the definition of *chose in action* or *chose in possession* be extended to cover it? The tradition of recognising commercial custom should guarantee that one of the above options is applied in common law jurisdictions.

---

100 Kim, T. (2018), "Jamie Dimon says he regrets calling Bitcoin a fraud and believes in the technology behind it", *CNBC,* 09/01/2018, https://www.cnbc.com/2018/01/09/jamie-dimon-says-he-regrets-calling-Bitcoin-a-fraud.html, accessed 02/02/2018.
101 Loeys, J. & Chang, J. (2018), *Decrypting cryptocurrencies: Technology, applications and challenges*, New York, J.P. Morgan.
102 Micheler, E. and Davies, S., "The future of money and the impact of Fintech and cryptocurrencies", London School of Economics. Speech at conference, London, 26/11/2018.
103 *Goodwin v Robarts* (1876) 1 App. Cas. 476.
104 Supra, note [103].

2.7.8 Scale risk

At present blockchain-based systems are slow, taking an average of ten minutes per Bitcoin transaction, and relatively small in scale with under a quarter of a million transactions a day compared with 150 million a day at Visa alone, each carried out in a fraction of a second.[105] To compete, blockchain-based systems are going to have to handle far greater numbers of transactions. As we have already seen blockchain-based transactions grow progressively and the networks and computers utilising it will thus need far greater capacity than at present to handle it all. In turn this will require a considerable investment of capital by users, especially at the retail end where such an increase in costs may be a deterrence to use. It may be possible to resolve this by processing transactions through payment channels which do not requiring validation by miners[106] or by the development of other approaches which reduce the need for such a vast increase in capacity. At present this is an area that remains uncertain.

---

105 Blockchain Info, "Bitcoin Charts" https://blockchain.info/charts/n-transactions; Daily Hodl, (2018), "Cryptocurrency Transaction Speeds: The CompleteReview", *The Daily Hodl*, 28/07/2018, https://dailyhodl.com/2018/04/27/cryptocurrency-transaction-speeds-the-complete-review/.

106 Poon, J and Dryja, T. (2016), "The Bitcoin Lightning Network: Scalable Off-Chain Instant Payments", *Lightning network*, 14/01/2016.

CHAPTER 3

A digital global currency

3.1 Introduction

When releasing his famous Bitcoin white paper, Satoshi Nakamoto announced that he had developed a new electronic cash system that was fully peer-to-peer with no trusted third party. In effect Nakamoto introduced a system of online exchange to enable two parties to exchange tokens of value without divulging vulnerable information about themselves or their financial accounts. The idea was to operate outside of the conventional banking structure and allow people to send digital money directly to each other – peer-to-peer (P2P) as the notion of middleman-free commerce is known – and where no banks or credit cards are needed, and no payments processors or other "trusted" third parties are involved.[1] This in essence is digital cash.

Whether Bitcoin could evolve as digital cash as intended, or take different directions are explored in the context of the following five scenarios.[2]

3.2 The case against

Mainstream economists, most central banks and most regulators recognised that money has three main characteristics: as a unit of account, a medium of exchange and a store of value. For Bitcoin and other cryptocurrencies to achieve these they need broad-based support from consumers and businesses. Despite being in existence for almost a decade, it is still an open question whether cryptocurrency usage has reached a critical mass, or is still held back by insufficient users, lack of sellers accepting it and insufficient reason to hold it due to price volatility.

Those critical of cryptocurrency point to extreme price volatility[3] which inhibits its function as a medium of exchange or store of value. It is not entirely convenient to buy a cup of coffee with Bitcoin even when some merchants are willing to accept them, as most items are priced in fiat currency like the US dollar. The quick and deep price changes within minutes could mean profit or loss

---

[1] Vigna, P. & Casey, M. J. (2015) *Cryptocurrency: How bitcoin and digital money are challenging the global economic order*, London, The Bodley Head.

[2] Supra, note [1], Vigna and Casey (2015).

[3] Periaky, A., Artigas, J. C., Hewitt, A. and Reade, J. "Cryptocurrencies are no substitute for gold." World Gold Council White Paper, 25/01/2018.

being exaggerated in terms of fiat currency value unless some kind of financial solution is available to cut down these swings. Research suggests that Bitcoin is mostly held for speculative rather than for transaction purposes and thus most current holders are less concerned at its utility to buy goods and services.

As the speculative element is very strong, Bitcoin as a store of value could be compared to gold or other precious commodities. Bitcoin dwarfs gold and other precious commodities in terms of the extent of price swings. Gold by comparison is less volatile, has a more liquid market, trades in an established regulatory framework, and has a well understood role in investment portfolios and little overlap with Bitcoin on many sources of demand and supply. These characteristics underpin gold's function as a mainstream financial asset that will probably continue to resonate in the new digital world.[4] Mainstream analysts generally support the contention that Bitcoin's extreme price volatility and relatively, much lower usage as a medium of exchange, disqualifies for the moment Bitcoin's claim as a potential global digital currency.[5]

As alluded to earlier, Bitcoin needs to facilitate transactions, be a store of value, and increasingly important in modern monetary system, be the lender of last resort in providing liquidity to financial institutions in times of crises.[6] Seashells, cigarettes, silver and gold have on previous occasions in the past operated as money as these, on many occasions, are scarce real assets with value to their users and are available in small units to facilitate easy transactions.[7] Hardly any economies use these as money any more. Instead the world has migrated to the use of fiat money, or a currency with no intrinsic value. They are paper printed by governments with quantities amplified by the financial system, and are valuable or sought after because governments guarantee them and want taxes to be paid in them. Fiat currency issued by central banks is superior to money based on real assets such as gold as it could be adjusted to better serve economies instead of being constrained by the production of a natural resource. In comparison the volume of cryptocurrency, including Bitcoin, like a natural resource, cannot be adjusted.

There have been past occasions when governments have abused fiat money and printed too much, as exemplified by the stagflation of the 1970s or the immediate years following the 2008 global financial crisis. In extreme cases the hyperinflation of Germany in the 1920s and 30s coupled with that of Zimbabwe in recent years and Venezuela today show how extreme this can get. There are therefore problems associated with fiat money as well, depending on the role of central banks as stewards of money.

---

4 Supra, note [3], Periaky, Artigas, Hewitt and Reade (2018).

5 Montag, A. (2017), "Kevin O'Leary explain one big thing people don't understand about bitcoin (but need to)", *CNBC*, 07/12/2017, www.cnbc.com/2017/12/07/kevin-oleary-bitcoin-is-an-asset-not-a-currency.html, accessed 02/02/2018.

6 Danielsson, J. (2018), "Why cryptocurrencies don't make sense" *World Economic Forum (WEF)*, 15/02/2018, www.weforum.oeg/agenda/2018/02/why-cryptocurrencies-dont-make-sense, accessed 18/02/2018.

7 Ferguson, N. (2012), *The Ascent of Money: A Financial History of the World*, 4th Edition, London, Penguin Books.

For now, Bitcoin is far less useful for commercial transactions.[8] With cash, transactions are costless, anonymous and immediate, while electronic transactions are very cheap and also immediate for most amounts. In contrast, Bitcoin transactions could require an hour or more at a cost of at least US$25 and are not fully anonymous. There are now other cryptocurrencies promising greater efficiency, privacy and speed. Still, it takes time to locate businesses or entities willing to accept Bitcoin, and probably considerably longer for other cryptocurrencies. The largest amount that could be transacted by cryptocurrencies are dwarfed by the scale of transactions in fiat currency.

As a store of value, neither cryptocurrencies nor fiat money have any intrinsic value. Their utilisation is based on belief, faith, credibility and the expectation that the money would retain its value over time. In the case of fiat money, most central banks are committed to keeping its value stable at a decreasing rate of 2% annually and most have been able at keeping their tracking errors small for sustained periods. Cryptocurrencies, including Bitcoin, are less successful in this regard, with values doubling or halving sometimes in a matter of hours. Thus, most holders hold cryptocurrencies, including Bitcoin, for speculative reasons. This leaves the lender of last resort issue. Central banks as lenders of last resort have been seen as essential ever since Walter Bagehot's 1873 analysis of the 1866 crisis. It was used more recently during the 2007 global financial crisis and could be needed again in the future. There appears at this stage of cryptocurrency evolution no real sign of any such equivalent facility. The three points taken together suggest that cryptocurrencies are less useful than existing fiat money.[9]

3.3 The evolution of Bitcoin

With its low cost, high speed, decentralised network, Bitcoin could become the first cryptocurrency to start to function as money. In the digital world, simplicity and cost savings are close to essential benefits. Many people believe that Bitcoin would gradually achieve the three essential features of modern-day money and so be as heavily utilised as the US dollar. It is argued that despite some public image issues and regulatory constraints, the ecosystem is not entirely unaccommodating for Bitcoin to flourish. Innovation friendly countries such as Switzerland, Singapore, UK, and Canada are fostering hubs of innovation to give the technology underpinning Bitcoin a strong forward momentum. In the US, thoughtful federal regulators are leaving space for innovation despite the controversy regarding the New York Department of Financial Services BitLicense concept. Various large and small emerging economies have not been too slow to participate in the evolution of Bitcoin as a global digital currency, especially for their large unbanked population such as can be found in India, Africa, and Indonesia.[10]

---

8 Supra, note [6], Danielsson (2018).
9 Supra, note [6], Danielsson (2018).
10 Carrick, J. (2016), "Bitcoin as a Complement to Emerging Market Currencies", *Emerging Markets Finance and Trade*, 52 (10), pp. 2321–2334.

It is therefore likely that Bitcoin will continue to evolve attached to the real economy, where blockchain (or its variant equivalent) underpinning Bitcoin is increasingly adopted by a variety of institutions and businesses to satisfy their requirements.

From a legal perspective, cryptocurrencies could be regarded as negotiable, performing an essential function of money through judicially recognised mercantile usage in the UK.[11] The judiciary's view of this is, however, based on the mercantile situation in the 19th century and before the emergence of digital currency. An indication of the current judicial view on the matter could come from the outcome of forthcoming cases where decisions would have to be made on the status of Bitcoin.[12]

Further, with regards to the UK, a Bank of England research report argues that whether digital currency could be considered to be money rests on the extent to which it serves as a store of value, a medium of exchange and a unit of account. On the basis of this, at its present stage of evolution cryptocurrencies are deemed to not yet reach that status[13] as was stated by the Governor of the Bank of England, Mark Carney in March 2018. For UK tax purposes however, cryptocurrencies are broadly treated as a foreign currency, and where its value appreciates this would be deemed as a foreign currency gain. Which further implies that gains on foreign currency held for personal use, or bought and held speculatively, would not attract tax while gains on trading might be taxable as capital gains.[14] Also, HMRC's guidance for Bitcoin is that it is not a form of economic activity and as such transactions involving it are not subject to value added tax (VAT).[15] The UK's position on the status of digital currency could be shaped differently if the country were ever to opt for the use of a central bank issued digital currency. Researchers at the Bank of England suggest significant benefits from central bank digital currency such as an increase of as much as 3% in GDP and improved stability when stabilising inflation and reducing the risk of "boom and bust," but they caution that further research is required.[16] Meanwhile, currently the Bank of England has no immediate plans to issue a digital currency.[17]

---

11 The House of Lords upheld he decision in *Goodwin v Robarts* (1875) L.R. 10 Exch. 337, Exchequer Chamber and approved in the *ratio decidendi* of the decision: (1876) 1 App. Cas. 476; Clarke, M. A., Hooley, R. J. A., Muday, R. J. C., Sealey, L. S., Tettenborn, A. M. & Tuners, P. G. (2017) *Commercial Law: Text Cases and Materials*, 5th Edition, Oxford, Oxford University Press.

12 Falvey, D. (2018), "Cryptocurrency latest: 'Unprecedented' Bitcoin legal battles BAFFLE top regulation lawyers." *Daily Express*, 15/02/2018. www.express.co.uk/finance/city/919207/cryptocurrency-news-bitcoin-legal-battle-regulation-litecoin-rille-etherium, accessed 18/02/2018.

13 Ali, R., Barrdear, J., Clews, R. & Southgate, J. "The Economics of Digital Currencies." *Bank of England Quarterly Bulletin*, 2014, Q3.

14 Wood, A. (2017), "Tax on Bitcoin Activity and other Cryptocurrencies" *Enterprise Tax*, 8/12/2017, https://www.etctax.co.uk/tax-on-bitcoin/, accessed 2/2/2018.

15 Supra note [14], Wood (2017).

16 Barrdear, J. & Kumhof, M. (2016), "The Macroeconomics of Central Bank Issued Digital Currencies", *Bank of England Working Paper No 605*, 18/07/2016. www.bankofengland.co.uk/working-paper/2016/the-macroeconomics-of-central-bank-issued-digital-currencies, accessed 2/02/2018.

17 Buntix, J. P. (2018), "Bank of England Cancels Plans to Issue Digital Currency." *The Merkle*, 8/01/2018. https://thebitcoin.pub/t/bank-of-england-cancels-plans-to-issue-a-digital-currency/22289, accessed 2/02/2018. Bruce, A. (2017), "BoE's Carney sees problems with

The *Spinoza* case,[18] a recent US example from the jurisdiction of Florida, took the view that Bitcoin is property not a currency, as it did not meet the definition of a "payment instrument". A "payment instrument" includes a cheque, draft, warrant, money order, travelers' cheques, electronic instrument, or other instrument, payment of money or monetary value whether or not negotiable.[19] The court's finding that Espinoza did not engage in the sale of a payment instrument is puzzling.[20] While Florida's money transmitter law does not define "money," many US state laws define "money" as a medium of exchange issued by a government, implying that Bitcoin is not "money" under state law. Decentralised digital currencies such as Bitcoin commonly fall within the definition of "monetary value". This is almost universally defined as medium of exchange whether or not redeemable in currency.

While "monetary value" is listed within Florida's definition of a "payment instrument", the circuit court moved past this analysis, focusing instead on determining whether Bitcoin is "money". Therefore, instead of considering whether Bitcoin could be something of monetary value, the court held that cryptocurrencies are not currently included in the statutory definition of a "payment instrument", nor does Bitcoin fit into one of the defined categories listed. The court went on further to state that even though it was not an expert in economics. It is very clear, even to someone with limited knowledge in the area, that Bitcoin has a long way to go before it is the equivalent of money.[21] The Florida circuit court's decision would eventually have to follow the opinions of its federal circuit and other superior federal courts.

An equivalent decision was also reached in one federal case drawing from "funds" as defined in 18 U.S.C. s.1960,[22] while in an earlier federal case,[23] the court concluded that in the light of the consensus as to the ordinary meaning of "funds" for the purposes of s.1960, it means "pecuniary resources which are generally accepted as a medium of exchange or a mean of payment." Applying this definition, the court held that it is clear that Bitcoins are funds within the meaning of that term. Two other subsequent federal cases also reached the conclusion that Bitcoin is a digital currency.[24] Differing opinions on Bitcoin will

---

central-bank issued cryptocurrencies", *Reuters*, 20/12/2017. https://uk.reuters.com/article/uk-britain-boe-carney-bitcoin/boes-carney-sees-problems-with-central-bank-issued-cryptocurrencies-idUKKBN1EE1ZO, accessed 2/02/2018.

18 Order Granting Motion to Dismiss, *Florida v Espinoza* (22 July 2016).

19 Fla. Stat. Section 560.125 (29) defines "Payment instrument" to include "a check, draft, warrant, money order, travelers check, electronic instrument, or other instrument, payment of money or monetary value whether or not negotiable."

20 Miller, K., Hansen, J. D. and Rosini, L. (2016), "Florida State Court Order in Espinoza Case Raises Questions about Classification of Bitcoin under Florida Law." *Perkins Cole Virtual Currency Report.* 26/07/2016.

21 Supra note [20]. Miller, Hansen and Rosini (2016).

22 *United States v Petix*, No 15-CR-227A, 2016 WL 7,017,919.

23 *United States v Murgio*, 209 F.Supp. 3d 698, 707 (SDNY, 19/11/2016).

24 *United States v Ulbricht*, 858 F. 3d 71, 82–83 (2nd Cir. 2017); *United States v Lord*, No CR 15-00240-01/02, 2017 WL 1,424,806 (W.D. La. 20/4/2017).

continue as it evolves or until the involvement of the US Supreme Court or when US Congress passes legislation that defines Bitcoin for legal purposes.

For the moment, US Federal regulators, such as the SEC, maintain that US federal securities law may apply to cryptocurrencies,[25] depending on the circumstances, and in particular because of the *"Howey* Test"[26] created by the Supreme Court as a means of determining whether certain transactions qualify as investment contracts or securities.[27] The *Howey* Test comprises a four part question. These ask whether there was an investment of money, whether this occurs in a common enterprise, whether it is undertaken with the expectation of profit, and whether any such profit arises from the managerial initiatives of others.

The SEC's investigative report on DAO's ICO concludes that the DAO tokens issued constituted a security or stock and should therefore be regulated under existing securities laws.[28] The SEC report advises that whether or not a particular transaction involves the offer and sale of security regardless of the terminology used will depend on the facts and circumstances, including the economic realities of the transaction.

The CFTC appears to have no intention of interfering with cryptocurrencies or blockchain, though that would no doubt change were derivatives structured in relation to cryptocurrencies or cryptoassets to emerge at a significant level. The CFTC envisions a future not only with Bitcoin and blockchain in it, but also with them having a transformative effect and it has stated that it has no intention of standing in the way of such innovation. It adds that until the US Congress chooses to act, it calls upon the investment community and advocacy community around digital currencies to create some kind of self-regulatory organisation to develop standards around cyber policy, and insider trading ethics code of conduct.[29]

While the SEC and bank regulators supervise specific institutions and discrete activities, and state regulators have jurisdiction in their respective jurisdictions over money transmission, the CFTC is the only federal regulator of cryptocurrency markets. In terms of CFTC regulation cryptocurrencies such as Bitcoins are treated as a commodity under the Commodity Exchange Act over which the SEC does not enjoy direct oversight. The CFTC has wide jurisdiction over derivatives markets, including futures in digital currencies, but only limited jurisdiction over spot markets where participants buy and sell virtual currencies for prompt delivery.

On 1 December 2017, the CFTC announced that the Chicago Mercantile Exchange Inc. (CME) and the Chicago Board Options Exchange (CBOE) Futures

---

25 The SEC ruling specifically related to etherium but the principle is worded in a manner which suggests that it is generally applicable to cryptocurrencies.

26 *SEC v W J Howey* Co. 328, US 293.

27 Churchhouse, T. (2017), "Is a cryptocurrency like a stock? This is what the SEC says...", *Stansberry Pacific Research*, 28/07/2017, https://stansberrypacific.com/asia-wealth-investment-daily/cryptocurrency-like-stock-sec-rules/, accessed 2/02/2018.

28 SEC (2017), "Report of an Investigation Pursuant to section 21(a) of the Securities Exchange Act 1934: The DAO", *SEC Release No 81,207*, 25/07/2017.

29 Terzo, G. (2018), "CFTC's Quintenz 'Bitcoin and Blockchain are Transformative'", *CCN*, 7/02/2018. www.ccn.com/cftc-quintenz-bitcoin–blockchain-transformative, accessed 18/02/2018.

Exchange (CFE) had been given the regulatory green light to list Bitcoin futures.[30] This is a significant step in allowing mainstream investors to buy and sell the highly volatile cryptocurrency. Both had also agreed to operate under a self-certified regime for their upcoming contracts. These future exchanges are also required to monitor for potential market manipulation and market dislocations like sudden drops and trading outages. The announcement led to an immediate surge in Bitcoin prices, as market participants hope that with the availability of Bitcoin futures through these futures exchanges, more institutional investors' funds would flow into the Bitcoin space to lift it mainstream as an asset class.[31]

The IRS virtual currency guidance treats virtual currency as property for US federal tax purposes and that general rules for property transactions would apply.[32] On 25 March 2014, the IRS defined Bitcoin as a convertible digital currency that functions as a medium of exchange and operates like a real currency but does not have legal tender status in any jurisdiction. Given that the announcement had less impact than expected, on 17 November 2016 the IRS requested the largest Bitcoin exchange in the US, Coinbase, to furnish records of all customers who had purchased cryptocurrency from the company between 2013 and 2015, so as to demand back taxes from the largest customers on the exchange. This resulted from the IRS discovering that the likelihood of under-reporting is significant, as Bitcoin transactions do not go through a third party, implying no good way to report the transactions, thereby making it easier for those involved to evade taxes. This realisation could likely push the IRS to further define Bitcoin and other cryptocurrencies so as to curb illegal activities. In the meantime, as alluded to earlier, the court ordered Bitcoin to report 14,355 users to the IRS on 29 November 2017.

The US Federal Reserve regards cryptocurrencies as highly speculative assets and not a stable source of value.[33] The Fed noted that Bitcoin remains a very small part of the overall payment system and that it did not have the authority to regulate cryptocurrencies.[34] Its regulatory powers extend only to those banking institutions that they already supervise. It does not play any regulatory role with respect to cryptocurrencies; other than assuring that banking organisations that

---

30 Stafford, P. (2017), "US Regulator Gives Green Light for Bitcoin Futures Trading. CME, CBOE and Cantor pass hurdle in preparing derivatives on volatile cryptocurrency", *Financial Times*, 2/12/2017.

31 Shen, L. (2017), "Bitcoin Futures are about to be a thing and it's sent prices soaring", *Fortune*, 1/12/2017.

32 Internal Revenue Service (IRS) "IRS virtual currency guidance: Virtual currency is treated as property for US federal tax purposes: General rules for property transactions apply." *IR-2014-36*, 25/03/14 https://www.irs.gov/businesses/small-businesses-self-employed/virtual-currencies, accessed 2/02/2018.

33 Buck, J. (2017), "US Fed Chair speaks out on bitcoin and national crypto", *Coin Telegraph*, 15/12/2017. www.cointelegraph.com/news/us-fed-chair-speaks-out-on-bitcoin-and-national-crypto, accessed 2/02/2018.

34 Melloy, J. (2017), "Fed chief Yellen says bitcoin is a 'highly speculative assets'", *CNBC*, 13/12/2017. www.cnbc.com/2017/12/13/fed-chief-yellen-says-bitcoin-is-a-highly-speculative-asset.html, accessed 2/02/2018.

they do supervise are attentive; that they are appropriately managing any interactions they have with participants in that market; and appropriately monitoring anti-money laundering and Bank Secrecy Act responsibilities that apply. The US Fed does not differentiate between decentralised currencies like Bitcoin that are neither issued nor given any value by any particular jurisdictions and digital currencies issued by governments themselves.

Though central banks are exploring the option of creating their own centralised digital currencies constituted as legal tender, the Federal Reserve has no current agenda of launching a digital dollar,[35] even as Venezuela, Catalonia, Russia and Dubai have announced plans in this direction.[36] The US Fed's tentative conclusions are that there are limited benefits and limited needs from introducing central bank issued digital currency that are counterweighed by other concerns.[37] China however is taking rapid steps towards issuing a state-backed cryptocurrency, initially in the cities of Shenzen and Suzhou. This is discussed later in the book.

The Financial Crimes Enforcement Network (FinCEN) of the US Department of the Treasury issued a guidance note on 18 March 2013 clarifying the differences between currency and cryptocurrency. Its guidance defines cryptocurrency as a medium of exchange that operates like a currency in some environments, but does not have all the attributes of a real currency. It also differentiated between specific entities and persons involved in cryptocurrency transactions in an initiative to clarify which Bitcoin participants could be defined as a money transmitter, but as alluded to earlier this contributed to a fluid interpretation in several federal cases.

It is unsurprising that Bitcoin, characterised by peer-to-peer transfers, relative anonymity, encryption and the absence of an administrative clearing house, is the cryptocurrency of appeal for those engaged in tax evasion and other illegal activities.[38] The potential for misuse goes well beyond this. With tax consequences associated with using Bitcoin having been settled in many jurisdictions, the focus is now likely to shift to whether taxpayers are properly reporting their gains when disposing of Bitcoins, at least in those jurisdictions where such profits are taxable.

It is right for central banks and other financial authorities to warn users that they are at risk of losing their money if the currency suddenly devalues. It is also a fact that cryptocurrencies could be used for illicit purposes such as drug dealing, tax evasion and money laundering. Equally, they are not too far removed from current forms of conventional money in other respects.[39] In the unlikely event that the US dollar were to lose its status as a world reserve currency, its

---

35 Supra note [34], Melloy (2017).
36 Supra note [34], Melloy (2017).
37 Supra note [34], Melloy (2017).
38 Larson, J. (2016), "Implications of bitcoin not being actual currency: The Espinoza Case", *ABA Tax Times,* 36 (1),002018/11/2016, pp. 1–10.
39 Bjerg, O. (2016) "How is bitcoin money?" *Theory, Culture and Society*, 33 (1), 01/12/2015, pp. 53–72.

value would also likely drop dramatically. Illicit activities such as drug smuggling; tax evasion and money laundering; fraudulent Ponzi-schemes; and other illegal activities are also associated with fiat currencies and in larger amounts at both offshore and onshore financial centres. Linking these common deficiencies of fiat currencies to cryptocurrencies is not really helpful.[40]

Satoshi Nakamoto's vision of Bitcoin evolving into a global digital currency might be realisable, albeit via a stablecoin format when Facebook's Libra is targeted to launch in mid-2020. On the 18 June 2019 Facebook released a white paper outlining Libra's mission, the blockchain technology that was going to be deployed, the governance structure and future planned activities. Facebook claims that this venture would enable a simple global currency and financial infrastructure to empower billions of people deprived of banking services access. The Libra cryptocurrency is targeted to be a global digitally native currency replicating the world's most stable fiats through the Libra Reserve mechanism. Further analysis of Facebook Libra will be taken up in the section covering international multilateral entities involved in the evolution and regulation of cryptoassets.

3.4 Beyond currency functions

Another scenario that could evolve involves cryptocurrencies assuming a vital role inside the national and global infrastructure of financial systems, but in the background, with fiat currencies as economies' main units of accounts and mediums of exchange. This would imply that cryptocurrency protocols and blockchain-based systems for confirming transactions could replace the cumbersome payment system currently run by banks, credit card companies, payment processors and foreign exchange traders. Eventually, some of these would disappear into oblivion, leaving others to apply cryptocurrency technology for their own business-to-business (B2B) transactions. Owing to real time conversion into fiat currencies after each transaction, businesses and end users' customers would continue to quote prices and pay money in the same currencies as in the past.

Were Bitcoin to become the top choice in this situation, its value as a currency or equivalent equity in the ecosystem would rise significantly, as it would be consistently in demand. Alternative cryptocurrencies might however challenge this assumption. For instance, Ripple Lab's system, designed to facilitate international transfers in fiat currencies and other units of value simultaneously eliminates all intermediary steps which currently make money transmission expensive, could be one such candidate. Those not keen on Ripple could take up Stellar, Ripple's notable clone.

Then, there is Ethereum, a decentralised platform for applications running exactly as programmed without any chance of fraud, censorship, or third-party interference. These apps run on a custom built blockchain, a hugely powerful shared global infrastructure that could move value around and represent the

---

40 Supra, note [39], Bjerg (2016).

ownership of property. This could enable developers to create markets, store registries of debts or promises, or move funds in accordance with prior established instructions, such as wills or futures contracts. All such activities could be facilitated without a middleman or counterparty risk and hence eliminating unnecessary costs.

Important Ethereum-based platforms include Cardano, EOS, Neo and Qtum, with respective market capitalisation as at mid-February 2018 of US$10.2 billion, US$6.5 billion, 8.4 billion and 2.4 billion.[41] Other competing alternatives include Realcoin, an altcoin (See Section 3.7.1 for explanation of altcoins) layered upon the Bitcoin blockchain that is transparently backed by auditable reserves of dollar-based assets. This transforms altcoins into a proxy for a fiat currency and an instrument by which people could simply transfer money to one another without Bitcoin's exchanges risks. Uphold (formerly Bit reserve) is a cloud-based financial services platform which facilitates users in converting deposits to their bank and credit card accounts and to retrieve them later. Then there are tokens from ICOs, where another currency or corporations goes crypto. Russia is said to be considering the crypto-ruble after Venezuela's apparent success with its Petro in March 2018. Camera Company Kodak pivoted to KodakCoins, while Long Island Iced Tea Corporation started mining bitcoins. Liberal US cities like Berkley in California became the first to develop its own digital currency for buying municipal bonds.[42]

Despite these competitive cryptocurrencies on the horizon, and despite falling from its highly dominant position of over 90% of market capitalisation at the beginning of its journey to something like 35% for now, Bitcoin enjoys the advantage of being the first cryptocurrency to emerge publicly, with brand recognition and a generally reliable reputation. Bitcoin's future as the internet native currency[43] could continue flourish at least in the short term as the preferred unit of exchange for online commerce.

On the other hand, one global US investment bank thinks most if not all cryptocurrencies would be likely to reduce in value to zero, since they have no intrinsic value.[44] This was echoed in March 2018 by Stefan Hofrichter, Alliance Global's Head of Economic Strategy. In his view, Bitcoin's intrinsic value must be zero or worthless and that a Bitcoin bubble will inevitably arise at some point. It remains to be seen whether the large decline in price in 2018 is a prelude to this. As at the start of 2020 this does not appear to be the case.

---

41 Chatrrvedi, S. (2018), "Our final etherium killers review-QTUM", *Daily Fintech*, 19/02/2018, https://dailyFintech.com/2018/02/19/our-final-ethereum-killers-review-qtum/, accessed 20/02/2018.

42 Holder, S. (2018), "To fund the Resistance, Berkley turns to Cryptocurrency", *City Lab*, 12/02/2018, www.citylab.com/equity/2018/02/berkeley-crypto/552884/, accessed 18/02/2018.

43 Popper, B. "Meet the man building for Fort Knox of bitcoin", *The Verge*, 11/01/14, www.theverge.com/2014/8/29/6082195/the-fort-knox-of-bitcoin-xapo-wences-casares, accessed 2/02/2018.

44 Kharpal, A. "most cryptocurrencies will crash to zero Goldman Sachs say", *CNBC*, 7/02/2018, www.cnbc.com/2018/02/07/most-cryptocurrencies-will-crash-to-zero-goldman-sachs-says.html, accessed 7/02/2018.

Counter arguments contend that groundbreaking technology and collaborations with established business could replace the current fear of missing out syndrome.[45] Other potential blockchain applications could compensate for scope limitations in cryptocurrencies in places where databases are employed, such as supply chains, medical records and logistics. This suggests why industry behemoths like Disney, Amazon and IBM have moved into proprietary blockchain. Bitcoin in particular is still by far the safest cryptocurrency. Its limitations as an effective currency exist because of its relative slowness and cost which could be solved with the onset of the Lighting Network. This is a protocol that generates an off-chain system by forming a network of payment channels that could be accessed by involved entities independent of the wider blockchain. This latch on to Bitcoin's blockchain is designed to solve scalability, speed and cost issues by lifting transactions off the main network onto a private system among users of the underlying payment channel.[46]

However, the key issue in the background is that governments are not going to unilaterally abandon their powers to issue sovereign currencies and so fiat currencies will persist as key pillars in the financial system alongside cryptocurrencies. This also means that concerns that the rising use of cryptocurrencies inducing deflation are likely to be off the mark.[47]

3.5 The multi-coin world

Given that blockchain could enable the attachment of a digital value to anything, it is possible that the global economy could end up with everything having its own currency. This would be a world where digitised claims to assets would be created via the technology behind the blockchain. This refers to the smart property notion[48] where all property is assigned a digital ownership token and a tradable title. These could be divided into various coin denominations required to facilitate easy exchange with other digitised asset claims. Such digital coins or tokens could be traded between each other through interlinked blockchain-based exchanges that would fairly and transparently formulate universally recognised prices.

Such a multi-asset global digital exchange would not need a common currency at all. It would operate as a sophisticated kind of barter, where its divisibility and flexibility overcome the original limitations found in the raw version. A coin-based economy such as this would allow goods and services to

---

45 Goss, S. (2017), "Commentary: Yes bitcoin may be a bubble, but not for the reason you think", *Fortune*, 4/12/2017, https://fortune.com/2017/12/04/bitcoin-value-today-bubble-burst/, accessed 2/02/2018.

46 Upson, S. (2019), "The lightning network could make bitcoin faster and cheaper", *Wired*, 19/01/2019, www.wired.com/story/the-lightning-network-could-make-bitcoin-faster-and-cheaper/, accessed 2/02/2018.

47 Buntix, J. P. (2017), "Cryptocurrency Inflation vs Deflation", *The Merkle*, 25/04/2017, https://themerkle.com/cryptocurrency-inflation-vs-deflation/, accessed 2/02/2018.

48 Bursell, M. "What is a blockchain smart contract?" *Open Source*, 11/12/2017. www.open-source.com/article/17/12/whats-blockchain-smart-contract, accessed 02/02/2018.

be transacted without needing the medium of exchange provided by fiat currencies. Where such a market is allowed to flourish, there would be little need for central banks and a centralised interest rate to operate, as tradable items would be priced against each other. The system could thus become more efficient as digital coins are exchanged in seconds without moving physical goods, in the absence of minimum transaction sizes, and without large fees penalising smaller transactions. A global marketplace for all asset classes and instruments could emerge levelling the playing field between users. Big companies with big brand names with large scale operations might not be favoured as in an electronic barter society, individuals and small groups could compete with them at no loss in efficiency thus igniting a wave of innovation and wealth creation.[49]

This digital barter economy[50] could avoid the economic distortions that lead to the 2007 global financial crisis, where prices, and especially wages, had been unable to find their natural levels, and where central banks had to intervene with interest rates to locate desirable economic balances, but which inevitably gave rise to new distortions leading to ongoing economic problems. The scenario under discussion potentially implies a much less crisis-prone economy which is the vision of most free market fundamentalists.[51]

This vision of a cryptocurrency-based digital barter economy could however face significant obstacles along the way. These include the logistical complexity of a global exchange system to provide market based valuations for an infinite range of digitised assets, and the unlikely happening for a world of entirely free floating prices because of almost insurmountable political barriers. Some elements of a digital barter economy are more likely to appear when digitised assets and blockchain exchanges become much more widely used.

3.6 Digital fiat currencies

Global consumer payments are still primarily carried out in cash and over two billion of those are at the bottom of the pyramid in terms of size because of the inaccessibility to financial services for those in some parts of the world. Globally, the use of cash has a cost for societies in terms of printing, distribution and destruction. Digital fiat currencies issued by central banks offer interoperable instruments, instant settlements and robust system security, but it would also mean sovereign denomination and greater accountability for central banks.

Cryptocurrencies' deflationary attributes backed by its 21 million capped supply differs crucially from the inflationary tendencies of digital currencies and in particular digital fiat currencies. Knowing the limited supply of Bitcoin

---

49 Olsen, R. & Mulchandani, S. (2017), "Blockchain will help society: Blockchain will become the notary of choice for these traditional financial assets, but there is something more exciting afoot", *BW Business World*, 08/09/2017.
50 Hastreiter, N. (2017),"The future of cash free barter economy for business", *Future of Everything*, October 2017, www.futureofeverything.io/future-cash-free-barter-economy-business/, accessed 02/02/2018.
51 Supra note [49] Olsen and Mulchandandi (2017).

and its eventual potential values prompts people to save Bitcoins to simultaneously strengthen its purchasing power. In contrast, in the world of digital fiat currencies central banks could, and often do, create more money through quantitative easing and bank bailouts that could lead to strong inflation that erodes purchasing power. Cryptocurrency supporters drawing on this crucial difference believe that this could lead to more financial freedom for everyone, while those on the other side of the fence stoke fears of financial insecurity, bubbles and frauds.

Finally, the internet has empowered a lot of ordinary people and many small businesses to drive the sharing and collaborative economy, and perhaps soon a digital barter economy that cryptocurrencies such as Bitcoin envision. This is a pure form of information technology. At its heart is the decentralised Bitcoin network and its public ledger, the blockchain, that represents a new manner for dealing with information. This involves extracting information concerning monetary transactions and economic exchanges, but outside the hands of monopolist institutions to lead to a decentralised mechanism for society to evaluate the validity of that information.[52]

In this sense cryptocurrencies could claim to be among the latest in a long line of technological developments that are perceived to have the potential to shift powers from centralised elites back to the common people. Yet, there are those who would use it to advance all kinds of illicit activities, but these Bitcoin anarchists could be relegated to minor participations when Bitcoin technology and applications overcome their present constraints and policymakers provide the enabling environment for cryptocurrencies' innovations to flourish. They could well end up amounting to less than the stateless third party, less utopian dream of its most ardent supporters.[53] However, the financial world would have a different kind of discipline imposed on it and were costs to come down dramatically then commerce and economic activity could grow along digital lines further expanding its impact.

Cryptocurrencies are backed by mathematics and only resemble the characteristics of money in terms of a unit of account, a store of value and a medium of exchange. It is also based on a decentralised P2P network that uniquely differentiates it from other virtual currencies. It is also worthwhile recalling that the 1899 English case of *Moss v Hancock*[54] defined money to be that which passes freely from hand to hand throughout the community in the final discharge of debts, and also being accepted equally without reference to the character or credit of the person who offered it and concurrently without the intention of the person who received it to consume it.

Neither the US Coinage Act nor the UK Bank of England Act 1833, nor any regulation in both jurisdictions state as such that the actual process must involve

---

52 Vigna, P. and Casey, M. J. (2015), *Cryptocurrency: How bitcoin and digital money are challenging the global economic order*, London, The Bodley Head.
53 Supra note [52], Vigna and Casey (2015).
54 [1899] 2 Q.B. 111.

payment in cash. Thus, the judicial interpretation is complemented by the economic perspective of money as anything that is widely accepted in payment for goods and services, used as a medium of exchange and articulated as the standard unit wherein prices and debts are calibrated.

Cryptocurrencies are therefore virtual currencies, i.e. a kind of unregulated digital money issued and generally controlled by its developers and used and accepted among members of a particular virtual community. Money in closed-in "game only schemes," with no link to the real economy or fiat currency; schemes with unidirectional flow whereupon the currency could initially be acquired with a fiat currency but not convertible back to it, such as Facebook credits; or schemes with a bidirectional flow allowing conversion in both directions, such as frequent flyer miles, are not truly virtual currencies. Money in such schemes exists in the form of an account balance rather than distinct identifiable items. These are less regarded as cryptocurrencies, but more as a variant of e-money.

At least in the EU e-money are characterised: firstly, by electronic storage, secondly by issuance upon receipt of funds and thirdly by acceptance as a means of payment by a legal or natural person other than the issuer. Bitcoin and similar cryptocurrencies as such are not deemed as e-money as they do not comply with the second criterion. They do however share two of the characteristics of e-money. They are also not issued in or linked to a sovereign currency, not the liability of any entity and not backed by any authority. Bitcoin and other cryptocurrencies operate along the lines of retail payment systems, except that non-banks rather than financial intermediaries are almost exclusively involved in the payment process.

The Bitcoin system enables users to exchange online credit for goods and services from retailers, contractors and online trading intermediaries that accept Bitcoin for payments. Competing currency systems are not altogether new as local, unregulated, community currencies came into being long before the digital age. The virtual currency system has positive features when it contributes to financial innovation and provides additional payment alternatives to consumers. Nevertheless, they also generate risks for their users in the absence of regulation.

Though cryptocurrencies resemble the key characteristics of currency, they also have the characteristics of a commodity of other property. As such their legal treatment varies from jurisdiction to jurisdiction and regulators within the same jurisdiction could also take differing approaches relative to the regulatory context under review. For example, New York actively regulates entities doing business and allows virtual currencies into the state's banking system, whereas in the UK such trading remains largely unregulated. China currently prohibits cryptocurrencies but has not been entirely effective as the ban was immediately followed by a large increase in the number of people accessing virtual currency systems on Hong Kong websites. For now, there appears to be no existing legal framework addressing the unique features and functionality of cryptocurrencies although as is seen later in the book, China is going to issue a state backed cryptocurrency.

Regulators are struggling with the option of prohibiting cryptocurrencies or isolating them from the regulated financial system. The concerns over their legal status and regulation arises because they have the potential to be used in illegal activities outside the reach of law enforcement and their extreme price volatility could hurt ill-informed investors. Importantly, they are complicated and complex financial instruments as they have features enabling them to function as a commodity, as demonstrated by a self-imposed scarcity limit of 21 million bitcoins and the extreme volatility of its value, and as security in the form of ICOs. Economic blocs such as the G20, and international or supranational regulators such as the International Monetary Fund (IMF) are planning consensus building forums to address the issue.

In part this struggle is the result of the disparate nature of cryptocurrencies. The most thorough categorisation of them would seem to be the following breakdown.[55] Many cryptocurrencies will have more than one of these characteristics.

3.7 Different types of cryptoassets

3.7.1 Altcoins

These are cryptocoins that are alternatives to Bitcoin and are a variant of it. They are created using either Bitcoin's open-sourced protocol with the underlying codes being changed resulting in a fork in the original blockchain, or they are the result of a separate blockchain and protocol that supports them.[56] There are currently 17 different types using the same hashing algorithms as Bitcoin (e.g. Namecoin, Peercoin, Devcoin and Terracoin), 19 using a script algorithm (e.g. Litecoin, Novacoin, Terracoin and Worldcoin) and 18 using other innovative algorithms (e.g. Etherium Cloud Mining, Primecoin, Securecoin and Quark). All altcoins have their own independent blockchain. The result of this is that their features are different.

3.7.2 Asset-backed tokens

These represent a claim on an underlying asset and are effectively a modern version of the certificates issued by medieval goldsmiths. Those not wishing to risk carrying their gold around could deposit it at a goldsmith's in return for a certificate. This could be used to pay for goods or services and a later owner could cash it in for the gold.[57] Put simply they are IOUs and unlike some other types of cryptocurrency are rooted in something of real value and the range that exists on

---

55 Crypto Utopia (2018), "The $20 billion Cambrian explosion of tokenized digital assets, and the emerging infrastructure being built to support them." *Autonomous Next*, 2018, https://next.autonomous.com/crypto-utopia, p. 79.

56 Aziz, "Coins vs Tokens: What's The Difference", *Master The Crypto*, https://www.masterthecrypto.com/differences-between-cryptocurrency-coins-and-tokens, accessed 14/02/2019.

57 Lewis, A. (2015), "A gentle introduction to digital tokens", *bitsonblocks*, 28/09/2015, https://bitsonblocks.net/2015/09/28/gentle-introduction-digital-tokens/, accessed 14/02/2019.

the current market is very wide.[58] Examples are LAToken, Tether, GoldMint and Ripple IOUs. It is worth flagging up at this point the difference between tokens and coins. Coins that are part of an e-currency can be used to buy things, e.g. tokens. The token itself can only be used however within the ecosystem of the blockchain concerned.[59]

3.7.3 Blockchain native tokens

These are tokens that are implemented on the blockchain at the protocol level. The investors will normally have had no prior involvement with each other and are a disparate group. They are an integral part of its consensus mechanism and necessary to operate the blockchain. Examples of this are Bitcoin, Ether and Steem.[60]

3.7.4 Commodity tokens

Rather like a hybrid of security tokens for commodities and futures contracts these have been mainly used so far for natural assets such as carbon.[61] It still remains a market in its very early stages and it remains to be seen whether or not it will develop significantly.

3.7.5 Crypto fiat currencies

Discussed elsewhere in the book, these are crypto versions of existing currencies. For reasons of financial desperation it was the Government of Venezuela that first expressed an interest in the idea, with China following more recently. Russia has also discussed it, while the UK have made clear they are not considering it at the moment. It will be an interesting idea to watch. The Governor of the Bank of England (BoE), though open to the idea of a Central Bank Digital Currency (CBDC), stressed that any such adoption would not happen while the BoE maintains that cryptocurrencies do not currently constitute money.[62] The BoE's recently released a staff working paper suggests that there is no reason to believe that introducing a crypto pound could have a negative impact on private credit or on total liquidity provision to an economy.

At this juncture, recent developments suggest taking note of potential digital currencies issued by central banks. Various central banks from Canada, Ireland,

---

58 midlifecroesus (2018), *midlifecroesus*, 23/02/2018, https://midlifecroesus.com/2018/02/what-is-an-asset-backed-token/, accessed 14/02/2019.

59 Bonpay (2018), "What Is the Difference Between Coins and Tokens", *Medium*, 13/03/2018, https://medium.com/@bonpay/what-is-the-difference-between-coins-and-tokens-6cedff311c31, accessed 14/02/2019.

60 www.blockchainhub.net, accessed 14/02/2019.

61 Tapscott, D. & Tapscott, A. (2018), *Blockchain Revolution*, Penguin Random House, p. xxxvi.

62 Wood, A. (2018), "Bank of England Governor: Open to the Idea of a Central Bank Digital Currency", *Coin Telegraph*, 26/05/2018. https://cointelegraph.com/news/bank-of-england-governor-open-to-the-idea-of-a-central-bank-digital-currency, accessed 5/03/2019.

Norway, to Switzerland and others are now considering the viability of these and are investigating their logistical and technical details. It has been argued that the progress of digital commerce could ultimately make the benefits seem overwhelming and it would strategically competitive to stay ahead of the curve instead of trying to catch up at the eleventh hour.[63]

For now the Federal Reserve Bank in the US nevertheless is not taking this position. The US Federal Reserve maintain that even though a crypto dollar might be able to overcome some of the special vulnerabilities that cryptocurrencies encounter, they too have significant challenges pertaining to cybersecurity, money laundering and the retail financial system.[64] A more positive stance is taken by the International Monetary Fund (IMF) as reflected by its call for central banks around the world to turn their fiat currencies digital.[65]

3.7.6 dApp tokens

These are tokens that are implemented at the application level on top of the blockchain. They are part of the apps' incentive mechanism and are tracked on an underlying blockchain to which they are not integral. They must have four key ingredients to be a distributed application token:

- The source code of the e-application must be open to everyone
- It must use a blockchchain type of cryptography
- It must operate itself on crypto tokens or digital assets
- It must generate tokens and have an inbuilt consensus mechanism[66]

Effectively, they facilitate access to the Blockchain for which the users will pay transaction fees.[67] Examples are: LiquidApps, CENT, Safecoin and SAFE Network (Safe effectively being a fork of the Komono and Zcash projects).

---

63 Bordo, M. D. & Levin, A. T. (2017), "Central bank digital money and the future of monetary policy", *National Bureau of Economic Research, (NBER)*, August 2017, Working Paper Series 23,711.

64 Brainard, L. (2018), "Cryptocurrencies, digital currencies and distributed ledger technologies: what are we learning?", *Paper presented by Lael Brainard, Member Board of Governors of the Federal Reserve System at the "Decoding Digital Currency" Conference, San Francisco, CA*, 15/05/2018. Kumhoff, M. & Noone, C. (2018), "Central bank digital currencies: Design principles and balance sheet implications", *BoE Staff Working Paper No 725*, May 2018.

65 Lagarde, C. (2018), "Winds of Change: the case for the new digital currency", *Paper presented by Christine Lagarde, IMF Managing Director at the Singapore Fintech Festival*, 14/11/2018. Mancini-Griffoli, T., Soledad, M., Martinez, P., Agur, I., Ari, A., Kiff, J., Popescu, A. & Rochon, C. (2018), "Casting light on central bank digital currency", *IMF Staff Discussion Note 2018 SDN/18/08*.

66 Agrawal, H. (2019), "What are DApps (Decentralized Applications)? – The Beginner's Guide", *Coinsutra*, 06/09/2019, https://coinsutra.com/dapps-decentralized-applications, accessed 3/06/2019.

67 Warren, W (2017), "The difference between App Coins and Protocol Tokens", *0x Blog*, 02/02/2017, https://blog.0xproject.com/the-difference-between-app-coins-and-protocol-tokens-7281a428348c, accessed 14/02/2019.

3.7.7 Hybrid tokens

These are hybridised usage and work tokens, such as Binance, Bitfinex LEO, Chainlink token and Maker.

3.7.8 Internal tokens

JP Morgan recently announced that they were creating a blockchain-based payments system purely for internal use.[68] It is too early to tell what the significance of this development is, but where one investment bank goes others tend to follow, so it is reasonable to expect others to adopt similar systems. What also remains to be seen is whether this is a first step to investment banks using such systems externally.

3.7.9 Security token offerings (STOs)

These are intended as passive investments in the issuing entity or in an asset which it owns. Unlike ICOs they grant a share in the profits and unlike equity tokens they do not grant part ownership of the company. They may go up in value and are saleable, e.g. Neufund Equity Tokens, Digix gold and DigixDAO. They can be seen as a subset of security tokens (see below).

3.7.10 Network tokens

These are designed to be used within a specific system or network rather than as a general currency. Every token in the network is convertible with each other. This can be useful for creating loyalty programmes or as tokens to take part in a game. They reduce the risk of fraud and increase functionality because unlike, say, a credit card the functionality is limited to each token, not transferred across all transactions on the same credit card. Examples would be Gnosis, Stacks and Blockstack.

3.7.11 Network value tokens

As their name suggests, these are tokens whose value is measured by the development of a network. They are communication protocols for a local area network on which they operate by way of a string of workstations. Ether, Etherium and Steem are examples.

3.7.12 Non-native protocol tokens

Tokens that are implemented in a cryptoeconomic protocol at the top of the blockchain. Again, they are an integral part of the blockchain's protocol consensus

---

68 Business Section, *Daily Telegraph*, 15/02/2019, p. 3.

mechanism. It is however tracked on an underlying blockchain to which it is not integral. Examples are Decentralised Oracle Protocol and Augur.

3.7.13 Pure cryptocurrencies

These are both a medium of exchange and a store of value. There is no central authority and they do not represent part ownership of anything. Effectively they are a type of money even if not legally categorised as such in most places. Examples are Bitcoin, Zcash and Litecoin.

3.7.14 Usage tokens

These function as an access key to a digital service. Beyond that the holders do not acquire any special rights. If the demand for the service is high and the number of tokens limited, then the token itself can acquire a high value.[69] Examples are Ether, Stacks and Blockstack.

3.7.15 Utility tokens

These offer the holders access to a utility, normally within a digital ledger system. They do not function as a currency but enable the holder to act as an investor in a future service or product, though their real value can be hard to assess, e.g. Steem. Purchase tokens might have been a better name.

3.7.16 Work tokens

These provide a right to contribute to the system by doing work in return for some type of reward. The work might be done on the blockchain or at a smart contract level. Rewards can be given for recommendations or building up a work profile on the system.[70] Examples are Reputation, Augur, Maker and Maker DAO.

The IMF in particular views cryptocurrency payments as immediate, safe, cheap and potentially semi-autonomous, and from this perspective urges central banks to consider issuing digital assets so that they can retain a sure footing in payments. The IMF, nevertheless, cautions central banks to consider their particular country circumstances, giving special attention to the risks and relative merits of alternative solutions. The Bank for International Settlements (BIS) cautioned that central banks eying a general purpose CBDC as an alternative to cash would need to ensure the fulfilment of anti-money laundering, and counter-terrorism financing (AML/CTF) requirements, simultaneously satisfying the public policy requirements of other supervisory tax regimes.[71] A recent BIS

---

[69] www.blockchain.hub.net, accessed 14/02/2019.
[70] www.blockchain.hub.net, accessed 14/02/2019.
[71] BIS (2018), "Central Bank Digital Currencies", *BIS Paper*, March 2018.

survey[72] suggests that most central banks appeared to have clarified the challenges of launching a CBDC, but are yet unconvinced that the benefits would outweigh the costs. Central banks from advanced and emerging economies are moving at different speeds. This could generate a potential risk for spillover effects across borders. However, the BIS survey evidence suggest that central banks are proceeding cautiously, collaborating and sharing the outcomes of their work. This implies that the world will have to wait to use a CBDC.

---

[72] Barotini, C. & Holden, H. (2019), "Proceed with caution. A survey on central bank digital currency", *BIS Papers*, 101, January 2019.

CHAPTER 4

Why are the regulators watching?

4.1 Introduction

Despite experimentation with privately issued currency by the US until the mid-19th century, the control by governments of money is now the norm. US banks used to issue private notes, but these were taken out of existence in favour of the US dollar in the civil war,[1] to be controlled by the Federal Reserve System (the Fed). Whilst there are arguments that governments should not be in complete control of money supply, alternative choices have not been available other than some local alternative currencies. The major reason for this is that, until recently, there has never been an alternative, apart from gold and silver, that could provide the security of fiat currencies with the convenience of financial institutions that facilitate worldwide commerce.[2] This was the situation until the onset of Bitcoin, the world's first digital private currency, exchangeable over the Internet via the employment of P2P networks, followed by the arrival of other cryptoassets.

As mentioned earlier, Bitcoin has no intrinsic value, and there is not government, company, or independent organisation upholding its value or monitoring its application, although as alluded to previously, there could be changes emerging as governments issue their own digital currencies as Venezuela did recently[3], and as China[4] seems to be moving towards more recently. Instead Bitcoin relies on P2P network to achieve value through demand and maintains security through the programs these users run on their computers.

Many governments, including the US and the UK, have not banned the use of transactions in Bitcoins other than some ICOs that have breached securities laws. However, there are some countries like China, Vietnam and India that have more or less outlawed Bitcoin, and yet others that have discouraged their

---

1 There was also a Confederate dollar that was used to finance the confederate states during the civil war.

2 Kaplanov, N.M. (2012), "Nerdy money: Bitcoin, the private digital currency, and the case against its regulation", *Temple University Legal Studies Research Paper*, 31/03/12.

3 Liao, S. (2018), "Venezuela's own oil-backed cryptocurrency is available for presale today", *The Verge*, 20/02/2018, www.theverge.com/2018/2/20/17031720/venezuela-cryptocurrency-petro-oil-reserves-diamonds-inflation, accessed 12/02/2018.

4 Palmer, D. (2019), "China's central bank 'close' to launching official digital currency", *Coin Desk* 12/08/2019, www.coindesk.com/chinas-central-bank-close-to-launching-official-digital-currency, accessed 15/08/2019.

employment, as in South Korea. US policymakers,[5] including its President[6] have chastised cryptoassets like Bitcoin. Through the vehicle of Twitter, the US President stated that he is no fan of Bitcoin and other cryptoassets. He explained that these cryptoassets are not money, are highly volatile, and are based on thin air. He added that unregulated cryptoassets could facilitate unlawful behaviour, including drug trade and other illegal activities. Equally, across the world others[7] have also denounced their use.

Complaints against complete government control of money have existed, especially in the US and Germany for decades. What is novel about the Bitcoin initiative is its response to the 2007 global financial crisis, with a decentralised ledger technology doing away with the trust provided by a central authority, and its offer of an avenue for a private currency to function globally.[8] Bitcoin is the unique confluence of technology and demand enabling it to be a serious contender as a viable global alternative currency. Though not perfect yet in terms of the main functions of modern fiat currencies, the blockchain technology behind it has spawned billions worth of Bitcoins in fiat currency valuations, without the need for government issues or any third-party transaction network. This quest for a private global currency is more recently joined by the Facebook Libra[9] and Venus[10] ventures that drew condemnations by major regulators and policymakers across the world.[11]

Both the retail use of Bitcoin by consumers and Bitcoin miners fall outside of the US federal banking and money transmission laws.[12] Arguments have been raised that Bitcoin transactions could be treated as a community currency under US law and elsewhere.[13] Rather than being prohibited by policymakers and the courts, it has been argued law enforcement, should become more acquainted with the technology behind cryptoassets particularly when they provide a public log of every transaction.[14]

---

5 Masnick, M. (2018), "Senator Schumer Says Bitcoin Is Money Laundering", *Techdirt*, 06/06/2018, www.techdirt.com/articles/20110605/22322814558/senator-schumer-says-Bitcoin-is-money-laundering.shtml, accessed 02/02/2018.

6 Ossinger, J. (2019), "Bitcoin tumbles as Trump critiques tests Stellar run for 2019", *Bloomberg* 15/07/2019, www.bloomberg.com/news/articles/2019-07-14/Bitcoin-tumbles-as-trump-s-critique-tests-stellar-2019-surgeBitcoin, accesses 16/07/2019.

7 Yen, N.L. (2017), "From China to Singapore, Asian countries are increasingly uneasy with the rise of BitcoinBitcoin", *CNBC*, 22/12/2017, www.cnbc.com/2017/12/22/Bitcoin-china-singapore-japan-issue-cryptocurrency-warnings.html Bitcoin, accessed 22/12/2017.

8 Farr, M. (2017), "Bitcoin … Future global currency", *Farr, Miller & Washington Investment Counsel*, 06/06/2017, https://farrmiller.com/2017/06/06/Bitcoin-future-global-currency/Bitcoin, accessed 20/02/2018.

9 Libra (2019), "An introduction to Libra", *libra.org*, 23/06/2019, https://libra.org/en-US/wp-content/uploads/sites/23/2019/06/LibraWhitePaper_en_US.pdf, accessed 20/08/2019.

10 Linver, H. (2019), "Binance Venus Aims to Outshine Libra and Chinese National Crypto?", *Coin Telegraph*, 21/08/2019, https://cointelegraph.com/news/binance-venus-aims-to-outshine-libra-and-chinese-national-crypto, accessed 23/08/2019.

11 Browne, R. (2019), "Facebook's cryptocurrency faced with regulatory warnings from global central bankers", *CNBC*, 20/06/2019, www.cnbc.com/2019/06/20/facebook-libra-cryptocurrency-faced-with-central-bank-warnings.html, accessed 25/02/2019.

12 Supra, note [1], Kaplanov (2012).

13 Supra, note [1], Kaplanov (2012).

14 Supra, note [1], Kaplanov (2012).

Such arguments, however, are not accepted by many governments. They are concerned that with its anonymity, cryptocurrencies could become the borderless engine of growth for illicit activities such as money laundering and tax evasion. The Silk Road[15] and Mt. Gox[16] Bitcoin scandals suggest that money laundering or other illicit forms of activities, including pyramid financial fraud, could become more common. These have triggered concerns over investors' losses from highly speculative and risky unconventional investments and linkages with the criminal world, in the US, EU, and UK which are perceived as the leaders in financial regulatory norms.

4.2 Practical issues with cryptoassets

There could also be other reasons why some countries are hostile towards Bitcoin and other cryptoassets. Bitcoin claims to be the first decentralised P2P network powered by users with no central authority or middlemen. This lack of central authority is believed by analysts to be the main reason governments are wary of cryptoassets.[17]

Conventional fiat currencies are backed by the full faith and credit of the governments that issued them and nothing more. To exchange for services, people need to exchange the fiat currencies in play with persons or entities possessing the items in question. Governments control fiat currencies and employ central banks, that are in many cases supposedly independent, to issue or destroy money out of thin air, making use of monetary policy to generate economic influence.[18]

They also decide how fiat currencies could be transferred, thereby enabling them to monitor currency movements and arguably decide who profits from the movements. They also gather taxes in it and trace criminal activities, to the extent that this is possible. Currency controls therefore have many downstream impacts, most notably to an economy's fiscal policy, business environment and initiatives to control financial crimes.

While crime captures the public interest, the role currency plays in an economy's monetary policy has the potential to land a far much larger impact. When governments intentionally expand or restrict the amount of money circulating in an economy so as to stimulate investment and spending, generate jobs, control inflation or avoid a recession, control over currency is a key element. The supposed central bank independence could be under threat in various economies,

---

15 McCoy, K. (2017), "Silk Road mastermind Ross Ulbricht losses legal appeal", *USA Today*, 31/05/2017, www.usatoday.com/story/money/2017/05/31/silk-road../102343063/, accessed 20/02/2018.

16 Gibbs, S. (2017), "Head of Mt Gox bitcoin exchange on trial for embezzlement and loss of millions", *The Guardian*, 11/07/2017, www.theguardian.com/technology/2017/jul/11/gox-Bitcoin-exchange-mark-karpeles-on-trial-japan-embezzlement-loss-of-millions Bitcoin, accessed 02/02/2018.

17 McWhinney, J. E. (2019), "Why Governments Are Afraid of Bitcoin", *Investopedia*, updated 01/11/2019, https://www.investopedia.com/articles/forex/042015/why-governments-are-afraid-bitcoin.asp, accessed 02/02/2018.

18 Supra, note [17], McWhinney (2019).

including that for the US where its President appeared to be putting pressure on the Federal Reserve through his Twitter messages.[19]

Cryptoasset users do not generally rely on the existing banking system. The digital currency is created in cyberspace where, in the case of Bitcoin and similar cryptos and as discussed elsewhere in the book, miners utilise their computers to solve complex algorithms serving as verifications for transactions. Their reward is a digital Bitcoin which is stored digitally and flows between buyers and sellers in the absence of an intermediary. Were cryptocurrencies to become sufficiently widely adopted the entire banking system could potentially cease to be financially viable.[20] This may at present seem a distant future given that financial institutions still carry out key activities such as overseeing timely, effective, and trustworthy asset transfers and their associated recordkeeping.[21] However, such institutions operate on narrow profit margins, and an alternative money system could rapidly render them non-viable. Fees earned from such operations also generate a large number of jobs and significant revenue.

The argument that, because of its anonymity, Bitcoin facilitates crime also applies to cash.[22] Yet, this is one of the core arguments that regulators and central banks use when advocating restrictions on, or an outright ban of cryptocurrencies. They are also considered financially harmful as their price volatility can cause serious financial damage to investors, both sophisticated and unsophisticated. It is worth adding, however, that this also applied to the fiat currencies used in many failing economies.[23]

The counter argument is that central banks' tinkering with the money supply has induced recessions, exacerbated unemployment and has on occasions unintentionally polluted the global banking system.[24] Insights from the aftermath of the 2007/8 global financial crisis regarding mortgage market failures suggest why disaffected and disenchanted consumers, especially in the US, would give support to the initiatives of anonymous software coders in challenging a system that is perceived to have failed them.[25]

This approach is not a new one, as the core argument that economic manipulation by central banks is not necessarily beneficial took root very much earlier in Austrian economic thinking.[26] It had then been argued that irresponsible and

---

19 Jolly, J. (2019), "Trump criticizes Fed chairman Powell for trying to be 'tough'", *The Guardian,* 26/06/2019, www.theguardian.com/business/2019/jun/26/trump-criticises-fed-chairman-powell-for-trying-to-be-tough, accessed 28/06/2019.
20 Supra, note [17], McWhinney (2015).
21 Supra, note [17], McWhinney (2015).
22 Bjerg, O. (2016), "How is Bitcoin money?", *Theory, Culture & Society*, 33(1), pp. 53–72.
23 Supra, note [22], Bjerg (2016).
24 Rouanet, L. (2017), "How central banking increased inequality", *Mises Institute*, 15/08/2017, https://mises.org/library/how-central-banking-increased-inequality, accessed 02/02/2018.
25 Nielsen, J. (2017), "What triggered the creation and success of cryptocurrencies?", *Coin Codex*, December 2017, https://coincodex.com/article/1072/what-triggered-the-creation-and-success-of-cryptocurrencies/, accessed 02/02/2018.
26 Ferrara, P. (2013), "Rethinking money: The rise of Hayek's private competing currencies", *Forbes*, 01/03/13, www.forbes.com/sites/peterferrara/2013/03/01/rethinking-money-the-rise-of-hayeks-private-competing-currencies/, accessed 02/02/2018.

dishonest governments have, at times, eroded the value of currencies through reckless inflationary tendencies.

An Austrian economic thinker came up with the idea of private currencies in competitive private markets that could compete to maintain their value. Since then, more than 4,000 unofficial private currencies are operational in the world today.[27] But, these are viewed as complementary or cooperative rather than competing currencies as they are not competing to replace the official currency, but to complement it where it is leaving available resources unused.[28] The most visible complementary currency is frequent flyer miles, presently issued by ninety-two airlines.[29] Apart from bonus or discount tickets in return for repeat flight business, increasingly such frequent flyer miles are redeemable for various services such as mobile phone calls, hotels, cruises and catalogue merchandise besides airline tickets. This explains why Singapore International Airlines, one of the few successful global airlines, plans to use blockchain technology to give its frequent flyers a new way to spend their accumulated miles, and why Qantas another respectable global airline, turns its Qantas points into a blockchain based cryptocurrency.

More than half of frequent flyer miles are, however, not earned by flying but via credit cards offering bonus miles with purchases. These have become the more popular avenue to earn frequent flyer miles. This suggests that frequent flyer miles have evolved into a kind of private currency issued by airlines.[30] Another related time-backed private currency model is exemplified by the Local Exchange Trading System (LETS)[31] popularised in Vancouver, Canada. WIR, a mutual credit system among businesses in Basel Switzerland exemplifies on the other hand a prominent regional private currency.

It is claimed that the starting point for all private currencies is potentially the Terra proposed by Belgian economist and monetary system expert Bernard Lietaer in 2010.[32] This is a global currency explicitly backed by a basket of a dozen or so precious commodities like gold, silver, oil and so on. Each Terra could be exchanged for the specified share of the basket of currencies that would be held as 100% backing of the currency under contract with producers of those commodities, the partners in the financial institution issuing the Terras. The producers would be paid in Terras for their contribution, which they could then use these to settle their suppliers and creditors.

A transaction fee of no more than 4% assessed against the face value of the currency would be levied annually thereby depreciating its backing by that amount.[33]

---

27 Lietaer, B. & Dunne, J. (2013), *Rethinking money: How new currencies turn scarcity into prosperity*, San Franscisco, Berrett-Koeler Publishers.
28 Supra, note [27], Lietaer & Dunne (20,130).
29 Supra, note [26], Ferrara (2013).
30 Supra, note [26], Ferrara (2013).
31 Supra, note [26], Ferrara (2013).
32 Lietaer, B. (2010), "The Terra TRC: A global complementary currency to stabilize the world economy", 04/01/10, www.lietaer.com/2010/01/terra/, accessed 02/02/2018.
33 Supra, note [33], Lietaer (2010).

This would go to finance the costs of issuing and maintaining the Terra including storage costs of the reserve commodities backing the currency. This would transform the Terra into an international global currency. No government permission is required to issue and trade in this currency, except to the extent that people try to settle their taxes in it.[34] In such an eventuality, it is up to the governments concerned to decide whether to accept.

Economic players worldwide could decide to denominate their contracts in Terras, without buying or selling Terras at all. The Terras would trade in every currency in the world on world markets, and payment due could then be in the Terra value for each currency. The rise of the Terra could boost global economic growth and prosperity, thereby empowering the world economy to trade in a currency not subject to inflation, devaluation and variation in real market value.[35] Such a fixed yardstick to calibrate commerce would promote global production, trade and economic growth. This could result in a game-changing 21st century breakthrough. However, the implementation of complementary currencies is highly improbable at this juncture because central banks currently have a monopoly on money creation and they are not in a hurry to give it away.[36] In addition, the inherently unstable value of some of the commodities suggested would inevitably leave the Terra with an unpredictable value.

It is an interesting observation that Bitcoin market capitalisation went from almost nothing to about US$11 billion in 2013 to close to a peak of US$641 billion in February 2019.[37] Bitcoin's price escalated beyond 1,400% from the beginning of 2017. Its extreme price volatility aside, Bitcoin showed that unlike the Terra that is largely still-born, it is fast evolving quickly across both emerging and advanced economies, even though critics counter argued that being a fraud, Bitcoin would eventually collapse. However, Bitcoin together with other cryptocurrencies are now no longer sideshows, with some enthusiasts arguing that the cryptocurrency would go beyond its US$1 trillion market capitalisation in 2018.[38] It never did though, but instead has now nosedived to US$270.52 billion in mid-July 2019, impacted significantly by the negative Twitter messages from the US President, as alluded to earlier. This demonstrated a significant decrease from the massive market cap of close to US$800 billion at its peak in December 2017, but also recall that this was only around US$16 billion back in 2016. The US$100 billion mark was breached only in the middle of 2017, suggesting phenomenal growth from the second half of 2017 onwards.

---

34 Supra, note [33], Lietaer (2010).
35 Supra, note [33], Lietaer (2010).
36 Crooks III, J.R. (2015), "Think 'thunk' about complementary currencies", Uncommon Wisdom Daily, 20/07/2015, www.uncommonwisdomdaily.com/think-thunk-about-complementary-currencies, accessed 02/02/2018.
37 www.statista.com/statistics/377382/Bitcoin-market-capitalisation, accessed 11/02/2019.
38 Browne, R. & Kharpal, A. (2018), "Cryptocurrency market will hit $1 trillion valuation this year, CEO of top exchange says", *CNBC*, 13/02/2018, www.cnbc.com/2018/02/13/cryptocurrency-market-to-hit-1-trillion-valuation-in-2018-kraken-ceo.html, accessed 20/02/2018.

The spectacular price fluctuations caused cryptocurrencies, and in particular Bitcoin, to be labelled as bubbles, speculation, and in some quarters as a fraud, by analysts including economics Nobel laureates, bank CEOs, and others. The OECD's[39] initial assessment views Bitcoin as something that must replace legal tender in order to be successful, and so is dismissive of Bitcoin as a monetary unit, but still acknowledges the potential of the blockchain technology driving Bitcoin. The IMF,[40] however, mentioned that in a world of billions of unbanked without access to the conventional banking system for various reasons, cryptocurrencies offer the alternative to join the global economy. These developments altogether drew the close attention of policymakers,[41] central banks[42] and regulators[43]. These issues have been explored elsewhere in the book.

Concerns over investors' risks, threats to sovereign control of monetary and fiscal policies, conduits for illicit activities, access for the unbanked and technology innovation opportunities between them focused the minds of those involved in financial regulation. Countries differ in their official positions toward cryptocurrencies, but generally they have become more aware that innovation is the primary driver of productivity, which in turn is a determinant of GDP and that Fintech upstarts and incumbent global banks are increasingly operating outside the current regulatory regime. While mindful of these, national regulators need also to protect their citizens and others from fraud and enforce the applicable laws to deter crimes. As they juggle and balance these challenging conditions, they are mindful that jurisdictional competition for technological innovation might present serious difficulties in terms of different levels of regulatory attention and coordination.

With respect to policymaking, laws and regulations, cryptoassets could be categorised into five types to facilitate analysis.[44]

---

39 Blundell-Wignall, A. (2014), "The Bitcoin question", *OECD Working Papers on Finance, Insurance and Private Pensions No. 37*, www.oecd.org/daf/fin/financial-markets/The-Bitcoin-Question-2014.pdf, accessed 20/02/2018.

40 Schulze, E. (2017), "'We are about to see massive disruptions': IMF's Lagarde says it's time to get serious about digital currency", *CNBC*, 13/10/2017, www.cnbc.com/2017/10/13/bitcoin-get-serious-about-digital-currency-imf-christine-lagarde-says.html, accessed 20/02/2018.

41 Morgan, D. (2018), "Congress sets sights on federal cryptocurrency rules", *Reuters*, 19/02/2018, www.reuters.com/article/us-crypto-currencies-congress/congress-sets-sights-on-federal-cryptocurrency-rules-idUSKCN1G31AG, accessed 20/02/2018; Palmer, D. (2018), "UK treasury launches inquiry into cryptocurrency", *Coin Desk*, 22/02/2018, www.coindesk.com/uk-treasury-launches-inquiry-into-cryptocurrencies-and-blockchain, accessed 23/02/2018.

42 Lam, E. (2017), "What the World's Central Banks Are Saying About Bitcoin", *Bloomberg*, 15/12/2017, www.bloomberg.com/news/articles/2017-12-15/what-the-world-s-central-banks-are-saying-about-cryptocurrencies, accessed 23/02/2018.

43 International Organization of Securities Commissions (IOSCO) (2018), "IOSCO board communication on concerns related to initial coin offerings (ICOs)", *IOSCO Media Release*, 18/01/2018; IOSCO (2017), "IOSCO research report on financial technologies (Fintech)", *IOSCO Report*, February 2017, https://www.iosco.org/library/pubdocs/pdf/IOSCOPD554.pdf, accessed 20/02/2018.

44 Lunn, B. (2018), "Some governments want to shut down Bitcoin but they don't know how" *Daily Fintech*, 03/02/2018, https://dailyfintech.com/2018/02/03/some-governments-want-to-shut-down-bitcoin-but-they-dont-know-how/, accessed 20/02/2018.

4.3 Countries with weak currencies and weak democracies

People in these jurisdictions do not trust their domestic fiat currency as a store of value prompting a stateless currency such as Bitcoin as a viable alternative. In weak democracies, governments could simply ban whatever they do not like. This develops into a vicious circle, where less trust leads to greater attempts at control, which in turn leads to less trust. For failing economies like Zimbabwe[45] and Venezuela,[46] fiats there have become next to useless owing to hyperinflation, or the prospect of hyperinflation.[47] It then becomes prudent to seek alternative stores of value such as a stable overseas currency, gold, Bitcoin, or some tangible commodity.

Countries facing such challenges usually ban cryptocurrencies, or move to a national digital currency as Venezuela has recently done. The African continent is home to many countries with weak currencies and weak democracies which is probably why many people there look towards cryptocurrencies as a way out. An equally important consideration is that the blockchain technology underpinning them could provide access to financial services for the 2.5 billion unbanked population around the world.[48]

4.4 Offshore countries positioning as global currency hubs

Lambasted as tax havens, many such jurisdictions are currently repositioning to attract cryptocurrency entrepreneurs.[49] They have little to lose and much to gain by doing this. To avoid being denounced by regulators, they need to avoid being tagged as havens for tax evaders, money launderers and other criminals. They focus on how people outside their jurisdictions use cryptocurrencies, and why overly restrictive regulations could drive cryptocurrency activities away. These refashioned offshore financial centres parade themselves as conducive international locations for the setting up of Bitcoin exchanges, Bitcoin mining and Bitcoin vaults. Examples of such jurisdictions include the Cayman Islands, Malta, Cyprus, Gibraltar and the Isle of Man.[50] The Cayman Islands, for example, is

---

45 Dzirutwe, M. (2017), "Think bitcoin's getting expensive? Try Zimbabwe", *Reuters*, 13/11/2017, www.reuters.com/article/us-zimbabwe-bitcoin/think-bitcoins-getting-expensive-try-zimbabwe-idUSKBN1DD0NF, accessed20/02/2018.

46 del Castillo, M. (2018), "Why Venezuela Should Worry About a National Crypto", *Coin Desk*,23/02/2018,www.cnas.org/press/in-the-news/why-venezuela-should-worry-about-a-national-crypto, accessed 26/02/2018.

47 Koesch, J. (2011), "Hyperinflation in Zimbabwe", *Globalization and Monetary Institute 2011 Annual Report*, www.dallasfed.org/~/media/documents/institute/annual/2011/annual11b.pdf, accessed 20/02/2018.

48 Vigna, P. & Casey, M. J. (2017), "Bitcoin for the Unbanked: Cryptocurrencies That Go Where Big Banks Won't", *Foreign Affairs*, 25/10/2017, www.foreignaffairs.com/articles/2015-02-26/bitcoin-unbanked, accessed 20/02/2018.

49 Palan, R. (2012), "Tax havens and offshore financial centres", *Academic Foresights*, 4 (April–June 2012), pp. 1–15.

50 Higgins, S. (2017), "ICOs welcome: Isle of Man to unveil friendly framework for token sales", *Coin Desk*, 20/09/2017, www.coindesk.com/icos-welcome-isle-of-man-to-unveil-friendly-framework-for-token-sales, accessed 02/02/2018; Milmo, C. (2016), "Bitcoin: How the Isle of Man

home to around 70% of the world's offshore investment funds.[51] With the absence of any direct taxation on companies or individuals, the Cayman Islands is well positioned to attract tech start-ups. Tech City, the special economic zone within Cayman Enterprise City hosts some of the world's leading blockchain and Fintech entities. The Cayman Islands also hosts significant numbers of investment funds investing in cryptoassets and distributed ledger technologies and entities undertaking token generation events.

4.5 Countries with a tendency towards freedom and innovation

Such countries have strong currencies and strong democracies. For example, Switzerland bears this characteristic. Not known by many, Switzerland is officially a multi-currency country, where an alternative currency known as WIR[52] was created in 1934 by people who wanted to create an alternative to its financial system when it failed miserably in 1929. Though WIR accounts for a tiny representation of the Swiss GDP, it is real and legal. Bitcoin resembles fiat currency in Switzerland as legal tender as people can pay taxes and fines and buy railway tickets in Bitcoin there. Bitcoin has not so far posed a threat to the national fiat currency which people continue to trust.

Switzerland has developed into a hub for cryptocurrency innovation and hence operates as more than just an offshore financial hub. It has gained recognition as a talent magnet and a good location to run a global business backed by a sophisticated domestic market with strong privacy laws and ranking as number one in the Global Innovation Index.[53] It has also shown the capacity to reverse the tide of European start-ups migrating to the US Silicon Valley with Xapo,[54] a US start-up moving to Switzerland first before shifting its headquarters to Hong Kong to be near to the potentially huge Chinese Fintech market. There are a rich variety of cryptoassets available in Switzerland, but there is no generally recognised classification of ICOs and the tokens arising from them. The Swiss Financial Market Supervisory Authority (FINMA) though differentiates between utility, payment, and asset tokens, and applying the concept of substance over form.[55] Japan is another example of an economy with strong currency and strong democracy that

---

is leading a cryptocurrency revolution", *Independent*, 03/01/2016, www.independent.co.uk/news/uk/home-news/bitcoin-how-the-isle-of-man-is-sparking-a-cryptocurrency-revolution-a6794756.html, accessed 02/02/2018.

51 Colegate, A. & Wisdom, A-L. (2019), *Cayman Islands: Fintech 2019*, London, ICLG.

52 Migchels, A. (2012), "The Swiss WIR, or: How to defeat the money power", *Real Currencies*, 19/04/2017, https://realcurrencies.wordpress.com/2012/04/19/the-swiss-wir-or-how-to-defeat-the-money-power/, accessed 02/02/2018.

53 Cornell University/INSEAD/WIPO (2017), *Global Innovation Index 2017: Innovation feeding the world*, Tenth Edition, New York/Paris, Cornell University/INSEAD/WIPO.

54 Parker, L. (2017), "Bitcoin, Switzerland, Xapo", *Brave New Coin*, 28/01/2017, www.bravenewcoin.com/news/xapo-edges-closer-to-switzerland, accessed 02/02/2018.

55 Liebii, M. (2019), "A primer on the regulation of trading in cryptocurrencies and asset management related to cryptocurrencies in Switzerland" *PwC Switzerland Paper*, www.cryptovalley.swiss/?mdocs-file=54694, accessed 02/07/2019; Haeberli, D., Oesterhelt, S. & Meier, U. "Blockchain and cryptocurrency regulation 2019: Switzerland", in J. Dewey (ed.), *Blockchain and cryptocurrency regulation 2019*, First edition, London, Global Legal Insights (GLI).

does not find Bitcoin or any of the cryptocurrencies a threat to their national fiat currency.[56] As alluded to earlier, the Japanese regulatory framework for cryptocurrencies is anything but restrictive to digital currency development.

4.6 Superpowers that may set the de facto standards for regulation

All the superpowers struggle with the competing agendas of protecting citizens and incumbents versus the fostering of innovation. The US has the current global reserve currency and enjoys the track record of being the locus of Fintech innovation. The country is seeing strong competition being fought between its two major Fintech hubs, namely California and New York. California believes cryptocurrency innovation through new start-ups could disrupt and replace incumbent financial services providers, while the New York hub takes cryptocurrency innovation as complementing the incumbents.[57] The US has taken a wait and see attitude towards cryptocurrencies even though the country has almost the highest concentration of cryptocurrencies activities in the world.[58] Despite various Securities Exchange Commission (SEC) enforcement actions against ICOs of late,[59] this has not slowed down significantly the pace of ICOs or restricted blockchain innovations there. Though lately because of the SEC's stance towards ICOs by categorising them as investments, the crypto community is feeling otherwise. The SEC surprised the crypto community when it recently gave Blockstack the go-ahead to undertake a US$28 million digital offering under Regulation A that allows smaller businesses to raise money publicly. This is the SEC's first approval for a token offering after a series of crackdowns the regulator led against unregistered ICOs it deems as securities.[60]

China on the other hand is preoccupied with capital flight, which makes the regime there seemingly anti-cryptocurrency,[61] even though many Chinese people there are known to be heavily involved in Bitcoin trading in over-the-counter markets, Bitcoin mining and Bitcoin exchanges.[62] The People's Bank of China

---

56 Blair, G. (2018), "US$1 billion down, why is Japan still in love with Bitcoin", *South China Morning Post*, 05/02/2018, https://www.scmp.com/week-asia/business/article/2131758/us1-billion-down-why-japan-still-love-bitcoin, accessed 20/02/2018.
57 Nicoletti, B. (2017), *The future of FinTech: Integrating finance and technology in financial services*, London, Palgrave Macmillan.
58 Hileman, G. & Rauchs, M. (2017), *Global cryptocurrency benchmarking study*, Cambridge, Cambridge University Press.
59 Securities Exchange Commission (2018), "SEC halts alleged initial coin offering scam", *SEC Press Release 2018–8,* 30/01/2018, www.sec.gov/news/press-release/2018-8, accessed 20/02/2018.
60 Chaparro, F. (2019), "Blockstack wins first-ever SEC approval for a token offering under Reg A+ listing", *The Block Crypto* 10/07/2019, www.theblockcrypto.com/daily/30770/blockstack-wins-first-ever-sec-approval-for-a-token-offering-under-reg-a-listing, accessed 12/07/2019.
61 Meyer, D. (2018), "China Enlists its 'Great Firewall' to Block Bitcoin Websites", *Fortune,* 05/02/2018, https://fortune.com/2018/02/05/bitcoin-china-website-ico-block-ban-firewall/, accessed 20/02/2018.
62 Clark, G. (2018), "Bitcoin and cryptocurrencies: Quick Take Q&A", *The Washington Post,* 16/01/2018, http://www.washingtonpost.com/business/how-chinas-stifling-bitcoin-and-cryptocurrencies-quicktake-qanda/2018/01/16/96984492-fb24-11e7-9b5d-bbf0da31214d_story.html, accessed 20/02/2018.

(PBOC) has also run trials of its own prototype cryptocurrency, taking it closer to being the first major central bank to issue digital money,[63] while the blockchain technology[64] driving Bitcoin is also being extensively pursued. With regards to cryptocurrency, China's vision seems to be based on taking full control of digital money transactions in contrast to the libertarian aspirations of Bitcoin.

Therefore, cryptocurrency development in China probably signals that this would be categorised as sovereign or official cryptocurrency, and non-sovereign cryptocurrency or private cryptocurrency. The CBIRC stated in June 2018 that the sovereign cryptocurrency would be treated as a legitimate digital currency issued by the PBOC that has value as a fiat currency and could be employed as a medium of exchange, whereas the non-sovereign cryptocurrency, particularly Bitcoin, would instead be treated as merely a digital symbol programmed and issued by market participants with agreed protocols and essentially similar to a kind of virtual commodity that can be circulated.[65]

It is to be noted that the PBOC Circular 2013 and Circular 2017 are the two primary government regulations governing private cryptocurrencies in China. Both together clarified the nature of Bitcoin, imposed restrictions on financial institutions and third-party payment agents participating in cryptocurrency transactions, and prohibit ICOs and cryptocurrency transactions through token financing and trading platforms.[66] These regulations have defined and referenced Bitcoin only, whereas the legal status of other cryptocurrencies including Ethereum are still vague with ICOs explicitly banned within the country. Thus far, the regulators have taken enforcement actions on most activities linked to cryptocurrency, but crimes and disputes nevertheless keep climbing, with cryptocurrency disputes-related cases already exceeding 1,000, and still growing.[67] Facebook's recent plan to design its own Libra cryptocurrency might be forcing the PBOC to stepping up research in the creation of its own central bank digital currency that first began in 2014 and was further developed in late 2019. This is attributed to the fear that Libra could potentially pose a challenge to Chinese cross-border payments, monetary policy and even financial sovereignty.[68] Though China recently announced that it would launched its own digital currency in response to Facebook Libra, mainstream argument is that the new digital currency would have many traits that makes it resembles

---

63 Supra, note [63], Clark (2018).
64 Gibson, W. (2018), "China on the blockchain, Part 2: A trillion dollars", *Hacker Noon*, 14/02/2018, https://hackernoon.com/china-on-the-blockchain-95336b5acbf9, accessed 20/02/2018.
65 Li, WH. & Jiang, Z. (2018), "The study of the development and regulation of distributed ledger, blockchain and digital currency", *CBIRC Working Paper June 2018*.
66 Gong, L. & Yu, LP. (2019), "Blockchain & cryptocurrency regulation 2019: China" in J. Dewey (ed.), *Blockchain & cryptocurrency regulation 2019*, 1st Edition, London, Global Legal Insights (GLI).
67 Supra, note [67], Gong & Yu (2019).
68 Tang, F. (2019), "Facebook's Libra forcing China to step up plans for its own cryptocurrency, says central bank official", *South China Morning Post*, 8/07/2019, www.scmp.com/economy/china-economy/article/3017716/facebooks-libra-forcing-china-step-plans-its-own, accessed 11/07/2019.

a centralised digital currency rather than a conventional cryptocurrency.[69] It is even more precise to argue that the PBOC is seeking to release digital cash with extra surveillance.

Given the situations in the US and China Switzerland[70] or the UK[71] could take leadership cryptocurrency roles given the leadership vacuum brought about by the positions in the US and China.

4.7 Countries that have competing agendas

Two countries with significant participation in the global economy facing competing agendas in the area of cryptocurrencies and assets are South Korea and India. Despite having a relatively strong currency, strong democracy and history of innovation South Korea is expected, along with other economies in the same category, to take a positive line. However, spatial reasoning weighs in on the decision in South Korea. It is located between China and Japan who compete strongly with it in the global economy and are sending mixed messages to South Korea with regards to Bitcoin. It has also faced Bitcoin hacking threats as well as a potential nuclear threat from North Korea.[72] This probably helps to explain why the country has a vast local enclave and in particular its younger population engaging in crypto activities.

India is transiting towards a modern global economy, has a historically weak currency, but is the largest democracy in the world. In 2016, the country withdrew high denomination notes from circulation in an effort to combat corruption, black market trade and tax evasion.[73] The country is now, however, focusing on innovation. With an abundant, talented tech workforce, India has the opportunity to become a leading Fintech hub that could include the fostering of cryptocurrencies. Recent statements from the country's central bank nonetheless appear to suggest that it is denouncing Bitcoin or at least the excessive speculative risks posed by the digital currency.[74] India's central bank along with other major central banks in the world is nevertheless appreciative of the

---

69 Huang, R. (2019), "China's Digital Currency Is Unlikely To Be A Cryptocurrency", *Forbes* 14/08/2019, www.forbes.com/sites/rogerhuang/2019/08/14/chinas-digital-currency-is-unlikely-to-be-a-cryptocurrency/, accessed 16/08/2019.

70 Cag, D. (2017), "The Case for Switzerland, and Particularly Zug, as the Global Blockchain and Cryptocurrency Hub", *Influencive,* 02/10/2017, www.influencive.com/case-switzerland-particulalry-zug-global-blockchain-cry, accessed 02/02/2018.

71 Dillet, R. (2015), "UK is leading the way to becoming a global Bitcoin hub", *Tech Crunch*, 31/07/2015, https://techcrunch.com/2015/07/31/uk-is-leading-the-way-to-become-a-global-bitcoin-hub/, accessed 02/02/2018.

72 Sulleyman, A. (2018), "Bitcoin latest: South Korea will not ban cryptocurrency trading, finance minister says after new rules send price crashing", *Independent*, 31/01/2018, www.independent.co.uk/life-style/gadgets-and-tech/news/bitcoin-latest-updates-south-korea-trading-ban-finance-minister-cryptocurrency-a8186831.html, accessed 20/02/2018.

73 Doshi, V. & Allen, K. (2016), "Your money's no good: Rupee note cancellation plunges India into panic", *The Guardian,* 10/11/2016, www.theguardian.com/world/2016/nov/10/rupee-note-cancellation-panic-in-india-banks-500-1000, accessed 20/02/2018.

74 Meyer, D. (2018), "India just caused the price of Bitcoin to slide again", *Fortune*, 01/02/2018, https://fortune.com/2018/02/01/bitcoin-price-india/, accessed 20/02/2018.

potential of blockchain technology.[75] The Reserve Bank of India's recent "Draft Enabling Framework for Regulatory Sandbox", unlike those in the UK, Australia, Hong Kong and Singapore, leaves out businesses involving cryptocurrency, cryptoasset services, crypto trading, crypto investing, ICOs and settling in cryptoassets, but similar to these named others would allow smart contracts and blockchain technologies.[76]

The crypto community in India in July 2019 received a shock when the Inter-Ministerial Committee of the government proposed a draft bill banning cryptocurrencies.[77] The draft bill would also make it illegal to deal in any cryptocurrency not regulated in the country. India's National Association of Software and Services Companies (Nasscom) opposed the proposal arguing the banning of all cryptocurrencies other than those backed by the state would not be a constructive move, and that it would be better for the state to work towards developing a risk-based framework to regulate and monitor cryptocurrencies and tokens. Other stakeholders in the industry argued that the bill would not be able to stop crypto users in the country. This would merely drive its use underground, and the better option would be for the currencies to be brought in through regulated channels to enable these to be traced and to stop illicit activities.

4.8 Government worries

In general, four matters worry governments:[78]

(1) When allowing cryptocurrencies to flourish, governments fear that their populations could be exposed to fraud and financial crime of the kind found in the earlier Silk Road and Mt. Gox cases. The risk of cryptoasset money laundering activities have not gone away and have continue to haunt the Fintech space, with crypto scams and frauds exceeding more than US$1 billion in the first quarter of 2019.[79] These range from exchange thefts, exit scams, fraud and misappropriation to ATM double-spend attacks. This concern could be mitigated by regular and active enforcements using existing securities and related financial services laws.

(2) The fear of citizens deserting their national fiat currencies. Responsible monetary and fiscal policies could prevent unwarranted erosion

---

75 Supra, note [75], Meyer, (2018).
76 Helms, K. (2019), "Supreme Court advocate suggests how to regulate crypto in India", *Bitcoin.com* 15/07/2019, www.news.Bitcoin.com/suppreme-court-advocate-regulate-cryptocurrency-india/, accessed 18/07/2019.
77 Banerjee, P. (2019), "Banning cryptocurrency in India not a solution: Nasscom", *Live Mint*, 30/07/2019, www.livemint.com/news/india/banning-cryptocurrency-in-india-not-a-solution-nasscom-1564476081539.html, accessed 09/08/2019.
78 Supra, note [45], Lunn (2018).
79 Cipher Trace (2019), "Cryptocurrency anti-money laundering report, 2019 Q1", *Ciphertrace*, April 2019, https://ciphertrace.com/wp-content/uploads/2019/05/ciphertrace-q1-2019-cryptocurrency-anti-money-laundering-report.pdf, accessed 18/06/2019.

through inflation. When excessive loose monetary policies and irresponsible fiscal policies are in play for whatever reasons citizens would switch to gold, other precious metals or other strong and stable currencies or digital currencies, but the switch does not arise because of the existence of cryptocurrencies. This is exemplified in the Venezuelan, Iranian, and North Korean economies more recently, and increasingly so as they use cryptoassets to bypass US sanctions and so on.[80]

(3) Governments are seeking ways to collect tax from cryptocurrency activities without inhibiting innovation. Guidance could be sought from those economies which have designed effective ways of dealing with this issue. For example, cryptocurrencies could be treated as an asset that enables capital gains from it to be taxed accordingly. Australia has a successful model meriting attention and perhaps replication,[81] and so has the UK[82] and others.

(4) The persistent fear that cryptocurrencies could be used to facilitate the undertaking of illegal activities, from money laundering to tax evasion. As mentioned earlier, these issues also arise with fiat currencies. Much could be gained by offering some benefits from using cryptocurrencies with know your customer (KYC) and know your transaction (KYT) routines commonly used in the banking sector. This is now happening in a widening range of countries, the latest of which involved a Danish bank operating in Estonia.[83]

Thus, central banks and regulators are concerned with financial and security risks attached to cryptocurrencies and whether the financial systems could suffer a negative impact were cryptocurrencies to continue with their growth trajectory. More importantly, other than for a few economies where they are not viewed as a threat to their national fiat currencies, most others are concerned with the threats cryptocurrencies pose to their central bank's control over monetary supply, monetary policies, and fiscal policies. Official attitudes depend on the contextual circumstances in different economies. The next and subsequent chapters will look more closely at how some selected advanced and emerging economies deal with the impact of cryptocurrencies in their financial systems.

---

80 Webb, S. (2018), "Iran, North Korea and Venezuela turning to cryptocurrency to bypass US sanctions, experts warn", *Fox News*, 07/09/2018, www.foxnews.com/tech/iran-north-korea-and-venezuela-turning-to-cryptocurrency-to-bypass-us-sanctions-experts-warn, accessed 10/10/2018.

81 Australian Taxation Office (2017), "Tax treatment of cryptocurrencies", *ATO*, 21/12/2017, www.ato.gov.au/General/Gen/Tax-treatment-of-crypto-currencies-in-Australia---specifically-bitcoin/, accessed 20/02/2018.

82 KPMG (2019), "Cryptoassets – Accounting and tax", *KPMG*, April 2019, https://home.kpmg/content/dam/kpmg/be/pdf/2019/06/cryptoassets-accounting-tax.pdf, accessed 26/07/2019.

83 Guerstelle, G.L. (2019), "Massive Danske Bank money laundering scandal continues to unfold", *Ballard Spahr* 04/03/2019, www.moneylaunderingnews.com/2019/03/massive-danske-bank-money-laundering-scandal-continues-to-unfold/, accessed 21/03/2019.

Individually, each regulator has examined various parts of the crypto domain, from mining to trading and evaluated how they should or could be regulated.[84] Pertaining to exchanges, regulators look at how these assets are traded, their classification as commodities or securities,[85] and also with regards to environmental concerns posed by the alleged high electricity consumption,[86] especially in China and elsewhere. Pertaining to ICOs[87], regulators are studying frauds, where founders of fake companies have disappeared with the money. With respect to financial products, regulators are looking into the bringing in of financial products onto the traditional market, as exemplified by the Bitcoin futures products in the US offered by the CME and CBOE, as well as the series of initiatives to get Bitcoin ETFs launched.[88] Each country seems to be looking at how the others distinguish and differentiate themselves as new Bitcoin or crypto hubs.

The Financial Stability Board (FSB) has compiled a registry of crypto regulators from across major crypto hotspots outlining the degree and kinds of intervention from each.[89] For example, the directory briefly highlights the crypto oversight function of the Swiss FINMA and its collaborative workings with the State Secretariat for International Finance (SIF), and the Money Laundering Reporting Office Switzerland (MROS).[90] The Swiss examples shows how and why the monitoring and overseeing of crypto activities would require inter-agency attention owing to the complexity and cross-border nature of cryptoassets. This international perspective provides helpful guidance for many economies looking to see how they could effectively deal with the threats flowing from the crypto space without harming genuine innovative initiatives. Comparative insights are also available from the US Library of Congress.[91]

Thus far, regulatory interventions cast a spotlight predominantly on the creation and distribution of pre-mined cryptoassets (like ICOs), together with cryptoasset exchange and trading intermediaries. Competent authorities' responses

---

84 Kharpal, A. (2018), "Cryptocurrencies: Regulating the new economy", *CNBC*, 9/08/2018, www.cnbc.com/2018/08/09/cryptocurrencies--regulating-the-new--economy.html, accessed 5/03/2019.

85 Demertzis, M. & Wolff, G.B. (2018), "The economic potential and risks of crypto assets: Is a regulatory framework needed?", *Bruegel Policy Contribution* Issue No 14/09/2018, 1–14, https://bruegel.org/wp-content/uploads/2018/09/PC-14_2018.pdf, accessed 20/10/2018.

86 De Vries, A. (2018), "Bitcoin's growing energy problem" *Joule 2*, 801–809, 16/05/2018, www.researchgate.net/publication/325188032_Bitcoin's_Growing_Energy_Problem, accessed 27/06/2018; Dilek, S. & Furuncu, Y. (2018), "Bitcoin mining and its environmental effects", 12/05/2018, https://dergipark.org.tr/download/article-file/641972, accessed 27/06/2018.

87 Liebau, D. & Schueffel, P. (2019), "Cryptocurrencies & initial coin offerings: Are they scams? – An empirical study", *The Journal of the British Blockchain Association*, 2 (1), pp. 1–7.

88 Brown, M.A. (2019), "Cryptocurrency and financial regulation: The SEC's rejection of Bitcoin-based ETPs", *University of North Carolina School of Law*, 23 (1), pp. 139–157.

89 FSB (2019), "Crypto-assets regulators directory", *FSB*, 05/04/2019, www.fsb.org/wp-content/uploads/P050419.pdf, accessed 18/05/2018.

90 Supra, note [90], FSB (2019): 21.

91 Library of Congress (2018), "Regulation of cryptocurrency in selected jurisdictions", *Library of Congress*, June 2018, www.loc.gov/law/help/cryptocurrency/regulation-of-cryptocurrency.pdf, accessed 26/07/2018.

extend from public warnings to regulatory guidance, selected enforcement actions against those not complying, outright bans, and legislative initiatives covering cryptoassets in offshore financial services hubs,[92] particularly since scandalous revelations from the Panama and Paradise Papers.[93]

Four kinds of regulatory interventions have been observed across the world. First, this involves the applications of existing laws and/or regulations to cryptoasset activities that typically come with various prior guidance that focuses mainly on the applicability/relevance of securities laws and to a lesser degree existing banking regulations and payment provider rules. This is exemplified by Australia's Information Sheet (INFO 225) on ICOs and cryptocurrency.[94] The second kind involves the deployment of retrofitted regulation involving amendments to existing laws or regulations to include specified crypto activities. This is exemplified by Estonia's amendment of its Money Laundering Act and Terrorism Financing Prevention Act to include cryptoasset exchanges and wallets.[95] The third kind or bespoke regulation involves new laws or regulations issued, especially to regulate cryptoasset activities. Bespoke regulations typically involve establishing a separate legal framework applicable only to cryptoasset activities. This is exemplified by Malta's Virtual Financial Assets Act.[96] The fourth kind involves distinct bespoke regulatory regimes generally applicable to Fintech activities that includes cryptoasset activities and are typically legislative instruments. This is exemplified by Mexico's Law to Regulate Financial Technology institutions.

Observations extracted from 108 selected jurisdictions suggest that the retrofitted regulation approach is popular in countries with higher levels of cryptoasset activities. This has been attributed to the benefits of quick solutions providing regulatory clarity relative to the bespoke regulatory framework. By contrast, jurisdictions with lower levels of cryptoasset activities show a preference for reliance on existing regulations or leaving these activities unregulated.

Interestingly, smaller economies with lower levels of cryptoasset activities prefer the deployment of the most advanced regulatory frameworks, meaning bespoke regulatory regimes or specific new regulations. These economies

---

92 Blandin, A., Cloots, A.S., Hussain, H., Rauchs, M., Saleuddin, R., Allen, J.G., Zhang, B. & Cloud, K. (2019), *Global cryptoasset regulatory landscape study*, Cambridge, Cambridge Centre for Alternative Finance (CCAF).

93 Shaxson, N. (2019), "The billions attracted by tax havens do harm to sending and receiving nations alike", *Finance & Development*, September 2019, pp. 7–10.

94 Australian Securities and Investment Commission (2018), "Information Sheet (INFO 225) on ICOs and crypto-currency", *Australian Securities and Investment Commission*, updated 30/05/2019, https://asic.gov.au/regulatory-resources/digital-transformation/initial-coin-offerings-and-crypto-assets/, accessed 19/08/2019.

95 Teataja, R. (2017), "Money Laundering and Terrorism Financing Prevention Act", *Riigi Teataja*, 26/10/2017, https://www.riigiteataja.ee/en/eli/517112017003/consolide, accessed 19/08/2019.

96 Justice Services (2018), "Virtual Financial Assets At-Laws of Malta", *Malta Justice Services*, http://justiceservices.gov.mt/DownloadDocument.aspx?app=lp&itemid=29079, accessed 12/12/2018; Pisani, W. (2018), "Guidance notes for the VFA sector", *Grant Thornton* November 2018, www.grantthornton.com.mt/industry/fintech-and-innovation/The-Malta-Virtual-Financial-Asset-Act/, accessed 12/12/2018.

appear also to correspond to jurisdictions with historically less rigid attitude towards business regulations. These crypto-friendly regimes appear to be at odds with the regulatory objectives of larger jurisdictions concerned with the harmful impacts of crypto activities and thus potentially generate risks for the latter owing to the cross-border nature of crypto activities.

In general, most jurisdictions apply activity-based rather than entity-based approaches.[97] The former refers to regulations applicable to particular types of crypto activity, in contrast to particular companies or entities as found in the latter. The idea behind activity-based approaches is that risks associated with crypto activities are correlated with the nature of the activities instead of the underlying entities undertaking these activities. This approach enables regulators to explicitly state which activities they are responsible for regulating and hence what kind of authorisation involved businesses would require. Activity-based approaches in some jurisdictions are complemented by the entity-based approach, especially when regulating systemic risk. This is shown when regulators issue restrictions to prevent existing regulated entities like commercial banks from dealing with cryptoassets, like the 2018 ban issued by the Reserve Bank of India.

In general, token creation activities appear to be mainly unregulated across most jurisdictions surveyed. This is attributed to the general absence of any precise reference to mining activities in regulators' guidance/regulations.[98] Distributions and exchange activities are regulated to some extent, especially with regards to ICOs in all of the jurisdictions surveyed. Payments and storage activities are respectively regulated in 45% and 23% of these jurisdictions.

There appear to be two enforced self-regulatory entities.[99] The Japanese Virtual Currency Exchange Association (JVCEA) was, in October 2018, approved by Japan's financial regulator as a self-regulatory body to oversee crypto activities in the country. The JVCEA assumes a wide range of responsibilities extending from the setting of industry standards to conducting on-site inspections and data gathering from its members. The other is the Investment Industry Regulatory Organisation of Canada (IIROC) that has incidentally included the preparation of regulation of blockchain applications and digital assets in it 2019 priorities. However, various industry groups could get involved with the development of crypto industry standards and best practices together with regulators, as exemplified by the US Virtual Commodities Association Working Group. The 2019 G20 Osaka Summit witnessed enhanced collaborations between such national association from across the world on the side lines of the Summit.

As alluded to earlier, there are three approaches to authorisation, namely bespoke authorisation, retrofitted authorisation, and existing authorisation. France stands out here with its unique forthcoming opt-in authorisation regime via its

---

97 Supra, note [93], Blandin et al. (2019).
98 Supra, note [93], Blandin et al. (2019).
99 Supra, note [93], Blandin et al. (2019).

Action Plan for Business Growth and Transformation (PACTE) bill that provides for ICOs and cryptoasset service providers. Affected market participants here are not compelled to apply for a licence and would be permitted to run lawfully without licences. This so called "whitelist approach" examining only voluntary licencing applications is envisaged to incentivise viable and trustworthy undertakings to seek regulator's approval and apply for a licence.[100]

The more pioneering and more extensively followed regulatory approach is the regulatory sandboxes (RSs) introduced by UK's Financial Conduct Authority (FCA) back in 2015. This has since grown with fifty jurisdictions participating globally.[101] Though RSs focus more on the Fintech space, they are also deployed for testing crypto products and services, especially testing for distributed ledger technology (DLT) based offerings. In the UK, some 30% of yearly cohorts are involved with DLT or the provision of cryptoasset related services. The Abu Dhabi Global Market Sandbox and those available in Singapore and Hong Kong are other good examples. Under the RS regime, the regulators are able to work with the entities involved in a controlled space to gather better insights of their business models and potential market impacts.

Various enforcement actions have been observed in most high crypto active jurisdictions, and in particular these covering the US, Japan, South Korea and Israel. The focus appears to be on ICOs, cryptoasset exchanges and on litigations involving consumers and investors.[102]

The near absence of harmonised and coordinated regulatory responses enables quick thinking market participants to take advantage of regulatory loopholes and circumvents stringent regulations.[103] More global regulatory coworking and cooperation are taking place to help mitigate potential harms of regulatory arbitrage via the formulation of more consistent, harmonised and coordinated regulatory frameworks, additional to enforcement actions across jurisdictions. The Financial Action TaskForce (FATF) in particular focuses on the facilitation of AML/CTF regulatory harmonisation among its member states. Other international multilateral supervisory organisations are also helping, as alluded to in previous chapters. Geopolitics though may contribute to divergent regulatory responses as national regulators seek regulatory strategy consistent with their national approach to the cyber world in general.[104] In turn, this could impact on the nature and scope of international regulatory cooperation.

---

100 This law is expected to be passed in the third quarter of 2019.
101 Financial Conduct Authority (2019), "The impact and effectiveness of Innovate", *Financial Conduct Authority*, 01/04/2019 www.fca.org.uk/publication/research/the-impact-and-effectiveness-of-innovate.pdf, accessed 08/04/2019.
102 Supra, note [93], Blandin et al. (2019).
103 De Araujo Consolino Almeida, Y.W. & Pedrosa-Garcia, J.A. (2018), "Regulation of cryptocurrencies: Evidence from Asia and the Pacific", *MPFD Working Papers WP/18/03*, 03/08/2018, 1–24.
104 Gurguc, Z. & Knottenbelt, W. (2018), "Cryptocurrencies: Overcoming barriers to trust and adoption" *Imperial College/eToro Paper*, https://www.imperial.ac.uk/media/imperial-college/research-centres-and-groups/ic3re/CRYPTOCURRENCIES--OVERCOMING-BARRIERS-TO-TRUST-AND-ADOPTION.pdf, accessed 12/12/2018.

The risks and potential harms posed by crypto activities to economies, businesses and investors/issuers are increasingly being addressed through investors and other alerts issued by many national and international regulators. In general, most of them take the position that the cryptoasset markets presently do not present systemic risks to existing financial systems.[105] Nevertheless, as cryptoassets continue to grow as an asset class and mainstream financial institutions get more involved, the risk momentum could gather and also be exacerbated by the cross-border nature of the asset class. There is the danger that financial entities of systemic significance might be exposed to related activities outside of the jurisdiction's regulatory oversight. Since, systemic risks are usually obvious only in hindsight, they may need to be addressed counter-cyclically,[106] and hence the benefit of regular monitoring of financial stability risks.

Overall, regulatory approach has to be adapted to the technical nature of cryptoassets that are premised on fully decentralised systems.[107] Cryptoassets like Bitcoin are not issued by known legal entities, but by a mere software code located in the Internet space. As such, it is impossible to regulate Bitcoin. Rather, it is more possible to regulate most entities operating with cryptoassets, like Bitcoin mines and crypto exchanges. Foremost, generalised regulation is argued to be not advisable given that the eventual use of cryptoasset classification could deter or prevent innovation or motivate regulatory evasion.[108] Also, the use of generalised regulation could prematurely provide legitimacy to the potential regulated entity. This is because, being regulated and supervised is a stamp of brand recognition giving a halo effect in the marketplace. Instead, the preferred option is concentrating regulatory initiatives on the interface between cryptoassets and the conventional financial system. However, the notion of isolating cryptoassets by focusing their regulation on the interface and limiting the ability of banks and funds to invest in cryptoassets has major limitations. The intervention could restrict the progress of cryptoassets much more than direct regulation of the assets. Deprived of access to investment and savings funds, cryptoassets market growth would be seriously threatened, while innovation would be confined at the fringes. Crypto exchanges on the other hand could be witnessing significant growth and profitability, and together with significant consumer/investor protection questions, are already held at very high standards. This has prompted Mark Carney, the governor of the Bank of England to argue for regulation of cryptoassets now rather than keeping them isolated from the conventional financial system. Also, while it is rational to limit the exposure of financial institutions to cryptoassets in advanced economies with well-functioning and accountable central banks, it needs highlighting that cryptoassets are high-risk assets that could generate financial stability risks when left to grow

---

105 ECB (2019), "Crypto-assets: Implications for financial stability, monetary policy, and payments and market infrastructures", *ECB Crypto-Assets Task Force Paper No 223/May 2019*, www.ecb.europa.eu/pub/pdf/scpops/ecb.op223~3ce14e986c.en.pdf, accessed 21/04/2019.
106 Supra, note [93], Blandin et al. (2019).
107 Supra, note [86], Demertzis (2018).
108 Supra, note [86], Demertzis (2018).

without controls. Going by this, it seems more sensible to treat them as highly risky assets that warrant strict disclosure regimes associated with such asset class.

The public policy approach to cryptoassets would secondly necessitate global coordination on key regulatory questions.[109] International coworking and cooperation initiatives from key multilateral institutions, like the FSB, BIS and FATF, as discussed in the earlier chapter are extremely helpful when seeking to contain money laundering and terrorism activities as well as tax evasion issues. Advice is also needed from these multilateral institutions to formulate global standards that could be compatible with different legal regimes.

For large federations of states like the US and more than two dozen member states like in the EU, the issues of getting the right institution to supervise the regulation is not necessarily an easy matter. While the US federal agencies involved in the financial services sector have clear designated mandates, in view of the hybrid characteristics of cryptoassets as an asset class and as some sort of global virtual currency, deciding on which institution to supervise the industry could be tricky there. The same goes for the EU, with its plethora of EU-level agencies.[110]

Finally, cryptoasset systems, wherever possible, should be kept free from fraud, error and ill intention. This means that there should be built-in processes for dealing with conflicts and/or disputes between market participants. It might be insufficient to just rely on peer review of the software code. Also, accountability is a big issue in decentralised systems associated with the underpinning blockchain technology. This suggests that the new technology is likely to be beneficial when it is integrated with systems that have strong ultimate accountability characteristics.[111]

---

109 Supra, note [86], Demertzis (2018).
110 Supra, note [86], Demertzis (2018).
111 Supra, note [86], Demertzis (2018).

CHAPTER 5

Global cryptoasset hubs

5.1 Introduction

The cryptoassets industry is a subset of the larger Fintech digital space. Some cryptoassets hub with heavy applications like Canada, Singapore and Hong Kong (SAR) are boosted by the presence of users from other nationals barred from using cryptoassets because of bans in their countries of origin, notably nationals from China. Some cryptoasset hubs with apparently low cryptoasset utilisations are due to inhospitable cryptoasset ecosystem such as India. Active and heavy cryptoasset hubs such as found in Western advanced economies are due to the strong pursuits of liberalism even though they have the most advanced and powerful banking systems in the world, as strongly exemplified in the US, UK and various continental European economies. Countries with relatively less developed banking systems, such as those in the African continent, leapfrog to cryptoassets and other subsets of the Fintech space because of the need to provide financial inclusiveness to large tracts of their populations. Multilateral financial institutions, such as the IMF in particular, supports cryptocurrencies and other Fintech subsets to help foster financial inclusiveness in emerging economies where there many less well off.

Forming a precise view of where the heaviest use of cryptoassets occur is not easy as many crypto entities and platforms will not share users' data for various reasons, including data protection laws, or the fact that some wallet providers prevent the gathering of location-based data. Combining available public resources with those others available from private sources could offer a crude estimate of where most crypto activity is occurring.[1] Indication of activity could be gleaned from local Bitcoin volumes, a P2P exchange platform connecting users across 249 countries. While volumes here are relatively smaller than those of large exchanges, they are reaching all-time highs in 2017 before subsequent price falls. High volume growth has been seen in emerging Asian economies such as China, India, Thailand and Malaysia; Latin America states such as Brazil, Chile, Colombia, Mexico and Venezuela; African and Middle Eastern states

---

1 Hileman, G. & Rauchs, M. (2017), *Global cryptocurrency benchmarking study*, Cambridge, Cambridge University Press.

such as Kenya, Nigeria, Saudi Arabia, Tanzania and Turkey; and Eastern Europe states such as Russia and Ukraine.[2]

The geographical distribution of cryptocurrency ATMs including Bitcoin in a recent global cryptocurrency benchmarking study suggests that some 94% of all publicly-known ATMs are based in North America and Europe, with the US and Canada having a total share of 59% and 15% respectively of all ATMs; Africa, the Middle East and Latin America have less than 1% of worldwide cryptocurrency ATMs.[3] Coinmap hosts some 9,000 known merchants across the globe that entertain cryptocurrencies suggesting that significant concentrations of merchants could be seen in North America and Europe. Some activity could also be observed in the Asia-Pacific belt, with concentrations in Australia, Japan, and South Korea; Latin America with concentrations in Brazil and Argentina; and Africa and the Middle East, notably in Kenya, South Africa, and Israel.[4]

Analysis of Bitcoin full nodes suggest that the US has the highest number of full node operators of all economies. User data analysis suggests that nearly 40% of cryptocurrency users are based in the Asia–Pacific, followed by Europe at 27%, with the US share notably low and inconsistent with the data alluded to earlier.[5] The data provided are from a very limited number of wallet providers and payment platforms, and excludes users from exchanges as well as mining pools. All in all, it would appear that cryptocurrencies adoption is most advanced in the US and Europe, but numbers are growing in other jurisdictions like those in the emerging economies of Asia, Latin America and the Middle East.[6]

The geographical distribution of study participants further suggests that Europe accounted for 29% of the study participation rate. Exchanges, wallets, payments and mining respectively there accounted for 37%, 42%, 33% and 13%.[7] The US accounted for 27% of the participation rate. Exchanges, wallets, payments and mining there respectively accounted for 18%, 39%, 19% and 33%. Asia–Pacific accounted for 36% of the study participation rate. Exchanges, wallets, payments and mining there respectively accounted for 27%, 19%, 33% and 50%. Latin America accounted for 6% of the study participation rate. Exchanges, wallets, payments and mining there respectively accounted for 14%, 0%, 11% and 4%. Africa and the Middle East accounted for 2% of the study participation rate. Exchanges, wallets, payments and mining there respectively accounted for 4%, 0%, 4% and 0%.

Cryptocurrency ICOs[8] also emerged from 2017 onwards as a popular and effective crowdfunding method for both start-ups and established companies

---

2 Supra, note [1], Hileman & Rauchs (2017).
3 Supra, note [1], Hileman & Rauchs (2017).
4 Supra, note [1], Hileman & Rauchs (2017).
5 Supra, note [1], Hileman & Rauchs (2017).
6 Supra, note [1], Hileman & Rauchs (2017).
7 Supra, note [1], Hileman & Rauchs (2017).
8 Cadigan, T.N., Frank, J. & Chin, K. (2017), "This is what you get when you invest in an initial coin offering", *Business Insider*, 09/11/2017, www.businessinsider.com/ico-initial-coin-offering-explained-bitcoin-ethereum-2017-11?r=US&IR=T, accessed 02/02/2018.

seeking to raise further capital. This drives further the publicity attaching to cryptoassets.[9] The rapid pace of development in the cryptocurrencies' sector in terms of technology, applications and economics have in turn attracted the attention of governments, international financial regulators and analysts. The surge in investments in cryptocurrency and assets, coupled with the incidences of theft and the perceived linkage with money laundering, tax evasion and drug transactions have ushered in disparate national attitudes towards cryptocurrencies. Cryptocurrencies and blockchain applications have also been touted by developmental experts as a viable instrument for helping the large underbanked populations in many emerging economies by enabling their access to finance which has been previously restricted in the more conventional forms of financing.[10]

The ten cities in the world with strongest Bitcoin presence are San Francisco (US), Vancouver (Canada), Amsterdam (the Netherlands), Ljubljana (Slovenia), Tel Aviv (Israel), Zurich (Switzerland), Tampa (US), Buenos Aires (Argentina), New York (US) and London (UK). The identification is based on the number of Bitcoin merchants in each city, the number of Bitcoin ATMs, and the population size relative to Bitcoin activity.[11]

Last year, 2019, was a remarkable time for Bitcoin in particular, due to its large financial correction from the earlier phenomenal price rise from less than US$1,000 at the commencement of 2017 to its peak of about US$20,000 in mid-December and then dramatically down again to less than US$10,000 as the year closed with further falls in 2018. While some made handsome profits to become crypto billionaires, many more suffered serious financial losses. It was also the year that saw cryptoasset hacks and thefts returning on a scale not seen since the notorious Mt. Gox incident in 2014. It was also the year that witnessed the unleashing of ransomware worm WannaCry which saw ultimate settlement of some £108,000 paid in Bitcoins by victims of the malware. Added to these are record levels of ICO scams and frauds. All these incidents, as discussed in the previous chapter, caught the attention of financial regulators across major economies of the world entrusted with the mission of looking after the interests of investors and consumers.

Finally, since the onset of Bitcoin, a pattern of rapid expansion and collapse marked the characteristic of the Bitcoin or cryptoasset ecosystem. A bubble could be defined as the market capitalisation of a cryptoasset, such as Bitcoin, appreciating by a multiple of ten or more times within a duration of six or less

---

9 Hackett, R. & Wieczner, J. (2017), "How high can Bitcoin's price go in 2018?" *Fortune*, 21/12/2017, https://fortune.com/2017/12/21/bitcoin-price-value-prediction-bubble/, accessed 02/02/2018.

10 Dale, O. (2017), "How Bitcoin & cryptocurrencies are helping developing countries", *Blockonomi*, 24/12/2017, www.blockonomi.com/cryptocurrencies-developing-countries, accessed 02/02/2018.

11 Blystone, D. (2018), "10 cities leading Bitcoin adoption", *Investopedia*, updated 19/09/2019, www.investopedia.com/articles/forex/042415/10-cities-leading-Bitcoin-adoption.asp, accessed 02/02/2018.

months. In turn, local ecosystem bubbles only impact on a particular cryptoasset and its ecosystem and are mainly isolated from the overall development of the global cryptoasset market, while in contrast, the global ecosystem remains prone to price instability.[12]

Thus far, most previous global bubbles were dwarfed by the market frenzy commencing in April 2017. Many first-time retail and institutional cryptoasset investors then flooded in. This was attributed to intense media spotlighting, the tempting promise of "get rich quick" ICO schemes and an oversupply of new coins and tokens. Aggregate cryptoasset market capitalisation catapulted more than 25-times peaking at about US$800 billion, before quickly subsiding throughout 2018.[13] This induced a media story wherein Bitcoin, cryptoassets and ICOs were declared bubbles and deemed dead. However, Bitcoin doomsayers have declared the downfall of the cryptoasset industry subsequent to every global ecosystem bubble. Though the 2017 was the biggest in Bitcoin's history, its market capitalisation and that of the cryptoasset ecosystem still exceeded its January 2017 levels prior to the bubble commencement.[14] Research further suggests speculation of the end of the market and ecosystem have been vastly exaggerated and that more probably only the industry's growth has been delayed.[15]

Not many governments could openly be seen to be very hospitable towards cryptocurrencies because of these controversies surrounding them. Also, no one is really sure of their eventual economic and technological potentials, despite the fact that they have been around since 2008. As a result, most governments assume a cautious stance. So rather than analysing which economies are more hospitable to cryptocurrencies, it could be more pragmatic to differentiate economies in terms of their tolerance levels towards this asset class. For the purpose of this chapter, economies with relatively higher level of tolerance will be spotlighted. These are referred to as Bitcoin-friendly economies in other research initiatives.[16] They refer to countries where the underpinning technology is being tested and applied with increasingly rapid momentum.[17] Western advanced economies in this category include the US, the UK, Canada, Australia, and the continental European economies of Germany, Switzerland and Estonia. Asian economies under this category include Japan, South Korea, and Singapore. The reasons behind surging interest in cryptoassets in each of these is examined below.

---

12 Rauchs, M., Blandin, A., Klein, K., Pieters, G., Recanatini, M. & Zhang, B. (2018), *2nd global cryptoasset benchmarking study*, Cambridge, *Cambridge Centre for Alternative Finance Paper*.

13 Supra, note [12], Rauchs, Blandin, Klein, Pieters, Recanatini & Zhang (2018).

14 Supra, note [12], Rauchs, Blandin, Klein, Pieters, Recanatini & Zhang (2018).

15 Supra, note [12], Rauchs, Blandin, Klein, Pieters, Recanatinin & Zhang (2018).

16 Dedi, D. (2017), "Top 10 most crypto-friendly countries", *Crypto Slate*, 16/09/2017, www.cryptoslate.com/top-10-most-crypto-friendly-countries, accessed 02/02/2018.

17 Scott, A. (2016), "These are the World's Top 10 Bitcoin-Friendly Countries", *Bitcoin*, 29/03/2016, www.bitcoin.com/worlds-top-10-bitcoin-friendly-countries/, accessed 02/02/2018.

5.2 Western advanced economies

5.2.1 The United States

The US unsurprisingly hosts the highest concentration of cryptocurrency users and Bitcoin trading volumes in the world.[18] The country has been home to crowdfunding technology at the cutting edge of digital currency from the beginning.[19] Spurred by the dynamism and innovative spirit of Silicon Valley as well as the New York Fintech prowess, the US is home to numerous cryptocurrency and blockchain related start-ups and the highest number of Bitcoin ATMs in the world.[20] Eleven of the biggest names in the cryptocurrencies' space are US based or US inspired. They are namely; Brian Armstrong of Coinbase, Vitalik Buterin of Ethereum, Juthica Chou of Ledger X, Jack Dorsey of Square, Terry Duffy of the CME Group, Charlie Lee of Litecoin, Naval Ravikant of MetaStable and CoinList, Elizabeth Rossiello of BitPesa, Barry Silbert of Digital Currency Group, Balaji Srinivasan of Earn.com, and Elizabeth Stark of Lightning Labs. In addition, there are many other smaller companies in the US still fighting for recognition.

Many economies look toward the US for guidance and inspiration pertaining to the technology underpinning cryptocurrencies as well as the law and regulations surrounding them, not only from Washington DC, but also from states better known for Fintech innovations, such as California, New York, and New Hampshire. It is therefore unsurprising for the US to serve as the testing ground for cryptocurrency regulation and direction.[21]

An indicator of organic demand in the US is the large population and number of Bitcoin users in the country. This is reflected by the steady growth in Bitcoin trading volume since 2013 as confirmed by the progress achieved by Localbitcoins[22], the major P2P Bitcoin trading service in the country.

5.2.2 The United Kingdom

The UK in general is competing successfully with the US and Singapore as a leading international Fintech hub that includes cryptocurrency innovations. Based on recent investment data, London appears to be Europe's leading

---

18 Hileman, G. & Rauchs, M. (2017), *Global cryptocurrency benchmarking study*, Cambridge, Cambridge Centre for Alternative Finance.

19 Pipikaite, A. & Grover, V. (2018), "US needs to lead digital currency revolution, or other nations will", *The Hill* 08/01/2018, https://thehill.com/blogs/pundits-blog/finance/313224-us-needs-to-lead-digital-currency-revolution-or-other-nations-will, accessed 02/02/2018.

20 Roberts,D.(2017),"The 11 biggest names in cryptocurrency right now",*YahooFinance*,30/11/2017, https://finance.yahoo.com/news/11-biggest-names-cryptocurrency-2017-110033921.html?guccounter=1, accessed 02/02/2018.

21 McKenna, F. (2017), "Here's how the U.S. and the world regulate Bitcoin and other cryptocurrencies", *Market Watch*. 28/12/2017, www.marketwatch.com/story/heres-how-the-us-and-the-world-are-regulating-bitcoin-and-cryptocurrency-2017-12-18, accessed 02/02/18.

22 Haig, S. (2017), "Localbitcoins markets set record trading volume", *Bitcoin*, 03/12/2017, https://news.bitcoin.com/localbitcoins-markets-set-record-trading-volume/, accessed 02/02/2018.

Fintech hub.[23] Over US$1 billion has been invested into UK financial technology companies in 2017, doubling the amount raised in 2016. The country has an active cryptocurrency community, numerous Bitcoins and blockchain related start-ups and Bitcoin BTMs (BTM or Bytom is blockchain project launched to develop a protocol to facilitate the standardised storing of different cryptocurrencies on a blockchain system, and promoting AI) to qualify as a Bitcoin-friendly destination. The country's central bank sees new payment solutions as inevitable.[24] The UK is preparing itself for mass-scale digital currency adoption in the future. In a place where pubs are such an important part of its community, it is unsurprising that many pubs in the UK are accepting Bitcoins.[25]

The Bank of England is closely looking at Bitcoin technology as the candidate to improve the country's monetary system. Mark Carney, the Bank of England's governor, nevertheless declared that Bitcoin cannot be considered a legitimate currency as it failed to meet two major requirements of a traditional currency.[26] He argued in March 2018 that Bitcoin is neither a means of exchange nor a store of value. It is not considered ideal as a medium of exchange because of high fees and slow confirmation times. However, he conceded that the cryptocurrency's underlying blockchain technology may still prove useful due to its decentralised nature.[27] As a senior member of the Financial Stability Board, Carney regularly takes the position that though cryptoassets do not presently posed serious risk to the financial system, this still warrants close monitoring owing to the inherent risk of cryptoassets. He surprised the crypto community in September 2019 at Jackson Hole in the US with the suggestion that central bankers could develop a network of national digital currencies to create a new basket-managed synthetic hegemonic money, a Libra-like digital currency. It has been argued though that his proposal should be treated as a thought exercise to inspire conversation around solutions to the risky imbalances brought about by the current system's dependence on dollar as the world's reserve currency. This and any other solutions are likely to be politically and technically difficult. Still, there are views that rather than contemplating a whole new global

---

23 London Partners (2017), "London is Europe's number one fintech hub for global investors", *London Partners Press Release*, 19/10/2017, https://media.londonandpartners.com/news/london-is-europe-s-number-one-fintech-hub-for-global-investors, accessed 02/02/2018.

24 Sagone, R. (2017), "Results of the Bank of England/Ripple Proof of Concept published today", *Ripple*, 10/07/2017, https://ripple.com/insights/results-of-the-bank-of-englandripple-proof-of-concept-published-today/, accessed 02/02/2018.

25 Hamil, J. (2018), "You can pay for your pint using Bitcoin-at a pub which doesn't accept cards", *Metro News*, 26/01/2018, https://metro.co.uk/2018/01/26/can-pay-pint-using-bitcoin-pub-doesnt-accept-cards-7262557/, accessed 02/02/2018.

26 Partz, H. (2018), "Bank of England Governor Claims Bitcoin 'Failed' As A Currency", *Coin Telegraph*, 20/02/2018, https://cointelegraph.com/news/bank-of-england-governor-claims-bitcoin-has-failed-as-a-currency accessed 22/02/2018.

27 Carney, M. (2018), "The future of money", *Governor of the Bank of England Speech at the inaugural Scottish Economics Conference*, Edinburgh University, 02/03/2018, www.bankofengland.co.uk/-/media/boe/files/speech/2018/the-future-of-money-speech-by-mark-carney, accessed 08/06/2018.

currency, central bankers should seriously consider developing digital currency interoperability.[28]

Prior to July 2019 the UK's financial consumer protection regulator, the Financial Conduct Authority (FCA), has taken the position to not yet regulate cryptoassets. This puts businesses in a limbo about how to proceed with integrating cryptoassets into their business model. This also raised concerns that UK's unclear policy could be hurting UK start-ups who depend on blockchain and cryptocurrency-like platforms. In the light of its consumer welfare protection agenda, the FCA cautioned UK investors that they could lose their funds when investing in Bitcoin as it carries risks similar to gambling. Since, Bitcoin is neither backed by central authorities nor regulated the FCA did not generally consider Bitcoin a safe investment.[29] However, the Cryptoassets Taskforce Final Report released in late 2018 tasked the FCA to provide guidance on cryptoassets in the context of its existing regulatory perimeter. The FCA accordingly on 31 July 2019 issued its finalised guidance on cryptoassets. Discussions on its legal implications would be taken up in the subsequent chapters on crypto regulatory policies.

The UK taxation authority generally treats Bitcoin as private money. Accordingly, VAT is imposed in the usual way from suppliers of any goods sold in exchange for Bitcoin or other cryptocurrencies, with the value being taken from Sterling at the time of the transaction.[30] Bitcoin is therefore likened to a "foreign currency" for most purposes, including value added tax. Bitcoin miners are not subject to VAT as the act of mining is not classed as an economic activity nor would VAT be added to Bitcoin when it is used as a currency for good or services. Much like the US, profitability outcomes from cryptocurrencies transactions are subject to applicable capital gains tax in the UK. Though not a legal tender, Bitcoin is not prohibited for use in the UK.

Last year, the UK Treasury Committee announced launching an inquiry into cryptocurrencies and the technology behind them.[31] This was in order for the country to better understand the risks and benefits of digital money following the explosion of interests and significant investments in them. The cryptocurrency inquiry would assess how consumers and UK's financial infrastructure could be better protected without stifling innovation.

For now, there are at least eleven Bitcoin start-ups in the UK meriting attention according to a recent Accenture Fintech study. This, together with other Fintech support systems, makes the UK the centre of European cryptocurrency

---

28 Casey, M.J. (2019), "A Crypto Fix For a Broken International Monetary System", *Coin Desk*, 02/09/2019, www.coindesk.com/a-crypto-fix-for-a-broken-international-monetary-system, accessed 09/09/2019.

29 Sundararajan, S. (2017), "UK's FCA Chief Warns Bitcoin Investors: Be Prepared to Lose Your Money", *Coin Desk*, 15/12/2017, www.coindesk.com/uks-fca-chief-warns-bitcoin-investors-be-prepared-to-lose-your-money, accessed 02/02/2018.

30 HM Revenue & Customs (2014), "Revenue and Customs Brief 9 (2014): Bitcoin and other cryptocurrencies", *HMRC*, 03/03/2014, www.gov.uk/government/publications/revenue-and-customs-brief-9-2014-bitcoin-and-other-cryptocurrencies, accessed 02/02/2018.

31 BBC (2018), "Bitcoin: MPs launch inquiry into digital currencies", *BBC News*, 22/02/2018, www.bbc.co.uk/news/business-43148180, accessed 23/02/2018.

space as they appear to be at the cutting edge of blockchain technology that underpins much of the cryptoasset space.[32]

5.2.3 Canada

Canada is generally perceived as a cryptocurrency host country. Various Bitcoin ventures and numerous ATMs have sprung up in Canada. It has two internationally-known Bitcoin hubs, one in Toronto and the other in Vancouver. This has resulted in cryptocurrency communities arguing that the country has the potential of becoming the Silicon Valley for Bitcoin, especially when Bitcoin miners now outlawed in China have taken domains there.[33] The Canadian central bank is looking into cryptocurrency regulation, but in the meantime, anti-money laundering and counter-terrorism laws are applicable. The central bank considers the blockchain technology behind Bitcoin a true piece of genius, but Bitcoin trading a form of gambling.[34]

The country hosts a thriving cryptocurrency community. Decentral, its first leading blockchain start-up makes Jaxx Cryptocurrency Wallet and hosts Toronto's first Bitcoin ATM. The Vanbex Group in May 2017 raised US$365,474 to finance the development of blockchain-based products including Etherparty, the company's easy-to-use smart contract creator.[35] Many businesses and retail outlets in Canada are also accepting Bitcoins, including KFC Canada, and Subway.[36] In August 2017, Impak Coin became the first Canadian approved cryptocurrency. This means that Montreal-based Impak Finance could go ahead with the public sale of its digital Impak Coin money. These aside, Canada has the potential to become a prime destination for Bitcoin mining because of a long list of benefits including stable government, cheap electricity and a cold climate that is helpful to Bitcoin mining.[37]

5.2.4 Australia

The country is a key Fintech hub within the Asia-Pacific region. Initially unappealing for Bitcoin start-ups because of heavy taxation and unreported bank

---

32 Ali, B. (2017), "11 Bitcoin start-ups from London you need to know in 2017", *Tech Flier*, 10/08/2017, www.techflier.com/2017/08/10/11-bitcoin-startups-from-london-you-need-to-know-about-in-2017/, accessed 02/02/2018.

33 Freeman, S. (2014), "Will Canada Become 'The Silicon Valley Of Bitcoins'", *Huffington Post*, 28/01/2014, https://www.huffingtonpost.ca/2014/01/28/bitcoin-canada_n_4676044.html?guccounter=1, accessed 02/02/2018.

34 Tso, K. & Kharpal, A. (2018), "Bitcoin is 'gambling' and regulations are needed, Canada central bank head says", *CNBC*, 25/01/2018, https://www.cnbc.com/2018/01/25/bitcoin-trading-is-gambling-canada-central-bank-governor.html, accessed 02/02/2018.

35 Vanbex (2017), "Vanbex Group raises C$500,000 in first seed round", *PR Newswire*, 30/05/2017, www.prnewswire.co.uk/news-releases/vanbex-group-raises-c500000-in-first-seed-round-625422734.html, accessed 02/02/2018.

36 Chokun, J. (2018), "Who Accepts Bitcoin as Payment? List of companies, stored, shops", *99 Bitcoins*, 14/01/2018, https://99bitcoins.com/bitcoin/who-accepts/, accessed 02/02/2018.

37 Vomiero, J. (2018), "Why Canada is poised to become prime destination for Bitcoin mining", *Global News*, 21/01/2018, www.globalnews.ca/news/3978151/canada-Bitcoin-mining-prime-destination, accessed 02/02/2018.

account freezes, there has been a turnaround since the recent Double Taxation Relief legislation.[38] Through this new legislation, Australians are no longer charged GST[39] on purchases of digital currency, allowing it to be treated the same way as physical money for GST purposes. This law change is retrospectively effective from 1 July 2017 and this initiative is widely seen as making it easier for new, innovative, digital currency business to operate so as to boost jobs and wages in the country.

There are now some eighteen cryptocurrency start-ups in the country. These include ACX, a Bitcoin exchange platform, Bata, a cryptocurrency platform, Bit Trade Australia, and Bitcoin Australia that buys and sells Bitcoins on customers' behalf.[40]

Two major factors are driving cryptocurrency start-ups away from the country, as well as causing the Australian Bitcoin exchange market to fall significantly behind growing markets like South Korea and Japan, which control more than half of the global Bitcoin exchange market. These refer to the termination of Bitcoin banking services by leading Australian banks and the double taxation of Bitcoin trading in Australia.[41] The double taxation problem was solved as from 1 July 2017, and Australian banks are now taking a more positive stance toward blockchain technology underpinning Bitcoin. Positive sentiments towards cryptocurrency technology are driven by the Austrian Securities Exchange's (ASX) willingness to trial distributed technology in its operation,[42] as well as by the Australia Post[43] to use this technology to store digital identities and other improvements to strengthen its services.

Subsequent to its earlier regulatory guidance for ICOs in 2017, the Australian Securities and Investments Commission (ASIC) in late May 2019 provided further guidance detailing the legal obligations for cryptocurrency firms under the country's Corporations Act (CA), the ASIC Act (AA), and other laws.[44] These regulatory requirements seek to maintain the integrity of the country's financial market and ensure consumer protection. The ASIC guidance explained

---

38 Higgins, S. (2017), "Bitcoin 'Double Taxation' Relief Bill Introduced in Australia", *Coin Desk*, 18/09/2017, www.coindesk.com/bitcoin-double-taxation-relief-bill-introduced-australia, accessed 02/02/2018.

39 This is a goods and services tax normally assessed at 10% of value.

40 Finder (2018), "Complete list of Australian cryptocurrency start-ups", *Finder*, 07/02/2018, https://www.finder.com.au/australian-cryptocurrency-startups, accessed 18/02/2018.

41 Young, J. (2017), "Australia will recognize Bitcoin as money and protect Bitcoin businesses, no taxes", *Coin Telegraph*, 11/05/2017, https://cointelegraph.com/news/australia-will-recognize-bitcoin-as-money-and-protect-bitcoin-businesses-no-taxes accessed 02/02/2018.

42 Mathes, S. & Irrera, A. (2017), "Australia's ASX selects blockchain to cut costs", *Reuters*, 07/12/2017, https://uk.reuters.com/article/us-asx-blockchain/australias-asx-selects-blockchain-to-cut-costs-idUKKBN1E037R, accessed 18/02/2018.

43 Bhunia, P. (2017), "Australia Post exploring Blockchain technology to secure food products supply chain", *Open Government Asia*, 06/06/2017, www.opengovasia.com/australia-post-exploring-blockchain-technology-to-secure-food-products-supply-chain/, accessed 02/02/2018.

44 Australian Securities & Investments Commission (2019), "Digital transformation: Initial Coin Offerings and crypto-assets", *ASIC,* 30/05/2019, https://asic.gov.au/regulatory-resources/digital-transformation/initial-coin-offerings-and-crypto-assets/ accessed 02/06/2019.

that ICOs and cryptoassets in many situations are financial products that are regulated under the CA. This means that a firm issuing a token that falls within the definition of a financial product like an interest in a managed investment scheme or a security, these laws would apply, including the requirement to hold an Australian financial services (AFS) licence.

These laws are extended to those giving advice, dealing, or providing other intermediary services for crypto-based financial products. Further, cryptocurrency wallet and custody services providers are required to ensure that they hold the suitable custodial and depository authorisations. The said laws also bound cryptocurrency miners when assisting the clearing and settlement of tokens that are financial products. The applicable rules including the holding of an Australian market licence also apply to cryptocurrency exchanges and trading platforms. In turn, cryptocurrency payment and merchant service providers are required to apply for an AFS licence when involved in providing a non-cash payment facility. Additionally, with regards to ICOs and cryptoassets that are not financial products, promoters must ensure that they do not partake in misleading or deceptive conduct or statements. ASIC commissioner, John Price[45] stressed that Australian laws would also apply even when the ICOs or cryptoassets are sold or promoted to Australians from offshore and that issuers of ICOs, cryptoassets and their advisers should not assume the deployment of these structures imply that main consumer protections under Australian laws do not apply or could be disregarded.

5.2.5 Germany

Germany, the EU's anchor economy, generally provides favourable government policies for cryptocurrencies, especially in activities connected with developing blockchain solutions. The virtual currency Bitcoin is recognised by the German Finance Ministry as a "unit of account" meaning it can be employed for tax and trading purposes in the country.[46] Unlike other European destinations that classify Bitcoin as e-money or a foreign currency, Germany's Finance Ministry specifies Bitcoin as a financial instrument under German banking rules, more closely resembling "private money"[47] that can be applied in multilateral clearing circles. This appears to be in support of Friedrich August von Hayek's scheme[48] to nationalise money so as provide competition in the production of money. Bitcoin represents the first step in this direction.

---

45 Supra, note [46], ASIC, 30/05/2019.
46 Clinch, M. (2013), "Bitcoin recognized by Germany as 'private money'", *CNBC*, 19/08/2013, https://www.cnbc.com/id/100971898, accessed 02/02/2018.
47 McElroy, W. (2017), "The Satoshi Revolution - Chapter 1: How And Why Government Outlawed Private Money (Part 2)", *Bitcoin*, 07/10/2017, https://news.bitcoin.com/the-satoshi-revolution-chapter-2-how-and-why-government-outlawed-private-money/-, accessed 02/02/2018.
48 Von Hayek, F.A. (1977), *Denationalisation of money: The argument refined (An analysis of the theory and practice of concurrent currencies series)*, London, The Institute of Economic Affairs.

The new ruling suggests that German authorities are preparing regulations on how to tax Bitcoin transactions. The legal classification of Bitcoin means that commercial profits arising from using the currency might be taxable. For now, though, Bitcoin held for a year or more is exempted from the 25% tax on profits achieved. Being legal in Germany, Bitcoin has had an impact on its value, due to the perceived legitimacy given to it by such government recognition. Germany is also home to one of the biggest Bitcoin marketplaces in the world. The country has also recently finalised plans to introduce Ethereum, the second most valuable cryptocurrency trading into the platform.

5.2.6 The Netherlands

Netherlands calls Arnhem its Bitcoin city with over 100 merchants.[49] The place has been touted as the place where those with Bitcoins can be used to get most things their owners need from petrol, accommodation and bicycles, to dental services. This means that within the Bitcoin City in Arnhem, Bitcoin is just like any fiat currency, a store of value and medium of exchange. As people engage in economic interaction using Bitcoins, a consciousness is generated within the general public that cryptocurrencies can function in a similar way to fiat currencies. Bitcoin for now does not fall under any identified regulation, but because of growing risks and in particular growing frauds linked to ICOs, the Dutch Finance Minister says the country is researching on the possibilities for a tighter rein on Bitcoin in the country.[50]

Numerous start-ups from Bitcoin ATMs to a Bitcoin embassy have sprung up in the country. The generally hospitable Bitcoin climate has fostered vibrant Bitcoin communities across the country that host regular conferences and other events.

The country's largest banks, ABN Ambro and ING, have also been increasingly looking at Bitcoin and blockchain to improve on their own technology and costs, and to transform to agile businesses. The idea is to self-disrupt their status-quo to avoid being swamped by newly emerging Fintechs.[51]

Globally known BitPay set up their European headquarters in Amsterdam in 2014. The business could support over 7,000 merchants in Europe. It has the

---

49 Scott, A. (2016), "How 'Bitcoin City' Arnhem Signed Up Its 100th Merchant, Burger King", *Bitcoin*, 20/02/2016, https://news.bitcoin.com/bitcoin-city-arnhem-signed-100th-merchant-burger-king/, accessed 02/02/2018; Juskalian, R. (2015), "A weekend in Bitcoin city: Arnhem, the Netherlands: Is it possible to live 48 hours on nothing but Bitcoin?", *MIT Technology Review*, 26/01/2015, www.technologyreview.com/s/534011/a-weekend-in-bitcoin-city-arnhem-the-netherlands/, accessed 02/02/2018.

50 de Witte, S. (2018), "Watchdog AFM and Minister of Finance plea for a ban on Bitcoin in the Netherlands", *Start-up Delta*, 04/02/2018, www.startupdelta.org/watchdog-afm-and-minister-of-finance-plea-for-a-ban, accessed 18/02/2018.

51 Petkovic, S. & Sinha, A. (2017), "Ideation to realization: How Dutch banks are harnessing blockchain", *Coin Desk*, 04/09/2017, www.coindesk.com/ideation-realization-dutch-bank-harness-blockchain, accessed 02/02/2018.

eventual mission of serving more than 30,000 merchants in Europe.[52] BitPay enables merchants to accept Bitcoin payments from customers, while receiving bank deposit settlements in their local currency, without price volatility or direct Bitcoin integration. The service provider claims that by accepting Bitcoin through BitPay, merchants gain access to a payment network and a new customer base as global as the internet but without the fees, country-by-country integrations costs and fraud risks of traditional online payment methods.

5.2.7 Finland

This is the home of Nokia,[53] once renown globally, but is now looking to exert its former glories through a strategic review action plan. Like its Scandinavian brethren, the country is also at the forefront of technological innovation.

The Finnish Central Board of Taxes has deemed Bitcoin as a category of financial services thereby exempting it and Bitcoin purchases from value added tax. It announced that Bitcoin does not meet the definition of a currency or even an electronic payment form in Finland, and as such the country's central bank has instead decided to categorise the software as a commodity.[54] Relative to its small population of 5.5 million, there are 21 Bitcoin ATMs in Finland, including six in its capital of Helsinki.[55]

Finland is also home to exchanges like FinCCX,[56] Bittiraha[57] and leading global P2P Bitcoin exchange LocalBitcoins. Interestingly, the most expensive Bitcoin sale for a luxury vehicle happened in 2016 at Helsinki involving a Tesla vehicle for over €140,000.[58]

5.2.8 Denmark

This is a very advanced economy in terms of living standards and technology. It is also at the forefront of the journey towards digital currency so as to eliminate

---

52 Gallippi, T. (2016), "BitPay opens European headquarters in Amsterdam", *BitPay*, 02/02/2014, https://bitpay.com/blog/bitpay-opens-european-headquarters-in-amsterdam/, accessed 02/02/2018.

53 Schroeder, P., Finkle, J. & McCool, G. (2018), "Nokia starts review of digital health business, cuts jobs in Finland" *Reuters*, 15/02/2018, https://uk.reuters.com/article/uk-nokia-strategy/nokia-starts-review-of-digital-health-business-cuts-jobs-in-finland-idUKKCN1FZ12C, accessed 18/02/2018.

54 Hajdarbegovic, N. (2014), "Finland classifies Bitcoin as VAT-exempt financial services", *Coin Desk*, 19/11/2014, https://www.coindesk.com/finland-classifies-bitcoin-vat-exempt-financial-service, accessed 02/02/2018.

55 Coin ATM Radar (2018), "Bitcoin ATMs in Finland", www.coinatmradar.com/country/72/Bitcoin-atm-finland, accessed 02/02/2018.

56 Coinalert (2015), "Finland Bitcoin exchange FinCCX now accepts Euros and stopped USD", *Coinalert*, 20/05/2015, http://coinalert.eu/2015024124-Finland+Bitcoin+Exchange+FinCCX+Now+Accepts+Euros+and+Stopped+USD.html, accessed 02/02/2018.

57 Barrier, E. (2013), "Finland gets its first Bitcoin ATM", *Coin Telegraph*, 19/12/2013, https://cointelegraph.com/news/finland_gets_its_first_bitcoin_atm, accessed 02/02/2018.

58 Redman, J. (2016), "€140,000 tesla bought for Bitcoin in Finland", *Bitcoin*, 23/01/2016, https://news.bitcoin.com/e14000-tesla-bought-bitcoin-finland/, accessed 02/02/2018.

the use of cash altogether.[59] Here, the digital currency aspiration is not a question of "if" but more of "when." For this country, the debate here is whether Bitcoin would function as a means of exchange or an alternative to the central bank monopoly or both.

The Danish Central Bank declared Bitcoin not to be a currency in March 2014, and as such would not regulate its use in the country.[60] Denmark is one of the first to declare Bitcoin trade to be tax free. Denmark is home to various Bitcoin start-ups and exchanges like the CCEDK, which has grown to be a prolific innovator in the crypto space with recent releases of Bitcoin 3.0 technology.[61] CCEDK's CEO Ronny Boesing stresses that the company's mission is to bring Bitcoin into mainstream acceptance in a responsible way.[62]

5.2.9 Sweden

Like Denmark, Sweden is also on a mission to be a cashless society.[63] With the recent introduction of a negative interest rate[64] in the country by the Swedish Riksbank, a surge in demand for Bitcoin is envisaged as citizens there seek safe refuge for storing their wealth. The Swedish Financial Supervisory Authority has legitimised Bitcoin a means of payment[65] and this could well spur the growth of the cryptocurrency industry in the country.

Sweden is home to various Bitcoin start-ups including the Safello Bitcoin exchange[66], and Stockholm-based KnCMiner[67], a well-known hardware developer that has been generating cutting-edge ASIC miners since 2013. The

---

59 Lyon, N. (2016), "Norway, Sweden and Denmark say 'No' to cash", *Coin Telegraph*, 25/01/2016, https://cointelegraph.com/news/cash-electronic-money-scandinavia, accessed 02/02/2018.

60 Bitcoin (2017), "Bitcoin in Denmark-Facts & figures", *Bitcoin*, 03/05/2017, https://news.bitcoin.com/bitcoin-denmark-facts-figures-2017/, accessed 02/02/2018.

61 Snook, C.J. (2017), "As Bitcoin passes $11,000 regulators are accelerating the adoption of blockchain 3.0 technology", *Inc.*, 29/11/2017, https://www.inc.com/chris-j-snook/as-bitcoin-passes-11000-regulators-are-accelerating-adoption-of-blockchain-30-technology.html, accessed 02/02/2018.

62 Thomas, C. (2015), "A conversation with Ronny Boesing, founder of CCEDK", Coin Report, 02/12/2015, https://coinreport.net/conversation-ronny-boesing-founder-ccedk/, accessed 02/02/2018.

63 Supra, note [61], Lyon (2016).

64 Megaw, N. (2017), "IMF backs Sweden's commitment to negative interest rates", *Financial Times*, 28/09/2017, www.ft.com/content/e91cf92b-4631-39bd-8d08-646422b9fd4c, accessed 02/02/2018.

65 John, U. (2017), "Countries That Love, Use and Understand Bitcoin", Politics & Society, 01/12/2017, https://thebitcoin.pub/t/countries-that-love-use-and-understand-bitcoin-moneybag/18083, accessed 02/02/2018.

66 Kallgren, J. (2014), "Swedish Exchange Safello Aims to be 'CoinBase for Europe'", *Coin Desk*, 03/04/2014, https://www.coindesk.com/safello-introduces-europe-wide-bitcoin-trading, accessed 02/02/2018.

67 Higgins, S. (2017), "The Swedish telecom that bought KnC is now mining Bitcoin", *Coin Desk*, 08/02/2017, www.coindesk.com/swedish-telecom-knc-mining-bitcoin, accessed 02/02/2018; Smolaks, M. (2015), "KnC miner to build fourth Bitcoin facility in Sweden", *Data Center Dynamics*, 14/12/2015, www.datacenterknowledge.com/archives/2015/12/14/bitcoin-mining-data-center-update, accessed 02/02/2018.

LocalBitcoins volume in Sweden also reflects continued surge in cryptocurrency demand.[68]

5.2.10 Estonia

This small Baltic former Soviet nation of 1.3 million people is globally known for its tech-friendly government and in particular for its digitisation processes that is said to save the state some 2% of its GDP annually in salaries and expenses.[69] This is unsurprising given that it has a significant tech-savvy population in the workforce. The government seems willing to implement blockchain initiatives[70] for health care and banking services. These are guided by competitive governance,[71] meaning unrestrictive borderless innovation so as not to miss out in the global innovation competition.

These measures together facilitate its citizens to become "e-Residents."[72] This gives Estonian citizens and businesses digital authentication. This is an ambitious project in technological statecraft that includes all members of the government and alters citizens' daily lives. Government services such as legislation, voting, education, justice, health care, banking, taxes, policing and so on have been digitally linked across one platform to wire up the nation.[73] The country is one of the first to apply a blockchain-based e-voting service which also enables people to become shareholders of NASDAQ's Tallinn Stock Exchange. It is also among the first economy in the world to go into robotics[74] in a big way.

Better known globally as the birthplace of Skype[75], Estonia now hosts many Bitcoin ATMs, and start-ups like Paxful, a global P2P buying and selling service for Bitcoin. Reinforced by one of the highest internet penetration rates in the world, the country is well-poised to be a location where cryptocurrencies' community can feel welcome.[76] Along with these, this EU

---

68 Haig, S. (2017), "Sweden sees record trading volume as MP Sundin joins Bitcoin exchange BTCX", *Bitcoin*, 09/06/2017, https://news.bitcoin.com/sweden-sees-record-trading-volume-as-mp-sundin-joins-bitcoin-exchange-btcx/, accessed 02/02/2018.

69 Heller, N. (2017), "Estonia, the digital republic", *The New Yorker*, 18 & 25/12/2017, https://www.newyorker.com/magazine/2017/12/18/estonia-the-digital-republic, accessed 24/01/2020.

70 Galeon, D. (2017), "Estonia's plans to build a digital nation using blockchain are taking shape" Futurism, 29/12/2017, www.futurism.com/estonias-plans-build-digital-nation-using-blockchain-taking-shape/, accessed 02/02/2018.

71 Supra, note [71], Heller (2017).

72 Hammersley, B. (2017), "Concerned about Brexit? Why not become an e-resident of Estonia", *Wired*, 27/03/2017, www.wired.co.uk/article/estonia-e-resident, accessed 02/02/2018.

73 OECD (2017*), OECD public governance reviews-Estonia: Towards a single government approach*, Paris, OECD.

74 Pettit, H. (2017), "Are robots more than just 'personal property'? Estonia works toward giving AI legal status", *Mail Online*, 10/10/2017, https://www.dailymail.co.uk/sciencetech/article-4965922/Estonia-working-giving-robots-AI-legal-status.html, accessed 02/02/2018.

75 Walt, V. (2017), "Is this tiny European nation a preview of our tech future?", Fortune, 27/04/2017, https://fortune.com/2017/04/27/estonia-digital-life-tech-startups/, accessed 02/02/2018.

76 Master, C. (2017), "Bitcoin in the Baltics: Estonia leads crypto-friendly region", *Coinspectator*, 12/10/2017, https://coinspectator.com/news/86099/bitcoin-in-the-baltic-estonia-leads-the-crypto-friendly-region, accessed 02/02/2018.

member state has the lowest business tax rate in the EU and fast becoming known for liberal regulations around technological research. In Estonia, it is legal to test Level 3 driverless cars where human drivers can take control, but Estonia is planning to advance ahead with Level 5 where cars drive on their own.[77]

Nevertheless, a major banking scandal in Estonia[78] recently may put some brakes on the state's cryptoasset initiatives. The scandal has tarnished the reputation of the tiny state that has marketed itself as a digital hub, offering electronic residency cards to foreigners including Pope Francis. Subsequent to the scandal, European regulators are more actively looking into the regulatory aspects of digital banking including those involving cryptoassets. This is unfortunate, as the incident involved a branch of a large bank from Denmark, an entity outside of Estonia.

5.3 Asian advanced economies

Other than those advanced Western economies discussed above, advanced economies in Asia, like Japan, South Korea, and Singapore are also known for relative high levels of cryptoasset and blockchain technology activities. These will now be explored.

5.3.1 Japan

Two countries not on the list of Bitcoin-friendly economies or places where people in general are actively using or investing in Bitcoin merit some attention as there is no official policy standing in the way of Bitcoin development. First, there is Japan which though now is no longer the commercial capital of Asia is fast evolving as the region's cryptocurrency's hub.[79]

As China and South Korea take steps to discourage Bitcoin-related activities, Japan has been provided with the opportunity to become the breeding ground for the growth of cryptocurrency including Bitcoin trading in Asia. Japan's amended Payment Services Act[80] is a framework that makes it legal to use cryptocurrencies for payment services. China dominated Bitcoin mining for some years until the present government policy compelled many Chinese Bitcoin

---

77 Estonia Ministry of Economic Affairs and Communications (2017), "Estonia allowing a number of self-driving cars on the streets starting today", *Estonia Ministry of Economic Affairs and Communications*, 02/03/2017, www.mkm.ee/en/news/estonia-allowing-number-self-driving-cars-streets-starting-today, accessed 02/02/2018.

78 O'Donnell, J. (2019), "Estonia warns of risks in wake of money laundering scandal", *Reuters*, 24/06/2019, www.reuters.com/article/us-moneylaundering-estonia/estonia-warns-of-risks-in-wake-of-money-laundering-scandal-idUSKCN1TP1VS, accessed 24/06/2019.

79 Pal, R. (2017), "Countries approving cryptocurrencies", *Hacker Noon*, 19/21/2017, www.hackernoon.com/countries-approving-cryptocurrencies-d1fb7fefa261, accessed 20/02/2018.

80 Global Legal Monitor (2016), "Japan: Bitcoin to Be Regulated", Global Legal Monitor, 04/11/2016, www.loc.gov/law/foreign-news/article/japan-bitcoin-to-be-regulated/, accessed 02/02/2018.

miners to move their operations elsewhere. Japan in contrast has the lion's share of cryptocurrency trading/exchange activities where the region is concern for some years now and still does. Japan's FSA, the country's financial regulator, has approved four new cryptocurrency exchanges[81] as well as cryptocurrencies that could be traded on these platforms.

Given the support from the Japanese government, cryptocurrency operations are thriving and it is envisaged that in the immediate years many ICOs could even opt to host their issuance campaigns in the country. Leveraging on the reticence and ambivalence of many economies with respect to cryptocurrencies, Japan is positioning itself to becoming a major global player in the market. Japan's case appears to suggest that for the infant industry to thrive it needs a supportive ecosystem and a well-balanced regulation. Japanese authorities acted swiftly when Coincheck, a large cryptocurrency exchange in Japan, lost some US$530 million through hacking.[82] Authorities quickly raided Coincheck's office and started investigating all cryptocurrency exchanges in the country for security gaps. They ordered Coincheck to raise its operating standards.[83]

Japan therefore continues to fascinate the world with its ability to maintain traditions while modernising. The Japanese habitually appear to prefer to transact in cash for their daily needs but yet, when it comes to digital currency, the country is able to embrace it at the same time. According to Yuko Kawai, the Fintech head of the Bank of Japan, cash is still king in Japan as cashless living is not making much progress.[84] The value of physical currency in circulation was equivalent to some 20% of Japan's economy in 2016, the highest among major nations according to the report by the Bank for International Settlements.[85] Credit and debit cards and e-money were used for less than 20% of transactions in Japan in 2015. Under present circumstances, it is not easy for Bitcoin or any cryptocurrency to become a major means of settlement. Still, Japan like most economies is keen to make available Fintech services like Bitcoin for tourists and other people visiting the country. This is why Japan hosts many facilities convenient for cryptocurrencies users.

More formally, on 31 May 2019, the Japanese House of Representatives officially approved a new bill to amend its national laws governing cryptoasset

---

[81] Althauser, J. (2017), "Japanese financial regulator legalizes four new cryptocurrency exchanges", *CoinTelegraph*, 04/12/2017, https://go2co.in/news/japanese-financial-regulator-legalizes-four-new-cryptocurrency-exchanges/amp, accessed 02/02/2018.

[82] Uranaka, T. & Wilson, T. (2018), "Japan raps Coincheck, orders broader checks after $530 million cryptocurrency theft", *Reuters*, 29/01/2018, www.reuters.com/article/us-japan-cryptocurrency/japan-raps-coincheck-orders-broader-checks-after-530-million-cryptocurrency-theft-idUSKBN1FI06S, accessed 18/02/2018.

[83] Shane, D. (2018), "$530 million cryptocurrency heist may be biggest ever", *CNN*, 29/01/2018, https://money.cnn.com/2018/01/29/technology/coincheck-cryptocurrency-exchange-hack-japan/index.html, accessed 20/02/2018.

[84] Fujioka, T. & Kidaka, M. (2018), "Japan's Central Bank Sees No Need To Mint a Digital Currency", *Bloomberg*, 29/01/2018, https://www.bloomberg.com/news/articles/2018-01-28/japanese-don-t-need-digital-currency-as-they-love-cash-boj-says, accessed 20/02/2018.

[85] Bank for International Settlements (BIS) (2017), *Statistics on payment, clearing and settlement systems in the CPMI countries*, Basel, BIS.

regulation.[86] This is expected to come into force in April 2020. These amendments are expected to tighten cryptocurrency regulation so as to promote user protection, more robustly regulate crypto derivatives trading, mitigate industry risks like exchange hacks and to establish a more transparent regulatory framework for the new asset class. The amendments further establish a legal name change for cryptocurrencies as cryptoassets that were previously identified as virtual currencies in the country. Additionally, the amendments provide for more robust legislation for crypto margin trading, limiting leverage to two to four times the initial deposit. Through its position as the G20 chair for 2019,[87] Japan seeks to promote its framework as the global benchmark for regulating the sector. It has accordingly prepared a handbook for the June 2019 G20 meeting in Osaka that each G20 country can use for regulations that includes measures to prevent the outflow of virtual currency.

5.3.2 South Korea

The rhetoric over the South Korean government's displeasure of Bitcoin's links to money laundering and other illicit activities plus the country's concerns over the extreme investment risk appear to suggest that cryptocurrency has no place in Korean society.[88] This is evidently not the case when the cryptocurrency space in the country is looked at more closely.

South Korea has a tech space that is conducive for cryptocurrency development. It has a tech-savvy population that is quick to adopt the latest gadgets. Its younger generation sees cryptocurrencies as a way to better life. When a minister recently mentioned that regulators were preparing legislation to halt cryptocurrency trading, global Bitcoin prices temporarily plummeted. A public petition to the country's President attracted overwhelming support such that the heavy internet traffic briefly crashed the President's website. This "online uprising" led to the President's office announcing that the minster's idea was a mere proposal under consideration.[89] The recent talk of Bitcoin banning and so on arises from the government's fear of the political disputes of being held accountable for doing nothing when Bitcoin investment risks and Bitcoin scams seem to be sprouting in many parts of the world, including its closely watched neighbour, China. Calm returned to the crypto community recently with the announcement of regulation over crypto exchanges.

---

86 Huillet, M. (2019), "Japan officially approves Bill to amend national legislation governing crypto regulation", *Coin Telegraph*, 31/05/2019, https://finance.yahoo.com/news/japan-officially-approves-bill-amend-093900306.html, accessed 02/06/2019.

87 Helms, K. (2019), "Japan to Provide G20 With Solution for Crypto Regulation", *Bitcoin.com*, 23/04/2019, https://news.bitcoin.com/japan-g20-cryptocurrency-regulation/, accessed 02/06/2019.

88 Kim, C. & Kim, D. (2018), "South Korea inspects six banks over virtual currency services to clients", *Reuters*, 08/01/2018, www.reuters.com/…southkorea-Bitcoin/south-korea-inspects-six-banks-over-vir, accessed 02/02/2018.

89 Kim, C. & Yang, HY. (2018), "Uproar over crackdown on cryptocurrencies divides South Korea", *Reuters*, 12/01/2018, https://www.reuters.com/article/us-southkorea-bitcoin/uproar-over-crackdown-on-cryptocurrencies-divides-south-korea-idUSKBN1F10YG, accessed 02/02/2018.

South Korea is home to global tech titans like Samsung and LG. It also has one of the highest smartphone penetration and mobile payment rates in the world. As the country seeks to find ways to regulate cryptocurrencies without restricting the tech innovations that underpin them, various related start-ups have already made the scene. This includes Korbit,[90] a secure and comprehensive Bitcoin exchange that also focuses on remittances and cross-border payments. Coinplug,[91] another South Korean Bitcoin exchange platform that enables people to buy Bitcoins at 7-Eleven stores across the country. A friendly climate is provided for the local Bitcoin community, while the country is also a regular host of Bitcoin conferences.

South Korea is the third largest market after Japan and the US, accounting for about 20% of all Bitcoin trading.[92] However, concerns over Bitcoin are growing at least within the government side in South Korea. These concerns are most profound across Asia, where cryptocurrency is also illegal in Kirgizstan, Bangladesh and Nepal. China, which at one time accounted 90% of all Bitcoin trading, banned ICOs in September 2017 and began to crackdown on exchanges and Bitcoin mining. The Bank of Japan in particular cited the dangers of speculative investing in Bitcoin. The Reserve Bank of India articulated concerns over tax evasion and other abuses and has been looking into ways to outlaw Bitcoin as a payment mechanism. Indonesia acted against ICOs. Vietnam might be banning cryptocurrency payments. Malaysia and Singapore warned speculative investors of the risks of losing their money in cryptocurrencies' investments and in ill-designed ICOs.[93]

There are, nevertheless, legitimate concerns about crypto and crypto-related frauds in Asia, where South Korea is located. In December 2017, South Korean police ended a US$200 million cryptocurrency Ponzi scheme named Mining-Max, and the Bitcoin exchange BitKRX that claimed to be a legitimate venture created by the Korean Exchange. The latter was subsequently revealed to be fraudulent.[94] Such incidents prompted the case for more Bitcoin regulation, but others claim that the country usually struggles with the acceptance of new technologies that could infringe on some of the major vested interests and it is suspected that Bitcoin would be no different.

---

90 Young, J. (2017), "South Korea's largest Bitcoin exchanges ready for strict regulations", *Coin Telegraph*, 14/12/2017, https://cointelegraph.com/news/south-korean-financial-authorities-plan-to-regulate-bitcoin-exchanges-soon, accessed 02/02/2018.

91 Helms, K. (2017), "South Korea's Coinplug launches new exchange and begins trading Bitcoin cash", *Bitcoin*, 03/09/2017, https://news.bitcoin.com/south-koreas-coinplug-launches-new-exchange-trading-bitcoin-cash/, accessed 02/02/2018.

92 Das, S. (2017), "$250 million ethereum mining scam? Korean prosecutors file charges", *CCN*, 22/12/2017, www.ccn.com/250-million-ethereum-mining-scam-korean-prosecutors-file-charges/, accessed 02/02/2018.

93 Volodzko, D.J. (2018), "Why is South Korea suddenly terrified of Bitcoin?", *South China Morning Post*, 01/01/2018, www.scmp.com/week-asia/business/article/2126189/why-south-korea-suddenly-terrified-bitcoin, accessed 02/02/2018.

94 Supra, note [95], Volodzko (2018).

What differentiates South Korea from the rest of the Bitcoin pack in Asia is the existential threat posed by North Korea.[95] For example, Youbit[96] became insolvent in in December 2017 after losing one fifth of its clients' holdings from hacking. North Korean hackers are believed to be behind the attacks on four South Korean Bitcoin exchanges in the summer of 2017. The North Korean regime is believed also to have begun Bitcoin mining in May 2017 and is likely to use what it mines or steals to circumvent present UN sanctions against the country. Despite such problems, shutting down Bitcoin exchanges or other equivalent actions to slow down Bitcoin adoption in South Korea is not viewed as a good economic decision by the country's younger tech-savvy population. Rather, what is needed for the country is for these various Bitcoin challenges to be managed by the right balance of regulation and support.[97]

5.3.3 Singapore

Alongside Hong Kong (SAR), Taiwan, South Korea and Japan, Singapore is an economic powerhouse despite being a small tiny island economy. Through good political governance, world class education, world class financial system, and generally innovative and pragmatic economic and industrial policies and strategies, Singapore was brought to the attention of the world in Michael Porter's "The Competitive Advantage of Nations" in the 1990.[98] The island city state generally fight shy of such publicity, but many multilateral institutions and many economies continue to speak positively of Singapore. With a small population of some 5.6 million, Singapore's GDP per capita averaged US$24,547 from 1960 to 2018, rising from a record low of US$3,503 to US$58,247.[99] It continues to progress drawing mostly on its generally stable political and legal system, as well as its forward-looking and pragmatic economic and industrial policies. In particular, it boasts one of the best and secure financial system in the world, where its three largest domestic banks have carved out a sound global reputation for innovation, safety and financial stability.

In the face of growing competition from regional and other economies Singapore is pushing forward its greater participation in the global Fintech industry, including the cryptoasset industry subset and inclusive of the underpinning blockchain technology. Singapore already functions like Hong Kong as a regional financial hub and now aspires to be the crypto hub of Asia.[100] In this, the

---

95 Supra, note [95], Volodzko (2018).
96 Castor, A. (2017), "After second hack this year, South Korean exchange Youbit closes down", *Bitcoin magazine*, 19/12/2017, https://bitcoinmagazine.com/articles/after-second-hack-year-south-korean-exchange-youbit-closes-down, accessed 02/02/2018.
97 Supra, note [95], Volodko (2018), citing the view of Business Administration Professor Yoo Bying-Joon of Seoul National University.
98 Porter, M. (1990), *The competitive advantage of nations*, New York, The Free Press.
99 Trading Economics (2018), "Singapore GDP per capita", *Trading Economics*, https://tradingeconomics.com/singapore/gdp-per-capita.
100 Yang, J. (2018), "Singapore is the crypto sandbox that Asia needs", *TechCrunch* 22/09/2018, https://techcrunch.com/2018/09/22/singapore-is-the-crypto-sandbox-that-asia-needs/, accesses 26/09/2019.

island state enjoys a relative advantage in that when compared to its brethren in the region or even much of the rest of the world, as the regulators in Singapore are relatively better-informed and more transparent about their thinking on blockchain and cryptoassets. Relative to the regulatory uncertainties in much of Asia and even some advanced economies like the US, the Monetary Authority of Singapore (MAS) has already released its guidance on digital token offering that shows the application of securities laws to digital token offerings and issuances.[101] This is not a new approach, as the young nation since its birth in 1957 has been pioneering economic and regulatory standards in Asia.

In respect of the crypto space, Singapore has successfully launched a "Token Day" marking the 10-year anniversary of cryptocurrency showing the potential for crypto addition across the island state.[102] Some 30 retailers in Singapore during a 19-day period then accepted cryptocurrency as payments. This led to increased discussion over the emergence of cryptocurrencies as an alternative for settlements in the payments space. Singapore was among first economies to commence regulating the employment of digital currencies in 2014 through the imposing of taxation on earnings.[103] However, prior to November 2018, the spotlight was on crypto earnings instead of the underlying technology.

MAS in late November 2018 finalised its regulatory framework to safeguard cryptocurrencies against counter-terrorism financing and to bolster cybersecurity. MAS, via the Payments Services Bill (PSB), will require crypto payment service providers to be licensed. Prior to this, crypto exchanges were an unregulated industry.[104] The PSB has therefore laid the foundations for absorbing blockchain into the securities framework and payment systems. This accelerated blockchain-based partnerships and investments that would eventually further the progress of the cryptocurrency asset class. In Singapore, ICOs set the trend, followed by blockchain, whereas in other economies blockchain adoption came after cryptocurrency.[105]

MAS has also issued a retail investor's guide to digital assets in May 2019, contrasting its earlier lukewarm position out of fear of their volatility. This might be the signal that Singapore is preparing for cryptocurrency's entry into mainstream payment solutions. MAS has also more recently announced the widening of its regulatory regime for payment providers to bring designated cryptocurrencies under its jurisdiction.[106] Its new legislative initiative is envisaged to come into force by the end of 2019, when cryptocurrency service providers will be licensed under the new regulatory framework. Thus, the implementation of crypto as a payment option is more a matter of when. These initiatives have

---

101 Supra, note [102], Yang (2018).
102 Deogawanka, S. (2019), "Is Singapore on the way to embracing cryptocurrency as part of the financial system?", *ASEAN Today*, 15/01/2019, www.aseantoday.com/2019/01/is-singapore-on-the-way-to-embracing-cryptocurrency-as-part-of-the-financial-system/, accessed 18/02/2019.
103 Supra, note [104], Deogawanka (2019).
104 Supra, note [104], Deogawanka (2019).
105 Supra, note [104], Deogawanka (2019).
106 Supra, note [104], Deogawanka (2019).

already attracted various high-profile exchanges to domicile in Singapore, while numerous innovative crypto-based ventures have also sprung up.

Branded as the Fintech capital of Asia, Singapore's landscape has become increasingly favourable for cryptocurrencies and a magnet for huge inflows of funds into crypto and blockchain technologies, especially with its closest competitor, Hong Kong, facing immense politico-socio problems. Hence, the envisaged influx of crypto exchanges into Singapore[107] is expected to make the island economy the crypto and blockchain capital in the region and perhaps the world. Singapore's reputation as a respectable global hub for financial innovation is recently boosted by remarks of Tim Berners-Lee, the creator of the world wide web, that the island state can lead the way when it comes to developing law with technology.[108]

5.3.4 China and India

The world's two biggest populations, China and India, both exceeding 1.3 billion people each are both in Asia. Over the last two decades both have had large and robust growing economies. Though lately China has had to contend with a trade war with the US and with some serious domestic economic challenges, while India too has some significant economic problems it has to deal with. On the geopolitical front, China has to grapple with political challenges in the South China Sea, whereas India has issues with Pakistan over Kashmir.

Both China and India are growing in GDP terms relatively better than most other economies, but unlike them their very large population bases mean that their GDP per capita put them as emerging middle-income economies. Both have relatively respectable banking systems supported by relatively well-managed monetary policies. However, large tracts of their populations are without access to banking services for various reasons. China has, to date, addressed this problem through the use of Fintechs in impressive fashion, while India is also doing the same though relatively less impressively.

Both economies are hostile towards cryptoassets even though they are highly supportive of other Fintech subsets. China being a Communist authoritarian regime is unable to condone the crypto industry as the decentralisation and democratisation principles behind the industry are not in sync with its political practices. India on the other hand is highly concerned over the use of cryptoassets for illicit activities, notably the corruption that is high on its national agenda.

---

107 Cox, D. (2019), "Binance CEO Hails Singapore's Crypto-friendly Jurisdiction on its 54th Birthday", *CryptoNewsZ*, www.cryptonewsz.com/binance-ceo-hails-singapores-crypto-friendly-jurisdiction-on-its-54th-birthday/35933/, accessed 08/09/2019.

108 Khan, A. (2019), "Singapore can be role model for how technology, law can develop, says Tim Berners-Lee", *Channel News Asia (CNA)*, 05/09/2019, www.channelnewsasia.com/news/singapore/singapore-can-be-role-model-for-how-technology-law-can-develop-11877308, accessed 06/09/2019.

The People's Bank of China, the country's central monetary and regulatory authority, has stated that it would block access to all domestic and foreign cryptocurrency exchanges and ICO websites.[109] It is the country's aim to clamp down on all cryptocurrency trading with a ban on foreign/offshore exchanges/platforms. It has over the past few years been issuing regular advisories and implementing initiative to deter the use of cryptocurrency in the country.

Together with the latest move, these could likely and completely eliminate cryptocurrency trading and mining activities in the world's most populous and soon to be world's second largest economy.[110] Still, this does not necessarily mean that crypto activities are altogether dead in the country, as it is an open secret that many of its population engaged with these through various means, including via virtual private networks through Hong Kong and via Canada and other places where Bitcoin mining is concentrated. For example, the country's Tron or TRX token pioneer Justine Sun paid US$4.7 million for lunch with Warren Buffett.[111]

Regulatory authorities have conceded that recent attempts to stamp out digital currencies by shutting down domestic exchanges have failed to completely eradicate crypto trading, as ICOs and virtual currency trading did not completely recede subsequent to the country's official ban on cryptocurrencies and the closure of domestic virtual currency exchanges, with many people turning to overseas platforms to continue transacting in virtual currencies. China's regulatory authorities are perturbed that oversea transactions and regulatory evasion have resumed, with many risks fuelled by illegal issuance, and even fraud and pyramid selling.[112]

The tough stance taken by the authorities, aside from its authoritarian agenda, was also prompted by the frenzy among retail investors that led to huge price volatility and various reports of major frauds that could potentially have led to social unrest. China though takes a less tough stand on the use of blockchain beyond cryptocurrencies. More recently, China's central bank said it is close to releasing its own digital currency as if in response to Facebook Libra[113] and IMF's positive stance on central bank digital currency. China is unlikely to be alone in this, as Sweden's Riksbank is another central bank looking into this idea.[114]

---

109 Seth, S. (2019), "Is Bitcoin Banned in China", *Investopedia*, 25/06/2019, www.investopedia.com/news/Bitcoin-banned-china/, accessed 28/06/2019.

110 Supra, note [111], Seth (2019).

111 Ablan, J. (2019), "Crypto pioneer Justin Sun pays $4.7 million for lunch with Warren Buffett", *Reuters*, 04/06/2019, www.reuters.com/article/buffett-lunch/crypto-pioneer-justin-sun-pays-4-57-million-for-lunch-with-warren-buffett-idUSL2N23A0V4, accessed 18/06/2019.

112 Xie, Y. (2018), "China to stamp out cryptocurrency trading completely with ban on foreign platforms", *South China Morning Post*, 05/02/2018, www.scmp.com/business/banking-finance/article/2132009/china-stamp-out-cryptocurrency-trading-completely-ban, accessed 19/09/2018.

113 Browne, R. (2019), "China's central ban says it's close to releasing its own digital currency", *CNBC*, 12/08/2019, https://www.cnbc.com/2019/08/12/china-central-bank-close-to-releasing-digital-currency-pboc-official.html, accessed 19/08/2019.

114 Browne, R. (2018), "People in Sweden barely use cash- and that's sounding alarming bells for the country's central bank", *CNBC*, 03/05/2018, www.cnbc.com/2018/05/03/sweden-cashless-future-sounds-alarm-bells-for-the-central-bank.html, accessed 19/08/2019.

India on the other hand opposes the greater use of cryptoassets for different reasons. The country has struggled over many decades to curb corruption in the country. It also struggled to provide banking services access to large tracts of its rural population. To deal with both problems, India first launched its AADHAR policy which is the world's largest biometric system. The AADHAR journey began in 2009. This is a unique 12-digit number provided to each and every registered Indian resident. The 12-digit number houses biometric details, address, dob and all major details of an individual. Some 1.19 billion or 93% of India's population have already been registered.[115]

AADHAR will enable digitalisation and centralisation of data. It will be linked to bank accounts. This is by no means a modest achievement, but it seems to violate privacy issues that are of vital importance elsewhere in other democracies.[116] India also launched its demonetisation move in 2016. It managed to withdraw the two largest banknotes that accounted for 86% of cash transactions from circulation in the country. The idea was to break the grip of corruption and black money (or money from gains unreported to the tax authorities).[117] Both are a rampant and persistent scourge in India. Since then, the tax base in India has gone up, while some cash transactions have gone down, and motivations to try out digital payments induced as seen by the spike in mobile wallets. These suggest some progress in terms of financial maturity and financial sophistication. Still, some 94% of other asset class were not impacted by the move.

More, importantly, however, cash that has a cost to society is gradually being replaced by a variety of alternatives like digital, electronic, credit cards that provides some kind of paper trail of payment transactions.[118] As digital currency has a relatively lower transparency and associated with various kinds of money laundering and related illicit activities, India having done much to curb these kinds of activities inevitably view these negatively. In April 2018, the Reserve Bank of India (RBI), the country's central bank issued a notice to Indian banks telling them to stop dealing with any cryptocurrency businesses, but peer-to-peer trading of virtual currencies remain legal in India.[119] The Internet and Mobile Association of India (IAMAI) though has challenged RBI's directive in the Supreme Court of India.[120]

---

115 Prabhu, J.R. (2018), "AADHAR-India's digital identity and world's largest biometric system", *Medium*, 20/10/2018, https://medium.com/@jairamrprabhu/aadhar-indias-digital-identity-and-world-s-largest-biometric-system-9ce81ebb4b8b, accessed 19/08/2019.

116 Supra, note [117], Prabhu (2018).

117 Chakravorti, B. (2018), "When India killed off cash overnight", *Harvard Business Review*, 27/08/2018, https://hbr.org/ideacast/2018/06/when-india-killed-off-cash-overnight.html, accessed 28/08/2019.

118 Supra, note [119], Chakravorti (2018).

119 Perez, Y.B. (2019), "Indian government ban on 'non-sovereign' cryptocurrency would see holders jailed for up to 10 years", *The Next Web*, 05/09/2019, https://thenextweb.com/hardfork/2019/07/22/indian-government-ban-cryptocurrency-jail-10-years/, accessed 08/09/2019.

120 The Economic Times (2019), "IAMAI says RBI has no authority to ban cryptocurrencies", *The Economic Times*, 14/08/2019, https://m.economictimes.com/news/economy/policy/iamai-says-rbi-has-no-authority-to-ban-cryptocurrencies/articleshow/70677612.cms, accessed 08/09/2019.

A government panel has more recently issued a recommendation to ban all cryptocurrencies created by non-sovereigns or entirely private enterprises. The panel recommended that anyone found dealing with digital currencies of any kind could face up to 10 years in jail as well as hefty fines.[121] The panel argued that there all these private cryptocurrencies have no underling intrinsic value and lack all the attributes of fiats, as they have no fixed nominal value and could neither act as any store of value nor as medium of exchange. The panel while largely critical of decentralised currencies is supportive of the possibility of a state-issued digital currency in the country. It also views decentralised ledger technology as an important and innovative technology that could play vital roles in ushering in the digital age and has even called for specific legislations to promote and regulate the use of blockchain in financial and related domains.

Thus, both China and India oppose the use of cryptoassets but from different perspectives. Both though are generally positive towards central bank digital currency, as well as blockchain technology.

5.4 Offshore financial centres (OFCs)

OFCs became highly controversial all over the world subsequent to the unofficial release of the Panama[122] and Paradise Papers[123]. Both cast bad connotations on various OFCs operating in various parts of the world because of the implications that various well-known politicians, royalties, businesses, and high-profile celebrities could be involved in stashing unaccounted for savings/funds in exotic OFCs. Various national and global financial regulators subsequent to the revelations began probing the named beneficiaries or holders all these accounts.

Various reports also alleged money laundering and related illicit activities through the deployments of various kinds of cryptoassets in these offshore accounts. Many of the named OFCs were condemned for helping to condone such activities. National regulators led by the US, and international global multilateral institutions like the OECD and the EU launched probes into the named OFCs. The regulators threatened to blacklist some of these OFCs, and the EU has in effect done so already. In response, and to avoid being blacklisted, some OFCs have come out with various initiative to deal with the sins of cryptoassets. Attention is drawn to two of these OFCs, namely the Cayman Islands and the Isle of Man.

The Cayman Islands seem to adopt a fairly flexible regulatory environment for cryptocurrencies and blockchain technology. Though there are no specific laws dealing with cryptocurrencies, there are laws that are in certain respects applicable. Among these are the 2015 (Revised) Securities Investment

---

121 Supra, note [121], Perez (2019).
122 Zaidi, S.H., Wang, X-Y, Ahamd, S., Tan, X.P. & Meng, Q. (2017), "Panama Papers and the dilemma of global financial transparency", *International Journal of Modern Research in Management (IJMRM)*, 1 (1), pp. 18–35.
123 Berglez, P. & Gearing, A. (2018), "The Panama and Paradise Papers: The rise of the global fourth estate", *International Journal of Communication*, 12(2018), pp. 4537–4592.

Business Law, the Anti-Money Laundering Laws and Regulations (2017), the Revised 2010 Money Services Law, and the Revised 2003 Electronic Transactions Law. The Cayman Islands legal community are of the opinion that more specific legislation would be eventually generated. For the time being, it seems that the regulators and lawmakers in the jurisdiction are keen to avoid rushing through any laws before the potentials and pitfalls of blockchain technology, cryptocurrencies and ICOs are properly understood.[124] The Cayman Islands are pitching blockchain entities from across the world to locate in the Cayman Enterprise City, which is a special economic zone targeting tech-related entities.

The Isle of Man is a UK Crown Dependency that has a robust online gambling industry and a burgeoning financial sector. Many businesses there accept Bitcoins as payments alongside its national fiat.[125] This jurisdiction was an early adopter of law to regulate cryptocurrencies within its borders. It amended its Proceeds of Crime Act 2015 to absorb virtual currency businesses within its regulated sector as a designated business.[126] The said legislative amendment meant that those seeking to offer ICOs within the confines of its AML laws will be required to use KYC practices.[127] Such businesses would be overseen by the Isle of Man FSA to ensure compliance.

The Isle of Man differentiates between digital, virtual, convertible, and non-convertible virtual currencies.[128] Also, the FSA has stated that it will not register an applicant where the ICO provides tokens that do not offer any benefit to the purchaser other than the token itself, because such features are generally considered by the FSA to pose an unacceptable high risk that the money raised from the ICO could be used for unanticipated and illegal purposes besides giving risk to consumers.[129] More recently, the Isle of Man has amended its online gambling laws to enable operators to accept virtual currencies.[130]

Finally, revelations from the Panama and Paradise Papers suggest that the tentacles of OFCs as tax havens are far bigger and more central to the world economy than previously thought and that the biggest havens are located not where previously thought. These tax havens collectively cost governments between US$500 billion and US$600 billion annually in lost corporate tax revenues

---

124 Humphries, C.A. & Smith, J. (2018), "Cayman Islands: Initial Coin Offerings (ICO) in the Cayman Islands", *Mondaq*, 19/02/2018, www.mondaq.com/caymanislands/x/667952/Commodities+Derivatives+Stock+Exchanges/Initial+Coin+Offerings+ICO+In+The+Cayman+Islands, accessed 25/03/2018.

125 Milmo, C. (2016), "Bitcoin: How the Isle of Man is leading a cryptocurrency revolution", *Independent*, 03/01/2016.

126 Isle of Man FSA (2018), "Questions & answers in respect of persons seeking to launch an Initial Coin Offering in or from The Island", *Isle of Man FSA*, 05/10/2018, www.iomfsa.im/media/2365/icoguidanceforapplicants.pdf, accessed 21/05/2018.

127 Supra, note [128], Isle of Man FSA (2018).

128 Isle of Man FSA (2018), "Virtual currency business: Sector specific AML/CFT Guidance Notes".

129 Supra, note [130], Isle of Man FSA (2018).

130 Online Gambling (Amendments) Regulations 2016, SD 2016/0341, reg. 11(1)-(2), www.gov.im/media/1354648/online-gambling-amendments-regulations-2016.pdf, accessed 28/08/2019.

through legal and not so legal means.[131] Of this, US$200 billion was accounted for by low income economies, a relatively larger loss as a percentage of GDP than that for the advanced economies. Trillions were also stashed away by individuals in these often-obscure tax havens.[132] Tax haven definitions vary, but they are commonly characterised by two key words, "escape" from financial regulations, disclosure, criminal liability, and more; and "elsewhere" implying offshore and across borders.[133] It has now been argued that tax losses aside, free capital flows across borders carry risks including the danger of financial instability in emerging market economies. Of surprise to many in the world, the Corporate Tax Haven Index[134] identified the British Virgin Islands, Bermuda and the Cayman Islands as the top three in the world. These are all British Overseas Territories, and they are followed closely by the Netherlands, Switzerland, Luxembourg, Jersey (British dependency), Bahamas and Hong Kong. In turn, the Financial Secrecy Index[135] ranks Switzerland, the US, and the Cayman Islands as the top three jurisdictions for private wealth. They are followed by Hong Kong, Singapore, Luxembourg, Germany, Taiwan, United Arab Emirates (Dubai), Guernsey, Lebanon, Panama, Japan, Netherlands, Thailand, the British Virgin Islands, Bahrain, Jersey, the Bahamas, Malta, Canada, Macao, UK, Cyprus, France, Ireland, China and Russia.

Subsequent to the 2008 global financial crisis, and the Panama and Paradise Papers revelation, the OECD suggest the use of tax havens for often illicit purposes and increased pressure for multilateral entities to do something. The OECD responded with the Common Reporting Standard (CRS)[136] and the Base Erosion and Profit Shifting (BEPS)[137] initiative targeted at multinationals. Resolving working problems associated with these two initiatives led to gradual global acceptance of four best practices. These are namely; the automatic exchange of financial information across borders, public registers of beneficial

---

131 Cobham, A. & Jansky, P. (2018), "Global distribution of revenue loss from corporate tax avoidance: Re-estimation and country results", *Journal of International Development*, 30 (2), pp. 206–232.

132 Henry, J. S. (2016), "Taxing tax havens", *Foreign Affairs*, April 12.

133 Shaxson, N. (2019), "The billions attracted by tax havens do harm to sending and receiving nations alike", *Finance & Development*, September 2019, 7–10.

134 Mansour, M.B. (2019), "New ranking reveals corporate tax havens behind breakdown of corporate tax system; toll of UK's tax war exposed", *Tax Justice Network*, 28/05/2019, www.taxjustice.net/2019/05/28/new-ranking-reveals-corporate-tax-havens-behind-breakdown-of-global-corporate-tax-system-toll-of-uks-tax-war-exposed/, accessed 08/08/2019.

135 VIDC, "Financial secrecy index 2018" www.attac.at/fileadmin/dateien/Presse/FSI_2018/Schattenfinanzindex_Ranking.pdf; Cobham, A., Jansky, P. & Meinzer, M. (2015), "The financial secrecy index: Shedding new light on the geography of secrecy", *Center for Global Development Working Paper 404* May 2015, 1–28.

136 OECD (2018), *Standard for automatic exchange of financial information in tax matters-Implementation Handbook-2nd edition*, Paris, OECD, www.oecd.org/tax/exchange-of-tax-information/implementation-handbook-standard-for-automatic-exchange-of-financial-information-in-tax-matters.pdf, accessed 08/08/2019.

137 OECD (2013), *Action plan on base erosion and profit shifting*, Paris, OECD, www.oecd.org/ctp/BEPSActionPlan.pdf, accessed 08/08/2019.

ownership of financial assets, country-by-country reporting and unitary tax with formula apportionment.

Subsequent to 2008, when the US found Swiss bankers assisting US citizens to evade tax, the US Department of Justice (DOJ) targeted Swiss bankers and banks that led to major concessions on banking secrecy.[138] This initiative suggests that any effective international responses needs to include strong sanctions against the private enablers, like solicitors and accountants particularly when they facilitate tax evasion.

More recent research by the BIS and the IMF[139] suggests the bane from too much finance, or financialisation of economies, where financial services, instead of serving businesses, become overly dominant. Research further suggests that most advanced economies including the US, the UK and other major tax havens have passed the point where financial services are beneficial.[140] Financialisation thus represents a shift from wealth-creating activities toward more predatory wealth extracting activities like monopolisation through the likes of major global tech firms; too big to fail banking, such as major global US and European banks; and the employment of tax havens, whether offshore or onshore. Indeed, financial flows looking for secrecy or fleeing corporate taxes are precisely the type that would exacerbate the financial bane associated with excessive financialisation. This is where and why many global regulators are worried about the anonymity and secrecy that cryptoassets can provide to users with assets to conceal.[141] Indeed, as tax havens come under closer international regulatory probing, cryptoassets offer, in many respects, a near perfect alternative to tax evaders. As such, it is reasonable to envisage that as the market volume of cryptoassets increased as they have over the past decade, so would the tax avoidance associated with it. There are now concerns that policymakers are embracing the faulty assumption that cryptocurrency-based economies are constrained by the virtual economy size. However, the only virtual aspect of cryptoassets, however, is their form. Their embeddedness within real economies, and as such their growth potential could be, ergo, infinite.[142] This kind of potential alongside recent developments in cryptoassets markets[143] are therefore likely to put the spotlight on the urgency of the latent challenges.

---

138 Lengwiler, Y. & Salijihaj, A. (2018), "The U.S. program for Swiss banks: What determined the penalties", *Swiss Journal of Economics and Statistics*, 154 (1), pp. 23–35.

139 Cecchetti, S.G. & Kharroubi, E. (2015), "Why does financial sector growth crowd out real economic growth?", *BIS Working Papers No. 490*, February 2015, 1–31, www.bis.org/publ/work490.pdf, accessed 08/08/2019; Arcand, J-L, Enrico, M. & Panizza, U. (2012), "Too much finance?", *IMF Working Paper WP/12/161*, June 2012, 1–50, www.imf.org/external/pubs/ft/wp/2012/wp12161.pdf, accessed 08/08/2019.

140 Smith, Y. (2015), "IMF paper finds that too much finance is bad for growth", *Naked Capitalism*, 20/05/2015, www.nakedcapitalism.com/2015/05/imf-paper-finds-that-too-much-finance-is-bad-for-growth.html. accessed 08/08/2019.

141 Marian, O. (2013), "Are cryptocurrencies super tax havens?", Michigan Law Review First Impressions, 112 (1/2), pp. 38–48.

142 Supra, note [143], Marian (2013).

143 FSB (2018), "Crypto-asset markets: Potential channels for future financial instability implications", *FSB*, 10/10/2018, www.fsb.org/wp-content/uploads/P101018.pdf, accessed 08/08/2019.

5.5 Comparative note

Alternative financing forms, like crowdfunding and so on developed quickly subsequent to the 2008 global financial crash. People and small businesses in particular were perturbed by the excesses of financialisation. Private money such as cryptocurrencies became the next order of business in the financial space. The US and the UK and major continental European economies took the lead in the mushrooming of cryptoassets hubs. It is still surprising to many people as all these alluded to Western advanced economies all boast having the best and most powerful banking systems in the world.

It would be unsurprising though for three major reasons. First, the widening financial gaps between the haves (meaning the powerful big corporations and other financial elites) and the have-nots (meaning the small businesses and the working class) identified the need to do something for the latter. Second, the latter argued for fairer and easier access to financial resources under more democratic means. Third, the squeeze and seize pressures from the said financial crisis induced many to question the infallibility of the monetary system controlled and manage by central authorities. These were said to be the main reasons behind the rise of the Fintech space, and its cryptoasset subset. The quest for private currency away from the sole controls of government together with the technological talents found in these advanced economies helped to usher in the world of cryptoassets.

Then the use of cryptoassets spread quickly to much of the rest of the world, given the inter-connectedness of global financial system, and importantly the cross-border features of blockchain and cryptoassets. While the advanced Western economies saw the use of cryptoassets as part of its more mature democratisation system, and to some degree inclusive participation by the disadvantaged, the reality is that cryptoassets are more fondly embraced by millennials, those with some secrets to shelter, those with nefarious intentions, and those simply with the greed for exponential profits. Taken together they have the effect of propagating the deployment of cryptoassets across other parts of the world, but especially in many of the more affluent as well as the very large economies in Asia, respectively Japan, South Korea, India and China.

As highlighted earlier the levels of cryptoasset activity are not necessarily linked to the kind of official attitude towards the use of cryptoassets. So, while China bans the use of cryptoassets, many of their nationals engaged with them via private virtual networks into other economies more tolerant towards the use of these assets. Thus, low official incidence of cryptoasset usage does not necessarily suggest low utilisation by the nationals in their respective jurisdictions, while high incidence could be attributed to utilisation by nationals beyond a designated jurisdiction. This thus marks out the cross-border nature of virtual currencies, and the reason why the FATF tightened its rules against the risk of money laundering via the use of these kinds of virtual currencies.

The way and the pace upon which cryptoasset hubs proliferate is therefore the outcome of the financial system and nature of particular economies concerned.

Globally, there are some concerns that the race to be premier Fintech or cryptoasset hubs could at some point later lead to enhanced risks to the stability of the global financial system. This is a reasonable view given that various businesses and national economies have exploited the more favourable attitudes towards the use of blockchain technology through shrewd messaging that they promote this rather than the use of cryptocurrencies, when in reality they could be relatively more involved with the propagation of the blockchain technology to promote the greater use of virtual currencies. The debate and controversies will likely continue unabated as long as there is the motivation to look for the lucrative alternative global virtual currency. This could further mean that such activities would gather momentum in tax havens even though lately some have provided laws and rules against the use of cryptoassets for illicit purposes. The next chapter will look at how national financial regulators grapple with the risks and dangers of cryptoassets.

CHAPTER 6

Cryptoasset policies of international bodies

6.1 Introduction

This chapter goes beyond the emerging national-based regulatory initiatives to multilateral regulatory approaches. It covers those focusing on economic advancement and anti-money laundering concerns such as the G20 economies and the OECD, those focusing on Fintechs and techfins like the BIS and the IMF, those focusing on capital markets like the IOSCO, and those focusing on anti-money laundering such as the FATF.

6.2 G20 economies

The G20 or Group of Twenty was formed in 1999. It is an international forum represented by the governments and central bank governors of Argentina, Australia, Brazil, Canada, China, France, Germany, India, Indonesia, Italy, Japan, Mexico, the Republic of Korea, the Russian Federation, Saudi Arabia, South Africa, Turkey, the UK, the US, and the EU as represented by the European Commission (EC) and the European Central Bank (ECB). The G20 engages in policies and actions to promote international financial stability; it hosts leaders summits; it has in recent years extended to cover forums involving finance ministers and foreign ministers. The G20 economies together account for about 85% of the world's gross domestic product (GDP), 75% of world trade, and some two thirds of the world's population.

Cryptoassets, and especially Bitcoin have attracted the attention of the G20. They have expressed concerns over the potential spillover of risks into the economies of the existing international financial system. G20 member nations, driven mainly by France and Germany made joint proposals to regulate cryptoassets at the March 2018 summit of the G20. These two advanced economies provided a joint Franco–German analysis of the relevant risks and included proposals for regulatory interventions. Arising from this development, arguments have been raised that there a could be a link between the evolution of cryptoasset regulations and the 80% decline in Bitcoin prices from its peak of US$20,000 in mid-December 2017 to the end of 2018.[1]

---

[1] Rivet, M., Le Guernigou, Y, Thomas, L. & Rose, M. (2018), "France, Germany to make joint bitcoin regulation proposal at G20 summit", *Reuters*, 19/01/2018, https://uk.reuters.com/article/us-global-bitcoin-france-germany/france-germany-to-make-joint-bitcoin-regulation-proposal-at-g20-summit-idUKKBN1F728X, accessed 02/02/2018.

The Franco–German initiative was supported by the US which did not then see cryptoassets as a serious threat to financial market stability and is more concerned over their deployment in money laundering and other illegal activities.[2] The US already has a functioning cryptoasset working group dedicated to the investigation of the market to ensure that these are not being misused. The US Treasury held Senate Hearings on 6 February and 4 March of 2018 where the respective roles of the SEC, the CTFC, cryptoasset exchanges and other market participants were examined. Recommendations from the Senate and Congressional Hearings are still being awaited. By comparison, the UK Select Committee Hearings have already made their recommendations pertaining to UK's regulatory stand on cryptoassets.[3]

The G20 communique issued on the 28–29 June 2019 at the Osaka Japan Summit stated that, whilst recognising that cryptoassets do not presently pose threats to global financial stability, they would nonetheless closely monitor their developments and remain vigilant to existing and emerging risks and have also requested standard setting bodies like the FSB to advise on further multilateral responses as when needed.[4] The G20 have also reaffirmed their commitments to applying the recently amended FATF Standards to cryptoassets and related providers for anti-money laundering and the countering of terrorism financing. The Virtual Asset Service Providers Summit (V20) held simultaneously in Osaka announced that a group of national trade associations representing virtual asset services providers signed a memorandum of understanding (MOU) for establishing an association that would assist in setting mechanisms to engage with government agencies and the FATF to ensure that their best interests are understood and appreciated at international forums. The G7 economies, comprising the world's most powerful economies (but excluding China and Russia for political reasons), have examined the risks posed by cryptoassets since 2015. The G7 would together with the G20 address the policy implications of cryptoassets, and in particular Facebook's Libra, as these could have an impact on the financial sovereignty of national economies.[5]

---

2 Skolimowski, P. (2018), "Coeure urges G-20 to discuss regulating Bitcoin at March Meeting", *Bloomberg,* 26/01/2018, https://www.bloomberg.com/news/articles/2018-01-26/coeure-urges-g-20-to-discuss-regulating-bitcoin-at-march-summit, accessed 02/02/2018.

3 HM Treasury/FCA/Bank of England (October 2018), *Cryptoassets taskforce: Final Report*, London, HM Treasury, https://assets.publishing.service.gov.uk/government/uploads/system/uploads/attachment_data/file/752070/cryptoassets_taskforce_final_report_final_web.pdf, accessed 02/11/2018.

4 G20 (2019), "Full text of the G20 Osaka leaders' declaration", *G20 Communique,* 29/06/2019, www.japantimes.co.jp/news/2019/06/29/national/full-text-g20-osaka-leaders-declaration/, accessed 02/07/2019.

5 Helms, K. (2019), "G7 Agrees on Crypto Action Plan Spurred by Facebook's Libra" *Bitcoin.com,* 24/08/2019, https://news.Bitcoin.com/g7-agrees-cryptocurrency-action-plan-facebooks-libra/, accessed 26/08/2019.

6.3 The Organisation for Economic Co-operation and Development (OECD)

The OECD's mission is to promote policies that would improve the economic and social wellbeing of people around the world. It provides a forum by which governments can collaborate to share experiences and seek solutions to common problems. It works with governments to understand the underlying forces that drive economic, social and environmental change. The OECD measures productivity and global flows of trade and investments. It also analyses and compares data to predict future trends.

The OECD sets international standards on a wide menu of matters, extending from agriculture and tax to the safety of chemicals. It also examines issues that directly impact on everyone's daily life, such as how much people pay in taxes and social security and how much leisure time they can have. The OECD's current agenda includes restoring confidence in markets and the institutions that makes them function; re-establishing healthy public finance as a basis for future sustainable economic growth; and the fostering of new sources of growth through innovation, environmentally friendly green growth strategies, and the development of emerging economies.[6] Hence cryptocurrency and blockchain technology attracted the OECD's attention.

A 2014 OECD paper suggested the following[7]:

(1) The 2008 GFC prompted extensive erosion of trust in all categories of financial services that move the needle toward greater positiveness toward deployment of alternative exponential technologies associated with Industry 4.0.

(2) Pertaining to application of the Blockchain technology in the design of virtual or cryptocurrency the OECD maintains that this would not undermine the ability and power of central banks in relation to monetary policy.

(3) The OECD, nevertheless, raised concerns over consumer welfare protection and bank secrecy priorities. In particular attention is drawn to Bitcoins' valuation and price volatility challenges including electronic thefts, contracts failures and so on that could lead to large losses for consumers with ultimate negative impact costs to taxpayers. The cryptocurrency's anonymity characteristic arguably facilitates money laundering and tax evasion that could snowball into significant public concerns.

(4) Blockchain as an innovative technology going beyond its use in Bitcoin as a virtual currency could transform the core trust element in financial transactions. The blockchain or decentralised ledger technology (DLT) enjoys the ability to shift to execute transactions without

---

6 OECD (2018), "About the OECD", *OECD*, www.oecd.org, accessed 02/02/2018.
7 Blundell-Wignall, A. (2014), "The Bitcoin question: Currency versus Trust-less transfer technology", *OECD Working Papers on Finance, Insurance and Private Pensions No. 37.*

needing to rely on a trusted intermediary thereby making the migration towards trust-less transactions. This could lead to transactions cost reductions particularly heralding healthy competition to incumbent financial services firms.

(5) Importantly, the general aims of national and global policy considerations should involve encouraging technologies that foster healthy competition in the payments system (especially in mobile payments), as well as ensuring the proper use of cryptocurrencies

Overall, various generic policy issues need to be explored.[8] Should there be a general ban on any form of the use of cryptocurrencies in the clearing system between banks and the central banks to ensure that the monetary system is not undermined. Should there be a recognition that a trust less transfer and ledger technology is separable from the notion of a cryptocurrency and that it is potentially very useful for future competition in the financial system. Finally, should there be some form of agreement for best practice registration that permits consumer protection, tax, and anti-money laundering authorities to verify the owner's identity.

The general aim of policy should be to encourage technologies that improve competition in the payments system, and to ensure that cryptocurrency use includes the revelation of the user's identity so as to avoid the darker aspects of Bitcoin use and to meet minimum requirements for consumer protection. The crypto community in general did not fully endorse the OECD's main suggestions.[9] Bans and prohibitions on cryptocurrencies in the interbank clearing system are likely to prove totally ineffective. A ban would enhance global awareness of cryptocurrencies, inspiring alternative and parallel clearing systems and as a consequence this could potentially end up harming the usefulness of existing clearing systems.

The technology supporting the Bitcoin network is distributed and decentralised for the reason that it had to be immune to plenary power shutdown and strong enough to sustain an attack from outside computational powers. The Bitcoin unit provides the incentive for maintaining the security and integrity of the blockchain, which makes it inseparable.

Cryptocurrency exchanges could be treated as financial institutions when exchange endpoints interface with national currencies and not merchants. Physical cash transactions do not typically demand owner identity verification, but when cryptocurrency exchanges are involved, the operating jurisdiction defines the required conditions around getting in and out of national fiat currency. These best practices registration could be conducted on an opt-in basis.

With respect to balance sheet and income statement reporting for networks, market competition could demand exchange solvency and reporting of financial

---

8 Supra, note [8], Blundell-Wignall (2014).
9 Matonis, J. (2014), "Why the OECD Needs to do its Homework on Bitcoin", *Coin Desk*, 01/07/2014, https://www.coindesk.com/oecd-needs-homework-bitcoin, accessed 02/02/2018.

status. In response to the suggestion that mandatory capital should be held by exchanges in the form of legal tender, the Global Policy Counsel at the Bitcoin Foundation suggested that consumer protection may differ in the future, as the assumption of government regulation providing sophisticated commercial oversight becomes challenged. Cryptographic proof of reserves could deliver a responsible public audit of exchange assets as Bitcoin's cryptography based public ledger allows an organisation to prove control of Bitcoin assets without disclosing private information about consumer or account holders. Multi-signature (Multi-sig) transactions are a second innovation that might assist with consumer protection. Multi-sig allows any combination of consumers and business entities to exercise control over a Bitcoin-based asset. Such innovations and others forthcoming would tend to render consumer oversight of Bitcoin businesses easier and government oversight a less important part of the mix. Consumers could be better placed to apply their own monitoring and in the best case to enjoy cryptographic proof that they are being properly served.

Requesting gold backing for Bitcoin suggests a gold-backed Bitcoin that would lead to centralisation in the manner of specific reserves and would irreparably damage the incentive structure for securing the distributed blockchain which precludes the process of new Bitcoin issuance. The sovereign power to collect taxes and declare legal tender imbues a currency with ultimate value, but it is still based on a state sanctioned illusion. The question of political control over the monetary system is the greatest litmus test for discovering those that seek control over others. In practice, it would be cloaked in terms such as full employment, price stability, temporary stimulus, quantitative easing and economic growth, but manipulation of money supply serves only to favour the issuers of that particular monetary unit. Here, Bitcoin is the primary value unit and requires backing from neither state sanction nor gold. It is freedom in the monetary standard untouched by the politicising process. At some level, money requires a leap of faith. The belief in gold requires this too as the non-monetary value assigned to gold is arguably no more than 5% of its market price. This, however is also what makes Bitcoin the ultimate social money because for its value it merely requires others to accept it, not the law.[10] Money is already the most viral thing on earth and the network effects exponentially reinforces that.

It is further argued that governments could no longer maintain a monopoly position over money because an alternative exists and that alternative does not rely on legal tender status for its legitimacy. It relies on global acceptance of the mathematics behind the protocol for its market-based legitimacy. Such arguments have their roots in the Hayek notion of private currency.[11]

---

10 Matonis, J. (2013), "The fiat emperor has no clothes", Forbes, 18/04/2013, https://www.forbes.com/sites/jonmatonis/2013/04/18/the-fiat-emperor-has-no-clothes/#40af66f26e9e, accessed 02/02/2018.

11 Ferrara, P. (2013), "Rethinking money: The rise of Hayek's private competing currencies", *Forbes,* 01/03/2013, Rethinking money: The rise of Hayek's private competing currencies, accessed 02/02/2018.

A subsequent OECD cryptocurrency analysis undertaken in the context of disruptive innovation in financial services teased out various issues.[12] The OECD treats virtual currencies as stores of value that can be traded between users. While Bitcoin is the best known, there are more than a hundred of others. The ECB estimated the combined value of cryptocurrencies around the world at about €3.3 billion as of February 2015. Trades of currency occur over currency exchanges on the internet often with the exchanges of cryptocurrency used as payment for real world goods. Cryptocurrencies have limited issuance, and they use digital techniques for securing the transactions. On the one hand, this provides confirmation of the ownership of each coin keeping track of the entire history of ownership in a blockchain to ensure that one unit of virtual currency cannot be sold multiple times by one owner. On the other hand, they do not necessarily identify the trader's full identity publicly.

Unlike nationally issued fiat currencies, cryptocurrencies are not backed by the full faith and credit of national governments, nor are they governed by a regulation that restricts activities such as legally preventing the sudden introduction of more currency. Provided the expectations of purchasers that others would accept the virtual currency as a store of value, they might be willing to purchase it. Cryptocurrencies differ from these in the ease with which they could be transformed back into legal tender currency, mainly through exchanges and trading platforms performing this conversion. They are alternatives to cash and other fiat currencies, and are smaller and more secure than paper currencies. Cryptocurrency owners have the potential to achieve profits both from the float and from issuing initial currency to themselves.

As a consequence of the apparent anonymity of transactions, some users of cryptocurrencies misused them for improper and illicit activities such as money laundering and a transfer of value for illegal goods. In response, some governments have taken measures that effectively rules out their use as currencies. These suggest a clear and implied possibility of governments' declaring cryptocurrencies to be illegal. The focus on them as mechanisms for fraudulent transactions could be attributed to a perceived high frequency of improper motives behind their use. This in turn is the consequence of the apparent anonymity built into the system. Arguably, cash functions as a more anonymous way of transferring value than virtual currencies. The ownership string of a cryptocurrency is public, but not the actual owner's name and address. Where that name and address are in some stages identified by law enforcers, the latter have a powerful instrument to track entire chains of value in manners that cash would never enable. Hence, the arguments against cryptocurrency anonymity could be much weaker than comparable arguments against cash.

Governments worry that virtual currencies could substantially supplant the fiat currency they issue as it could put at risks central banks' abilities to conduct

---

12 Emmis, S. (2015), "Hearing on disruptive innovation in the financial sector-Note by the (OECD) Secretariat", *OECD Secretariat Working Paper Party No. 20 on Competition and Regulation Paper*, 26/10/2015.

monetary policy, while the seigniorage from issuing currency could be reduced. However, it has been argued that cryptocurrencies cannot undermine the ability of central banks to conduct monetary policy, as long as taxes are paid in legal tender, that in turn necessitates that banks be able to clear with the government's bank or central banks. Supplanting does not appear to be a significant risk for now, as the level of public trust in virtual currencies is limited. Nonetheless, to the extent that a regulator is empowered to regulate virtual currencies in the future, it is debatable whether central banks should be given the role to regulate cryptocurrencies, or whether other bodies with less direct financial interest in the regulator outcome could be more apt. Central banks and finance ministries might have interests to maintain seigniorage, but they also have a counterbalancing experience with the oversight of money.

Undoubtedly the risks from using cryptocurrencies are real. Exchanges could be breached as has already happened in a few cases recently. For cryptocurrencies to succeed and grow, rules would be needed providing clear guidelines on registration and KYC rules. Their repudiation as a currency as has happened in China, Germany, France, South Korea and Thailand would clearly make operating cryptocurrencies as a virtual currency a challenge. Even where they are permitted, only an estimated 3 out of 10,000 merchants accept them.

Where competition between cryptocurrencies is encouraged, a clear identification of them as currencies would be needed. The UK, for instance for now exempts them from VAT, thus treating them in and of themselves as currencies and not as goods and services. Simultaneously, the UK requires cryptocurrencies to provide mechanisms to prevent money laundering. Australia treats them as currencies, while the US IRS issued guidance treating them as property, and the US CFTC treats them as a commodity.

To the extent possible regulations should ensure that a level playing field exists between banks and P2P lenders, but that the relevant regulations should be proportionate to the perceived risks and needs. Only time will confirm whether such a regulatory approach will yield clear benefits or allow pent up risks to develop. Regulation alone might not generate the desired result if not complemented by sufficient information, awareness and education for investors, issuers, users, or borrowers.

The OECD 2019 Global Blockchain Policy Forum (OECD GBPF) highlighted the helpfulness for policymakers and pertinent stakeholders to fully understand what blockchain is and where its applications can value-add, and hence the importance of the education aspects of blockchain. The OECD GBPF reinforces the need for a collaborative multi-stakeholder policy approach that both protects the rights of citizens and the flow of innovations. By extension, such collaborations need to embrace the borderless nature of blockchain itself, implying that governments and innovators globally should share data pertaining to the outcomes of pilots, regulatory sandboxes and other excursions into DLT applications. Instead of exacerbating inequality and environmental issues, the OECD GBPF advocated the tapping of blockchain technology for the advancement of sustainable development and human rights. These are particularly evident where financial inclusion and supply chain due diligence are concerned. The OECD GBPF also drew attention to the Facebook-initiated Libra project that has sovereignty impact implications for national economies, as well the potential rise and impact of central bank digital currencies.[13]

It needs to be determined that the opinions articulated above, including the earlier 2014 paper, may or may not reflect the views and official opinions of the OECD or the governments of its member countries. That said, it merits noting that the EU's European System of Accounts, 2010 contains a section on "Borderline Cases" which requires the inclusion and reporting of the so-called illegal trade in its respective members' GDP. This working paper contented that even when a cryptocurrency is not declared illegal, discussing the possibility that it could be made so might undermine its value.[14]

The OECD's Special Advisor, Joseph Weinberg commented positively on the quality of due diligence undertaken by cryptocurrency exchanges with regards to KYC/AML compliance. He added that most crypto exchanges processing fiat to crypto transactions are very compliant, and in some cases even more so than banks. He cited a recent review that stated that Australian banks make potential customers go through a less stringent due diligence process than crypto exchanges, while for crypto exchanges the challenge lies in how little formal guidelines there are from regulators, and as a consequence, most of the industry has been engaging in self-compliance in the absence of clear procedures and as a consequence overregulate themselves to err on the safe side.[15] This phenomenon of strict self-regulation coupled with a rather vague regulatory feedback is not unique to Australia as it is being observed around the world, notably in China and South Korea. Not many businesses wish to operate in a legal grey area, thus, the lack of clear regulations has led many cryptocurrency exchanges to over regulate themselves to err on the side of caution and to show their commitment to legitimate operations.[16]

The OECD have now started looking at the accounting implications starting at the meeting of the Working Party on Financial Statistics on 3 November 2018.[17] They have also called for a global ICO regulation, stressing the high risks and asking for a standardised set of regulations to avoid money laundering.[18] This

---

13 OECD (2019), "The policy environment for blockchain innovation and adoption: 2019 OECD global blockchain policy forum summary report", *OECD Blockchain Policy Series*, http://www.oecd.org/finance/2019-OECD-Global-Blockchain-Policy-Forum-Summary-Report.pdf, accessed 07/02/2020.

14 Cohen, B. (2015), "OECD: Simply 'Discussing' Bitcoin illegality is mutually damaging", *Coin Telegraph*, 03/01/2015, www.cointelegraph.com/news/oecd-discussing-possible-Bitcoin-illegality-is-mutually-damaging, accessed 02/02/2018.

15 Munro, A. (2018), "OECD advisor: Cryptocurrency exchanges are over-regulating themselves", *Finder*, 28/02/2018, https://www.finder.com.au/oecd-advisor-cryptocurrency-exchanges-are-over-regulating-themselves, accessed 03/03/2018.

16 Supra, note [15], Munro (2018).

17 OECD (2018), "Joint meeting of the Working Party on Financial Statistics and the Working Party on National Accounts", OECD COM/SDD/DAF/A(2018)2, 03/11/2018, http://www.oecd.org/officialdocuments/publicdisplaydocumentpdf/?cote=COM/SDD/DAF/A(2018)2&docLanguage=En, accessed 07/02/2020.

18 Supra, note [1], Helms (2020).

appears to be happening anyway as evidenced by the 5th EU Anti-laundering Directive.

The OECD's further insights on ICOs suggest that ICOs by their nature are not the optimal solution for every venture.[19] For instance, blockchain enabled products/services have a higher opportunity of benefiting from an ICO offering. Specifically, ICOs are especially beneficial for products/services underpinned by networks.

The OECD is of the view that clarity in the regulatory and supervisory framework could be a good stepping stone to the safer deployment of token issuance for financing purposes. These could include standardised disclosure requirements and expanded investor protection for retail investors, together with enhanced awareness of risks by retail investors that could fortify their informed participation in such financing.[20] In the context of unique risks posed by cryptoassets, as highlighted by the FBI,[21] AML/CTF requirements on ICO issuance are of particular importance.

The OECD is presently working on cryptoassets and applications of DLT in financial services and its Committee on Financial Markets released its report on January 2019 looking at the potential benefits from the deployment of regulated ICOs for small business capital formation, the issuing and trading of tokens, tokenomics, limitations in ICO designs, together with the risks to which investors subscribing to ICO offerings and SMEs issuing tokens are exposed to. Insights were also generated on the potential of ICOs as mainstream financing instruments for SMEs, regardless of project types or business models used by the business.[22] This latest OECD report on cryptoassets called for clarity and proportionality in the regulatory and supervisory framework applied to ICOs. The 2nd annual OECD Blockchain Policy Forum held on 12–13 September 2019 included high level discussion of these as well as the outcome of the OECD study on tokenisation of assets and the impact a possible proliferation of such a mechanism would have on financial markets, as well as around the benefits and risks of stablecoins.[23]

The above suggests that a delicate balance is needed when developing regulatory and supervisory requirements that would not deprive the ICO mechanism of its speed and cost benefits in relation to smaller size offerings. In this respect, a proportional application of regulatory requirements such as those deployed in small public equity offerings merits positive consideration.[24] Co-operation at the global level is needed given the global nature of ICO issuing and cross-border

---

19 Nassr, I.K. (2019), "Initial coin offerings (ICOs) for SME financing", *OECD* January 2019, http://www.oecd.org/finance/ICOs-for-SME-Financing.pdf, accessed 05/03/2019.

20 Supra, note [20], Nassr (2019).

21 Supra, note [20], Nassr (2019).

22 OECD (2019), *Initial coin offerings (ICOs) for SME financing*, Paris, OECD.

23 FSB (2019), "Crypto-assets: Work underway, regulatory approaches and potential gaps", *FSB*, 31/05/2019, www.fsb.org/wp-content/uploads/P310519.pdf, accessed 02/07/2019.

24 Ruggeieri, N. (2019), "Making a list and checking it twice: The FBI highlights key features in SCO scams", Eth News, 20/02/2019, www.ethnews.com/making-a-list-and-checking-it-twice-the-fbi-highoights-key, accessed 05/03/2019.

trading. This would prevent regulatory arbitrage and enable ICOs to achieve their potentials for the funding of blockchain based SMEs, while protecting investors appropriately.

6.4 The International Monetary Fund (IMF)

The IMF recognises both the benefits and perils of cryptocurrencies. It said that regulatory responses to cryptocurrencies are still at an early phase because they are difficult to regulate, as they cut across the responsibilities of different agencies at the national level and function on a global scale.[25] Many cryptoassets are seen to be opaque and operate outside of the conventional financial system making it difficult to monitor their operations. The IMF raised several issues.[26] Cryptocurrencies are digital representations of value, issued by private developers and denominated in their own unit of account. They can be obtained, stored, accessed and transacted electronically. The expression "cryptocurrencies" covers a broad range of currencies from simple IOUs of issuers like mobile coupons, to airline miles, cryptocurrencies and those backed by gold.[27] Cryptocurrencies are used interchangeably with cryptoassets and vice-versa in most mainstream policy and research papers. The ECB, the European Banking Authority (EBA), the ESMA, the World Bank, the IMF, and the FATF classify cryptocurrencies as a subset of virtual or digital currencies or a form of unregulated digital money, while the BIS qualifies crytpocurrencies as digital currencies or digital currency schemes characterised by asset with value, use of distributed ledgers and not operated by any particular institution. There is thus no generally accepted definition of cryptocurrencies in the regulatory domain other than those provided by the World Bank and the FATF, while most policymakers avoid defining the term and treat cryptocurrencies as a kind of virtual or digital currencies. The FATF and the World Bank, as alluded to earlier though, provided more precise definitions. Some mainstream legal scholars have defined a cryptocurrency as

> a digital representation of value that (i) is intended to constitute a peer-to-peer ('P2P') alternative to a government-issued legal tender, (ii) is used as a general-purpose medium of exchange (independent of any central bank), (iii) is secured by a mechanisms known as cryptography and (iv) can be converted into legal tender and vice-versa.

Still, for reasons mentioned earlier they too prefer to use cryptocurrencies, digital currencies and cryptoassets interchangeably. Much therefore depends on the ultimate direction of the research and the disciplinary perspective used. As digital representation of value, cryptocurrencies fall within the wider category

---

25 He, D., et al (2016), "Virtual currencies and beyond: Initial considerations", *IMF Staff Discussion Note SDN/16/3rd January 2016*.

26 Supra, note [25], He (2016).

27 Houben, R. & Snyers, A. (2018), "Cryptocurrencies and blockchain: Legal context and implications for financial crime, money laundering and tax evasion", *European Parliament Study PE 619.024 July 2018*, www.europarl.europa.eu/cmsdata/150761/TAX3%20Study%20on%20cryptocurrencies%20and%20blockchain.pdf, accessed 01/02/2019.

of digital currencies, but differentiated from the others such as e-money, a digital payment system for and denominated in fiat currency as cryptocurrencies are not denominated in fiat currency and have their own unit of account.

Non-convertible cryptoassets (or closed system ones) function exclusively within self-contained environments where the exchange of cryptocurrencies with fiat currencies or other virtual ones, or their use in payment for goods and services outside of the virtual domain, is significantly restricted.[28] Convertible cryptocurrencies, or open schemes, facilitate their exchange with fiat currency or other cryptos and for the payment of goods and services in the real economy. Interaction levels between convertible cryptocurrencies and the real economy are more extensive than in closed schemes. They can function via centralised, decentralised or hybrid models. Cryptocurrency schemes include their issuance and redeemability, mechanisms to implement and enforce internal rules on the use and circulation of the currency, and the payments and settlement process. Each of these could be managed by a trusted agency and private party or in decentralised among participants. Hybrid schemes exist where some functions are undertaken by a central authority with others distributed among market participants.

The IMF argues that decentralised schemes employ techniques from cryptography for their operations and thus it is appropriate to call them "cryptocurrencies". In decentralised schemes there is no central party such as a central bank administering the system or issuing them. These systems could allow for the issuance of a limited or unlimited number of currency units. Most cryptocurrencies are pseudo anonymous, where the transactions are publicly recorded but users are known only by their virtual currency addresses, which cannot be traced back to the users' real-world identities. They are as such more transparent than cash but more anonymous than other kinds of online payment. Cryptocurrencies challenge the standard concept of fiat currencies. The latter are backed by the creditworthiness of the central bank and the government. The value of privately issued virtual currencies have historically been supported by the private issuers' credibility and commodity reserves. The value of cryptocurrencies, however, does not enjoy backing from any sources and derive their value solely from the expectation that others would also value and use them.

When deliberating the role of cryptoassets as money, questions arise as to whether they satisfy the legal definition of money and fulfil all the economic roles of money such as store of value, medium of exchange and unit of account? Questions are also raised as to how they compare to other privately issued monies that existed historically and whether they qualify as substitutes for fiat currencies when used more widely. Both historic and economic theory seem to support a monetary regime with public provisions of currency over a competitive private system. The historical track record of containing inflation is mixed

---

28 FATF (2014), "Virtual currencies: Key definitions and potential AML/CTF risks", *FATF Report July 2014*, www.fatf-gafi.org/media/fatf/documents/reports/Virtual-currency-key-definitions-and-potential-aml-cft-risks.pdf, accessed 02/03/2019.

across both public and private systems, but public systems appear to function when there is a systemic liquidity shortage at the time of a financial crisis and the need arises for a lender of last resort.

Cryptocurrencies fall short of the legal concept of currency or money.[29] The legal notion of currency is associated with the power of the sovereign to establish a legal framework providing for central issuance of banknotes and coins. This being the case, the value and credibility of a sovereign currency are intrinsically linked with the ability of the state to support that currency. It is also based on the power of the state to regulate the monetary system. The concept of money as a legal matter is wider than the concept of currency, as it includes not only banknotes and coins but also instruments such as demand deposits. While money could be created by private parties like banks as well as central banks, it must be generally denominated in a currency issued by a sovereign authority and must be intended to serve as a generally accepted medium of exchange within that state.

For now, the IMF and others argue that cryptoassets do not completely fulfil the three economic roles associated with money. Their high price volatility limits their ability to serve as a reliable store of value and their use as a medium of exchange is restricted by the small size and limited acceptance network of those who will accept them. There appears to be little evidence that cryptocurrencies are used as independent units of account. Rather than measuring the value of goods and services directly they instead represent the value in fiat currency based on the cryptocurrencies' exchange rate. Retailers quote prices in fiat currency, with the price in cryptocurrency based on the exchange rate at a particular point in time.

Along with other developments in financial technology, distributed ledger modalities could herald important structural shifts in the financial industry.[30] In play already are growing numbers of blockchain-based financial services provided by non-bank start-ups, while some e-commerce firms are actively exploring the technology. Simultaneously, large global banks are also participating. Large technological changes have historically led to significant adjustments in market shares, with new firms often gaining at the expense of established ones. At the minimum, the internal structure and staffing of conventional financial intermediaries is likely to focus on technology skills.

Cryptoassets are a relatively novel phenomenon and have surfaced in the absence of effective regulation.[31] This led to their potential benefits, like low

---

29 Carney, M. (2018), "The future of money", *Mark Carney, Governor Bank of England, Speech Delivered at the inaugural Scottish Economics Conference Edinburgh University*, 02/03/2018, www.bankofengland.co.uk/-/media/boe/files/speech/2018/the-future-of-money-speech-by-mark-carney, accessed 08/03/2018.

30 Garg, G., Vudayagiri, Pillai, S.G. & Sharma, R. (2017), "Top 10 Trends in Payments 2018: What You Need to Know", Capgemini Paper October 2017, www.capgemini.com/wp-content/uploads/2017/12/payments-trends_2018.pdf, accessed 12/12/2018.

31 IOSCO (2019), "Issues, Risks and Regulatory Considerations Relating to Crypto-Asset Trading Platforms", *IOSCO Consultation Report CR02/2019*, May 2019, www.iosco.org/library/pubdocs/pdf/IOSCOPD627.pdf, accessed 03/06/2019.

transaction fees and processing time, but has left unaddressed the risks they pose. These risks are most serious with respect to cryptocurrencies but are not limited to them. Risks fall into a continuum, with immediate and pressing concerns about financial integrity pertaining to money laundering and terrorism financing (AML/CTF), consumer protection, tax evasion and the regulation of capital movements. Concerns about financial stability or the implications of monetary policy are less immediate, but would require further analysis and monitoring. The growing interest in blockchain technology, separate from a cryptoassets scheme, a priori raises fewer policy concerns as the technology could be used in a closed system administered by regulated financial institutions.

The effective regulation of cryptocurrencies poses unique challenges in various ways.[32] They posed a definitional challenge to regulators as they combined properties of currencies, commodities and payment systems. Their classification as one or the other could have implications for their legal and regulatory treatments, such as determining which national agencies should regulate them. The disparity of treatment within and among jurisdictions may hamper coordination and could lead to inconsistencies. Cryptocurrency schemes are difficult to monitor too due to their opaque nature by design. The transactional reach of virtual currencies complicate regulation as national regulators may find it difficult to enforce laws and regulation in a virtual online environment. Questions swirl around who to regulate because of their decentralised nature: individual users or other participants within the system.

Different regulatory responses have surfaced to address the risks posed by this new technology, while paying attention to the policy priorities of each jurisdiction.[33] Policymakers often seek to find the balance between solving the risks and vulnerabilities posed by virtual currencies, while not stifling innovation. Some economies ban their use; others address particular risks pertaining to financial integrity, tax evasion and consumer protection, in particular by amending or clarifying the interpretations of existing laws and regulations; and yet others by issuing consumer warnings. Various jurisdictions have yet to take a formal position. When deliberating on who to regulate, national authorities have mostly targeted cryptocurrency market participants and financial institutions interacting with them. The interface between cryptocurrencies and the wider economy would often go through a virtual currency exchange or other relevant service provider. Also, because of the limited size of the cryptoasset network, virtual currency users would at some point need to "cash out", meaning converting their cryptocurrency into fiat currency. Taking cognisance of these practices

---

32 Poskriakov, F., Chiriaeva, M. Cavin, C. Christophe, & Staehelin, L. (2019), "Cryptocurrency compliances and risks: A European KYC/AML perspective", In J. Dewey (ed.), *Blockchain & Cryptocurrency regulation* (162–173), London: Global Legal Insights.
33 Blandin, A. Cloots, A.S., Hussain, H., Rauchs, M., Saleuddin, Allen, J.G., Zhang, B. & Cloud, K. (2019), *Global cryptoasset regulatory landscape study,* Cambridge, Cambridge Centre for Alternative Finance (CCAF).

and features of the current market, regulators have targeted the gatekeepers by regulating cryptoasset market participants providing an interface with the wider economy, such as cryptocurrency exchanges, and by restricting the ability of regulated entities like banks to interact with cryptocurrencies and their market participants.

The effectiveness of emerging regulatory initiatives would depend on how the cryptoasset market evolves. Their more widespread use might warrant a more comprehensive regulatory response. For instance, where the system operates more on a P2P basis, regulating cryptoasset gatekeepers might be inadequate. In this respect, a few regulators have gone further and are regulating a wider range of virtual cryptoasset market participants, such as wallet service providers operating entirely within the system. The evolving nature of the technology requires regulation to be flexible to adapt to the evolving circumstances.

Regulatory responses are also being adopted at the global level. These tend to focus on achieving consensus on the potential benefits and risks of virtual currencies and seeking areas for future cooperation. Some have provided forums to discuss cryptocurrency matters and have contributed to the issuance of reports, guidance, and manuals in their areas of expertise. The FATF has contributed the AML/CTF standard setter,[34] while the UN Office on Drugs and Crime (UNODC) focuses on the prevention and law enforcement response to the money laundering risks they pose.[35] The Committee on Payments and Market Infrastructures (CPMI)[36] reviews the implications of cryptocurrencies as a means of exchange and distributed ledger technologies for central banks. Others contributing to the dialogues and debate include the OECD, the EBA, and the Commonwealth Secretariat.

More initiatives could be taken at the international level to facilitate the development of suitable policy responses. With experience, developing international standards and best practices could be considered to provide guidance on the most suitable regulatory responses in different fields to promote harmonisation across jurisdictions. These standards could also offer frameworks for cooperation and coordination across economies over questions like the sharing of information and the investigation and prosecution of cross border offences.[37] Specific risks are attached to cryptocurrencies pertaining to financial integrity, consumer protection, tax evasion and treatment, enforcement of exchange controls, financial stability, and monetary policy.

---

34 FATF (2019), "FATF report to the G20 Leaders' Summit", *FATF Report June 2019*, www.fatf-gafi.org/media/fatf/content/images/G20-June-2019.pdf, accessed 03/07/2019.

35 UNODC (2017), "The global programme against money laundering, proceeds of crime and the financing of terrorism 2011–2017", *UNODC Report GLOU40 Global*, 02/10/2017, www.unodc.org/documents/evaluation/indepth-evaluations/2017/GLOU40_GPML_Mid-Term_In-Depth_Evaluation_Final_Report_October_2017.pdf, accessed 08/10/2018.

36 CPMI (2018), "Cryptocurrencies: Looking beyond the hype", *BIS Annual Economic Report 2018 91–114*, 17/06/2018, www.bis.org/publ/arpdf/ar2018e5.htm, accessed 08/10/2018.

37 Helms, K. (2019), "G20 Leaders Issue Declaration on Cryptoassets-A Look at Their Commitments*", G20 Osaka Summit 2019 Communique*, Bitcoin, 01/07/2019, https://news.bitcoin.com/g20-leaders-declaration-crypto-assets-commitments/, accessed 11/08/2019.

Financial integrity, i.e., the anonymity and cross-border reach of cryptocurrencies raises genuine concerns from a financial integrity perspective.[38] These vulnerabilities are not merely theoretical but are exploited in practice. Cryptocurrencies are frequently the currency of choice in cyber-related criminal activity. Bitcoin was used in Silk Road, a dark web market place for illegal goods that was eventually shut down by US law enforcement authorities in 2013. Applying AML/CTF controls to cryptocurrency transactions can help to prevent such abuses. The FATF, the international standard-setter for AML/CTF, has provided some guidance on the application of the AML/CTF standards to virtual currencies. Their stance reflects the current knowledge of the money laundering/terrorism funding (ML/TF) risks, but might eventually need to be expanded to other virtual currency network participants, such as wallet service providers and payment processors, operating entirely within the system. Such entities could be treated as covered entities required to implement the preventive AML/CTF measures.

Enforcement would remain challenging despite dealing with these changes. In decentralised virtual currency schemes, law enforcement may not have a counterparty like a central administrator to deal with for investigative purposes and to implement freezing and seizing orders on funds held in virtual currencies. It is thus difficult for regulators to take enforcement actions like the freezing of assets and the seizure and confiscation of illicit assets in such circumstances. FTAF guidance has helped to clarify the suitable responses to the ML/TF risks generated by cryptocurrencies, but different jurisdictions have taken different approaches to regulating them. The US, Germany, UK and Canada have acted to clarify the applicability of existing AML/CTF obligations to certain cryptocurrency businesses, usually finding that their administrators and exchanges fall within covered entities for the purpose of AML/CTF preventive measures. Other jurisdictions usually do not, while China bars interaction between virtual currency businesses and the formal banking sector.

The regulatory uncertainty and lack of transparency in virtual currencies generate significant consumer vulnerabilities. Such risks could be in relation to cryptocurrency systems, virtual currency intermediaries and service providers, scams, or those risks related to the irreversibility of transactions. Policy responses focus on increasing awareness[39] of users and investors about these risks and clarifying the scope of relevant legislation.

Cryptocurrencies have high potential to be used as a vehicle for tax evasion,[40] more so where participants need not disclose their identity, transactions are P2P

---

38 Katarzyna, C. (2019), "Cryptocurrencies: Opportunities, Risks and Challenges For Anti-Corruption Compliance Systems", *OECD Paper Presented at OECD Conference Centre Paris 20–21st March 2019*, www.oecd.org/corruption/integrity-forum/academic-papers/Ciupa-Katarzyna-cryptocurrencies.pdf, accessed 23/06/2019.

39 Securities Exchange Commission (SEC) (2018), "Investor Alert: Ponzi schemes Using Virtual Currencies", *SEC Pu. No. 153 (7/13)*, www.sec.gov/investor/alerts/ia_virtualcurrencies.pdf, accessed 10/03/2019.

40 Hardy, P.D., Went, A.M. & Pierson, S. (2019), "IRS highlights international efforts to tackle cryptocurrency abuse, money laundering and tax evasion", Ballard Spahr LLP 09/12/19, https://www.moneylaunderingnews.com/2019/12/irs-ci-highlights-international-efforts-to-tackle-cryptocurrency-abuse-money-laundering-and-tax-evasion/, accessed 07/02/20.

and can occur across borders. To the extent that they are performing as store of value or a medium of exchange they raise potential tax implications. A key issue concerns whether they should be treated as a form of non-monetary property or as a form of currency. The former could pertain to capital gains or losses and the latter foreign exchange gains or losses. Additional issues include the tax treatment of newly created cryptocurrencies obtained through mining as against acquiring already ones that already exist, and the VAT and sales tax treatment of transactions they involve.[41] Greater international consistency should be promoted in these and related areas. Record keeping requirements for virtual currencies could be substantial and may reduce their appeal in everyday use.

Cryptocurrencies may also be used to circumvent exchange and capital requirements as reported in the media, notably in China, Venezuela, Cyprus, Greece, North Korea and possibly other jurisdictions too.[42] Cryptocurrencies have arguably as yet to enter the mainstream financial system to pose significant systemic financial risks as per present positions of various national and global regulators. They have, however, cautioned that as cryptocurrencies achieve larger scale use and greater interconnectedness with other parts of the financial system especially via the mobile payments landscape, various financial risks could arise.[43] However, their potentially larger scale use and greater interconnectedness with other parts of the financial sector could in due course give rise to significant systemic financial risks.[44] Cryptocurrency users face payment system risks such as operational risk, credit risk, liquidity risks and legal risk.[45] Cryptocurrencies and blockchains are also vulnerable to cryptographic risks. Under a tail risks scenario, some schemes or blockchains could become too big, too interconnected to fail, and could also be difficult to resolve.

Regulatory responses to financial stability concerns are still at the nascent stage. These raise a number of challenges for policymakers and regulators at both the national and international levels. Questions at the national level revolve around whether some cryptocurrency intermediaries could replace the functions of a bank, requiring them to be regulated in a similar fashion, or whether cryptocurrencies in virtual currency wallets should be considered as deposits protected by deposit insurance schemes.[46] At the international level, given the cross border nature of virtual currency networks, questions arise as to who should oversee the

---

41 HM Revenue & Customs (HMRC) (2018), "Tax on cryptoassets", *HMRC*, 19/12/2018, www.gov.uk/government/publications/tax-on-cryptoassets, accessed 21/02/2019.

42 Redman, J. (2019), "Venezuelan Government Accused of Using Bitcoin to Bypass US Sanctions", *Bitcoin.com*, 25/07/2019, https://news.Bitcoin.com/venezuelan-government-accused-of-using-Bitcoin-to-bypass-us-sanctions/, accessed 27/07/2019.

43 Supra, note [37], Helms (2019).

44 Inman, P. & Monaghan, A. (2019), "Facebook's Libra cryptocurrency 'poses risks to global banking'", *The Guardian*, 23/06/2019, www.theguardian.com/technology/2019/jun/23/facebook-libra-cryptocurrency-poses-risks-to-global-banking, accessed 25/06/2019.

45 Thackeray, J. (2018), "Breaking Down the Inherent Risks of Cryptocurrencies", *academia.edu*, www.academia.edu/37252500/Breaking_down_the_inherent_risks_of_Cryptocurrency, accessed 18/01/2019.

46 Library of Congress (2019), "Regulation of cryptocurrency around the world", www.loc.gov/law/help/cryptocurrency/world-survey.php, accessed 18/09/2019.

cryptocurrency and asset markets and others using the blockchain technology in payment, settlement and other activities.[47] While internationally agreed regulatory principles and cooperation among national authorities would be beneficial, the appropriate framework for such cooperation remains to be defined.

Cryptocurrencies do not currently have significant implications for monetary policy, but some concerns could arise where they become more widely used. By design, cryptocurrencies such as Bitcoin have limited inflationary risks unlike other private currencies that came before it. That said, current systems lack other critical features that stable monetary regimes would typically be expected to provide. These include guarding against the risk of structural deflation, flexibility to respond to temporary shocks to money demand, and the capacity to function as a lender of last resort (LOLR).[48] Moreover, the near fixed supply of cryptocurrencies could lead to deflation in the same manner as gold standard. In general, in an economy with a high share of cryptocurrencies the ability of monetary policy to manage the business cycle could be diminished. Importantly, they would be unable to replace the LOLR function of central banks. Experience and economic theory suggest that a public agency is needed to solve the externalities and coordination failures that arise in such cases. In the absence of regulatory measures and other interventions, cryptocurrencies would be more readily adopted in countries with less credible monetary policies.

Cryptocurrencies are still rapidly evolving and the future landscape remains difficult to predict. They offer benefits and perils. The development of effective regulatory responses are still at an early phase. National authorities' potential regulatory responses should be commensurate to the risks without stifling innovation; adapt to the challenges emerging in the cryptocurrency landscape; have design approaches that take into account the novel business models inherent in such schemes; and address not only market conduct issues such as AML/CTF and fraud but also the financial adequacy of relevant intermediaries. They should also provide due consideration to the degree of integration between the conventional financial system and the cryptocurrency market. In respect of the last issue, regulators should consider whether to prohibit any interaction between the financial institutions and the virtual currency markets, allow a certain level of integration, or allow full integration.[49]

Much more could be done at the international level to help develop an effective international framework for the regulation of cryptocurrencies. International bodies have a role to play in strengthening the international community's understanding

---

47 Silva, D. (2017), "Cryptocurrencies: International regulation and uniformization of practices", *United Nations Commission on International Trade Law (UNCITRAL) Paper*, www.uncitral.org/pdf/english/congress/Papers_for_Congress/29-DOLES_SILVA-Cryptocurrencies_and_International_Regulation.pdf, accessed 19/01/2019.

48 Claeys, G., Demertzis, M. & Efstathiou, K. (2018), "Cryptocurrencies and monetary policy: Monetary Dialogue", *European Parliament Paper PE 619.018 June 2018,* www.europarl.europa.eu/cmsdata/150000/BRUEGEL_FINAL%20publication.pdf, accessed 28/07/2018.

49 Peprah, W.K., Afriyie, A.O., Abandoh-Sam, J.A. & Afriyie, E.O. (2018), "Dollarization 2.0 a cryptocurrency: Impact on traditional banks and fiat currency*", International Journal of Academic Research in Business and Social Sciences,* 8(6), 341–349.

them more broadly. More work could be done to study their evolution and their potential impact on the conventional banking and payments system to understand the risks they pose and to identify the most effective regulatory responses taking into view national circumstances. As experience is gained, consideration could be given to developing standards and best practices to provide guidance on the most suitable regulatory responses to different virtual currency schemes.

An important agenda is the need to involve ongoing monitoring and analysis of the way in which cryptocurrencies are evolving and the policy challenges that they pose.[50] Further insights are needed as to how virtual currency schemes and their underlying distributed ledger technologies change existing business models in financial services and the kind of risks that could evolve from such developments. This could arise through the use of digital learning technologies in the mainstream financial system giving rise to new specific risks necessitating regulatory responses and what potential implications cryptocurrency schemes could have for IMF and other multilateral financial institutions in the future.

While cryptocurrencies have potential benefits such as payment efficiency, the IMF argues that their losses go beyond losses for individual investors. They can pose considerable risk as potential vehicles for money laundering, terrorist financing, tax evasion and fraud. The IMF has evolved since its inception into a lender of last resort (LOLR) for indebted nations and its views on currencies still carry special weight. In mid-January 2018, IMF spokesman Gerry Rice called for global coordination on cryptocurrencies as it warned of the risks from surging prices.[51] Though no elaboration on the kind of coordination needed was given, the push for action came as cryptocurrencies such as Bitcoin became an investment phenomenon and household name since their spectacular rise in value at the commencement of 2017 and less spectacular advance in the first half of 2019. This not only attracted participation from mainstream investors but also a lot from off mainstream ordinary unsophisticated investors. Rice added that when asset prices go up quickly, as they did in 2017, risks can accumulate, especially if market participants are borrowing money to buy and hence the importance of people being aware of the risks and taking the necessary risk management measures.

On 29 September 2017, IMF Managing Director Christine Lagarde advocated a balanced approach on cryptocurrency regulation.[52] She advised that they may give traditional government-issued currencies a run for their money and hence it was not wise to ignore them. She stressed further that cryptocurrencies could bring potential disruption and cautioned that central banks and financial services need to pay close attention to the technology. Lagarde also suggested that cryptocurrencies posed little or no challenge to the existing order of fiat

---

50 Supra, note [37], Helms (2019).
51 Hagan, S. & Mayeda, A. (2018), "IMF calls for global talks on cryptocurrencies" *Bloomberg*, 18/01/2018, www.bloomberg.com/news/articles/2018-01-18/imf-calls-for-global-talks-on-digital-fx-as-Bitcoin-whipsaws, accessed 23/02/2018.
52 Sundararajan, S. (2018), "IMF Calls for International Cooperation on Crypto", *Coin Desk*, 22/01/2018, www.coindesk.com/imf-calls-for-international-cooperation-on-cryptocurrencies, accessed 02/02/2018.

currencies and central banks. This is a consequence of them being too volatile, too risky, too energy intensive and the underlying technology not yet scalable, while many are too opaque for regulators and some have even been hacked. Such challenges could also be addressed over time as a repetition of the dotcom decade.[53] Also, cryptocurrencies have the potential to become more stable, provide better payment services, or more effective new models of financial intermediation. In the face of such possible potential, the best response by central bankers is to continue running an effective monetary policy, whilst being open to fresh ideas and new demands as economies evolve.

More lately, Lagarde has called for a different approach in dealing with the challenges posed by cryptocurrencies. She opines that IMF needs to "fight fire with fire", meaning she seeks to use blockchain analysis to track cryptocurrency users' behaviour.[54] In so doing, the IMF could address any concerns regarding money laundering and tax evasion. This initiative when implemented could bring more legitimacy to cryptocurrencies as a whole. She argued that those having shared interests in maintaining safe online transactions need to be able to communicate seamlessly. Technologies enabling instant global transactions could be applied to create registries of standards and verify customer information along with digital signatures. More effective employment of data by governments could also help free up resources for priority needs and reduce tax evasion, including evasion related to cross-border transactions. She appears to be leaning towards using AI, biometrics and cryptography. Bitcoin supporters immediately seized this as evidence of IMF supporting Bitcoin as a form of money.

To make things smoother, dialogues are needed between experienced regulators and those regulators just beginning to tackle Fintech, between policymakers, investors and financial services firms, and between economies. As the focus of regulation widens from national entities to borderless activities, from local bank branch to quantum encrypted global transactions, reaching across borders would be critical and crucial. The IMF with a global membership of 189 economies is the ideal platform for these dialogues.[55] It fits within the IMF's remit as being a focal point for economic and financial stability and the safety of the world's global payments and financial infrastructure.

Their most recent position was Christine Lagarde's suggestion on 13 November 2018 that governments should create their own cryptocurrencies to avoid the existing ones becoming a vehicle for fraudsters and money launderers.[56] This

---

53 Lagarde, C. (2017), "Central Banking and Fintech–A Brave New World", *Speech by Christine Lagarde, the IMF Managing Director at Bank of England Conference London*, 29/09/2017, www.imf.org/en/News/Articles/2017/09/28/sp092917-central-banking-and-fintech-a-brave-new-world, accesses 02/02/2018.

54 Lagarde, C. (2018), "Addressing the dark side of the crypto world" *IMF Blog*, 13/03/2018, https://blogs.imf.org/2018/03/13/addressing-the-dark-side-of-the-crypto-world/, 21/03/2018.

55 Supra, note [53], Lagarde (2017).

56 Inman, P. (2018), "IMF says governments could set up their own cryptocurrencies", *The Guardian*, 14/11/2018, www::/guardian.com/business/2018/nov/14/imf-says-governments-shouod-set-up-their-own-cryptocurrencies, accessed 02/03/2019.

does not seem entirely rational, whilst national currencies created as cryptocurrencies would have a more stable value than the existing cryptocurrencies this would not necessarily deter fraudsters and launderers. Neither would necessarily wish to hold the currency for a long period to satisfy their illegal activities and in the case of those wishing to engage in market manipulation of cryptocurrencies or of investments priced in relation to them, the more stable national cryptocurrencies would be less attractive. Likewise, those holding cryptocurrency as an investment asset are likely to see the existing ones as offering more opportunity.

The IMF has also shown recent concerns that the rapid increase in the holding and use of cryptocurrencies could create vulnerabilities in the world's financial system.[57] Specifically, in the IMF's Global Stability Report of September 2018:

> Despites its potential benefits, our knowledge of its potential risks and how they might play out is still developing. Increased cybersecurity risks pose challenges for financial institutions, financial infrastructure and supervisors. These developments should act as a reminder that the financial system is permanently evolving, and regulators and supervisors must remain vigilant to this evolution and be ready to act if needed.[58]

Put in a wider context, in the words of CEO Brad Garlinghouse, the IMF has also vowed to continue "devoting attention to blockchain and cryptocurrency."[59] "... but we think it is difficult to talk about blockchain without considering it in the light of the other new technologies that are forming part of the fintech debate." It is clear from other comments that these are taken to include artificial intelligence and cryptoassets.[60] The IMF's recent fintech policy paper, suggests further work on international dimensions of data policy frameworks, and evaluations of new international standards by standard setting bodies including cryptoassets, mobile money service, and P2P lending.[61] Thus, further developments in the IMF's views are awaited.

6.5 The Financial Stability Board (FSB)

The FSB is an international body that monitors and makes recommendations concerning the global financial system. Significant economies, international financial institutions, standard setting and other bodies and the G20 are

---

57 Hasan, S. (2018), "How the IMF and central banks are taking on cryptocurrencies", *Trtworld*, 16/11/2018, www.trtworld.com/magazine/how-the-imf-and-central-banks-are-taking-on-cryptocurrencies, accessed 02/03/2019.

58 International Monetary Fund (2018), "Global Financial Stability Report April 2018: A Bumpy Road Ahead", April 2018, www.imf.org/en/Publications/GFSR/Issues/2018/09/25/Global-Financial-Stability-Report, accessed 02/03/2019.

59 Speaking at Singapore Fintech 2018.

60 Suberg, W. (2018), "IMF Vows to Continue 'Devoting Attention' to Blockchain, Cryptocurrency in Fintech Drive", *Coin Telegraph*, 13/11/2018, www.cointelegraph.com/new/imf-vows-to-continue-devoting–attention-to-blockchain-cryptocurrency, accessed 02/03/2019.

61 Adrian, T. & Mancini-Griffoli, T. (2019), "The rise of digital money", *IMF Fintech Note/2019/01*, 01/07/2019, www.imf.org/~/media/Files/Publications/FTN063/2019/English/FTNEA2019001.ashx, accessed 22/08/2019; IMF (2019), "Fintech: The experience so far", *IMF*, 17/05/2019, www.imf.org/~/media/Files/Publications/PP/2019/PPEA2019024.ashx, accessed 02/07/2019.

represented in the FSB. The FSB promotes international financial stability. It does this by coordinating national financial authorities and international standard setting bodies as they collaborate toward developing strong regulatory, supervisory and other financial sector policies. The FSB fosters a level playing field by encouraging coherent implementation of these policies across sectors and jurisdictions.[62]

Specifically, the FSB assesses vulnerabilities impacting on the global financial systems. It promotes coordination and information exchange among authorities responsible for financial stability; monitors and advises on market developments and their implications for regulatory policy; monitors and advises best practice in meeting regulatory standards; undertakes joint strategic reviews of the international standards setting bodies; and coordinates their respective policy development work to address gaps in timely coordinated fashion. The FSB also sets out guidelines for establishing and supporting supervisory challenges; supports contingency planning for cross-border crisis management; collaborates with the IMF to conduct early warning exercises; and promotes member jurisdictions' implementation of agreed commitments, standards, and policy recommendations.[63]

With the emergence of Fintech activities, including cryptocurrencies, there would be both opportunities and risks to financial stability that policymakers, regulators, supervisors and overseers could consider.[64] This is important as many Fintech innovations have not been tested through a full financial circle and decisions taken in this early stage could set important precedents. The FSB in this context advises policymakers to continue assessing the adequacy of their regulatory frameworks as the adoption of Fintech increases with the aim of reaping the benefits while mitigating risks. The FSB has been mandated during the German G20 Presidency to build on the monitoring to date and identify supervisory and regulatory issues of Fintech meriting authorities' attention from a financial stability viewpoint.[65]

Currently, any evaluation of the financial stability implications of Fintech is challenging given the limited availability of official and privately disclosed data.[66] It would be important to account for materiality and risks when evaluating new areas such as Fintech. In this regard, it is necessary to understand how business models of start-ups, incumbents and the market structure are evolving.

The FSB has developed a framework that defines the scope of Fintech activities and their potential gains and risks to financial stability.[67] This is to draw out

---

62 FSB (2018), "About the FSB", FSB, www.fsb.org/about/, accessed 03/03/2018.

63 Supra, note [62], FSB (2018).

64 FSB (2017), "Financial stability implications from Fintech: Supervisory and regulatory issues that merit authorities' attention", *FSB Working Paper*, 27/07/2017, www.fsb.org/wp-content/uploads/R270617.pdf, accessed 02/02/2018.

65 Van Hulst, N. (2017), "Germany's successful G20 presidency", *OECD Insights*, 13/07/2017, http://oecdinsights.org/2017/07/13/germanys-successful-g20-presidency/, accessed 18/08/2017.

66 Supra, note [64], FSB (2017).

67 Supra, note [64], FSB (2017).

the supervisory and regulatory issues of Fintech. The analysis focuses on conceivable benefits and risks as most Fintech activities for now are small relative to the overall financial system. Still, international bodies and national authorities should consider accounting for Fintech in their existing risk assessments and regulatory frameworks. There are clear benefits for greater international cooperation given the commonalities and global dimensions of many Fintech activities. This is important when mitigating risks of fragmentation or divergence in regulatory frameworks that could impede the development and diffusion of beneficial innovations in financial services and limit the effectiveness of initiatives to promote financial stability.[68]

Back in 2017, drawing from the prevailing view, the FSB concluded that there were no compelling financial stability risks from emerging Fintech innovations. Ten issues, however merit the authorities' attention, of which three are seen as priorities for international cooperation.[69] They believed that resolving these is important to the promotion of financial stability, fostering responsible innovation and preventing any derailment of authorities' initiatives to achieve a more inclusive financial system. Though many of these issues are not new, they could be accentuated given the speed of growth of Fintech, new kinds of interconnectedness and increased dependencies on third-party service providers. The issues identified are building blocks for ensuring a strong, sustainable and resilient financial system as innovations in financial services evolve and adopted.

The ten issues were as follows[70]:

(1) Authorities should determine whether current oversight frameworks from important third-party service providers are appropriate, and in particular if financial institutions rely on the same third-party service providers. This may entail greater coordination globally across financial authorities and with non-traditional partners.

(2) Recent reports of significant and successful cyber-attacks underscore the difficulties of mitigating cyber risks.

(3) While there are currently no compelling signs of macro financial risks materialising, experience shows that they can emerged quickly if left unchecked. Authorities should consider developing their own capacity to access existing and new sources of information. The seven items featured next cover other issues that were thought to merit authorities' attention.

(4) Innovations in cross border lending, trading and payment transactions, including via smart contracts as these raise questions about the cross jurisdictional compatibility of national legal frameworks.

(5) Giving attention to governance and disclosure frameworks for big data analytics.

---

68 Supra, note [64], FSB (2017).
69 Supra, note [64], FSB (2017).
70 Supra, note [64], FSB (2017).

(6) The issue of assessing the regulatory perimeter and updating it on a timely basis.
(7) The issue of shared learning with a diverse set of private sector parties.
(8) The growing importance of Fintech activities and the interconnections across the financial system may lead authorities to consider developing further their lines of communication to ensure preparedness.
(9) Supervisors and regulators should consider placing greater emphasis on ensuring they have adequate resources and skillsets to deal with Fintech.
(10) Relevant authorities should analyse the potential implications of virtual currencies for monetary policy, financial stability and the global monetary system including the use of virtual currencies for illegal activities and cyber-attacks.

The FSB framework applies to particular Fintech activities including wholesale payments innovations, digital currencies, AI and so on to assess potential benefits and risks to financial stability. The lack of data and information poses constraints to assessing the significance of the financial stability implications of Fintech. The gathering of data in industry and academic associations on specific Fintech activities on a voluntary basis is at a nascent stage. The nature of information needed by regulators and supervisors may be different. The five key observations on possible implications for Fintech stability include considerations over the complementarities and trade-offs between financial stability, competition, consumer-investors protection and financial inclusion.

The degree to which regulators will respond to Fintech activities may be a function of whether current regulatory frameworks cover emerging risks. Macro-financial issues related to systemic importance are embedded in the FSB policy framework for addressing systemically important financial institutions (SIFIs), while some micro-financial risks of certain Fintech activities may be within the FSB policy framework for strengthening oversight and regulation of shadow banking activities. The FSB's stock take of regulatory approaches to Fintech finds that a majority of jurisdictions surveyed have already taken or plan to take regulatory measures to respond to Fintech activities. In general, the policy objectives pursued are mostly consumer and investor protection, market integrity, financial inclusion and promoting innovation or competition. Interestingly, financial stability was often not cited as an objective for recent or planned regulatory reforms with respect to Fintech.

In 2017 the FSB's position was affected by events unfolding over the previous two years. In October 2018 they published a report "Cypro-asset markets: Potential channels for future financial stability implications"[71] where they expressed concern at the risks cryptocurrencies posed, which they balanced against the

---

71 FSB (2018), "Crypto-asset markets: Potential channels for future financial stability implications", *FSB Paper*, 10/10/2018, www.fsb.org/wp-content/uploads/P101018.pdf, accessed 11/10/2018.

potential advantages that blockchain could bring. The risks they were concerned about were:

- risks to consumers and market protection. This was sub categorised as being made up of market liquidity, volatility, leverage, technological and operational risk
- market integrity
- sanctions evasion
- fraud
- tax evasion
- circumventing capital controls.

FSB's Chairperson, Randal Quarles commented at the BIS special governors meeting in Hong Kong in February 2019 that "developments like the emergence of crypto-assets may challenge any framework." Quarles went on to suggest what further needs to be done.[72] As the FSB continues to assess that cryptoassets do not pose materials risks to global financial stability, it nevertheless acknowledges that these products raise various further policy issues beyond financial stability. The FSB takes the position that vigilant monitoring remains justified especially as a variety of new products and services appear to be under development. Thus, a further monitoring note was submitted to its Standing Committee on the Assessment of Vulnerabilities (SCAV) in September 2019, incorporating developments in stablecoins and tokenisation.[73] In general, the FSB enjoys the opportunity to impact on the financial policies of influential economic blocs like the G20. Thus far, it has submitted three reports to the G20 Finance Ministers and Central Bank Governors Meetings. The first provided a directory of cryptoassets regulators, the second detailed standard-setting focuses on the financial stability, regulatory and governance implications of decentralised financial technologies.[74]

6.6 The Bank for International Settlements (BIS)

The BIS is an international financial organisation owned by its 60 member central banks, representing countries that together make up about 95% of world GDP. Its mission is to serve central banks in their pursuit of monetary and financial stability, to foster international cooperation in those areas, and to act as a bank for central banks. The BIS pursues its mission by fostering discussion and facilitating

---

72 Quarles, R.K. (2019), "Ideas for order: Charting a course for the financial stability board", *Remarks by Randal K. Charles, Chair FSB at BIS Special Governors Meeting*, Hong Kong, 10/02/2019, www.moodysanalytics.com/regulatory-news/feb-10-19-fsb-chair-randal-quarles-speaks-about-the-upcoming-work-of-fsb, accessed 03/03/2019.

73 FSB (2019), "Cryptoassets: Work underway, regulatory approaches and potential gaps", FSB, 31/05/2019, https://www.fsb.org/2019/05/crypto-assets-work-underway-regulatory-approaches-and-potential-gaps/, accessed 02/07/2019.

74 Helms, K. (2019), "G20 leaders issue declaration on crypto assets- A look at their commitments", Bitcoin.com, 01/07/2019, https://news.bitcoin.com/g20-leaders-declaration-crypto-assets-commitments/, accessed 07/02/2020.

cooperation among central banks, supporting dialogue with other authorities promoting financial stability, carrying out research and policy analysis on issues of relevance for monetary and financial stability, acting as a prime counterparty for central banks in their financial transactions, and serving as an agent or trustee in connection with international financial operations. The BIS does not think for now that cryptocurrencies can substitute for some forms of money. It claims to be seeing the fraudulent behaviour that brought down other private currencies starting to appear in the Bitcoin space. The BIS mentions the following flaws of cryptocurrencies.[75] Modern day clipping and culling takes the form of forks, a kind of spin off where developers clone the relevant cryptocurrency's software, release it with a new name and a new coin after tinkering with the algorithms' parameter. The objective often is to capitalise on the public's familiarity with the cryptocurrency to make profit. In 2017 alone, 19 Bitcoin forks came out including Bitcoin cash, Bitcoin gold, and Bitcoin diamond. Forks can fork again and more could occur. Such modern day clippings could dilute the value of existing ones to the extent such cryptocurrencies have little if any economic value at all.

Cryptocurrencies are not the liability of any individual or institution, nor are they backed by any authority. Governance weaknesses[76] such as the concentration of their ownership could make them even less trustworthy. To use them often means resorting to intermediaries such as cryptocurrency exchanges to which users have to trust. Often, they piggyback on similar institutional infrastructure serving the overall financial system and on the trust it provides. This reflects the challenge to set up their own trust in the face of cyber-attacks, loss of customers' funds, limits on transferring funds and inadequate market integrity. Novel technology such as Bitcoin blockchain does not necessarily equate with better technology or better economics. Bitcoin's volatility renders it as a poor means of payment and an unwise way to store value. Few use it for payments or less even as a unit of account.

To the extent that they are used, Bitcoins and other cryptocurrencies appear more attractive to those seeking to make transactions in the black or illegal economy rather than in everyday transactions. This is unsurprising since individuals who massively evade taxes or launder money are those willing to adapt to Bitcoin's volatility. Central bank experiments show that in practice the distributed ledger technology based systems are very expensive to run and much less efficient to operate than conventional payment and settlement systems. Electricity used in Bitcoin mining is estimated to equal to Singapore's daily electricity consumption thereby making it socially wasteful and environmentally undesirable.[77]

---

75 Carstens, A. (2018), "Money in the digital age: What role for central banks?", *Lecture by Augustin Carstens, BIS General Manager at the House of Finance Goethe University,* Frankfurt, 06/02/2018.

76 Nagarajan, M. (2018), "An analysis of cryptocurrency governance", *Joseph Wharton Scholars*, https://repository.upenn.edu/joseph_wharton_scholars/51/, accessed 19/01/2019.

77 Küfeoğlu, S. & Ozkuran, M.A. (2019), "Energy Consumption Bitcoin Mining", *Cambridge Working Papers in Economics No.1948,* 04/06/2019, www.researchgate.net/publication/333564703_Energy_Consumption_of_Bitcoin_Mining, accessed 05/06/2019.

The above suggests that the current fascination with cryptocurrencies seems to have more to do with a speculative mania than any use as a form of electronic payment, other than for illicit activities. It is unsurprising that authorities are accordingly inching closer to clamping them down to mitigate the risks related to virtual currencies. There is a strong case for policy intervention. These assets, according to many securities markets and regulatory and supervisory agencies, can raise concerns related to consumer and investor protection. Relevant authorities have a duty to educate and protect investors and consumers, and be alert to act. There are moreover further concerns relating to tax evasion, money laundering and criminal finance. Authorities should welcome or even promote innovation, but they also concurrently have a duty to ensure that technological advances are not applied to legitimise profits from illegal pursuits.

Central banks acting on their own and/or in coordination with other financial authorities such as bank regulators and supervisors, ministries of finance, tax agencies and financial intelligence units may also need to respond given their roles in providing money services and the safeguarding of money's real value. Working with commercial banks, authorities have a part to play in policing the digital frontier. Commercial banks operate in the front line as they provide the real liquidity that keeps exchanges going and interacting with customers, which means authorities need to watch with concerns those banks offering Bitcoin ATMs. Central banks also need to safeguard payment systems. To date cryptocurrencies are not functional as a means of payment and are essentially trading apps that link users to conventional bank accounts. Where the only business case is used for illegal transactions, central banks cannot allow such tokens to rely on much of the same institutional infrastructure serving the overall financial system and freeload on the trust that it provides.[78]

Authorities should apply the same principles that the Basel Process has held on to for years to provide a level playing field to all participants in financial markets, banks and non-banks alike, besides simultaneously fostering innovative, secure and competitive markets. This means ensuring the same high standards that money transfer and payment service providers have to comply with are also met by Bitcoin-type exchanges. It further implies ensuring that legitimate banking and payment services are only offered to those exchanges and products meeting these high standards. A further justification for financial authorities to intervene is the need to ensure financial stability. There are suggestions that, given cryptocurrencies' small size and limited interconnectedness, concerns about them have not reached a systemic level, but if authorities do not act pre-emptively they could become more interconnected with the main financial system and eventually become a threat to financial stability.[79]

---

78 Chiu, J. & Koeppl, T.V. (2018), "The economics of cryptocurrencies", *Bank of Canada/Queen's University Working Paper.*

79 Heald, J. (2018), "Regulating virtual currency risk", *Review of Banking & Financial Law*, 37 (2018), 567–578.

Importantly, the spectacular rise of cryptocurrencies should not divert attention from the important role central banks play as stewards of public trust. Private digital tokens masquerading as currencies must not be allowed to subvert this trust. History has shown there simply is no substitute. Central banks nevertheless are embracing new technologies as appropriate. Fintech and Techfin with reference to established technology platforms venturing into financial services are changing financial services deliveries in many economies, especially in payments in emerging economies such as Kenya and China. Even as these produce the possibility of non-banks introducing money-like instruments and raises a familiar set of regulatory questions they do offer the potential for many benefits.

Overall, while cryptocurrencies may pretend to be currencies, they fail the basic textbook definitions. Most would agree that they do not function as a unit of account, while their volatile valuations make them unsafe to rely on as a common means of payment and stable store of value. Importantly given their many fragilities, cryptocurrencies are unlikely to satisfy the requirement of trust to make them suitable forms of money. It is not invariably the case that new technologies improve lives and economies. Central banks have the obligation to intervene when it is needed.[80] After all, cryptocurrencies piggyback on the institutional infrastructure serving the wider financial system, thereby gaining a semblance of legitimacy from their links to it. This is clearly central banking territory. It further suggests that central banks and financial authorities need to focus foremost on the ties linking virtual currencies to real currencies to ensure a non-parasitic relationship, and second, with reference to the level playing field principle of same risk same regulation, with no exceptions.

The BIS' view on cryptocurrencies and in particular Bitcoin drew extensive financial media attention, especially coming a day after the ECB's chief's description of Bitcoin as a very risky and entirely speculative asset. Media reporting focuses on BIS's call for a clampdown on Bitcoin to stop them piggybacking on mainstream institutions and becoming a threat to financial stability.[81]

Additional BIS revelations suggest that Bitcoin counterfeiting through double spending attacks is inherently profitable, rendering payment finality premised on proof of work highly expensive. Further, the transaction market is unable to generate a sufficient level of "mining" income through fees as users freeride on the fees of other transactions in a block and in the subsequent blockchain. Newly minted cryptocurrencies, known as block rewards instead accounted for the bulk of mining income to date. These two constraints would imply that liquidity could

---

80 Carstens, A. (2018), "Money in the digital age: what role for central banks?", *Lecture by Augustin Carstens, General Manager BIS at House of Finance Goethe University Frankfurt, 06/02/2018*, www.bis.org/speeches/sp180206.pdf, accessed 10/11/2018.

81 Arnold, M. (2018), "Head of BIS calls for clampdown on Bitcoin: Cryptocurrency has lost more than half its value since start of 2018", *Financial Times*, 06/02/2018, www.ft.com/content/78bf5612-0b1a-11e8-839d-41ca06376bf2, accessed 03/03/2018; Bosley, C. & Speciale, A. (2018), "BIS Chief Sees 'Strong Case' for Cryptocurrency Intervention", *Bloomberg*, 06/02/2018, www.bloomberg.com/news/articles/2018-02-06/bis-chief-sees-strong-case-for-intervening-on-cryptocurrencies, accessed 03/03/2018.

fall significantly as these block rewards are phased out. Preliminary estimates suggest that at the moment block rewards are zero. It would require months before a Bitcoin payment is final, unless new technologies were available to expedite payment finality. Lightning Network second-layer solutions could assist, but the only fundamental remedy would require departing from proof-of-work, and this would likely need some kind of social coordination or institutionalisation.

Their most recent publication on the matter "Proceeding with caution - a survey on central bank digital currency"[82] shows that 70% of central banks are studying cryptocurrencies, but none are currently planning to introduce them. At some point, this may change. Agustin Carstens, BIS chief subsequent to previously issuing statements and report strongly critical of cryptocurrencies, has conceded that central banks would likely soon need to issue their own digital currencies.[83] He recently stated that BIS is supporting global central bank initiatives to research and develop digital currencies based on national fiat currencies. His comments came soon after Facebook's announcement of its planned Libra cryptocurrency – headlines that astonished regulators worldwide.[84] This is because of the fear that a tech firm with billions launching its own money potentially poses a threat to national currencies. The Finance Minister of France has argued that Libra must not be allowed to become a sovereign currency, while the US Congress has asked Facebook to halt development of the Libra projects as it subjects the tech firm to a Congressional hearing ongoing since mid-July 2019. BIS itself maintains that initiatives like Libra pose a long term threat to central banks' control of money. Importantly regulators need to ensure a level playing field between big techs and banks taking into account big tech's wide customer base, access to information and broad ranging business models. The BIS chief added that the simple way to regulate such cryptocurrency networks is to start addressing immediate and very obvious laundering concerns.[85] The latter concern was echoed by the US Treasury Secretary.[86]

6.7 The International Organisation of Securities Commissions (IOSCO)

The IOSCO website describes it as the international body that brings together the world's securities regulators and is recognised as the global standard setter for securities and their regulation. IOSCO develops, implements and promotes

---

82 Barontini, C. and Holden, H. (2019), "Proceeding with caution - a survey on central bank digital currency" *BIS Paper No 101*, 08/01/2019, https://www.bis.org/publ/bppdf/bispap101.htm, accessed 20/01/2020.

83 Palmer, D. (2019), "BIS Chief: Central Bank May Issues Digital Currencies 'Sooner Than We Think'" *Coin Desk*, 01/07/2019, https://www.coindesk.com/central-banks-may-issue-digital-currencies-sooner-than-we-think-bis-chief, accessed 02/07/2019.

84 Supra, note [83], Palmer (2019).

85 Supra, note [83], Palmer (2019).

86 De, N. (2019), "US Treasury Secretary Mnuchin is 'not comfortable' with Facebook's Libra", *Coin Desk*, 15/07/2019, https://www.coindesk.com/us-treasury-secretary-mnuchin-is-not-comfortable-with-facebooks-libra, accessed 16/07/2019.

adherence to international recognised standards for securities regulations. It collaborates extensively with the G20 and the FSB on the global regulatory reform agenda. IOSCO's total membership regulates more than 95% of the world's securities markets in more than 115 jurisdictions. Securities regulators in emerging markets account for 75% of its ordinary membership.

IOSCO's objective and principles of securities trading are endorsed by the G20 and FSB as the relevant standards in this area. They represent the overarching core principles guiding it in the development and implementation of internationally recognised and consistent standards of regulation, oversight and enforcement. They are the basis for the evaluation of the securities sector for the Financial Sector Assessment Programmes (FSAPs) of the IMF and the World Bank.

Through providing high quality technical assistance, education, training and research to its members and other regulators, IOSCO seeks to build sound global capital markets and a robust global regulatory framework. IOSCO members agree to cooperate in developing, implementing and promoting adherence to internationally recognised and consistent standards of regulation. These include oversight and enforcement to protect investors; maintain fair, efficient and transparent markets; and seek to address systemic risks. They also agree to exchange information at both global and regional levels on their respective experiences so as to assist the development of markets, strengthen market infrastructure and implement suitable regulations.

IOSCO's Fintech study covers DLT that underpins the workings of Bitcoin and other cryptocurrencies.[87] DLT are technologies used to implement distributed ledgers. A distributed ledger is a consensus of replicated, shared and synchronised digital data geographically spread across multiple sites, countries and/or institutions. The DLT term is used to include blockchain technologies and shared ledgers. DLT attracts the interests of financial services for various reasons, including the possibility that permissioned DLT present an opportunity to save costs when they are employed to replace legacy systems and associated back office processes. Permissionless DLT, on the other hand, could potentially present risks when they are applied to disintermediate financial institutions and central counter-parties.

DLT has grown significantly in the market place. Over US$1.4 billion venture capital (VC) investments poured in to DLT since 2013. Also, more than 2,500 DLT patents were filed since 2013 including many by financial institutions. Now, more than 24 economies invest in DLT, more than 90 central banks engaged in DLT dialogues, more than 90 corporations joined DLT consortia, and some 80% of banks are forecasted to initiate a DLT project by 2017.[88]

---

87 IOSCO (2017), "IOSCO research report on financial technologies (Fintech)", *IOSCO Research Report*, February 2017, accessed 26/03/2018.

88 World Economic Forum (2016), "The future of financial architecture: An ambitious look at how blockchain can reshape financial services", *World Economic Forum,* 2016, www3.weforum.org/docs/WEF_The_future_of_financial_infrastructure.pdf, accessed 02/02/2018.

A distributed ledger is a decentralised database accessible and collectively controlled by multiple users. This contrasts with a traditional ledger which is a centralised database accessible by designated users and is overseen by one or more system notaries who regulate access to and integrity of the data contained in the ledger. Blockchain technology is one kind of DLT providing a digitally-signed time-series of data or records assembled together as blocks with the linkage also digitally signed thereby making it hard to tamper with. The Bitcoin blockchain is the first, the world's largest and the most widely researched DLT.[89] Bitcoin's blockchain capacity expanded from 60,000 confirmed Bitcoin transactions per day in August 2014, to 120,000 in August 2015, and 220,000 in August 2016.[90]

Noteworthy publicly announced proofs of concepts in the securities industry include keeping corporate records, making corporate actions processes more efficient, revamping post-trading operations of exchange-traded equities, or trading and settling OTC derivatives, facilitating loan syndications, tracking repo transactions and re-hypothecation, trading short term debt, automation of KYC and AML compliance processes among financial institutions, individual digital ID, and alternative financing. Extending from these, the more frequently cited potential benefits as they apply to financial services include cost reduction in settlement, faster speed of settlement, reliability and traceability of records, automatic and real-time filings to regulators, inclusion of new asset classes, efficiency enhancement, and enhancement in security.[91]

DLT implementation in the securities markets could raise various technological, operational, business and regulatory challenges.[92] Technological challenges involve matters such as scalability, interoperability and cyber resilience. Operational challenges involved matters such as governance and smart contracts. Trading and settlement related challenges involve matters such as management of the cash leg of transactions, recourse mechanism, position and collateral netting, and transparency. Implementation of distributed ledger technology and smart contracts in the securities markets may raise several legal questions including but not limited to the validity of tokens as a representation of ownership and legal finality of smart contracts.

Though DLT is still evolving various authorities have issued their views.[93] In June 2016 ESMA issued a discussion paper; also in June 2016 the French

---

89 Goldman Sachs (2016), "Blockchain-Putting theory in practice", *Goldman Sachs*, 2016, https://www.academia.edu/38946070/Goldman_Sachs_Blockchain_putting_theory_to_practice, accessed 02/02/2018; UK Government Office for Science (GOS) (2016), "Distributed ledger technology: Beyond block chain", *GOS*, 2016, https://www.gov.uk/government/news/distributed-ledger-technology-beyond-block-chain, accessed 02/02/2018; McKinsey & Co. (2015), "Beyond the hype: Blockchains in capital markets", McKinsey Working Paper December 2015, https://www.mckinsey.com/~/media/McKinsey/Industries/Technology%20Media%20and%20Telecommunications/High%20Tech/Our%20Insights/Beyond%20the%20hype%20Blockchains%20in%20capital%20markets/Beyond-the-hype-Blockchains-in-capital-markets.ashx, accessed02/02/2018.
90 Supra, note [87], IOSCO (2017).
91 Supra, note [87], IOSCO (2017).
92 Supra, note [87], IOSCO (2017).
93 Supra, note [87], IOSCO (2017).

Parliament enacted a law that allows some securities vouchers to be issued and exchanged on a DLT. The US Financial Industry Regulatory Authority (FINRA) in January 2017 issued a paper as its contribution to the ongoing dialogue about their use in the securities industry. It requested comments on matters for which it would be suitable to consider additional guidance, consistent with the principles of investor protection and market integrity based on the applications and their implications for FINRA rules.[94]

While firms can operate globally, regulation is overseen within national or sub-national borders. This could generate challenges in terms of regulatory consistency, as well as cross-border supervision and enforcement. It also generates risks of regulatory arbitrage. The global nature of Fintech could therefore contribute to challenges that might be addressed by international cooperation and the exchange of information among regulators.

Regulators have engaged in greater multilateral collaboration on the topic of digital innovation at IOSCO, FSB and the BIS. Regulators could additionally continue to enter into bilateral memoranda of understanding to collaborate, thereby enabling regulators to share information about financial services innovations in their respective markets, including emerging trend and regulatory issues. Emerging new Fintech activities such as DLT and cryptocurrencies sometimes cut across different industries within the wider economy thereby impacting on current regulatory perimeters within jurisdictions. Many jurisdictions have engaged in greater national regulatory coordination. For instance, in Japan a new Working Group of the Financial System Council was formed. This is the advisory body of the Japan Financial Services Agency that helped to spawn major legislative amendments to the Payment Services Act and the Banking Act.[95]

On 18 January 2018, IOSCO issued an ICO cautionary note.[96] It described ICOs also known as token sales or coin sales as typically involving the creation of digital tokens using DLT and their sale to investors by auction or through subscription, in return for a cryptocurrency such as Bitcoin or Ether or more rarely for official fiat currency. The IOSCO does not consider these offerings as standardised and as such their legal and regulatory status is likely to depend on the circumstances of the individual ICO.

The IOSCO further cited clear risks associated with these offerings.[97] ICOs are deemed as highly speculative investments wherein investors are putting their entire invested capital at risk. Though some operators are providing legitimate investment opportunities to finance projects/businesses, the enhanced

---

94 FINRA (2017), "Report on distributed ledger technology: Implications of blockchain for the securities industry", *FINRA*, January 2017, www.finra.org/industry/report-distributed-ledger-technology-implications-blockchain-securities-industry, accessed 02/02/2018.

95 Supra, note [87], IOSCO (2017).

96 IOSCO (2018), "IOSCO board communication on concerns related to initial coin offerings (ICOs)", *IOSCO Media Release*, 18/01/2018.

97 Supra, note [96], IOSCO (2018).

targeting of ICOs to retail investors via online distribution channels by parties often located outside an investor's home jurisdiction that might not be subject to regulation or could be operating illegally in breach of existing laws raises investor protection concerns. There have been instances of frauds and, as a consequence, investors are cautioned to be very careful when deliberating whether to invest in ICOs.

In a related development, the IOSCO cautioned its member countries over the regulation of cryptocurrencies saying that such regulation might confer undue legitimacy on the products. At a recent two day meeting in Madrid, Spain, the gathering of regulators with IOSCO leadership opined that regulating virtual currencies would deceive the general public into believing that there is a regulatory faith in the products.[98] The gathering reached a consensus to conduct a deep analysis of the nature of the products to enable a clear appreciation of the depth of regulation required to ensure adequate protection of investors. They further agreed to launch intensive public awareness initiatives to boost investor education and understanding, and accelerate the development of the right regulatory framework as may be necessary. Regulators especially in emerging markets are further advised to better prepare for the incursion of cryptocurrencies into their markets by putting in place the appropriate regulatory frameworks that would ensure transparency, efficiency and protection for investors.

The IOSCO's consultation report of 28 May 2019, described the risks and issues that it has identified pertaining to cryptoasset trading platforms (CTPs). The report outlined key considerations that are intended to assist regulatory authorities when evaluating CTPs within the context of their regulatory frameworks.[99] These primary matters to be addressed include access to CTPs, safeguarding participant assets, conflicts of interest, CTPs operation, market integrity, price discovery, and technology. Many of these are also common to conventional securities trading venues, but could be heightened by how CTPs are operated. Where regulatory authorities have determined that a cryptoasset is a security and falls within their remits, the basic principles or objectives of securities regulation would apply. The IOSCO seeks to continue monitoring the evolution of the markets for cryptoassets to ensure the issues, risks and key considerations identified in the report remain pertinent and appropriate. Its approach ergo aligns with the G20's 2018 communiques calling on international standard setting entities to continue their monitoring of cryptoassets and their risks according to their respective mandates and assess multilateral responses as required.[100]

---

98 Nnorom, N. (2018), "IOSCO warns on regulation of virtual currencies", *Vanguard*, 27/02/2018, www.vanguardngr.com/2018/iosco-warns-regulation-virtual-currencies/, accessed 03/03/2018.

99 IOSCO (2019), "IOSCO requests feedback on key considerations for regulating cryptoasset trading platforms", *IOSCO*, 28/05/2019, www.iosco.org/news/pdf/IOSCONEWS530.pdf, accessed 02/07/2019.

100 Supra, note [99], IOSCO (2019).

6.8 Financial Action Task Force (FATF)

In October the FATF 2018 adopted changes to its pre-existing Recommendations to explicitly clarify that they applied to financial activities pertaining to virtual assets, and also provided definitions for virtual asset and virtual asset service providers (VASP).[101] Recommendation 15 requires VASPs be regulated for AML/CTF. Purposes, licensed or registered, and subject to effective systems for monitoring purposes. Subsequently in June 2019, FATF adopted an Interpretative Note to Recommendation 15 to further clarify how the FATF requirements should apply pertaining to VAs and VASPs, especially with regard to the application of the risk-based approach RBAO to VA activities or operations and VASPs; supervision or monitoring of VASPs for AML/CTF purposes, licensing or registration; preventive measures, like customer due diligence, recordkeeping and suspicious transaction reporting, among others; sanctions and other enforcement measures; and international co-operation.[102] The FATF also adopted the present Guidance on the deployment of RBA to VAs and VASPs in June 2019. The intention is to assist both national authorities in understanding and developing regulatory and supervisory responses to VA activities and VASPs, and to assist private sector businesses engaging in VA activities, in understanding their AML/CTF obligation and how they could effectively comply with these requirements.

The Guidance further demonstrates how VA activities and VASPs fall within the scope of these Recommendations.[103] It analyses the five kinds of activities covered by the VASP definition and gives instances of VA related activities that fall within the VASP definition and that would be excluded from the FATF scope. As such, it highlights the key elements required to qualify as a VASP, namely acting as a business on customers' behalf and actively facilitating VA related activities. The Guidance also clarifies the application of the FATF Recommendation to countries and competent authorities including VASPs and other obliged entities that partake in VA activities and including financial institutions like banks and securities broker dealers. The G20 in the June 2019 Osaka Summit reaffirmed that cryptoassets do not pose a threat to global financial stability, and requested further work done by standard setting bodies like the FATF.[104]

6.9 The challenge of Facebook's Libra

This chapter would be incomplete without commentaries on why most of these multilateral institutions stand strongly against Facebook's plan to issue Libra,

---

101 FATF (2019), *Guidance for a risk-based approach and virtual asset service providers*, Paris, FATF.
102 Supra, note [101], FATF (2019).
103 Supra, note [101], FATF (2019).
104 Helms, K. (2019), "G20 Leaders Issue Declaration on Crypto Assets - A Look at Their Commitments", *Bitcoin,* 01/07/2019, https://news.bitcoin.com/g20-leaders-declaration-crypto-assets-commitments/, accessed 16/07/2019.

its own cryptocurrency.[105] The idea is to transform how people use and expend money across the world through a cryptoasset, in this case Facebook's Libra. The plan is to launch this by mid-2020. The cryptocurrency would be pegged against a vault of global currencies and short-term government securities to trim price volatility generally linked to most cryptoassets thus far, but in particular, Bitcoin. Libra would not have a fixed exchange rate against conventional fiats, and therefore differs from existing stables of stablecoins that do. Libra would run on the Libra blockchain capable of handling some 1,000 transactions per second. This is enormously higher than the seven seen in Bitcoin blockchain, but relatively lower than the 1,700 transactions per second found in Visa.

A non-profit, the Libra Association (LA) headquartered in Switzerland would manage Libra.[106] Expected founding members extend from payments giants like Mastercard and Visa to e-hailing services like Uber and Lyft, with each said to be committing at least US$10 million and incorporating tech into their services. At least one hundred members are expected by the time Libra go official. LA members would function as nodes that verify transactions and keep records in this blockchain network. All LA members enjoy equal power in helping to govern the system. Calibra, the wallet app for the venture will be a Facebook subsidiary, thus enabling Facebook Messenger and WhatsApp users to migrate Libra between themselves, and to buy and sell – in effect a payments system. This immediate functionality though would expand into P2P and/or lending and so on at the later stages.

The evolution of Libra is unsurprising given Facebook's need and intention to broaden its earnings base beyond advertising. Facebook could achieve new income through a slice of the transactions done when integrating payments solutions and e-commerce into its platform comprising more than 2.38 billion users.[107] The business model involving the integration of payments systems into social media platforms is not altogether new as exemplified by the likes of those already profiting in China and elsewhere.[108] Facebook's initiative, backed by various precautionary and governance mechanisms on a global scale, is relatively novel because of the use of blockchain tech together with a cryptocurrency. With Libra, Facebook and the founding members of Libra could leverage their services to huge numbers of people globally without access to bank facilities, said to go beyond 1.7 billion.[109] However, things are relatively murky for

---

105 Libra "An introduction to Libra", *Libra White Paper 2019*, https://libra.org/en-US/whitepaper/?noredirect=en-US, accessed 16/07/2019.
106 Libra (2019), "The Libra Association", www.libra.org/en-US/association/, accessed 16/07/2019.
107 Noyes, D. (2019), "The top 20 valuable Facebook statistics-Ipdated July 2019", *Zephoria Digital Marketing* July 2019, https://zephoria.com/top-15-valuable-facebook-statistics/, accessed 16/07/2019.
108 Huang, E. (2019), "WeChat is setting blueprint for the world's social networks", Quartz 29/10/2019, https://qz.com/1613489/how-wechat-put-the-internet-in-chinas-hands/, accessed 07/02/2020.
109 The World Bank (2018), "Financial inclusion on the Rise, But gaps remain, Global Findex Database shows", The World Bank Press Release No: 2018/130/DEC, 19/04/2018, https://www.worldbank.org/en/news/press-release/2018/04/19/financial-inclusion-on-the-rise-but-gaps-remain-global-findex-database-shows, accessed 07/02/20.

Libra's potential in advanced economies. While the idea of extending seamless services to Facebook users to include payments this still has to compete with many other financial options currently available online.[110]

Facebook appears to be going beyond its agenda of helping to bring billions of people into the global financial system or the launching of a price stable cryptocurrency for the masses. It seems to be about transforming the manner in which people trust each other on the Internet. Buried within the more exciting features of the Libra White Paper is the mention of the additional goal of the Libra Association to develop and promote an open identity standard, or a decentralized and portable digital identity that is deemed crucial for financial inclusion and competition.[111] This matter needs to be elaborated upon. Though Libra mention the separation of financial data from Facebook users' other data, industry experts still harbour data privacy and regulatory concerns.[112]

Countries across the world vary in their responses to the Libra venture. Regulators though take sterner views. The US Fed chief warned that the Libra proposition raises many serious concerns pertaining to privacy, money laundering, consumer protection and financial stability. He feels that the venture cannot advance without addressing these concerns adequately. The Fed has set up a working group to monitor the projects and is also coordinating with other central banks across the globe on this matter.[113] Meanwhile, Libra's CEO David Marcus was severely grilled in the July 2019 Congressional hearing. Representatives from both sides of the aisle were mostly against the notion of this proposed global private currency.[114] Marcus though stood his ground maintaining that Libra was not designed to compete with conventional fiats or interfere with monetary policies and that Facebook will only offer the Libra cryptocurrency upon fully addressing regulatory concerns and receiving the appropriate approvals.[115] Thus, the world awaits the further progress of this global cryptocurrency project.

---

110 Shah, B. (2019), "Glut of payments sector mergers reflects pressure to offer diverse global payment acceptance services", *Computer Business Review* (CBR) 30/05/2019, www.cbronline.com/opinion/payments-market-deals, accessed 16/07/2019.

111 Allison, I. (2019), "Buried in Facebook's Libra White Paper, a Digital Identity Bombshell", *Coindesk*, 26/06/2019, www.coindesk.com/buried-in-facebooks-cryptocurrency-white-paper-a-digital-identity-bombshell, accessed 16/07/2019.

112 R. Wolfson (2019), "Facebook's cryptocurrency Libra validates blockchain, but industry experts voice concerns", *Forbes*, 19/06/2019, accessed 16/07/2019.

113 Helms, K. (2019), "How 10 countries respond to Facebook's Libra Cryptocurrency", *Bitcoin*, 17/07/2019, https://news.bitcoin.com/how-countries-respond-facebooks-libra-cryptocurrency/, accessed 16/07/2019.

114 De Silva, M. (2019), "Five major issues raised by Facebook's Libra hearing before Congress", *Quartz*, 16/07/2019, https://qz.com/1667568/five-major-issues-raised-by-facebooks-libra-hearing/, accessed 17/07/2019.

115 Marcus, D. (2019), "Testimony of David Marcus, Head of Calibra Facebook", *Hearing before the United States Senate Committee on Banking, Housing, and Urban Affairs*, 16/07/2019, www.banking.senate.gov/imo/media/doc/Marcus%20Testimony%207-16-19.pdf, accessed 18/07/2019.

6.10 A brief comparative note regarding multilateral cryptoasset regulators

This chapter demonstrates how economic blocs like the G20 and G8 look at the potential risks posed by cryptoassets to the conventional financial system, to businesses and to investors. It also examines how international financial standards setters like the IMF, the BIS, FSB, and the IOSCO approach this issue. In particular, the impact of ICOs on the capital markets as perceived by the IOSCO and other large national regulators like the SEC and the FCA were also analysed.

It would appear that economic blocs such as the G20 and G8 are taking the position that cryptoassets are not posing a threat to global financial stability and are focusing on close monitoring of existing and emerging risks in the context of consumer and investor protection and AML/CTF. Their goal is to use the multilateral approach effectively applied to help quell the 2008 global financial crisis. To this end, they have directed the FSB and other standard setting bodies to advise on further multilateral responses when appropriately needed. Of late, they have become concerned over the risks posed by the wider employment of new kinds of cryptoassets for retail payment purposes that might necessitate close examinations by the competent authorities to ensure compliance to high standards of regulation. On this issue, FSB's September 2019 report on stablecoins and tokenization is likely to get a response from them with regards to these items and Facebook Libra. In the meantime, they confirm adherence to FATF reporting standards for cryptoassets.

Drawing from previous experiences, other than the 2008 Global Financial Crisis, G20 and G8 summits are unlikely to focus enough on the cryptoasset risk threat to the global financial system as other high profile agendas are likely to draw greater relative attention. These happened during the recent 2019 Osaka Summit and the earlier summit in France. But, the G20 and G8 forums do provide the platform for multilateral solutions to potential cryptoassets issues in relation to the global financial system. In contrast, the EU takes a more disciplined approach to the potential harm posed to market participants and financial systems and the main reason why they have, under the guidance from the FSB, taken initiatives to gather an early appreciation of how blockchain innovation unleashed through the cryptoassets industry could transform markets and financial institutions to be ready with risk containment measures, including serious reflections on how the industry is to be regulated in the EU.

The OECD acknowledged both the benefits and risks from deployment of cryptoassets and has called for a balanced and harmonised approach to deal with the problem. The OECD's larger membership base enables it to reach out to more economies with its various guidance, the latest of which included the call for the use of blockchain technology to support and assist the further growth of SMEs. Other than these, it has a relatively lower profile than the G20 or G8 both of which enjoys greater global attention.

The FSB though focuses more on the issue of financial stability and in this has the ear of the G20 and G8 and other forums. It continues to provide helpful insights onto the workings of cryptoassets covering both the perils and the opportunities they bring. The BIS, the central bank for central bankers, initially took a very conservative ultra-negative stand on cryptoassets. From the perspective of their mission, this is rightly so, as the success of private money globally such as that proposed by Facebook Libra could suggest the potential end for central banking. Lately, they have shifted their position when the IMF and some central banks started to explore the potential of using CBDC, the latest of which came from the Governor of the Bank of England. The BIS stand is understandable as Facebook Libra has accelerated various central banks to seriously consider CBDCs, as exemplified by the stance from China's central bank and others.

While the IMF urges caution with regards to the cryptoasset industry, it has in recent years become slightly more positive towards it. The IMF has even called upon economies and central banks around the world to take a more balanced approach that takes into account both perils and the innovation opportunities unleashed by cryptoassets and the blockchain technology underpinning. In contrast to all the others the FATF issued specific guidance focusing on AML/CTF reporting precautions that most policymakers and regulators take seriously. Compared to the others that tend to take general stands AML/CTF is a high priority agenda for the FATF. Most regulatory institutions tend to follow FATF standards as deviations from these tend to attract blacklisting response in the global financial arena.

The potential heightened cryptoasset AML/CTF risks aside, all the multilateral global regulators discussed here agree that the blockchain technology behind cryptoassets could extend its value to areas where trusted authority is mandatory for coordination of socio-economic activities as it could offer the supporting infrastructure in substitution for these activities. This suggests a set of protocols and code-based rules inserted on top of blockchain-based networks for deployments in financial institutions, capital markets, online operators, content providers and including government systems. This technology therefore enables the on setting of new self-contained and autonomous systems of rules that install order without law in the direction of private regulatory frameworks, referred to as "lex cryptographica" that enables people and institutions to organize, communicate, and exchange value on P2P format without intermediary actors.[116]

Though "lex cryptographica" in some respects is similar to other conventional means of regulation by code, it nevertheless differs from current code-based regimes, as it runs autonomously of any centralised authority. Blockchain's decentralised systems and applications could therefore be governed almost entirely

---

[116] Davidson, S., De Filippi, P. & Potts, J. (2016), "Disrupting Governance: The New Institutional Economics of Distributed Ledger Technology", *SSRN Electronic Journal*, January 2016, www.researchgate.net/publication/323980958_Disrupting_Governance_The_New_Institutional_Economics_of_Distributed_Ledger_Technology, accessed 18/08/2018; Wright, A. & De Filippi, P. (2015), "Decentralized blockchain technology and the rise of lex cryptographica", *Cryptocurrency Research Group (CRG) Paper*, 12/03/2015, www.researchgate.net/publication/314892724_Decentralized_Blockchain_Technology_and_the_Rise_of_Lex_Cryptographia, accessed 18/08/2018.

by code rules, unlike other current technological systems in use in the Internet. These could portend various risks as they operate by going around conventional systems of control. Blockchain technology, however, does not necessarily suggest the end for the rule of law as, despite its potential widespread deployments, governments still maintain their holds over laws, codes, social norms and market forces that could ultimately indirectly or directly regulate this emerging technology.[117]

Both conventional systems and the blockchain decentralised system have their fair shares of constraints, ambiguity and uncertainty. Conventional technological systems in employment in the Internet and blockchain system have their fair shares of constraints, ambiguities, and uncertainties. As blockchain widen its applications and grip on the economy,[118] the option for the world could potentially straddle between the conventional rules of law systems that are not perfectly enforceable, but also more flexible. Or, the world could opt for the benefits of liberation from the tyranny of centralised intermediaries and trusted authorities via decentralised blockchain technology, but that could also bring with it a tyranny of codes. In the meantime, with pilots going into production, expansion of real world smart contract applications and preparations for state backed digital currencies, blockchain is argued to be ready to leave the hype behind and transition to a more mundane but useful phase.[119]

All in all, multilateral policymakers and regulators, for the most part, call for a balanced approach when dealing with cryptoassets. At the same time, owing to several high-profile illicit deployments of cryptoassets, FATF crypto-related AML/CTF standards are now in place for the world to follow. These are unlikely to diminish innovations flowing from the cryptoasset industry. It is also likely that regulatory response would converge gradually as the multilateral institutions continue to impact the views of national institutions with innovative insights. For the moment though, the regulatory response across the world is split into three camps, namely the wait and see camp, the deployment of new cryptoassets law camp and those relying on the tweaking of existing rules to deal with the emerging technology.

---

117 De Filippi, P. & Wright, A. (2018), *Blockchain and the law: The rule of code*, Cambridge, Massachusetts, Harvard University Press.
118 Hacker, P., Lianos, I., Dimitropoulos & Erich, S. (2019), *Regulating blockchain: Tecno-social and legal challenges,* Oxford, OUP; Finck, M. (2019), *Blockchain regulation and governance in Europe*, Cambridge, Cambridge University Press.
119 Wlasawsky-Berger, I. (2019), "Blockchain, yesterday's hype, transitions into something else", *Wall Street Journal,* 07/03/2019, https://blogs.wsj.com/cio/2019/03/07/blockchain-yesterdays-hype-transitions-into-something-else/, accessed 08/08/2019.

CHAPTER 7

Cryptoasset regulatory policies in selected advanced western economies

7.1 Introduction

In general almost all western advanced economies are marked by strong well established banking systems. This chapter focuses on cryptoasset regulatory policies in the advanced economies of the US, UK, Australia, Canada, EU, and Switzerland. The two national economies of the US and the UK, and those are selected for study as, in general, they play dominant roles in the advancement of Fintechs and in particular, the crypto industry. The US leads the world as the most active Fintech hub. The implications flowing from Brexit makes the UK an interesting country case study as the country leans on Fintech startup developments to spur growth. Australia and Canada are selected mainly because of their general aggressiveness toward cryptoasset development in general, and Bitcoin to some extent. Both economies are also part of the UK led Commonwealth of nations adhering to common law practices. The EU is selected as it is one of the largest economic bloc in the world with substantial global influence on financial regulatory development. Switzerland is one of the world's leading financial enclaves with strong banking and finance traditions. It would be interesting to see how it copes with the global impact of the crypto industry. Therefore, how regulators deal with cryptoassets in these respective national and regional economies are of interest to the world as these economies are sophisticated and generally well regulated.[1]

The analysis regarding regulatory approaches for an emerging and potentially private global currency starts with a discussion on the evolution of sovereign or fiat currencies. Fiat money has a hierarchical nature.[2] It is a promise to pay and stands as the ultimate form of money, and it achieves this as it has the most credible promise. Rather than having any kind of natural value, money's value depends on the credibility of its issuers, and that credibility relies upon an elaborate institutional infrastructure. Where confidence in that institutional structure

---

[1] Blandin, A., Cloots, A.S., Hussan, H., Rauchs, M., Saleuddin, R., Allen, J.G., Zhang, B. & Cloud, K. (2019), *Global cryptoasset regulatory landscape study*, Cambridge: Cambridge Centre for Alternative Finance (CCAF).

[2] Johnson, M. (2015), "Is money in your pocket same as money in the bank?", *Investopedia*, 24/12/2015, www.investopedia.com/../money-your-pocket-worth-same-bank.asp, accessed 02/02/2018.

is disturbed, so would the value of money. Cash and bank deposits are examples of different forms of money. An exchange rate is involved when switching from one form of money to another. In all these alluded to advanced economies, money could be exchanged between cash and deposit amounts, one for one, or at par rate. This, however, might not always be the case as US history and recent events in Greece can confirm.

7.2 Historical background

When capital controls were imposed in Greece in 2015, the value of a Euro in a Greek bank account was undermined.[3] This resulted in merchants offering discounts from customers paying in cash. This was because the capital controls in effect made Euro deposit accounts less liquid than euros in cash notes. Liquidity is one of the essential features of money and the value it claims to hold. Restrictions arising from capital controls demonstrate how the liquidity of different forms of money cause the value to deviate. Apart from the matter of liquidity, another factor that can have this effect is the credibility of the issuer.[4]

In times of crisis, such loss in liquidity becomes more apparent as occurred in Greece and elsewhere recently.[5] In the US antebellum period from the adoption of the US Constitution in 1789 to the commencement of the civil war,[6] it was gold and silver acting as government sanctioned forms of money; while for Greece, they are paper note euros, liabilities of the ECB, rather than Euro denominated Greek bank deposits, liabilities of private Greek banks.

The hierarchical nature of money[7] is reflected by the differentiation between the liabilities of public institutions and those of private institutions. During the time of the gold standard when gold functioned as the means of final payment with everything else merely a promise to pay, gold sat at the top of the hierarchy. For a fiat backed monetary system, the state issued currency is at the top of the hierarchy. It is money by decree which has value because the state is promising to enforce its exchangeability for goods and services, and its ability to store value is bestowed to it by law.

For the general public, the ability to make payments directly from their deposit accounts at par value with cash transactions implies that these are equivalent forms of money, where bank deposits are deemed a more secure

---

3 Kambas, M. & Gregorio, D. (2017), "Greece to further ease restrictions on individual bank withdrawals", *Reuters*, 04/08/2017, www.reuters.com/../greece-capital-controls/greece-to-further-ease-restrictions-on, accessed 02/02/2018.

4 Ashton, M. (2016), *What's wrong with money?: The biggest bubble of all*, New York, John Wiley & Sons.

5 Supra, note [4], Ashton (2016).

6 Bodenhorn, H. (2015), "Antebellum banking in the United States", *Economic History Association Paper*, www.eh.net/encyclopedia/antebellum-banking-in-the-united-states, accessed 02/02/2018.

7 Kelton, S.A. (1998), "The hierarchy of money", *Levy Economics Institute of Bard College Working Paper No. 231 April 1998*.

storage for cash. Banks, in contrast, see the same deposit account as their own ability or promise to pay the state issued currency. In practice, banks need to hold only a fraction of their customers' deposits in the form of that currency.

Thus far, cryptoassets are treated as a private digital money or a commodity depending on the jurisdiction concerned. Digital money exists only in digital form and does not have any physical equivalent in the real world, but it can have the key essential characteristics of conventional or fiat money, as it can be obtained, transferred or exchanged for another currency or used to transact in goods and services. Above all, it is not geographically restricted.[8] A cryptoasset is an asset that can be used as a means of exchange. It is deemed reliable as it is based on cryptography, which primarily seeks to make communications secure. Its mathematics based and algorithmic protocol ensures reliability. Cryptoassets use blockchain and a decentralised ledger that operates without any supervisory authority controls. They ergo differ from the conventional digital money in being decentralised and being anonymous in nature, but are transparent.[9]

Digital currencies are a non-physical representation of traditional fiat money. This contrasts with cryptoassets that represent a truly online assets that does not have value other than in its virtual world.[10] Notable examples of virtual currency are Pokecoins found in the Pokemon Go game, Facebook credit for in-platform game, and K Star within the Kardashian Game app. In each of these, traditional fiat currency in digital form must be exchanged for the virtual currency; but it is a one way flow as there is no easy way to exchange these items back to traditional fiat currency or used to buy things in the real world as their use and value reside within the platform they have been created in.

Digital currency by comparison is a digital representation of a physical asset such as money in a PayPal wallet that can be used to buy K Stars. Importantly, digital currency is owned and controlled by central banks and governments. Virtual currency, on the other hand, is decentralised and can be created by any corporate app maker or individual. It thus falls under a bespoke set of creation and usage rules external to national fiscal policy.

Bearing in mind the above, cryptocurrency regulatory policies would depend on how particular economies view it. Since the treatment of Bitcoin for now appears to differ between economies, their regulatory approach is likely to differ until perhaps when a more universal consensus is achieved. This chapter focuses on regulatory policies in the US, UK, Australia, Canada, the EU, and Switzerland for the reasons mentioned earlier.

---

8 Tar, A. (2017), "Digital currencies vs. cryptocurrencies", *Coin Telegraph*, 13/12/2017, www.cointelegraph.com/expllained/digital-currencies-vs-cryptocurrencies-explained, accessed 02/02/2018.

9 Annison, T. (2017), "Virtual vs digital currency-What's the difference?", *The Market Mogul*, 22/07/2017, www.themarketmogul.com/difference-virtual-digital-crypto-currencies, accessed 02/02/2018.

10 Supra, note [9], Annison (2017).

7.3 The US cryptoasset regulatory policy

It is still too soon to determine what the US Federal Reserve's regulatory attitude to cryptocurrencies will be. Their Vice Chair for Supervision recently stated that the central bank has no policy towards such regulation, but that it was worth further consideration.[11] The incoming new Federal Reserve Chair, Jerome Powell conceded that at some level of cryptocurrency volume traded, it could matter to monetary policy, but for now that position has not been reached.[12] Powell further maintained that technical issues with the technology remain, and governance and risks management could be critical. With regard to a central bank cryptocurrency, he argued that privacy issues could be a problem, but that private sector initiatives might do the job. The outgoing Chair, Janet Yellen said the equivalent at her departure conference. She added that they are highly speculative assets, not a stable store of value, does not constitute legal tender, and for now play a very small role in the payment system. She appears to downplay cryptocurrencies ability to impact on the wider financial markets.[13] In July 2019, Powell, however, told the US House Financial Services Committee that Facebook's push into finance posed many serious concerns, especially with regards to privacy, money laundering, and consumer protections.[14] The US Treasury Secretary and Congress raised similar concerns.

The US SEC has not approved any exchange-traded products such as the exchange-traded funds holding cryptocurrencies or related products for listing or trading,[15] and has not registered any ICOs.[16] Pertaining to ICOs, the SEC stated that whether or not a particular token or cryptocurrency falls foul of securities

---

11 Lam, E. (2018), "What the world's central banks are saying about Bitcoin", *Bloomberg*, 29/01/2018, www.bloomberg.com/news/articles/2017-12-15/what-the-world-s-central-banks-are-saying-about-cryptocurrencies, accessed 02/02/2018.

12 Supra, note [11], Lam (2018).

13 Disis, J. (2017), "Fed chair calls Bitcoin highly speculative", *CNN*, 13/12/2017, www.cnn.com/2017/12/13/investigating/Bitcoin-janet-yellen-federal../index.html, accessed 02/02/2018.

14 Barber, G. (2019), "The Fed chair says Facebook's Libra raises 'serious concerns'", *Wired*, 10/06/2019, www.wired.com/story/fed-chair-facebooks-libra-raises-seirous-concerns/, accessed 12/07/2019.

15 Graham, N. (2019), "VanEck-Cboe Bitcoin ETF on SEC's calendar", Eth News, 22/02/2019, www.ethnews.com/vaneck-cboe-Bitcoin-etf-on-secs-calendar, accessed 5/03/2019. The VanEck SolidX ETF recent submissions to the Cboe and the SEC are being awaited.Carrell, L. (2018), "What the US can learn from Sweden about how to launch a Bitcoin fund: The SEC has rejected all Bitcoin ETF filings to date: In Sweden, exchange-traded products tracking Bitcoin have been available for two years: The Swedish Bitcoin investments have attracted more than $1.3 billion, and their structure points to another way US ETF could get Bitcoin portfolios approved", *CNBC*, 17/01/2018, www.cnbc.com/../sec-frets-over-Bitcoin-etfs-but-swedes-figured-it-out-years-a, accessed 02/02/2018; De, N. (2018), "Bitcoin ETF proposals withdrawn after SEC pushback", *Coin Desk*, 10/01/2018, www.coindesk.com>US&Canada, accessed 02/02/2018.

16 Young, J. (2018), "SEC hints at tighter regulation for ICOs, smart policies for 'true cryptocurrencies'", *Coin Telegraph*, 09/02/2017, www.cointelegraph.com/../sec-hints-at-tigher-regulation-for-icos-smart-policies-for-, accessed 18/02/2018; Shin, L. (2017), "SEC Chairman statement on crypto and ICOs offers no bright line tests", Forbes, 11/12/2017.

laws depends on the facts and circumstances of each case.[17] According to Joshua Ashley Klayman, Chair of the Wall Street Blockchain Alliance's Legal Working Group[18] this means that existing facts and circumstances based enquiries and not bright line tests[19] should continue to apply to token sales. The SEC states that whether a particular investment transaction would constitute a security offering would depend on the case's facts and circumstances, including the economic realities of the transaction, regardless of the terminology or technology used.[20] So far, its enforcement actions against ICO sponsors included halting one,[21] and exposing two alleged frauds.[22] The SEC Chairman Jay Clayton has articulated concerns about market participants who extend customers credit and ICO gatekeepers like lawyers,[23] and celebrities who help to promote ICOs.[24] On 25th July 2017 the SEC issued an investor bulletin regarding ICOs, stating that these could be fair and lawful investment opportunities but might be used improperly.[25] This adds to their two earlier investor alerts,[26] one in 2013 and the other in 2014. In an effort to advanced ICO development, the SEC has provided a dedicated ICO guide.[27] The contents basically mirrored the SEC's ICO perspective discussed earlier. Jay Clayton in an earlier testimony to the US Senate hearing has stated that most ICOs he came across previously were essentially securities requiring SEC registration.[28] The SEC further mentioned that the delay thus far

---

17 SEC (2017), "SEC issues investigative report concluding DAO tokens, a digital asset, were securities: U.S. securities laws may apply to offers, sales and trading of interests in virtual organizations", *SEC Press Release 2017–131*, 25/07/2017, www.sec.gov/news-press-release/2017-131, accessed 02/02/2018; SEC (2017a), "Report of Investigation pursuant to section 21(a) of the, *SEC*, 25/07/2017, www.sec.gov/litigation/investreport/34-81207.pdf, accessed 02/02/2018. The SEC concluded that the DAO token is a security offering needed registration.

18 Supra, note [16], Shin (2017).

19 These are strictly interpreted legal or regulatory rules which have little or no scope for flexible interpretation.

20 Supra, note [17], SEC (2017a).

21 SEC (2018), "SEC halts alleged initial coin offering scam", *SEC Press Release 2018–8*, 30/01/2018, www.sec.gov/news/press-release/2018-8, accessed 02/02/2018.

22 SEC (2017), "SEC exposes two initial coin offerings purportedly backed by real estate and diamonds", *SEC Press Release 2017–85*, 29/09/2017, www.sec.gov/news/press-release/2017-186-0, accessed 02/02/2018. Here, the SEC charged REcoin, a cryptocurrency-backed real estate company and DRC World, a diamond company with fraud.

23 Zinman, D., Walker, J.Q., Myers, M.W. & O'Byrne, W. (2018), "SEC issues warning to lawyers on ICOs", *Big Law Business*, 23/02/2018, www.biglawbusiness.com/sec-issues-warning-to-lawyers-on-icos/, accessed 25/02/2018.

24 SEC (2017), "SEC statement urging caution around celebrity backed ICOs", *SEC Public Statement*, 01/11/2017, www.ec.gov/news/public../statement-potentially-unlawful-promotion-icos, accessed 02/02/2018.

25 SEC (2017), "Investor bulletin: Initial coin offerings", *Investor Alerts and Bulletins*, 25/07/2017, www.sec.gov/oiea/investor-alerts-and-bulletins/ib_coinofferings, accessed 02/02/2018.

26 Supra, note [17], SEC 2017a).

27 Suberg, W. (2019), "US SEC highlights dedicated ICO guide amid ongoing regulatory debate", *Coin Telegraph*, 11/02/2019, www.cointelegraph.com/news/us-sec-highlights-dedicated-ico-guide-amid-ongoing-regulatory-debate, accessed 5/03/2019.

28 Clayton, J. (2018), "Testimony on "Oversight of the U.S. Securities and Exchange Commission", *SEC's Chairman's Testimony before the U.S. Senate Committee on Banking, Housing, and Urban Affairs*, 11/12/2018, www.sec.gov/../testimony/testimony-oversoght-us-securities-and-exchange-co, accessed 5/03/2019.

in framing crypto regulation would provide more time for the industry to advance on its own.[29] As alluded to earlier, SEC surprised the crypto community with giving approval to Blockstack,[30] a startup exploring to design a new version of the Internet using blockchain that give users control over their personal data. Blockstack would be allowed to raised US$28 million via token sales that would comply with Regulation A+, which is applicable only to small companies.

The CFTC confirms that Bitcoin and other digital currencies are commodities covered by the Commodity Exchange Act (CEA), specifically under Section 1a (9) of the CEA. This defines commodity to include "... all services, rights, and interests in which contracts for future delivery are presently or in the future dealt in."[31] New York Law School Professor Houman Shadab, an expert in cryptographic technologies cautioned however, that the CFTC's oversight of the technology is limited to these applications, but this puts to rest any notion that all virtual currencies qualify as securities, as otherwise the SEC would have taken the action against Coinflip, a provider of ATM machines that enable people to trade cash to cryptocurrency and vice versa. This entity is said to have violated Section 4c of the CEA and Part 32 of the CFTC's regulations.[32]

Professor Shadab and co-authors Jerry Brito and Andrea Castillo of a legal paper on Bitcoin suggest that initial Bitcoin-related regulations have mainly focused on the application of "know your customer" anti-money laundering rules including consumer protection licensing on the intermediaries involved.[33] They expect the next wave of Bitcoin regulation will probably aim at financial instruments, including securities and derivatives as well as prediction markets and gambling. They also argue that following the Financial Crimes Enforcement Network's (FinCEN) approach, other financial regulators should consider exempting or excluding certain financial transactions denominated in Bitcoin from the full broadly in line with the scope of the regulations regarding the treatment of private securities offerings and forward contracts.[34] The US Treasury announced in November 2017 that it planned to review FinCEN's cryptocurrency practices as they relate to money laundering and terrorism financing risks. Shadab, Brito, and Castillo suggest also that to the extent that regulation and

---

29 Berman, A. (2019), "SEC 'crypto mon': Delay in crypto regulation may allow more freedom for technology" *Coin Telegraph*, 10/02/2019, www.cointelegraph.com/../sec-crypto-mom-delay-in-crypto-regulation-may-allow, accessed 5/03/2019.

30 Erlich, S. (2019), "Blockstack prepares for its true test following SEC approval to raise $28 million on a blockchain" *Forbes*, 16/07/2019, www.forbes.com/sites/stevenehrlich/2019/07/16/blockstack-prepares-for-its-true-test-following-sec-approval-to-raise-28-million-on-a-blockchain/, accessed 18/07/2019.

31 CFTC (2015), "Order instituting proceedings pursuant to sections 6 (c) and 6(d) of the Commodity Exchange Act, making findings and imposing remedial sanctions", *Order CFTC Docket No. 15–29*, 17/09/2015.

32 Rizzo, P. (2015), "CFTC ruling defines Bitcoin and digital currencies as commodities", *Coin Desk*, 18/09/2017, www.coindesk.com>Regulation, accessed 02/02/2018; Brito, J., Shadab, H. & Castillo, A. (Fall 2014), "Bitcoin financial regulation: Securities, Derivatives, Prediction markets, and gambling", *The Columbia Science & Technology Law Review"*, XVI (Fall 2014), pp. 144–221.

33 Supra, note [32], Brito, Shadab & Castillo (Fall 2014).

34 Supra, note [32], Brito, Shadab & Castillo (Fall 2014).

enforcement becomes more costly relative to their benefits, policymakers could consider and pursue strategies consistent with that new reality such as initiatives to foster resilience and adaptation.[35]

The CFTC therefore claims jurisdiction over fraud and manipulation involving Bitcoin traded in interstate commerce and the regulation of commodity futures linked directly to Bitcoin. The CFTC allowed the Chicago Mercantile Exchange (CME[36]) and Chicago Board Options Exchange (CBOE)[37] to launch Bitcoin futures. It also approved a platform for the trading and clearing of virtual currency derivatives for LedgerX,[38] a swap execution facility and derivatives clearing organisation.

The US IRS 2014 Virtual Currency Guidance treats Bitcoin as property for federal tax purposes. This means, a capital gain or loss should be recorded as if it were a transaction involving property. If held for resale it should be treated as an inventory and ergo an ordinary gain or loss recorded. When used for payment, Bitcoin should be treated like a foreign currency that must be converted and its fair exchange value verified on an exchange. The IRS thus appears to treat Bitcoin as a hybrid, depending on the manner of use or intention.[39]

The US is a federal republic comprising 50 states, a federal district (namely Washington, D.C.), five major territories, and various minor islands. Federal regulations and state-led legislation are in play where virtual currencies such as Bitcoin are concerned. Several US states plan to approve the acceptance and promotion of the use of Bitcoin and blockchain technology. Some states like Arizona[40] recognises smart contracts and allows payment of local taxes in Bitcoin, while Vermont[41] recognises blockchain as evidence, and Delaware authorises the registration of shares in Delaware[42] companies in blockchain form.

On the 14th July 2017, the National Conference of Commissioners on Uniform State Laws approved a model Act providing for the regulation of digital currency businesses at the state level.[43] The Uniform Law Commission (ULC)

---

35 Supra, note [32], Brito, Shadab & Castillo (Fall 2014).
36 Price, M. & McCrank, J. (2017), "U.S. regulator says it will allow CME Group, CBOE to list Bitcoin futures", *Reuters*, 01/12/2017, www.reuters.com/../Bitcoin/u-s-regulator-says-it-will-allow-cme-group-cboes-to, accessed 02/02/2018.
37 Supra, note [36], Price & McCrank (2017).
38 CFTC (2017), "CFTC grants DCO (Derivatives Clearing Organization) Registration to LedgerX LLC", *CFTC Press Release pr7592-17*, 24/07/2017.
39 IRS (2014), "IRS virtual currency guidance: Virtual currency is treated as property for U.S. federal tax purposes; General Rules for property transactions apply", IRS Notice IR-2014-36, 25/03/2014; IRS (2014a), "IRS Notice 2014–21", *IRS Notice 2014–21*, 14/04/2014.
40 Morris, D.Z. (2018), "Arizona state votes to accept tax payments in Bitcoin", *Fortune*, 10/02/2018, www.fortune.com>TheLedger>Bitcoin, accessed 18/02/2018; *Arizona Senate Bill 1091*, 20/02/2018.
41 Higgins, S. (2018), "Vermont could collect taxes in crypto under proposed law", Coin Desk, 08/01/2018.
42 Roberts, J.J. (2017), "Companies can put shareholders on a blockchain starting today", *Fortune*, 01/08/2017, www.fortune.com>Tech>Blockchain, accessed 02/02/2018.
43 Uniform Law Commission (ULC) (2017), "Regulation of Virtual Currency Businesses Act", *ULC*, 14/07/2017, www.uniformlaws.org/../regulation%20of%20virtual%20currencies/URVCBA_Final_, accessed 02/02/2018.

defines virtual currency as a form of electronic value that depends on the market. It is not backed by a government which means it lacks status as a legal tender. Interests in cryptocurrencies have grown because of the beliefs that they are relatively safe from hacking, often cheaper and faster and have finality of payment. Cryptocurrencies have legitimate purposes and can be bought, sold, and exchanged with other kinds of virtual currencies or fiat currencies. Responding to the absence of an overarching federal payments regulatory framework, state laws in play needed to be harmonised to the extent possible. The model Act as approved by the National Conference of Commissioners on Uniform State Laws covers licensing requirements, reciprocity, consumer protection, cybersecurity, anti-money laundering, and supervision of licensees.[44]

The above are regulatory initiatives at the federal and state levels in the US. Regulatory watchers are eagerly awaiting further initiatives from the SEC and the CFTC following the joint authorship of a paper[45] looking at cryptocurrency rules. The paper's key points are as follows:

(i) Transparency, investor protection and market integrity are critical to ensuring that innovation continues.

(ii) At the beginning of 2018, the collective market capitalisation of cryptocurrencies reached some US$700 billion. Direct participation by US investors in cryptocurrencies is significant, although the Federal Reserve takes the view that for now market participation in cryptocurrencies has yet to reach a level warranting a response. Cryptocurrencies' prices are set by trading on spot platforms. Many of these platforms are based offshore where none of them are registered with either the SEC or CFTC.

(iii) A cryptocurrency is initially designed as a payment facilitation alternative to fiat currencies, but it lacks the sovereign backing available to the latter. A cryptocurrency also lacks other fiat currencies' hallmarks such as governance standards, accountability, and oversight, and regular and reliable reporting of trading and related financial data. Importantly, cryptocurrencies are now being promoted, pursued, and traded as investment assets, with their purported utility as an efficient medium of exchange being a distant secondary characteristic.

(iv) Many of the internet based cryptocurrency trading platforms have registered as payment services and are not subject to direct oversight by the SEC or the CFTC. Both agencies welcome policy initiatives to review existing frameworks and ensure that they are efficient and effective for the digital era.

(v) For some areas the federal authority to police cryptocurrencies is clear. The Bank Secrecy Act and its implementing regulations set up federal

---

44 Supra, note [43], ULC (2017).
45 Clayton, J. & Giancarlo, J.C. (2018), "Regulators are looking at cryptocurrency: At the SEC and CFTC, we take our responsibility seriously" *The Wall Street Journal*, 24/01/2018.

anti-money laundering obligations that apply to most activity in the business of accepting and transmitting, selling, or storing cryptocurrencies. In other areas though federal authority obligations are unclear. Some would point to the absence of US and other government market regulations on the matter.

(vi) Two large CFTC regulated exchanges were permitted to self-certify and commence trading futures products without CFTC approval. They do now expend considerable time engaging with CFTC staff and have agreed to implement risk mitigation and oversight measures, including heightened margin requirements and a further requirement that the exchanges have information sharing agreements in place with underlying Bitcoin trading platforms. This enabled the CFTC to gain oversight over the US Bitcoin futures market and access to data that could facilitate the detection and pursuit of bad participants in underlying spot markets.

(vii) The SEC does not have direct oversight of transactions in currencies or commodities, though some products tagged as cryptocurrencies have the characteristics of securities. Where this is the case, the offer, sale, and trading of such products must be undertaken in compliance with existing securities laws. The SEC has shown that it will vigorously pursue those who seek to evade the registration, disclosure, and anti-fraud requirements of US securities laws. The SEC additionally monitors the cryptocurrency related activities of the market participants it regulates, including broker–dealers, investment advisers, and trading platforms.

(viii) The SEC is dedicating a significant portion of its resources to the ICO market. The SEC has made it clear through various announcements that federal securities laws apply irrespective of whether the offered security is tagged as coin, utility token rather than a stock, bond or investment contract. The SEC has cautioned market participants of its concerns over many examples of form being elevated over substance. The use of such form based arguments has deprived investors of mandatory protections.

(ix) The CFTC, SEC, together with other federal and state regulators and criminal authorities will continue to collaborate to ensure transparency and integrity in these markets, and importantly to deter and prosecute fraud and abuse.

(x) Going by past tech journeys in the US, distributed ledger technology is likely to be followed by many more major innovations, but the SEC, CFTC and others with similar obligations will not allow it or any other tech advancements to disrupt regulators' commitment to fair and sound markets.

(xi) The CFTC has also approved a platform for the trading, i.e., a swap execution facility and derivatives clearing organisation. It is now requesting industry feedback so as to better comprehend the markets, mechanics and technology for cryptoassets beyond Bitcoin and in particular the ether and Ethereum networks.[46]

At the 6th February 2018 Senate Hearing, the SEC provided the following testimony[47]:

(i) The SEC's mission is to protect investors, maintain fair, and orderly and efficient markets, and facilitate capital formation. These are achieved through the SEC's enforcement of the federal securities laws and oversight of the securities markets and their participants. The SEC regulates securities transactions and certain individuals and firms participating in the securities markets, but it does not have direct oversight of transactions in currencies or commodities including currency trading platforms.

(ii) The emerging cryptocurrency and ICO markets have grown rapidly and attracted significant capital from retail investors. These can benefit the economy and investors, but when laws are not adhered to, the risks to all investors are high. Such risks include risks caused by or related to poor, incorrect or non-existent disclosures, extreme price volatility, manipulation, frauds and thefts from hackings.

(iii) Regardless of the promise of technology, those investing in opportunities falling within the scope of federal securities laws deserve full protection under those laws. Enthusiasms get heighten by the "missing out" syndrome. Fraudsters and others prey on such enthusiasm.

(iv) The SEC together with the CFTC as federal market regulators are charged with establishing a regulatory environment for investors and market participants that fosters innovation, market integrity, and ultimately, confidence. The SEC in relation to cryptocurrencies, ICOs and related assets have taken various initiatives and actions. A cornerstone of such initiatives is to ensure that investors make informed decisions, a core principle of federal securities laws embodied in the SEC's registration requirements. Investors must note that for now (other than the July 2019 Blockstack case) no other ICOs have been registered with the SEC and the SEC also has not approved for listing and trading any exchange-traded products such as exchange-traded funds holding cryptocurrencies or other assets related to cryptocurrencies.

(v) These market products span national boundaries and significant trading may occur on systems and platforms outside the US, meaning that the funds involved might migrate quickly overseas without notice of investors' knowledge. This means risks could be amplified including

---

46 CFTC (2019), "CFTC's Technology Advisory Committee to meet on 27th March 2019", *CFTC Press* Release, 27/02/2019, www.cftc.gov/PressRoom/PressReleases/7880-19, accessed March 2019.

47 Written Testimony of Jay Clayton, Chairman of SEC Before the Senate Committee, Washington, D.C., 06/02/2018.

the risks that US market regulators such as the SEC and state securities regulators may not be able to effectively pursue participants who do not follow the rules or recover funds. There are also significant security risks arising from the loss of investment and personal information due to hacks of online trading platforms. Recent insights suggest that 10% of proceeds generated by ICOs or the equivalent of US$400 million has been lost to such attacks. A Japanese crypto market recently lost over US$500 million in an apparent hack of its systems. To deal with these and related risks, the SEC has issued investor alerts, bulletins and statements on ICO and crypto-related investments, the marketing of certain offerings and investments by celebrities, and others. Such warnings are not for undermining innovation, but for educating the general public to the effect that many promoters of ICOs and other cryptoassets are not complying with securities laws. These consequently suggest that the risks involved are significant.

(vi) Many cryptocurrencies are touted as having the same functions as fiat currencies, but without the backing of governments. Their beneficial features generally claim to include the ability to make transfers without an intermediary and without geographic limitations and with lower transactions costs compared to other forms of payment. Critics counterclaim that these benefits are unproven, while the other touted benefits such as the anonymity of buyers and sellers, and the absence of government oversight could also facilitate illicit trading. The proliferation and popularity of cryptocurrency markets gives rise to questions as to whether the country's historical regulatory approach could deal with such financial products that look and sound like conventional financial products. In reality, investors trading on such crypto platforms are not protected by market protections that they have taken for granted when transacting through brokers-dealers on registered exchanges or alternative trading systems like best executions, prohibitions on front running, short sale restrictions, and custody and capital requirements.

(vii) It seems that many US based cryptocurrency trading platforms have elected to be regulated as money transmission services. Such predominantly state regulated payment services are traditionally not subject to direct oversight by the SEC and CFTC. Traditionally, such money transfer services have not quoted prices or offered other services similar to securities, commodities, and currency exchanges. The current applicable regulatory framework for cryptocurrency trading was not designed with trading of the kind seen today. The SEC together with the CFTC are open to exploring with Congress as well as other federal and state agencies whether increased federal regulation of cryptocurrency trading platforms is necessary or appropriate.

(viii) Currently, the SEC is monitoring the crypto-related activities of the market participants it regulates, including brokers, dealers, investment advisers and trading platforms. Participants that allow for payments in cryptocurrencies, allow customers to purchase cryptocurrencies including on margin or otherwise use cryptocurrencies to facilitate securities transactions are expected to exercise caution including ensuring that their cryptocurrency activities are not undermining their anti-money laundering and know your customer obligations.

(ix) Financial products linked to digital assets including cryptocurrencies could be structured as securities products subject to federal securities laws even if the underlying cryptocurrencies are not themselves securities. Market participants have sought SEC approval for new products and services of this type that are focused on retail investors, including cryptocurrency linked exchange-traded funds. The SEC, however, needs to resolve various matters before permitting exchange-traded funds and other retail investor-oriented funds to invest in cryptocurrencies in a manner consistent with their obligations under federal securities laws. These include matters surrounding liquidity, valuation and custody of the funds' holdings, as well as creation, redemption and arbitrage in the exchange-traded funds area. Until such and other matters are resolved, the SEC is concerned whether it is appropriate for fund sponsors investing substantially in cryptocurrencies and related products, to register.

(x) Almost US$4 billion was raised through ICOs in 2017, but this could be an underestimate given that many ICOs fail after they are issued, which means potential losses could be far larger. All market participants need to know whether a particular coin or token is a security. The SEC's observations of many ICOs suggest that most involved the offer and sale of securities and directly suggest that the securities registration requirements should be met.

(xi) On 25th July 2017 the SEC issued a report regarding an ICO or DAO tokens, where the SEC concluded that these tokens were securities based on the basis of longstanding legal principles and hence subject to federal securities laws. This Report further clarified that issuers of distributed ledger or blockchain technology-based securities must register offers and sales of such securities, unless a valid exemption from registration applies. Platforms providing trading in such securities must too register with the SEC as national securities exchanges or operate pursuant to an exemption from such registration.

(xii) Various market professionals have touted the utility or voucher like characteristics of their proposed ICOs to differentiate them from conventional securities, by elevating form over substance. The SEC considers the rise of such form based arguments as a disturbing trend depriving investors of mandatory protections that clearly are required as a consequence of the structure of the transaction. The SEC cautions that merely calling a token a utility token or structuring it to provide some utility does not prevent the token from being a security. It is particularly more troubling when promoters of such offerings emphasise the secondary market trading potential of these tokens or the ability to sell them on an exchange for profit. This implies that prospective investors are being sold on the potential for tokens to increase in value and with the ability to lock in those increases by reselling the tokens on a secondary market or otherwise profit from the tokens based on the efforts of others. The SEC considers all these as key hallmarks of security and securities offerings.

(xiii) Gatekeepers and others including securities lawyers, accountants and consultants are cautioned to focus on their responsibilities, and be guided by the principal motivations for SEC registration, offering process and disclosure requirements, and investor protection. Engaging in the business of selling securities generally requires a licence. Experience suggest that excessive touting in thinly traded and volatile markets could be indicators of scalping, pump and dump, and other manipulations, and frauds. Those who operate systems and platforms that effect or facilitate transaction in crypto-products could be operating unregistered exchanges or broker–dealers in violation of the Securities Act of 1934. The SEC acknowledges the responsible steps taken by social media platforms such as Facebook to restrict the ability of users to promote ICOs and cryptoassets on their platforms. Nevertheless, subsequent to this banning of blockchain-related ads, the platform giant in May 2019 is reopening to ones for blockchain technology, industry news, education or event pertaining to cryptocurrency without the need for pre-approval.

(xiv) The SEC's Division of Enforcement set up a new Cyber Unit in September 2017 focusing on misconduct involving distributed ledger technology and ICOs, the dissemination of false information through electronic and social media, brokerage account takeovers, hacking to obtain nonpublic information, and threats to trading platforms. The Cyber Unit collaborates closely with the cross divisional Distributed Ledger Technology Working Group.

(xv) In September 2017 the SEC took enforcement proceedings against an individual for defrauding investors in a pair of ICOs purportedly backed by investments in real estate and diamonds, when neither companies had real operations. The SEC obtained an emergency asset freeze to halt an alleged ICO fraud operated by a recidivist securities law violator that purportedly raised up to $15 million from thousands of investors in August 2017. Another company in December 2017 halted its ICO after being told by the SEC that its ICO was an unregistered offering and sale of securities. More recently, the SEC halted an allegedly fraudulent ICO that targeted retail investors promoting what it claimed as the world's first decentralised bank. The SEC is also increasingly concerned with recent instances of public companies without a meaningful record in pursuing distributed ledger technology or blockchain technology changing their business models and names to reflect a focus on these without adequate disclosures to investors about their business model changes and the risks involved. The SEC is therefore now monitoring this closely, especially as to whether the disclosures comply with federal securities laws.

The CFTC Chairman submitted the following testimony to the Senate Banking Committee on the 6th February 2018[48]:

(i) Virtual currencies or cryptocurrencies are a digital representation of value that function as a medium of exchange, a unit of account, and/or store of value. Cryptocurrencies may be all things to all people, for some, potential riches through rapid increase in value; for others, the next big thing, a technological revolution, and an exorable value proposition; but for some others, a fraud, a new form of temptation and allure, and a way to take the money of the unsuspecting.

(ii) The total value of all outstanding Bitcoins on 5th February 2018 was about $130 billion against a Bitcoin price of $7,700. Bitcoin's market cap or even digital currencies' market cap of US$365 billion is relatively much smaller than the US stock market cap, or that for gold estimated at some $8 trillion. Yet, despite being a relatively small asset class, virtual currencies present novel challenges for regulators.

(iii) The CFTC's mission is to foster open, transparent, competitive and financially sound derivatives markets. By working to avoid systemic risks, the CFTC aims to protect market users and their funds, consumers, and the public from fraud, manipulation, and abusive practices related to derivatives, and products subject to the CEA.

(iv) The CFTC began with the oversight of agricultural commodities, but gradually its organised commodity future markets evolved to include those for energy and metals commodities collectively including crude oil, heating oil, gasoline, copper, gold, and silver. The CFTC also now oversees commodity futures markets for financial products such as interest rates, stock indexes, and foreign currency. The CEA's definition of "commodity" is broad. It can mean physical products such as agricultural products or natural resource like gold or oil, a currency or interest rate; or all services, rights, and interests in which contracts for future delivery are presently or in the future dealt with. The Dodd-Frank Act of 2010 empowers the CFTC to oversee most of the US swaps markets[49] in addition to exchange-traded futures markets.[50]

---

48 Written Testimony of J. Christopher Giancarlo, Chairman Commodities Futures Trading Commission (CFTC) Before the Senate Banking Committee, 06/02/2018.

49 These are markets made up of parties engaged in contracts for differences. These are contracts where the two parties pay or receive money from each other according to the amount by which a price or value has gone up or down. They are primarily used to hedge a financial risk.

50 A futures contract is one where a party pays or receives money according to whether an underlying asset goes up or down in value. These can be traded privately (OTC) or on an exchange, as though it were a share.

More than 90% of Fortune 500 companies use derivatives[51] to manage commercial or market risks in their worldwide business operations. When properly used derivatives serve the needs of society to help moderate price, supply, and other commercial risks to free up capital for economic growth.

(v) The CFTC regulates derivatives market participants and activities. It oversees a variety of individuals and organisations. These include swap execution facilities, futures commission merchants, commodity pool operators, and other entities. The CFTC prosecutes derivative market frauds and manipulations, including misconducts in underlying spot markets for commodities. In 2015 the CFTC stipulated that cryptocurrencies such as Bitcoin met the definition of "commodity" under the CEA. However, the CFTC does not have regulatory jurisdiction under the CEA over the markets or platforms undertaking cash or spot transactions in virtual currencies or other commodities or over participants in such platforms. Current US laws in fact do not provide any US federal regulator with such regulatory oversight authority over spot[52] virtual currency platforms operating in the US or abroad. Nevertheless, the CFTC does have the jurisdiction to enforce civil enforcement actions concerning fraud and market manipulation in virtual currency derivatives markets, and in underlying virtual currency spot markets through subpoena and other investigative powers. The CFTC in contrast to the spot markets have both regulatory and enforcement powers under the CEAs over derivatives on virtual currencies traded in the US. For derivatives on virtual currencies traded in US markets, the CFTC conducts comprehensive regulatory oversight, including imposing registration requirements and compliance with a full range of requirements for trade practice and market surveillance, reporting and monitoring standards for conduct, capital requirements, and platforms and systems safeguards.

(vi) The CFTC has been direct in asserting its area of statutory jurisdiction concerning virtual currencies derivatives. In 2015, the CFTC took enforcement action to prohibit wash trading[53] and prearranged trades on a virtual currency derivatives platform. A year later, the CFTC took action against a Bitcoin futures exchange operating in the US that failed to register with it. In 2017, the CFTC issued proposed guidance on what a derivative market is, and what is a spot market in the virtual currency context. The CFTC also issued warnings about valuations

---

51 A generic term to cover futures, options and contracts for differences which are all contracts where parties can trade against the change in value of an underlying asset, currency or interest rate.
52 The current price for an asset, i.e., one quoted for the next 48 hours as opposed to a price for future delivery.
53 A "wash trade" is an artificial trading activity where a participant simultaneously buys and sells the same investment to create an artificial price. In some states, e.g., the US, the UK, the EU and Hong Kong this will amount to market manipulation.

(vii) and volatility in spot virtual currency markets, besides launching an unprecedented consumer education effort.

(vii) The CFTC has been especially assertive of its enforcement jurisdiction over virtual currencies. Its virtual currency enforcement task force garners and deploys relevant expertise in this evolving asset class; and shares information with counterparts at the SEC with similar virtual currency expertise. The CFTC took enforcement action against a virtual currency Ponzi scheme. Between January and February 2018, the CFTC filed a series of civil enforcement actions against perpetrators of fraud, market manipulation, and disruptive trading involving virtual currency. These include My Big Coin Pay Inc., The Entrepreneurs Headquarters Limited, and Coin Drop Markets.

(viii) As for Bitcoin futures, as of 2nd February 2018, the open interest at CME of 6,695 Bitcoin and 6,695 Bitcoins at CBOE Futures Exchange are relatively small. At a price of around $7,700 per Bitcoin, the notional value came to about $94 million. By comparison, the notional amount of the open interest in CME's WTI crude oil futures was more than a thousand times bigger, or about US$170 billion as of 2nd February 2018, while the notional amount represented by the open interest of Comex gold futures was about $74 billion.

(ix) Futures exchanges may self-certify new products on 24-hour notice prior to trading under CEA and CFTC regulations and related guidance. This is to enable futures exchanges to quickly bring new products to the marketplace. Prior to their certifying and launching of Bitcoin futures in December 2017, both the CME and CBOE had numerous discussions and exchange numerous draft product terms and conditions with CFTC over some months. CFTC staff also secured voluntary co-operation of CME and CBOE with a set of enhanced monitoring and risk management steps.

(x) Subsequent to the launch of Bitcoin futures, criticisms were directed at the self-certification process by market participants. They questioned why the CFTC did not hold public hearings prior to the launch. However, the CFTC focus is on how the futures contract and cash settlement indices are design to bar manipulation and the appropriate level of contract margining to meet CEA and CFTC regulations; rather than seeking to solicit and address stakeholder concerns in new product self-certification, appropriately the function of the futures exchanges and futures clearinghouses. The CFTC's response to the self-certification of Bitcoin futures has been a balance one that culminated in the world's first federally regulated Bitcoin futures market. Blocking self-certification would not have stopped the rise of Bitcoin or other virtual currencies. It would instead ensure that virtual currency spot markets continue to operate without effective and data enabled federal regulatory surveillance for fraud and manipulation.

(xi) The CFTC has sufficient authority under the CEA to protect investors in virtual currency derivatives. With regards to virtual currency spot markets, the CFTC has only enforcement jurisdiction to investigate, and where appropriate conduct civil enforcement actions against fraud and manipulation. Any extension of the CFTC's regulatory authority to virtual currency spot market would require statutory amendment of the Commodity Exchange Act.

(xii) The CFTC believes that the responsible regulatory response to virtual currencies must begin with consumer education. The CFTC has produced an information primer on virtual currencies, consumer and market advisories on Bitcoin investing and other virtual currencies, a dedicated CFTC Bitcoin webpage, several podcasts regarding virtual currencies and underlying technology, the weekly publication of Bitcoin futures, and analysis of Bitcoin spot market data. CFTC's Office of Consumer Education and Outreach (OCEO) engages actively with responsible outside partners to educate consumers on Bitcoin and other virtual currencies. The OCEO is in working partnership with the Consumer Finance Protection Bureau, the American Association of Retired Persons, the North American Securities Administrators Association (NASAA), the National Attorneys General Training and Research Institute and the Federal Reserve Bank of Chicago.

(xiii) The CFTC's enforcement jurisdiction over virtual currencies is not exclusive. This means that the US approach to oversight of virtual currencies is evolving into a multifaceted, multi-regulatory approach that includes the SEC, State Banking Regulators, the IRA, and the Treasury's Financial Crimes Enforcement Network (FinCEN). The CFTC also actively communicates its approach to virtual currencies with other federal regulators including the Federal Bureau of Investigation, the Justice Department and the Financial Stability Oversight Council. Additionally, the CFTC is in communication with overseas regulatory counterparts through bilateral discussions and in meetings of the Financial Stability Board and the IOSCO.

(xiv) DLT has the potential to enhance economic efficiency, mitigate centralised systemic risk, defend against fraudulent activity and improve data quality and governance. It is also likely to have a wide and lasting impact on global financial markets in payments, banking, securities settlement, title recording, cyber security, and trade reporting and analysis. When attached to virtual currencies, it aims to serve as a new store of value, facilitate secure payments, enable asset transfers, and power new applications.

(xv) Distributed ledger technology might enable financial market participants to manage the significant operational, transactional, and capital complexities brought about by the many mandates, regulations and capital requirements stipulated by regulators in the US and elsewhere in the context of financial stress. Distributed Ledger technology could, according to one estimate, eventually enable financial institutions to save some $20 billion in infrastructure and operational costs annually. Blockchain could also cut trading settlement costs by a third or some $16 billion annually, and trim capital requirements by some $120 billion. Migrating from systems of record at the firm level to an authoritative system of record at the market level is an enormous opportunity to improve existing market infrastructure. Beyond financial services, distributed ledger technology can benefit international trade, to charitable initiatives, and social services. Other distributed ledger technology applications include legal records management, inventory control and logistics, charitable donation tracking and confirmation, voting security and human refugee identification and relocation.

(xvi) The "do no harm" approach for the development of the internet over the last two decades is well recognised, as is the fact that the enlightened regulatory underpinning of the internet helped bring about many profound changes to society. It was without doubt the right approach for the development of the internet and the rest is history. This could also be the right approach for distributed ledger technology. Virtual currencies nevertheless require more attentive regulatory oversight in key areas, especially to the extent that retail investors are attracted.

(xvii) The risks of cryptocurrencies and ICOs to all investors are very high and caution is merited. A key concern is whether the historic approach now in play for the regulation of currency transactions is suitable for the cryptocurrency markets.

(xviii) The CFTC together with the SEC would support policy initiatives to review existing frameworks and ensure that they are effective and efficient for the digital era. Considerations should be given to shortcomings of the current approach of state by state money transmitter licensures that leaves gaps in protection for virtual currency traders and investors. Proposed federal regulation of virtual currency platforms would need to adjust to the risks posed by relevant trading activity, and enhance the efforts to prosecute fraud and manipulation. Suitable federal regulatory oversight could include data reporting, capital requirements, cyber security standards, measures to prevent fraud and price manipulation, and anti-money laundering and know your customer protections. The resulting rationalised federal framework may be more effective and efficient in ensuring the integrity of the underlying markets.

Interestingly, previous announcements by the SEC and CFTC on Fintech financial products gave the message of the intention to apply a light touch approach to provide space for experimentation and innovation. Both these testimonies give a clear indication that the SEC and CFTC intend to facilitate the expansion of federal oversight on primary and secondary cryptocurrency markets. It is likely that the sway is prompted by the extreme price volatility of cryptocurrencies, the expansive participation of retail investors, the significant thefts and hackings of Bitcoins in cryptocurrency exchanges across the world, perceived increase Bitcoin use in illicit activities, signals of failing economies relying on cryptocurrencies, the avoidance of sanctions and other challenges; as well as the periodic surging of cryptocurrency capitalisation suggesting that its potential evolution into a mainstream asset class that might pose a threat to sovereign fiat currencies.

7.4 Potential cryptoasset regulation in the US

The price volatility of cryptocurrencies, together with the risk of theft for retail investors and allegations of price manipulation, as well as the lack of regulatory oversight, prompted regulatory intervention in the US. The next step was the Cryptocurrency Senate Hearings of February 2018. There had been a previous session in 2013, but that ended with cryptocurrencies unregulated because of the strong belief in the potential of their blockchain technology.

The Senate cryptocurrency hearings essentially show that the SEC views ICOs as being similar in nature to the securities that it traditionally polices, while the CFTC sees markets for cryptocurrencies as commodities and therefore subject to its jurisdiction. This is hardly surprising as each organisation is seeking to strengthen its own regulatory control. Although the basic categorisation scheme is clear: ICO equals SEC regulation and the quasi-derivative nature of cryptocurrencies that of the CFTC, detailed practical criteria for differentiating between which products fall into which category was not discussed in the hearing. It seems that the general rule for differentiating a security from a commodity focuses on substance over form analysis. Thus, according to the SEC, simply describing something as a currency or a currency-based product does not mean that it is not a security. The hearing suggests that the SEC views ICO regulation from a different vantage point compared to that of the CFTC. These deep-seated philosophical differences[54] shape, or are reflective of an internal consensus pertaining to policy at the respective institutions and could likely have major outcomes for the markets wherein these different products are traded.

The differing perceptions of intrinsic value inevitably impact on peoples' assessment of whether cryptocurrencies as a whole are a fundamentally positive or negative phenomenon, and hence whether they should be regulated with a light or heavy touch.[55] The SEC's view essentially is that although there is some public pressure for a cryptocurrency based on international exchange, it is not yet seeing those benefits manifesting themselves in the market place. The CFTC though points out that economists posit that there is a relationship between

---

54 Felsenthal, D. & Overall, J. (2018), "A tale of two cities: SEC & CFTC Heads testify before the Senate Banking Committee", *Crowdfund Insider*, 07/02/2018, www.crowdfundinsider.com/2018/02/128129-tale-two-cities-see-heads-testify-senate-banking-committee/?utm_source=Auto, accessed 18/02/2018.

55 Supra, note [54], Felsenthal & Overall (2018).

Bitcoin value and the difficulty or cost of mining, and that there is thus a floor price where the level set is above zero.

The SEC sees ICOs as a new form of an existing concept, ie, that tokens issued in ICOs constitute securities under existing federal securities laws and would not require Congress to grant new powers to the SEC via new legislation as the Commission already possesses the authority to regulate them under existing laws. To date, the SEC sees most ICOs as securities. The SEC considers the use of blockchain technology in ICOs to be an example of old wine in new bottles, or a cosmetic change involving novel facts that does not affect the legal substance of an ICO transaction, meaning a typical security.[56] Though market participants and certain gatekeepers such as securities lawyers and accountants frequently say that the law is not clear, the SEC does not align with this view as most ICOs it comes across is a security.

As ICO's were not being registered with the SEC, the implication is that the typical ICO is illegal under federal securities laws, unless a registration exemption applies. That would however require marketing restrictions that ICOs do not to date appear to have been observing. Legally, failure to register by itself leaves the issuer open for the SEC to pursue an enforcement action against them, thereby imposing liability for registration failures as reliance on affirmative fraud would not be necessary.[57] This seems to be the consequence of the SEC's *Munchee* enforcement action in December 2017. Here, despite the absence of fraud the SEC halted the ICO because of the issuer's failure to register.[58] Such registration failure could also result in liability for intermediaries who facilitated an ICO, but fail to register with and be supervised by the SEC as securities exchange or broker–dealers. Given that virtually all ICOs to date have very probably been conducted illegally, when asked whether it intends to pursue enforcement action against already completed ICOs, the SEC has said that it counted on gatekeepers to do their job.[59] The SEC have now issued a string of subpoenas against ICO offerors who had not made sure that only accredited investors bought them.[60] It is therefore highly likely that ICOs will have to start functioning as a normal part of the shares and bonds issuance regime.

The CFTC stance differs philosophically from the SEC in three ways.[61] Firstly, the CFTC believes that cryptocurrencies are CFTC jurisdictional commodities which constitute a fundamentally new asset class. Cryptocurrencies are not simply old wine in new bottles, but instead a commodity unlike any the

---

56 Supra, note [54], Felsenthal, D. & Overall, J. (2018),.
57 Supra, note [54], Felsenthal & Overall (2018).
58 SEC (2017), "Company halts ICO after SEC raises registration concerns", *SEC Press Release* 2017–227, 11/12/2017; SEC Order, Munchee Inc., Release No. 10,445/December 11,2017, Administrative Proceeding File No. 3–18,304, www.sec.gov/litigation/admin/2017/33-10445.pdf, accessed 02/02/2018.
59 Supra, note [54], Felsenthal & Overall (2018).
60 https://hackernoon.com/cryptocurrency-regulation-update-november-2018-d9b17837aeec, accessed 26/02/2019.
61 Supra, note [54], Felsenthal & Overall (2018).

CFTC has dealt with in the past, and hence a genuinely new phenomenon not just cosmetically but substantively.

Secondly, the CFTC is of the opinion that because Bitcoin and other virtual currencies are a genuinely new economic and financial phenomenon, their characteristics are not captured by and not subject to existing law. Since existing laws were not designed with cryptocurrencies' unique properties in mind, the jurisdictional deficit applies not just to the CFTC, but to all federal regulatory agencies as well.[62] The CFCT believes that a change in the law is needed for it to be able to comprehensively regulate the cryptocurrency spot markets where trades are for prompt delivery the same way that it regulates the cryptocurrency derivatives market where trades are made for future delivery or may never result in physical delivery, settling instead by cash or netting. Pertaining to the derivatives markets, the CFTC can impose liability on entities for failing to register or to obey business conduct requirements. In the spot markets, the CFTC is restricted to policing fraud and manipulation and this impacts on the kinds of enforcement actions the CFTC can take. This view implicitly recognises that such markets are not presently illegal under existing laws. If new laws are required to regulate them, then the applicable law currently in effect could not declare them wholly illegal.[63]

Thirdly, the CFTC holds that the optimal regulatory regime for spot markets for cryptocurrencies is one involving the lightest possible regulatory touch to avoid stifling the market for digital assets through excessive regulation.[64] Unlike the SEC's preference for declaring virtually the entire ICO market illegal and the apparent focus on policing registration and marketing violations whenever taking place even in the absence of fraud, the CFTC believes that a lighter touch approach is appropriate though with enhanced protections for retail investors for blockchain based assets. This resembles the laissez faire attitude adopted during the birth of the internet. It may also reflect the ongoing turf war which arises from time to time between the two institutions.

Following the Senate Banking Committee hearing, there is an inter-agency conferral between the CFTC, SEC, Federal Reserve, Treasury, IRS and state banking regulators, to identify gaps in their respective regulatory frameworks and whether new legislation is needed. Another observation of the Senate Cryptocurrency Hearing is the open admission by the CFTC that the cryptocurrency hearings are impacting on those currencies price movements. The prices of Bitcoin and other cryptocurrencies rose during and after the Senate Hearing, reflecting the widespread sense that it brought the asset class one step closer to mainstream adoption, even if legal strategies around token issuance may have to shift. It suggests that the industry is finding ways of meeting the demand from both the general public and Wall Street.[65] Meanwhile, rumours have been

---

62 Supra, note [54], Felsenthal & Overall (2018).
63 Supra, note [54], Felsenthal & Overall (2018).
64 Supra, note [54], Felsenthal & Overall (2018).
65 Eha, B.P. (2018), "Crypto exchanges welcome regulators as they woo institutional clients", *American Banker*, 21/02/2018, www.americanbanker.com/news/crypto-exchanges-welcome-regulaors-to-attract-institutional-clients, accessed 25/02/2018.

circulating in the media that US regulators have sent a number of subpoenas to firms they suspect might be violating securities laws.

A review of federal and state laws that might impact on cryptocurrencies is necessary so as to ascertain whether they could be regulated under existing provisions. Foremost, as cryptocurrencies operate as an alternative currency with individual users, banking concepts and regulations appear feasible. There are close similarities between some cryptocurrencies such as Bitcoin and money transmission services as defined under federal and state laws, electronic fund transfers as dictated by the Federal Reserve Board's Regulation E, and the applicability of US legal tender laws with respect to state contract law.[66]

Foremost, people use cryptocurrencies as a banking device or pseudo-bank account, while money under modern banking times are issued by a central bank and/or created by a central bank via monetary policies or by licensed commercial banks. The general consensus is that a bank is firstly a financial establishment for the deposit, loan, exchange, or issue of money and for the transmission of funds. Secondly, under securities laws, a bank includes any financial institution whether or not incorporated, doing business under federal or state law if a substantial portion of the institution's business consist of receiving deposits or exercising fiduciary powers equivalent to those permitted to national banks.[67] Thirdly, the business of banking includes discounting and negotiating promissory notes, drafts, bills of exchange, and other evidences of debt, receiving deposits, buying and selling exchange, coin and bullion, loaning money on personal security, and obtaining, issuing, and circulating notes.[68]

The key concept of a bank under US federal and state law is that it is an institution, it accepts deposits, and provides loans. A cryptocurrency, for example Bitcoin has to demonstrate these three key characteristics to fall under these general requirements of a bank. Bitcoin is not an institution, business, or person but primarily a collection of users making use of a payment mechanism. This makes Bitcoin simply a medium of exchange. The Federal Reserve, being in charge of the US dollar, conducts the monetary policy for the country. In contrast Bitcoin conducts its monetary policy through software without the intervention of a central institution. Its value is secured by users and not by government, business or any kind of institution. When it comes to accepting deposits, the Bitcoin software just distributes currency. Bitcoin is stored in personal computers or in an online wallet, not on the Bitcoin network, and hence the notion of using Bitcoin as a kind of offshore bank account is unworkable. Bitcoin is acquired through mining, exchange or by purchase and not through loan making. Taking these three Bitcoin characteristics into consideration, it is likely that federal and state banking laws are inapplicable to Bitcoin and other cryptocurrencies.

---

66 Kaplanov, N.M. (2012), "Nerdy money: Bitcoin, the private digital currency, and the case against its regulation", *Temple University Legal Studies Research Paper*, 22/07/2012.
67 *Black's Law Dictionary (2014)*, Tenth Edition, Eagan, Thomson West.
68 12 U.S.C. S.24 (West Supp. 2010).

Bitcoin transfers virtual currency between parties through a system managed by other individual users who create blocks and blockchains necessary to carry out the transfer.[69] This could suggest that Bitcoin resembles a money transmitting service which is regulated by the US Treasury and individual states,[70] even though Bitcoin is unlikely to be a money transmitter under federal laws or the US Code. The determination of a money transmission service is similar to a money transmission business but is more loosely defined and a subject of facts and circumstances. Money transmission services are any operation accepting currency or funds for transmission to another place. A money transmission service as drawn from statutes and case laws include a person or business that controls an operation engaging in funds transfers or other value substituting for currency, frequently for profits that require licensing under state law. As such, Bitcoin technology is unlikely to fall within this take on money transmitter services, as Bitcoin is not a legal entity nor is it operated for profit. However, Bitcoin users controlling and operating the Bitcoin software could fall within the regulator's definition of a person who transfers value that substitutes for currency. Bitcoin miners though could potentially satisfy the "for profit on a frequent basis" criterion, as they are rewarded with Bitcoins for their efforts. This is however arguable as they are not directly transferring payments for specific individuals or in charge of an operation transferring funds for others like conventional money transmission service.

The Financial Crimes Enforcement Network (FinCEN) announced on 8th March 2013 that it would make no distinction between fiat currency and cryptocurrencies such as Bitcoin for the purpose of the money transmission laws.[71] This means that individuals and businesses merely exchanging for goods and services and vice versa are not money transmitters. Businesses that accept cryptocurrency from one person and send it to another or back to the same person are money transmitters and are not exempt from money transmission regulation simply because they do not deal in fiat currencies. Also, any business that exchanges fiat currencies for one kind of cryptocurrency to another is a money transmitter. Payment processors who accept cryptocurrency from a merchant's customers and pass fiat currencies to the merchants are usually money transmitters.

As FinCEN regulates money transmitters in accordance with the Bank Secrecy Act, which includes elements of the Patriot Act, money transmitters must consequently register with FinCEN, undergo initial risk assessment and adopt a written anti-money laundering policy based on those risks. As such, money transmitters have to appoint a qualified compliance officer, train

---

69 Vigna, P. & Casey, M.J. (2015), Cryptocurrency: How Bitcoin and digital money are challenging the global economic order, London, The Bodley Head.

70 Santori, M. (2015), "What is money transmission and why does it matter?: Attorney Marco Santori explains how the current state of money transmission laws in the US can affect digital currency startups", *Coin Center*, 07/04/2015, www.coincenter.org/entry/what-is-money-transmission-and-why-does-it-matter, accessed 02/02/2018.

71 FinCEN (2017), "Important information for Money Services Businesses (MSB)", FinCEN, 11/02/2017, www.fincen.gov/resources/financial-institutions/money-services-businesses, accessed 02/02/2018.

employees on compliance procedures, and undergo regular testing and review of their business's compliance programme.[72]

While federal law requires mere registration, state law requires licensure, but thus far no state laws mention cryptocurrencies. Some states like Texas and Kansas have published official guidance on whether and how their laws apply to digital currency businesses. The New York State Department of Financial Services (NYSDFS) released its final BitLicense rules on 3rd June 2017. The NYSDFS emphasises that the regulations are not targeted at passive investors, and companies also would not need prior approval from NYSDFS for every new round of venture capital financing. In general, a company would only need prior approval if the investor wants to direct management and policies of the firm as a controlled person. Cryptocurrency businesses only need to obtain prior approval from the NYSDFS for any new material product, service or activity, rather than for all new products, services or activities. The final rules eliminate any obligation on them to file currency transaction reports and suspicious activity reports with the NYSDFS, where such reports must already be submitted to the federal governments.

While FinCEN sees itself as money laundering preventers, state regulators see themselves as consumer protectors. This explains why the state licence application process seeks to ensure safety, soundness, and solvency; and includes a heightened kind of substantial background check and substantial financial reporting obligations.[73]

Financial services in the US is heavily regulated with regulations written for business models that have not significantly altered for decades. There arise two real world consequences because of this. First, some new business models that could significantly improve businesses either move offshore to innovate elsewhere or simply quit and move on to a different product. For those businesses able to fit into the existing regulations, the costs of determining how these obligations apply combine with the ongoing compliance costs acts as a barrier to entry for bootstrapped virtual currency software companies. Thus, the stifling of innovation becomes the result of the policy.[74]

The exchange of cryptocurrency might constitute an electronic funds transfer since they function as a medium of online payment, and this is regulated by the Federal Reserve under the Electronic Fund Transfer Act of 1978 (EFTA). The aim of EFTA is to provide a basic framework establishing the rights, liabilities and responsibilities of participants in electronic fund transfer systems.[75] The statute seeks to provide a framework of law regulating the rights of consumers against financial institutions in electronic funds transfers,[76] and to help bring certainty to an era of banking which was fast becoming faceless.[77]

---

72 Supra, note [70], Santori (2015).
73 Supra, note [70], Santori (2015).
74 Supra, note [70], Santori (2015).
75 15 U.S.C. SS. 1601–1693 (West 2006).
76 Shawmut Worcester County Bank v. First American Bank & Trust, 731 F. Supp. 57, 61 (D. Mass. 1990).
77 Spain v. Union Trust, 674 F. Supp. 1496, 1500 (D. Conn. 1987).

Under the EFTA, an electronic fund transfer includes any transfer of funds, other than a transaction originated by cheque, draft, or similar paper instrument, which is initiated through an electronic terminal, telephone instruments, or computer, or magnetic tapes, so as to order, instruct, or authorise a financial institution to debit or credit an account.[78] Under the EFTA, a financial institution includes a state or national bank, savings and loan association, mutual savings bank, a state or federal credit union, or any other person who directly or indirectly holds an account belonging to a customer.[79] The regulations implementing EFTA also includes access devices and electronic fund transfers into their definition of financial institutions.[80] For Bitcoin to come within the Regulation E regulatory framework, Bitcoin has to be an institution conducting electronic funds transfers. While the Bitcoin software would not qualify as a financial institution under Regulation E as it is not a legally cognisable entity, a digital wallet company though might.

Other than financial regulatory provisions as discussed above, there are other legal concerns such as whether the use of Bitcoin causes any contractual problems, whether Bitcoin resembles complementary currencies under the law, or if securities provisions prohibit the use of Bitcoin. In respect of these, there are some useful illustrations.[81] A fiat currency such as the US dollar is legal tender for all debts, public charges, taxes, and dues. If a cryptocurrency is not deemed to be a currency, then any sale of a good or services for Bitcoins would essentially be a barter contract. Barter contracts are covered under the Uniform Commercial Code (UCC).[82]

Other equivalent examples are community currencies which are notes issued by a nongovernmental group within a confined locality that have a monetary value designed to develop local economies. This medium of exchange is then accepted for goods and services within the community according to the parameter of the system. The Time Dollar system,[83] and the Ithaca HOURS[84] are good examples of these. These could be considered as bills of credit. The US constitution prohibits states from issuing these, but the prohibition does not apply to private persons or private partnership, or private corporations. The creator of Liberty Dollar was convicted not because he tried to create a new form of currency, but that he violated the rules by coining real metal coins and passing them off as a US currency.

Since cryptocurrencies are purchased and exchanged in person, on online exchanges and over the internet and are interpreted variously as a currency,

---

78 15 U.S.C. S.1693(a)(6).
79 15 U.S.C. S. 1693a.
80 12 C.F.R. S. 205.2(i) (2010).
81 Supra, note [66], Kaplanov (2012).
82 Lord, R. A. (1989), *Williston on contracts*, Eagan, Thomson Reuters.
83 Cahn, E.S. (2017), "Time dollars: A new currency in community building", *Time Bank*, September 2017, www.tbmw.org/tag/time-dollar/, accessed 02/02/2018.
84 Ellis, B. (2012), "Funny money? 11 local currencies", *CNN Money*, 27/01/2012, www.cnn.com/galleries/2012/pf/1201/gallery.community-currencies/3.html, accessed 02/02/2018.

an investment, or even a future contract, they could likewise be regulated in a variety of manner. When looking for the meaning and scope of "security" in the Securities Act 1934, form should be disregarded for substance and the stress should be on economic reality.[85] This principle has been applied in many areas within securities by the courts thereby providing a foundational rationale to approaching financial regulation.[86]

Where cryptocurrencies are deemed as a security, then the SEC has wide powers to regulate or even prohibit the exchange of Bitcoins. The US Supreme Court defined the basic test applied to distinguish an investment contract falling within the definition of a security from a traditional commercial transaction. The Howey test to determine the presence or absence of an investment contract under the securities statutes is whether the scheme involves an investment of money in a common enterprise with profits to come solely from the efforts of others.[87] Primarily, the distinction is whether the investors are attracted solely by the prospects of a return on their investment. The court also created a family resemblance test in *Reeves v. Ernst & Young*,[88] where it was held that a note is presumptively assumed to be a security and thus regulated under federal law so long as it does not meet one of the Reeves' mitigating factors. As cryptocurrencies are created to be a kind of online currency, it might be best to treat them as such in the securities realm. Foreign currencies are generally not viewed as a security, and there are precedents providing an exception for currency trading under the definition of security as alluded to earlier in the *Reeves v. Ernst & Young* case. A cryptocurrency is not a foreign currency in the formal sense, since it is not designed or maintained by a foreign government. It does however function like a national currency by facilitating exchange and serving as a store of value in the marketplace.

Cryptocurrencies could also be classified as commodities and its exchange could therefore be a commodity futures contract. The definition of a commodity futures contract, however, is not provided for in the CEA or in CFTC regulations. The CES nevertheless negatively define "future delivery" to not include any sale of any commodity for deferred shipment or delivery. The Supreme Court held in Dunn v. Commodity Futures Trading Commission that futures contracts are agreements to buy or sell a specified quantity of a commodity at a particular price for delivery at set future dates and these are governed by the CFTC.[89] However, even though commodity futures trading is regulated by the CFTC and must be done in compliance with market rules on a designated exchange, the CEA does not include an agreement, contract or transaction in foreign currency. This means that though the CFTC does have authority to regulate any commodity contracts involving futures contracts, where contracts involving

---

85 *Tcherepnin v. Knight*, 389 U.S. 332, 336 (1967) (citing S.E.C. v. W.J. Howey Co., 328 U.S. 293, 298 (1946).
86 *United Hous. Found., Inc. v. Forman*, 412 U.S. 837, 838 (1975).
87 *Securities & Exchange Commission v. W.J. Howey Co*. 328 U.S. 293 (1946).
88 *Reeves v. Ernst & Young* 494 U.S. 56,57 (1990).
89 *Dunn v. Commodity Futures Trading Commission*, 519 U.S. 465 (1997).

foreign currency are concerned, the CFTC only maintains a limited regulator capacity compared with other commodities.

Whilst cryptocurrencies are technically not a foreign currency, they function in the same manner. The Securities Exchange Act of 1934 exempts currencies from its definition of a security, but it is generally understood that currency is not a security. Market participants that conduct a sufficient amount of currency trading are nevertheless permitted to do so off market, but may be required to register with the CFTC.[90]

Overall, under US law and regulation, Congress and the Executive have the ability to prohibit or limit the use of cryptocurrencies in the markets. However, they fall within a grey area under US law in which they are not necessarily outlawed but still give rise to contractual obligations. Hence, they could be treated as a local or community currency under the law; receiving full authority as a medium of exchange under contract law; requiring taxation on income; and not implicating securities regulations.

The position at case law unfortunately remains confused and so far, at least, is limited to decisions in the lower courts. In the *SEC v Trenton T Shavers and Bitcoin Savings and Trust Co*,[91] Texas state Amos L Mazzant said "It is clear that Bitcoin can be used as money ... The only limitation of Bitcoin is that it is limited to those places that accept it as currency. However, it can also be exchanged for conventional currencies ....Therefore, Bitcoin is a currency or form of money."

The position in New York however is less clear. In *US v Failella*,[92] it was determined that Bitcoin qualified as money, but in *US v Petrix*,[93] Judge Hugh B Scott held that it is not money, but private property along the same lines as special metals. Legislation to clarify the point, or a Supreme Court decision would make matters a great deal clearer.

Those arguing that since any prohibition on cryptocurrencies are unlikely to be effective, outright prohibition on their use would be ill advised and not practical, as they are an open source project and given their characteristics there is no cryptocurrency company to raid, subpoena, or shut down. Even if the website and the source code information underlying services were erased, there would be no impact as the database supporting cryptocurrencies exist only in the distributed P2P network designed by its users and removing any of the individual computer that constitute the P2P network would have hardly any impact on the rest of the network. Instead, there appears to be a more persuasive case for federal and state officials to develop a familiarity with the technology underlying cryptocurrencies and the nature of their transactions that could provide adequate information to reasonably investigate and counter any illegal activity.[94]

---

90 CFTC (2010), "Final rules regarding retail forex transactions", CFTC Press Release, 30/08/2010.
91 2014) 4:13-CU-416.
92 (2014) 39 F Supp 3d 544.
93 2016) No 15-CR-227A.
94 Supra, note [66], Kaplanov (2012).

Though there is unlikely to be a viable way to outlaw them, policymakers could stop the use and transfer of cryptocurrencies by outlawing the activity itself by making interstate transactions using Bitcoin invalid.[95] Outlawing the use and distribution of any P2P electronic currency, or any options between these two extremes could also signal a clear message that it is illegal to use them. The crackdown method as used in China could also be explored, but this ignores the prospect that cryptocurrency like technology could be developed that does not have the advantage that they now possess in assisting law enforcement. Such a new system could be solely maintained by foreign users and in a way that does not disclose all transactions publicly.[96]

Better ways of preventing criminal activity involving cryptocurrencies include looking at its public database as this provides the opportunity to track and locate those using them for illicit activity. The publicly available information inherent to the Bitcoin system is likely to be more effective tracking criminal activity than a system lacking such information. Such measured investigations could help to stop illegal activity without punishing those using the technology in legal ways.

The more important reason to resist prohibiting cryptocurrencies lies in the fundamental notion of the internet itself. Cryptocurrencies are unfettered by substantial regulation and can help to contribute to economic growth and job creation. Though in existence for only a few years, many kinds of businesses are flourishing because of cryptocurrency activities or because of their underlying blockchain technology. To a significant extent, cryptocurrencies have drastically reduced the cost of online transactions in a secure, anonymous, and efficient way.

Despite their price volatility, cryptocurrency thefts at exchanges, and some reported links to illicit activities, there are those who prefer a system outside of any government control or influence. Importantly, modern and advanced economies such as Switzerland[97] and Japan[98] are taking to cryptocurrency in significant ways, while Germany[99] is turning into a development hub for virtual currencies and blockchains, even though they are outlawed in some economies and discouraged in others because of fears of fraud and illegal activity.

---

95 Johnsont, M. E., McGuire, D. & Wiley, N.D. (2008), "The evolution of the peer-to-peer file sharing industry and the security risks for users", *Tuck School of Business Dartmouth College Paper Presented at the Proceedings of the 41St Hawaii International Conference on System Sciences.*

96 Touloumis, T. (2009), "Buccaneers and Bucks from the internet: Pirate bay and the entertainment industry", *Seton Hall Journal of Sports and Entertainment Law*, 19 (2008), pp. 253–258.

97 The Economist (2018), "Tales from the crypto-nation: Digital currency", *The Economist*, 426(9080), pg.69; The Miller, H. (2017), "Welcome to crypto valley: The Swiss city of Zug embraces digital currency", Bloomberg, 01/01/2017, www.bloomberg.com/news/articiles/2017-10-10/welcome-to-crypto-valley, accessed 02/02/2018.

98 Yagami, K. (2017), "Japan: A forward thinking Bitcoin nation", Forbes, 02/11/2017, www.forbes.com/sites/outofasia/../japan-a-forward-thinking-Bitcoin-nation, accessed 02/02/2018.

99 Turner, Z, 92,018), "Bitcoin finds a home in cash-loving Germany: Country is turning into a development hub for virtual currencies and blockchains", *The Wall Street Journal*, 17/01/2018, www.wsj.com/articles/Bitcoin-finds-a-home-in-cash-loving-germany-1515330000, accessed 02/02/2018.

Cryptocurrencies cannot survive in a viable form without enforceable contracts and a stable rule of law. When smothered by excessive regulation or an uncertain legal and regulatory environment, the promises and potential benefits would be lost. They present a particularly difficult and unique jurisdictional challenge to existing regulatory and enforcement agencies because of their ability to transcend borders in seconds and their anonymity due to encryption.[100] As said so by so many people, a proper balance between law, regulation, and freedom is essential.[101]

The regulators have become more active with the SEC announcing on 18th October 2018 that they have set up a collaborative programme with blockchain and cryptocurrency start-ups. It is called FinHub, or the Strategic Hub for Innovation and Financial technology.[102] At present, both state and federal level bills are being put forward to both regulate and facilitate this new area. It is too early to tell how this is going to map out in its final form.

Recent research suggests advancing the regulatory path through the Congress empowering the SEC or alternatively the CFTC with the authority to regulate the offering, distribution, and trading of cryptoassets, including the regulation of trading platforms, custodians (wallets), brokers and advisers.[103] The expanded powers should also be accompanied by the expansion the resources of both the SEC and the CFTC to enable both to implement more effectively existing as well as new authorities. Also, the Congressional legislations should focus on core principles equivalent to those undertaken for the futures industry and crowdfunding. Core principles should at the minimum cover the protection of customer assets, governance standards, conflicts of interest, periodic reporting, pre- and post-trade transparency requirements, prevention of fraud, manipulation, and abusive practices, pertinent disclosures to platform users, risk management, cybersecurity, and AML, KYC and other relevant measures to minimise nefarious activity risk and to ensure transparency.[104] As for offshore platforms[105] that offer or provide access to US investors, Congress should empower the relevant agencies with the authority to decide whether such platforms should be required to comply with US standards, or demonstrate compliance with comparable standards, or to disclose explicitly that they do not adhere to such standards.

7.5 The EU's cryptoasset regulatory policy

EU institutions and some individual Member States have issued various statements, guidance and regulations potentially applicable to blockchain,

---

100 Trautman, L.J. & Harrell, A.C. (2017), "Bitcoin versus regulated payment systems: What gives?", *Cardoza Law Review*, 38 (3), 1041–1097.

101 Eha, B.P. (2017), *How money got free: Bitcoin and the fight for the future of finance*, London, One World Publications Ltd.

102 https://hackernoon.com/cryptocurrency-regulaion-update-november-2018-d9b17837aeec, accessed 26/02/2019.

103 Massad, T.G. (2019), "It's time to strengthen the regulation of crypto-assets", *Brookings Economic Studies Paper March 2019*, www.brookings.edu/wp-content/uploads/2019/03/Economis-Studies-Timothy-Massad-Cryptocurrency-Paper.pdf, accessed 25/06/2019.

104 Supra, note [103], Massad (2019).

105 Supra, note [103], Massad (2019).

cryptoassets, and ICOs. For example, the ECB does not regard cryptoassets as a full form of money or currency from a legal perspective. The ECB defines a cryptocurrency/cryptoasset as a digital representation of value, not issued by a central bank, credit institutions or e-money institutions, which in some circumstances could be employed as an alternative to money.[106] The ECB refers to cryptocurrency schemes to describe both the aspect of value and that of the inherent or inbuilt mechanisms ensuring that value can be transferred.

The cryptocurrency systems ecosystem specifically comprises new categories of participants not previously present in the payments environment. Emerging business models are now developing around obtaining, storing, accessing and transferring units of cryptocurrencies. These come and go, but in 2015 there were already 500 in existence. Some new systems are built with slightly different characteristics that could improve the functionality or some elements in the ecosystem. For others, the purpose is unclear as it seems only a few are used or intended to be used for payments. Acceptance of cryptocurrency systems is not widespread, though some e-commerce merchants have announced their willingness to accepting payments with Bitcoin. It appears that Bitcoin is used for around 69,000 transactions daily worldwide, compared to a total of 274 million non-cash retail payment transactions daily for the EU alone.[107]

Users further encounter payment system-like risks owing to their direct participation in the cryptocurrency systems as well as risks associated with their particular characteristics, such as the counterparty risks discussed, price volatility and the risks of investment fraud associated with the lack of transparency. There are no safeguards for now to protect users against such risks.[108]

On the other hand, the ECB notes that cryptocurrency systems present some advantages as perceived by users. They could pose a challenge to retail payment instruments and innovative payment solutions pertaining to costs, global reach, anonymity of the payer and speed of settlement. New, improved cryptocurrencies could overcome the current barriers to widespread use more successfully than the current ones, especially for payments within virtual communities/closed-loop environments like Internet platforms and for cross-border payments.[109]

As discussed earlier in Chapter 6, international authorities such as the FATF have taken an interest to virtual currency systems because of the potential risks to the integrity of the international financial system. Various central banks and financial and supervisory authorities across the world have cautioned users of the risk pertaining to holding and transacting virtual currencies.[110] Some have provided clarifications on the legal status, started regulating certain activities or issued outright bans. Responses vary depending in part on the part of the world from which they originate and on the kind of authority.

---

106 ECB (2015), "Virtual currency schemes – a further analysis", *ECB Paper*, February 2015, www.ecb.europa.eu/pub/pdf/other/virtualcurrencyschemesen.pdf, accessed 02/02/2018.
107 Supra, note [106], ECB (2015).
108 Supra, note [106], ECB (2015).
109 Supra, note [106], ECB (2015).
110 Supra, note [106], ECB (2015).

The ECB in advancing further from its 2012 Virtual Currencies Report[111] suggested that though cryptocurrency systems can have positive aspects in terms of financial innovation and the offer of additional payment alternatives for consumers, they also clearly entail risks. The ECB, with regards to its monetary policy and price stability and related agendas, maintains that the materialisation of these risks depends on the volumes of cryptocurrency systems issued and their connection to the real economy, including their traded volume and acceptance of supervised institutions involved with them. For now, all these risk drivers remained low, implying no material risks for any of ECB's tasks as yet.[112] However, an incident involving cryptocurrency systems and a subsequent loss of trust in them could also undermine users' confidence in electronic payment instruments, in e-money, and/or in particular payment solutions, like those in place for e-commerce. Therefore, the ECB intends to continue to monitor payments-related developments in cryptocurrency systems.[113] It has been argued that the building of an effective cryptoassets monitoring framework would require caution because of data issues, as well as a stepwise approach to filling gaps.[114]

The ECB Crypto-Assets Task Force (ECBCTF) meanwhile concluded that present market conditions suggest that cryptoassets risks or potential implications are limited and/or are manageable within the context of existing regulatory and oversight frameworks.[115] It nevertheless cautioned that its evaluation is subject to further insights from its continuous monitoring of cryptoassets and the need to raise awareness and develop preparedness. By way of example, ECB's analysis of different kinds of stablecoins suggests a trade-off between the novelty of the stabilisation mechanism-applied initiatives extending from mirroring the conventional electronic money approach, to the introduction of an algorithmic central bank and their capacity to maintain a stable market value.[116] Stablecoins in general claim to stabilise the value of major currencies in the volatile cryptoasset market. Thus, relatively less innovative stablecoins could offer reliefs to users seeking a stable store of value, particularly when legitimised by the adherence to standards that are typical of payment services. But, confirmation on the potential future role of more innovative stablecoins outside their core user base is still being awaited.

---

111 ECB (2012), "Virtual Currency Schemes", *ECB Paper*, October 2012, www.ecb.europa.eu/pub/pdf/other/virtualcurrencyschemes201210en.pdf, accessed 02/02/2018.

112 Supra, note [106], ECB (2015).

113 Supra, note [106], ECB (2015).

114 Chimienti, M.T., Kochanska, U. & Pinna, A. (2019), "Understanding the crypto-asset phenomenon, its risks and measurement issues" *ECB Economic Bulletin*, 5(2019) 07/08/2019, www.ecb.europa.eu/pub/economic-bulletin/articles/2019/html/ecb.ebart201905_03~c83aeaa44c.en.html, accessed 08/08/2019.

115 ECB (2019), "Crypto-assets: Implications for financial stability, and monetary policy, and payments and market infrastructures", *ECB Occasional Paper Series No. 223*, May 2019, www.ecb.europa.eu/pub/pdf/scpops/ecb.op223~3ce14e986c.en.pdf, accessed 08/081/9.

116 Bullman, D., Klemm, J. & Pinna, A. (2019), "In search for stability in crypto-assets: are stablecoins the solution?", *ECB Occasional Paper Series No. 230*, August 2019, www.ecb.europa.eu/pub/pdf/scpops/ecb.op230~d57946be3b.en.pdf, accessed 29/08/2019.

In the meantime, the ECBCTF argues that in the absence of a common taxonomy, uncoordinated regulatory approaches could motivate regulatory arbitrage. It suggests that an EU level regulation should first target the cryptoasset gatekeepers like custody, trading and exchange services providing the entry point to retail customers and regulated entities.[117] It cautioned the unsuitability of the approach focusing on intermediaries in the decentralised networks and proposed subjecting these to a minimum set of principles that seek to ensure the network's technological integrity, transparency of algorithms and protocols, cyber-resilience, and regulatory compliances. The ECBCTF stressed that unintended consequences could result from regulating gatekeepers only and that decentralised networks should be evaluated in a holistic cost-benefit framework.

The EBA's mandate in Article 9 of its founding regulation covers the monitoring of existing and new financial activities so as to provide guidelines and recommendations with the agenda of promoting the safety and soundness of markets and convergence of regulatory practice. Subsequent to its analysis of virtual currencies, on 13 December 2013 the EBA issued a public warning advising consumers that cryptocurrencies are not regulated and as such there are significant risks in using them.[118] The outstanding question at that point of time was whether cryptocurrencies should or could be regulated. On the 4 July 2014, the EBA Opinion on this matter was addressed to the European Parliament, the Council and the Commission.

The EBA considers cryptocurrencies as digital representations of value that is neither issued by central banks or public authorities, not necessarily attached to fiat currencies, but are accepted by natural or legal persons as a means of payment and could be transferred, stored or traded electronically.[119] Main participants in the cryptocurrency space are users, exchanges, trade platforms, inventors and e-wallet providers. Potential benefits attached to virtual currencies include reduced transactions cost, faster transaction speed and financial inclusion. Such benefits though might be less relevant in the EU due to the existing and pending EU regulations and directives that are explicitly targeted at faster transactions speeds and costs and increasing financial inclusion.

Relative to the benefits identified, there are some 70 kinds of risks involved across several categories including risks to users; risks to nonuser market participants; risks to financial integrity, such as money laundering and other financial crimes; risks to existing payment systems in conventional fiat currencies; and risks to regulatory authorities.[120] Various casual drivers for such risks were

---

117 Supra, note [115], ECB (2019).
118 European Banking Authority (2013), "Warning to consumers on virtual currencies", *EBA/WRG/2013/01*, 12/12/2013, https://eba.europa.eu/sites/default/documents/files/documents/10180/598344/b99b0dd0-f253-47ee-82a5-c547e408948c/EBA%20Warning%20on%20Virtual%20Currencies.pdf, accessed 02/02/2018.
119 EBA (2014), "EBA Opinion on 'virtual currencies'", *EBA/Op/2014/08*, 04/07/2014, https://eba.europa.eu/sites/default/documents/files/documents/10180/657547/81409b94-4222-45d7-ba3b-7deb5863ab57/EBA-Op-2014-08%20Opinion%20on%20Virtual%20Currencies.pdf, accessed 02/02/2018.
120 Supra, note [119], EBA (2014).

identified, as these suggest regulatory measures that could be employed to contain them. These include the scenario that a cryptocurrency scheme could be created, then its function subsequently altered by anyone and, in the example of decentralised schemes such as Bitcoins, by anyone with an adequate share of computational power; that payer and payee could remain anonymous; that cryptocurrency schemes are not restricted by jurisdictional boundaries and could ergo undermine financial sanctions and seizure of assets; or that market participants lack sound corporate governance arrangements.[121]

The EBA noted that a regulatory approach addressing risk drivers comprehensively would necessitate a substantial body of regulation where some components are untested. Amongst other elements, it would need to comprise governance requirements for several market participants; the segregation of client accounts; capital requirements; and importantly, the design of a scheme governing authorities that are accountable for the integrity of a virtual currency scheme and its key components including the protocol and transaction ledger.[122] Though such a long-term structural scheme is yet to be available, some of the more pressing needs as identified would need to be addressed in other manners. As an immediate measure, the EBA recommended that national supervisory authorities discourage credit institutions, payment institutions and e-money institutions from buying, holding or selling cryptocurrencies.[123]

The EBA further recommends that EU lawmakers consider declaring market participants at the direct interface between conventional currencies and cryptocurrencies, such as virtual currency exchanges, to become obliged entities under the EU anti-money laundering Directive and ergo subject to its anti-money laundering and counter terrorism financing requirements.[124] Such immediate responses could insulate regulated financial services from cryptocurrency schemes and could mitigate those risks arising from the interactions between them and regulated financial services. It would, however, be unable to mitigate those risks that arise within or between cryptocurrency schemes themselves.[125] Ceteris paribus, these immediate responses would enable cryptocurrency schemes to innovate and develop outside of the financial services sector, including the design of solutions that could comply with regulatory demands of the kind as mentioned.[126] They would also enable financial institutions to maintain, for instance, a current account relationship with businesses active in the virtual currency space.

The 5th Anti-Money Laundering Directive (5AMLD)[127] extended the scope of sectors and persons to include electronic custodian wallet providers, cryptocurrency exchange services providers partaking in exchange services between

---

121 Supra, note [119], EBA (2014).
122 Supra, note [119], EBA (2014).
123 Supra, note [119], EBA (2014).
124 Supra, note [119], EBA (2014).
125 Supra, note [119], EBA (2014).
126 Supra, note [119], EBA (2014).
127 Directive (EU) 2018/43.

virtual and fiat currencies, and others. The 5AMLD is expected to strengthen existing Directives through the above, by enabling better identification of politically exposed persons (PEPs), by restricting the anonymous use of virtual currencies, by enhancing information-sharing between financial supervisory authorities, and by increasing transparency pertaining to the beneficial ownerships of companies. It remains to be seen how effective this can be.

Additionally, the EU proposes to subject these entities to registration or licensing requirements and subject those who own or hold a management function in these entities to the fit and proper testing. The EU published proposals in response to the EU Council's conclusion of February 2016 on the fight against the financing of terrorism for targeted amendments to EU law. The European Securities and Markets Authority (ESMA) took note of the parallel resolution and report published by the European Parliament (EP) in May 2016 where the EP proposed that the EU develop recommendations for any legislation needed to regulate the cryptocurrency space.

The EBA reiterated that in order for these amendments to reduce the risks of cryptocurrencies being abused for money laundering or terrorist financing activities, the EU and co-legislators should ensure that competent authorities have the right tools at their disposals to ensure the effective supervision of custodian wallet providers' and cryptocurrency exchange platforms' compliance with the AML/CTF obligations. Owing to their transnational nature, it is necessary for Member States and competent authorities to approach the new AML/CTF regime for these facilities consistently across the EU in alignment with one of EBA's statutory objectives.

The EBA's Opinion is based on Article 34(1), Article 56, and Article 9(2) of Regulation (EU) No. 1093/2010 (the EBA Regulation), as AML/CTF relate to the EBA's area of competence. The EBA Opinion fulfils its mandate in Article 9 of the EBA Regulation. The EBA proposals as set out below address issues related to the unclear transposition deadlines of the amendments; the limited suitability of the revised Payment Services Directive; the public's unclear perception of the legal status of the new entities; the need for amendments to facilitate the cooperation between national competent authorities; the lack of specification of fit and proper tests of the new entities; and the unclear scope of the registration and licensing regime[128]:

(i) The transposition deadline of amendments to Directive (EU) 2015/849 should be framed such as to facilitate the adoption of a consistent approach to the AML/CTF supervision of custodian wallet providers and virtual currency exchange platforms across Member States.

---

128 EBA (2016), "Opinion of the European Banking Authority on the EU Commission's proposal to bring Virtual Currencies into the scope of Directive (EU) 2015/849 (4AMLD)", *EBA-Op-2016-07*, 11/08/2016, https://eba.europa.eu/sites/default/documents/files/documents/10180/1547217/32b1f7f2-90ec-44a8-9aab-021b35d1f1f7/EBA%2520Opinion%2520on%2520the%2520Commission%25E2%2580%2599s%2520proposal%2520to%2520bring%2520virtual%2520currency%2520entities%2520into%2520the%2520scope%2520of%25204AMLD.pdf?retry=1, accessed 02/02/2018.

(ii) The EBA agrees with the EC's decision not to bring virtual currency transactions into the scope of Directives in financial services such as the Payment Services Directive (Directive (EU) 2015/2366 (PSDS2)) for now.
(iii) The status of cryptocurrency exchange platforms and custodian wallet providers needs clarification as consumers and business partners of these entities might be unaware that the imposition of requirements on cryptocurrency exchange platforms and custodian wallet providers for AML/CTF purposes does not include or imply consumer protection or prudential safeguards including capital requirements, calculation of own funds, safeguarding requirements, separation of client accounts and the extensive authorisation liability.
(iv) The amendments should enable competent authorities to easily exchange information pertaining to cryptocurrency exchange providers and custodian wallet providers.
(v) The amendments should provide more detail on how competent authorities could undertake fit and proper tests of owners and controllers of cryptocurrency exchange providers and custodian wallet providers.
(vi) The amendments to the Directive should clarify the scope of the proposed licensing or registration regime for cryptocurrency exchange providers and custodian wallet providers.
(vii) The proposed extension of national sanction powers to cryptocurrency exchange providers and custodian wallet providers should be retained.

The ESMA on 13 November 2019 issued two statements on ICOs, one for risks of ICOs for investors and one on the rules applicable to firms involved in ICOs.[129] ESMA notes the rapid growth of ICOs globally and in Europe and is concerned that investors might be unaware of the high risks that they are assuming when investing in ICOs. Further, ESMA is concerned that firms involved in ICOs might undertake their activities without complying with relevant applicable EU laws.

ESMA calls ICO an innovative way of raising funds from the public using coins or tokens. ICOs can also be referred to as initial tokens offering or tokens sales.[130] A business or individual issues coins or tokens and offers them for sale in exchange for fiat currencies or more often cryptocurrencies such as Bitcoin or Ether.

As discussed above, ICOs are highly speculative investments and, depending on how they are structured, they could fall outside the regulated space, in which case investors do not benefit from the protection accruing to regulated

---

129 European Securities and Markets Authority (2017), "ESMA highlights ICO risks for investors and firms", *ESMA Press Release*, 13/11/2017, www.esma.europa.eu/press-news/esma-news/esma-highlights-ico-risks-investors-and-firms, accessed 02/02/2018.
130 European Securities and Markets Authority (2017), "Statement: ESMA alerts investors to the high risks of Initial Coin Offerings (ICOs)", *ESMA50-157-829*, 13/11/2017, www.esma.europa.eu/document/esma-alerts-investors-high-risks-initial-coin-offerings-icos, accessed 02/02/2018.

investments. ICOs are also vulnerable to fraud or illicit activities because of their anonymity and their capacity to access large sums of money within a short time window. ESMA's view is that investors as such are exposed to the following key risks[131]:

(i) ICOs operating in an unregulated space are vulnerable to fraud or illicit activities.
(ii) There is a high risk of losing all the invested capital as most ICOs are launched for start-ups at early phase of their developments, with many of such coins and tokens issued having no intrinsic value other than the possibility to use them to access or use services/products that are to be developed by the issuer.
(iii) The lack of exit options and extreme price volatility in many cases.
(iv) Some ICOs do not come with full prospectuses. For those that do, the information provided is not verified independently and may be incomplete, unbalanced or even misleading. They tend to focus on the potential benefits but not the risks.
(v) The DLT underpinning the coins is largely untested and more generally the technology may not function quickly and securely especially during peaks of activity.

ESMA also draws the attention of firms involved in ICOs that they need to give due consideration to whether their activities constituted regulated activities, as well as to the high risks involved. Where the coins or tokens qualify as financial instruments it is probable that businesses involved in ICOs conduct regulated investment activities like placing, dealing in or advising on financial instruments, or managing or marketing collective investment schemes. They could also be involved in offering transferable securities to the public. Other than national rules, the following key EU rules could likely be applicable[132]:

(i) The Prospectus Directive
(ii) The Markets in Financial Instruments Directive (MiFID) 1 and 2
(iii) The Alternative Investment Fund Managers Directive; and
(iv) The Fourth and Fifth Anti-Money Laundering Directives

The European Supervising Authorities (ESAs) comprising ESMA, the EBA, and European Insurance and Occupational Pensions (EIOPA) issued a pan-EU warning on 12 February 2018 to consumers pertaining to the risks of buying virtual currencies.[133] The warning is based on Article 9(3) of the three ESA's

---

131 Supra, note [119], ESMA (2017).
132 ESMA (2017), "Statement: ESMA alerts firms involved in Initial Coin Offerings (ICOs) to the need to meet relevant regulatory requirements", ESAMA50-157-828, 13/11/2017, www.esma.europa-eu/sites/default/../eama50-157-828_ico_statement_firms.pdf, accessed 02/02/2018.
133 European Banking Authority (EBA) (2018), "ESAs warn consumers or risks in buying virtual currencies", EBA Press Release, 12/02/2018, www.eba.europa.eu/esas-warn-consumers-of-risks-in-buying-virtual-currencies, accessed 02/02/2018.

founding Regulations and follows the publication of two ESMA statements on ICOs in November 2017 as well as an earlier warning to consumers and two opinions on virtual currencies published by EBA in December 2013, July 2014 and August 2016 respectively. Virtual currencies emerge in many forms and, as we have seen, most are based on a DLT, the first of these being Bitcoin in 2009.

The ESAs warn consumers that virtual currencies are highly risky and unregulated products and are unsuitable as investment, savings or retirement planning products. The ESAs are concerned about the growing numbers of consumers buying virtual currencies while unaware of the risks involved.[134] They draw the attention of consumers to the following[135]:

(i) They cautioned that virtual currencies such as Bitcoin are subject to extreme price volatility and have demonstrated clear signs of a pricing bubble and consumers buying cryptocurrencies should note the high risk that they could lose a large portion or even all of their money invested.

(ii) They pointed out that cryptocurrencies and exchanges where consumers can trade are not regulated under EU law. This means that consumers buying them do not benefit from any protection associated with regulated financial services. For instance, where a cryptocurrency exchange goes out of business or consumers have their money stolen because their account is subject to a cyber security attack, there is no EU law applicable to cover their losses.

(iii) Various cryptocurrency exchanges have been subject to severe operational problems in the past. During such disruptions, consumers have been unable to buy and sell cryptocurrencies when they needed to and have suffered losses due to extreme price fluctuations during the disrupted period.

EU Commissioner Pierre Moscovici on 18 December 2017 stated that the EU was not looking to regulate cryptocurrencies,[136] although this seemed inconsistent with prior and consequential statements by other EU officials. Valdis Dombrovskis, the Vice-President of the EC, on 20 December 2017 stated that there are clear risks for investors and consumers associated to price volatility, including the risks of complete loss of investment, operational and security failures, market manipulation and liability gaps.[137] Calls for greater cryptocurrency regulation reverberated across Europe in January 2018. Bruno Le Maire, French Minister of the Economy, announced on 15 January the creation of a

---

134 Supra, note [133], EBA (2018).
135 Supra, note [133], EBA (2018).
136 Nelson, A. (2018), "Cryptocurrency Regulation in 2018: Where the World Stands Right Now", *Bitcoin Magazine*, 01/02/2018, https://bitcoinmagazine.com/articles/cryptocurrency-regulation-2018-where-world-stands-right-now, accessed 18/02/2018.
137 Supra, note [136], Nelson (2018).

working group with the purpose of regulating them.[138] A day later, Joachim Wuermeling, board member of the German Bundesbank, called for effective regulation of cryptocurrencies on a global scale.[139] Dombrovskis, on 22 January 2018, advanced his regulatory agenda further by warning three of EU's financial watchdog of a bubble.[140] The UK's prime minister joined the fray at Davos on 25 January 2018 saying that the world needs to watch cryptocurrencies seriously and warning about them being used particularly by criminals.[141]

Crackdowns on cryptocurrencies in the EU are not likely to happen until sometime in 2020 when new directives like the 4th Anti Money Laundering Directive, as amended by the 5th, have been transposed into national law.[142] Regulating cryptocurrencies presents formidable difficulties. One reason for their rise is the entry of nefarious users. The way cryptocurrencies, especially Bitcoin, work makes them ideal for money laundering, drug money and the funding of terrorism. This suggests that ultimately new laws would need to end the anonymity of wallet addresses as well as making exchanges and their users more transparent to the world. Such new laws might not be able to solve the issue of anonymity as those engaged in tax avoidance or in the criminal world generally have power and influence,[143] and importantly, the access to expert professional advice, demonstrated clearly in the Panama and Paradise Papers leaks.[144]

The other difficulty that the EU has highlighted is that suspicious transactions made through cryptocurrencies are not sufficiently monitored by the authorities, who are unable to link the transactions to identified persons. This is a serious practical difficulty when implementing the new rules. The EU's definition of cryptocurrencies may present difficulties as the rules considered make no mention of the "cryptocurrency" word. Blockchain technology, the digital ledger behind them is virtually tamper-proof and does not require monitoring.[145] This raises the possibility that with the new rules this might generate the unintended intention of pushing dirty money further behind the firewalls and into the dark web.

Germany, the most powerful of the EU Member States, has taken an attitude towards cryptocurrencies that could offer glimpses of the EU's potential regulatory path. Germany's Federal Ministry of Finance formally recognises Bitcoin as a unit of account – a form of private currency usable for private transactions.

---

138 Supra, note [136], Nelson (2018).
139 Supra, note [136], Nelson (2018).
140 Supra, note [136], Nelson (2018).
141 Supra, note [136], Nelson (2018).
142 Meyer, D. (2017), "Here's When Europe's New Bitcoin Rules Will Come Into Effect", *Fortune*, 04/12/2017, www.fortune.com/2017/12/04/eu-Bitcoin-anti-money-laundering-uk, accessed 02/02/2018.
143 Business World (2018), "Will EU regulation of Bitcoin and other cryptocurrencies succeed?", *Business World*, 30/01/2018, www.businessworld.ie/news/Will-EU-regulation-of-bitocin-and-other-cryptocurrencies-succeed-570220.html, accessed 02/02/2018.
144 Yeoh, P. (2018), "Financial secrecy business offshore and onshore", *Company Lawyer*, 39 (9), 279–285.
145 Supra, note [143], Business World (2018).

It is not treated as a foreign currency or as e-money. It, however, means that the Ministry would now be able to tax virtual currency creators or users. Nevertheless, businesses seeking to use them for commercial transactions would need permission from the Ministry. As Bitcoins are not on a similar footing as formal fiat currencies, the German move implies that people who have speculated in online cryptocurrencies could be liable for capital gains taxes when they sell them less than a year since acquiring them, while those holding them longer would not be liable.

In a public message the Ministry subsequently on 27 February clarified that it would not tax cryptocurrencies such as Bitcoin when they are applied in payments. When used for purchases they would receive the same treatment as legal tender. Taxes for purchases would be calibrated in accordance with EU's VAT Directive. Taxes may be imposed on fees collected by providers of digital wallets and other kinds of services pertaining to cryptocurrencies. Taxes are not imposed on block rewards sent to miners, or those intermediaries facilitating their conversion to or from fiat currencies. The European Court of Justice ruled such kinds of conversion as tax exempt supply of services. Those intermediaries that purchase or sell cryptocurrencies would also be tax exempt as would blockchain miners.[146]

Germany's Federal Financial Supervisory Authority (BaFin) treats cryptocurrencies such as Bitcoin as units of accounts within Section 1 (11) of the German Banking Act. They are financial instruments comparable to foreign exchange, with the difference that they do not refer to a legal tender. Comparable cryptocurrencies and online exchanges are accordingly subject to regulatory supervision. As such they are not currency, foreign notes or coins and nor are they e-money within the interpretation of the German Payment Supervision Act. Nor do they constitute a claim on an issuer, as in effect one does not exist. Digital means of payments in contrast are backed by a central entity which issues and manages the units. BaFIn generally is critical of cryptocurrencies especially in the context of murky ICOs.

The Bundesbank, Germany's central bank, generally rules out the idea of an official digital money for the Euro zone. It is also concerned over the risks of losses from investments in cryptocurrencies. It argues that any initiative to regulate them has to be a concerted global basis so as to be effective with the greatest possible international cooperation. Germany's call to the G20 for regulatory intervention quickly received support from France and the US.

As virtual currencies continue to creep into the mainstream through the launch of crypto futures, cryptocurrency index funds, etc, opportunities could continue to flourish. A way to gain control of cryptocurrencies could be via the ending of net neutrality. The US has started this initiative, but it is not a straightforward process. It is also uncertain whether the new regulations could enable the effective monitoring of those bent on having less government oversight, after

---

146 *Skatteverket v. David Hedqvist*, 22 October 2015. C-264/14.

all the very rationale for their introduction was the avoidance of government oversight.[147]

Additional oversight certainly exists in the form of the amendments to the 4th EU Anti-Money Laundering Directive enclosed in the 5th.[148] Cryptocurrencies are defined as "a digital representation of value that can be digitally transferred, stored or traded and is accepted ... as a medium of exchange."[149] Cryptocurrencies and cryptocurrency exchanges are determined to be "obliged entities" for the purposes of anti-laundering and terrorist financing regulations.[150] In addition, the reporting obligations are extended to the cryptocurrency area by Financial Intelligence Units having the obligation to make sure the names and addresses are taken of the owners of cryptocurrency.[151] Finally, the financial regulators in the EU are required to regulate the providers of cryptocurrency exchanges and wallets. Thus, for the purpose of the anti-money laundering laws and financial regulation, cryptocurrency has entered the financial services mainstream.

ESMA's most recent report on cryptoassets and ICOs sought to clarify current EU rules for cryptoassets that qualify as financial instruments, including pointing up various regulatory gaps that EU policymakers would need to take note of. In a nutshell, ESMA essentially advised the European Commission and national competent authorities (NCAs) that the current phase of cryptoasset development should focus on the regime for cryptoassets that are not financial instruments, warning buyers of the risks involved, rather than building a more elaborate regime legitimising cryptoassets and bringing them into the same regime for cryptoassets qualifying as financial instruments under current EU rules.[152]

Between January 2018 and the first half of 2019, ESMA conducted two surveys to collect evidence from NCAs on the licensing regimes of Fintech entities. These surveys confirmed that NCAs do not distinguish between Fintech and conventional business models in their authorising and licensing activities as they authorise financial activities and not a technology. The survey findings suggest that the primary area where regulatory gaps and issues have been identified by NCAs and where Fintech entities do not fall squarely within existing rules pertained to cryptoassets, ICOs, and DLT. More clarity at the EU level is sought by the NCAs with regards to the definition of financial instruments and cryptoassets' legal nature. NCAs' responses support ESMA's Cryptoasset Advice that those tokens that are financial instruments are, ergo, subject to the full applicable regulation, whereas those tokens not treated as financial instruments would be subjected to some minimal level of regulation. Therefore, ESMA

---

147 Supra, note [143] Business World (2018).
148 2015/849 EUR-Lex-32018L084-EN-EUR-LEX.
149 5th EU Anti-Money Laundering Directive at Art. 1(d)(18).
150 5th EU Anti-Money Laundering Directive at Art. 1(c).
151 5th EU Anti-Money Laundering Directive at Art. 13(1).
152 ESMA (2019), "Advice: Initial coin offerings and crypto-assets", *ESMA Report ESMA50-157-1391*, 09/01/2019; Maijoor, S. (2019), "Crypto-assets: Time to deliver", *Paper Presented by Steven Maijoor ESMA Chairman at the 3rd Annual Fintech Conference in Brussels*, 26/02/2019, www.esma.europa.eu/sites/default/files/library/esma71-99-1120_maijoor_keynote_on_crypto-assets_-_time_to_deliver.pdf, accessed 5/03/2019.

continues to foster supervisory convergence pertaining to the domain of cryptoassets across Member States.[153]

The other European supervisory authority, namely the EBA, also published its take on the suitability and applicability of EU rules on cryptoassets. The EBA analysis similarly mentioned that typically cryptoassets fall outside the scope of EU financial services regulation, other than for a few limited cases that could qualify as electronic money.[154] The former refers to specific services pertaining to cryptoasset custodian wallet provision and cryptoasset trading platforms that do not come under EU regulated financial services. These activities have triggered divergent regulatory approaches, giving rise to potential issues including consumer protection, operational resilience, market integrity and a level playing field.

The EBA accordingly advised the European Commission on the need for a comprehensive cost/benefit analysis to ascertain what actions would be required at the EU level, specifically pertaining to the opportunities and risks presented by cryptoasset activities and new technologies that could involve the deployment of cryptoasset activities. The EBA would be enhance its monitoring activities in 2019, especially pertaining to consumer-facing disclosure practices. The EBA together with ESMA are taking the position that anti-money laundering rules should apply to all activities pertaining to cryptoassets. They were responding to the FATF statement calling on the need for economies to implement coordinated actions to stop virtual currencies being deployed to finance crime and terrorism.[155]

The FSB in its briefing to G20 members in Osaka in June 2019 recapitulated that the EC, the EBA, the European Insurance and Occupational Pensions Authority, and ESMA are the four regulators for cryptoassets in the EU. This aside, individual member states are passing their own domestic legislation to fill the gap that exists at the EU level. This suggests that the existing EU regulatory framework gives rise to the risks of inconsistent interpretations across EU Member States and the potential for regulatory arbitrage. Accordingly, the EC takes the position that a review of existing legislations and a feasibility study would be undertaken to find a common EU approach for an EU-wide regulatory cryptoasset policy.[156] Tangible proposals for an EU-wide cryptoasset framework is likely to follow thereafter. This would take time, unless pressured by events or

---

153 ESMA (2019), "Licensing of Fintech business models", *ESMA Report ESMA50-164-2430*, 12/07/2019.

154 EBA (2019), "Report with advice for the European Commission on crypto-assets" *EBA Report*, 09/01/2019, https://eba.europa.eu/file/40451/download?token=dD44Fb9A, accessed 5/03/2019.

155 Bedell, C. (2018), "FATF adds new definitions of virtual assets and virtual asset providers to its international standard recommendations", *Bedell Christin*, 29/10/2018, https://www.bedellcristin.com/newsexperience/2018/fatf-adds-new-definitions-of-virtual-assets-and-virtual-asset-providers-to-its-international-standard-recommendations/, accessed 07/02/2020.

156 Daniel, C., Srivastava, A., Moffatt, N., Kaplan, L. & Kaplan, L. (2019), "The EU regulation of crypto-assets-Fit for purpose?", *Paul Hastings April 2019*, www.paulhastings.com/publications-items/details/?id=eb0fd56c-2334-6428-811c-ff00004cbded, accessed 05/06/2019.

scandals causing serious harm to cryptoassets investors and so on. The regulatory stand taken would likely be a fair balance between the continuous need for Fintech innovations and the risk of harm to market participants. It would also likely be an exemplary regulatory standard of the kind and quality seen in the General Data Protection Regulation (GDPR) that commands respect from much of the world.

7.6 The UK's cryptoassets regulatory policy

The FCA and the regulator which deals with the capital requirements relating to relevant UK financial institutions, namely the Prudential Regulation Authority (PRA), are primarily responsible for the supervision of financial services in the UK. The Treasury (HMT) has overall authority regarding financial services and legislation in the country. The FCA, PRA and Bank of England (BoE) together in close collaboration, but working independently, maintain and advance UK's financial services and legislative and regulatory framework,[157] that includes cryptoassets and market participants in the industry.

Under English common law, a cryptoasset is in general a digital form of personal property or a change in possession[158] where the rights of the owner of that property is derived from the capacity to physically possess it and transfer title to it to others, although these cryptoassets are intangible. As the nature and characteristics of cryptoassets continue to evolve, their legal status would persist in a state of flux. In the absence of a formal statutory definition for cryptoassets/cryptocurrencies/virtual currencies, it would be guided by 5AMLD that states that a virtual currency "is a virtual representation of value that is not issued or guaranteed by a central bank or public authority, is not necessarily attached to a legal established currency, but is accepted by natural or legal persons as a means of exchange, and which can be transferred, stored, or traded electronically".[159] This therefore would include various kinds of digital representation of value extending from cryptoassets and others as almost all of these under EU's taxonomy of cryptocurrencies have a digital representation of value, are decentralised, not attached to a legally established currency, not possessing the legal status of currency or money, and are electronically transferable, storable and tradeable.

Potential controversies could arise with regards to cryptocurrencies having to be a means of exchange. First, it does not say anything about a cryptocurrency

---

157 Penn, B., "Banking regulation in the UK: Overview", *Thomson Reuters Practical Law*, 01/08/2018, https://uk.practicallaw.thomsonreuters.com/w-008-0211?transitionType=Default&-contextData=%28sc.Default%29; Mwenda, K.K. (2018), *Legal aspects of financial services regulation and the concept of a unified regulator*, Washington, DC, The International Bank for Reconstruction and Development/The World Bank.

158 Financial Markets Law Committee (2016), "Issues of legal uncertainty arising in the context of virtual currencies", *FMLC Paper* July 2016, http://fmlc.org/wp-content/uploads/2018/03/virtual_currencies_paper_-_edited_january_2017.pdf, accessed 26/11/2017.

159 Houben, R. & Snyers, A. (2018), "Cryptocurrencies and blockchain: Legal context and implications for financial crimes, money laundering and tax evasion", *European Parliament Paper PE 619.024*, July 2018, pg.68.

that is not accepted as a means of exchange now, but where there is no intrinsic limitation preventing them from becoming a means of exchange in the future.[160] This then depends on the willingness of parties to accept the cryptocurrency as a standard of value in their mutual dealings. However, as soon as that happens, they transform into a means of exchange and fall under the definition of 5AMLD. Thus, from the perspective of combating money laundering, terrorist financing and tax evasion this will not be a problem, as normally when committing one of these offences via cryptocurrencies the activity will potentially have been carried out on an exchange. Second, it does not say anything about a virtual currency that is a medium of exchange, but which is also an investment instrument.[161] Though cryptocurrencies in general are marked by high volatility, mainstream finance increasingly considers them as a financial asset class. Moreover, the 5AMLD definition does not say that this should be the only or predominant function of the cryptocurrency. Cryptocurrencies as such should be covered by the definition provide in 5AMLD. In any case, even in the fiat currency framework, a fiat can also be acquired and held for investment or speculation purposes and this does not alter the fiat's primary status of being a fiat currency. Hence, the 5AMLD's definition of virtual currencies is adequate to combat money laundering, terrorist financing and tax evasion through the cryptocurrencies included in the taxonomy in use in the EU,[162] and UK.

After more than a decade of various initiatives[163] to resolve the regulatory issues in cryptoassets, in July 2019 the FCA issued its Final Guidance on Cryptoassets.[164] This does not seem to vary materially from its initial consultation. Still, this provides enhanced clarity in some important parts, including when particular kinds of cryptoassets would fall under the regulator's remit. The Final Guidance, ergo, seeks to help firms to ascertain whether their cryptoasset activities fall under FCA's regulation and also whether they need to be authorised, as well as the compliance process involved.

Foremost, the FCA Final Guidance categorises cryptocurrencies into three types. Firstly, exchange tokens such as Bitcoin, which are used as both media of exchange and as investments. Secondly, security tokens, which may entitle the holder to ownership or a share of property rights. These are caught by both the Financial Services (Regulated Activities) Order 2001[165] as they are categorised as financial instruments.[166] Finally, utility tokens which can be redeemed for a specific product using a DLT platform.

---

160 Supra, note [159], Houben & Snyers (2018).
161 Supra, note [159], Houben & Snyers (2018).
162 Supra, note [159], Houben & Snyers (2018).
163 Cryptoassets Taskforce: Final Report, October 2018.
164 Financial Conduct Authority (2019), "Guidance on Cryptoassets: Feedback and Final Guidance to CP 19/3", *FCA Policy Statement PS19*, 22/07/2019, www.fca.org.uk/publication/policy/ps19-22.pdf, accessed 08/08/2019.
165 SI 2001/544 as amended.
166 They will also be caught throughout the EU by the Markets in Financial Instruments Directive II (MiFID II).

Cryptocurrency derivatives[167] will be caught under the financial services regulatory regime as all three categories of derivative are "specialised investments" under the Financial Services and Markets Act 2000 (Regulated Activities) Order 2001.[168] The three categories are:

- Cryptocurrency futures which exist where two parties agree that one will transfer an amount equal in value to a cryptocurrency's future price on a stated or determinable future date in return for a determinable payment in the other direction. Essentially if the cryptocurrency rises in value in the interim one party will gain, if it falls then the other will.
- Cryptocurrency options are in essence a variation on this arrangement. Here one party pays a deposit in return for the right to notionally sell a cryptocurrency to the other party or to buy it from them. In the event of the price moving in favour of the depositor they will make a profit. In the event of its value moving the other way they will suffer a loss, but if this exceeds the amount of the deposit they can forfeit the deposit and their loss will be limited to that amount. As this contract is somewhat one sided in terms of risk compared with a futures contract, the terms offered will not be as attractive.
- Cryptocurrency contracts for differences are an arrangement where two parties agree to exchange payments equal in value to the difference between the price of a cryptocurrency and a stated item of other value for a fixed or determinable period of time.

This means that the party arranging, selling, advising or managing in relation to them will have to be regulated by the FCA.[169] The regulatory concerns, although real, have not yet come to an overall completed regulatory approach. The speed of development of the marketplace, coupled with a realisation by those inside the regulators that significant investment and job opportunities might be tied up in the new developments, has resulted in a considered approach. The Cryptoassets Taskforce (CAT) has been set up, including the FCA, HM Treasury and the Bank of England with a view to analysing the impact not only of cryptocurrencies but also cryptoassets generally and DLT. Their Report[170] was carried out against a background of not wishing to obstruct innovative developments in these areas.[171] This is evidenced by the

---

167 Essentially futures, options and contracts for differences where the underlying "commodity" is a cryptocurrency; Soylemez, Y. (2020), "Cryptocurrency derivatives: The case of bitcoin" in U. Hacioglu (ed.), *Blockchain economics and financial market innovations: Financial innovations in the digital age*, Basel, Springer.

168 SI 2001/544 as amended.

169 And for capital adequacy purposes the Prudential Regulation Authority (PRA) if they are a bank or insurance company.

170 Cryptoassets Taskforce: *Final Report*, October 2018.

171 Department for Digital, Culture, Media and Sport (2017) "Executive Summary: Our Plan for Britain" *Department for Digital, Culture, Media and Sport*, 01/03/2017. https://www.gov.uk/government/publications/uk-digital-strategy/executive-summary, accessed 31/01/2020.

government investing over £10 million to support a range of DLT projects including analysing its potential for use in the public sector and joining the EU Blockchain Partnership, which will require a national approach following the UK's departure from the EU. In addition, £20 million has been made available through the GovTech Catalyst Fund to explore both this and the potential of DLT in the financial services area. There are already 12 cryptoasset spot exchanges in the UK of which only four post daily trading volumes of over US$30 million equivalent. The 12 only amount to 2.66% of worldwide daily trading, though it should be added that some overseas exchanges have subsidiaries or branches here.[172]

The Taskforce determined that key issues were:

- Maintaining the UK's international reputation as a safe and transparent place to do business;
- Ensuring that there are high regulatory standards in the financial marketplace;
- Protecting consumers;
- Guarding against future threats to financial stability; and
- Allowing those who innovate within the rules to prosper.

The FCA have created an "Innovation Hub and Regulatory Sandbox" to allow businesses to test "innovative products, services, business models and delivery mechanisms in the real market, with real consumers."[173] A significant, if currently small, number of firms have used this facility.[174]

The Bank of England have created a Fintech hub to consider how the policy implications of the new developments might work out. One development was the work with 18 firms relating to proof of concepts to assist in understanding how the new technologies might be adopted. There has also been an analysis of the existing payments system[175] to see how comparable it will be with DLT-based payment systems. The Financial Policy Committee have also considered the financial stability implications of cryptoassets.

Within the current regulatory regime certain areas will be relevant for any regulated firms working with cryptocurrency as their business requires these elements from all regulated firms in the carrying out of their business activities.

- The FCA Principles for Business and in particular the requirement that a firm maintain sufficient financial resources, maintain adequate systems and controls and also that they deal with the FCA in an open and cooperative way.

---

172 Cryptoassets Taskforce: *Final Report*, October 2018, p 15.
173 Cryptoassets Taskforce: *Final Report*, October 2018, p 5.
174 89 firms used it including over a third of these who used DLT and/or cryptoassets.
175 The Bank of England's new RTGS service.

- The Senior Managers and Certification regime (SMCR) which means that the regulator can hold senior management of the relevant firms responsible even if the activity concerned was an unregulated one.
- The Systems and Control Provisions which deal with organisation, risk control, record keeping and employee requirements, to name the most important.
- The Financial Promotions Rules which require that promotions be clear, fair and not misleading. This requires behaviour to be in line with the Financial Promotions Order 2005.[176] Essentially, this divides communications with the public into unsolicited real time, solicited real time and non-real time communications.
- The first of these essentially covers cold calling by speaking to someone in person or over the phone. The second covers doing so after the receipt of evidence that the member of the public wishes to be contacted on the matter and the final one covers other methods of communication such as writing, email and leaving and answerphone message. The further down this list of three communication goes, the less vulnerable the recipient, and therefore the less protection they receive. The nature of the investment concerned is also a factor with those involving longer term and larger risks providing greater protection, mostly in terms of the risk warnings that have to be provided.

In addition, a firm which is not licensed to carry on investment business will be committing a criminal offence[177] if they induce anyone to enter into business involving regulated investments, which as we have seen will include some of the examples of cryptocurrency. A problem that arises here is that the newness of the cryptocurrency market means that it may not be entirely sure whether some products are going to be caught by the regulators or not. If in doubt a firm should seek the regulator's view.

The main concern of the CAT was that there were key risks to the public. They were: the risk of large-scale losses to the public, losses due to market manipulation and also that the products might be used as vehicles for financial crime.[178] As yet though they are not seen as posing a potential threat to financial stability.

What then do the regulators see as their perceived benefits? Firstly, their use as a means of exchange opens up the possibility of increased efficiency in the international financial transfer markets as a result of fewer intermediaries being involved. There is also the possibility that they could improve the traceability and transparency of financial transactions and increase stability as there would be no central system which might be disrupted. It may also lower barriers to

---

176 SI 2005/1529 as amended.
177 Section 21 of the Financial Services and Markets Act 2000.
178 Cryptoasset Taskforce (2018), "Cryptoassets taskforce final report", Cryptoassets Taskforce Final Report, October 2018, https://assets.publishing.service.gov.uk/government/uploads/system/uploads/attachment_data/file/752070/cryptoassets_taskforce_final_report_final_web.pdf, accessed 5/03/2019, p 41.

entry, encourage competition and provide an alternative to traditional payment methods.

When cryptoassets are used as an investment, they may also widen access, but subject to what are seen at present as an unacceptable degree of risk. When cryptoassets are used to raise capital there are potential benefits. ICOs may be supporting new business models and provide incentives for improvements in the traditional process of raising capital. They may also improve efficiency as they directly link issuers with investors and this is a particular benefit with small issuances. In particular, there could be a benefit in that it can help address the funding gap. Firstly, many high-risk projects find it difficult to raise funds in the early stages of projects and the direct connection may help here. In addition, there is the classic funding gap of between around £1 million and £10 million where funding has traditionally been hard to raise. The new ICO market could change this. Finally, the international basis of ICOs will mean that smaller firms can tap into the international financial markets in a way in which they could not have done in the past.

The key risk they found was that there was a concern expressed that money launderers and terrorist financiers would benefit because "of their accessibility online, their global reach and their pseudo-anonymous nature."[179] The UK Government's analysis[180] suggested that the risk of this remained low though a fear was expressed that cryptoassets could assist in crime related to computer technology. Concerns also relate to the anonymity of cryptoassets ATMs, peer-to-peer exchange facilities and the relative privacy of some coins. Europol's latest analysis suggests that around £3 to 4 billion is laundered using cryptoassets, which is only 3% to 4% of the amount laundered in Europe alone.[181]

The risk of financial losses for investors has already been mentioned, but in addition there is the risk of products being marketed with poor or unclear pricing material. There is also no recourse to the Financial Ombudsmen Scheme or the Financial Services Compensation Scheme. Also mentioned was the lack of clarity of ICO offerings due to the lack of standardisation such as that exists with regard to prospectuses in relation to the public offering of shares or bonds. Indeed, a recent report suggested that around 25% of ICOs could be fraudulent.[182] Around 46% of those issued in 2017 have already failed.[183] Those derivatives involving cryptoassets could also cause an investor to lose more than the amount they invest and retail investors may not be cognisant of this.

---

179 Supra, note [178] Cryptoassets Taskforce [2018], p. 33.
180 In the form of the National Risk Assessments of Money Laundering and Terrorist Financing 2015 and 2017.
181 Silma, S. (2018), "Criminals Hide Billions in Cryptocash – Europol." BBC, 12/02/2018. www.bbc.co.uk/news/technology-43025787. See also the FATF report to the G20 Finance Ministers and Central Bank Governors, Financial Action Task Force, 2018.
182 BIS Annual Report, Bank for International Settlements, 2018.
183 Hankin, A. (2018), "Nearly half of all 2017 ICOs have failed", *Market Watch*, 26/02/2018, https://www.marketwatch.com/story/nearly-half-of-all-2017-icos-have-failed-2018-02-26, accessed 07/02/2020.

The London Stock Exchange has not yet approved a listing which references any of these three categories and will only do so where they have confidence in the integrity of the underlying product. That said there have been 56 ICOs used for raising capital in the UK which accounts for 4.3% of the world market during the relevant period.[184] What is also significant is the location of those investing by this means but unfortunately this is not known. A comparison with the geographical spread of investors in conventional bond or share issues would be of interest.

The conclusions reached by the Taskforce were that they would:

- Implement comprehensive responses relating to the illicit use of cryptocurrency;
- Consider prohibiting the sale to retail investors of derivatives which refer to cryptocurrencies;
- Provide guidance clarifying how cryptoassets fall within the existing regulatory perimeter;
- Consider whether the regulatory perimeter requires extension in relation to cryptoassets;
- The Taskforce also believed that exchange tokens posed particular risks and HM Treasury are therefore going to engage in consultation in 2019 to see how they, together with exchanges and wallet providers can be best regulated.

These steps are now awaited and any steps will also inevitably involve international cooperation. The FCA together with the other members of the UK's CAT, namely the Treasury and the BoE would in response to the Final Crypto-Asset Final Report[185] consult on cryptoassets guidance so as to provide firms with additional clarity concerning the present regulatory perimeter that differentiates regulated and unregulated financial activities. The FCA consultation would also review potentially banning the sale to retail consumers of derivatives referencing particular kinds of cryptoassets, tax treatment of cryptoassets and the extension of the 5AMLD pertaining to the application of cryptoassets for illicit activities.[186]

As alluded to earlier, the main impediment to the design of new rules and policies could be attributed to the lack of a common lexicon around cryptoassets.[187] Global Digital Finance, an industry grouping is trying to resolve this issue. Meanwhile, it has been said that countries with a higher level of domestic cryptoasset activity usually have retrofitted regulation.[188] This response is justifiable in the context of the fast-moving new space that

---

184 Coinschedule market research in association with the Taskforce, 20 August 2018.
185 Supra, note [178] Cryptoassets Taskforce [2018].
186 FCA (2019), "Guidance on cryptoassets", *FCA Consultation Paper CP19/38*, January 2019.
187 Bladin, A. et al (April 2019), *Global cryptoasset regulatory landscape study*, Cambridge, Cambridge Centre for Alternative Finance (CCAF).
188 Supra, note [187], Bladin (April 2019).

encountered early signs of fraudulent activity. Malta and Luxembourg have been able to develop crypto-friendly regulatory and tax regimes, but their ability to achieve this is intrinsically linked to their relative lack of cryptoasset activity.

Compared to conventional systems where regulators are able to deal with individual nodes of firms or individuals on a case-by-case basis, networks premised on DLT, on the other hand, operate according to consensus and encryption might not be reliant on any one node. Here, regulators have the conundrum of resolving whether node operators have responsibility for the assets traded or the private key holders that made the transaction.[189] This is because a majority group of participants in a distributed network could collude to reach a consensus and undo a transaction or block a particular private key from transacting thereby making their digital assets useless.

Thus far, this pivotal point has not been resolved sufficiently and where node operators assumed responsibility they might have to be regulated. Importantly, when involving cross-jurisdictional transactions, purpose-built rules could be needed to counter this. Self-regulated industry-led entities for this reason play important roles as initiatives for setting up appropriate regulations continue.[190] Meanwhile, the regulatory sandbox is viewed in the UK and many other jurisdictions across the world as a fine example of a collaborative and structured approach to innovation and innovative products. Eighty-nine entities across four past cohorts have been able to test innovative products, services, business models and delivery mechanisms with real consumers under regulator monitoring. A further 29 entities were led into the frame at end of April 2019, including eight DLT-focused businesses. This is by far FCA's more successful story, as the national regulatory sandbox is now a global regulatory sandbox[191] with participations of many economies and would soon include the US too. The willingness of other jurisdictions to join in is due to their recognition that this is probably the best approach to deal with Fintech start-ups that deal with financial instruments characterised by cross-border features.

The FCA, as mentioned earlier, proposed rules in July 2019 to address harm to retail consumers arising from the sale of derivatives and exchange-traded notes referencing particular kinds of cryptoassets. Due to the inherent nature of the underlying assets that have no reliable basis for valuation, the prevalence of market abuse and financial crimes in the cryptoasset secondary market, extreme

---

189 Marshall, S. (2019), "Cryptoasset compliance in the UK: The story so far", *Torca*, 23/05/2019, https://www.torca.io/blog/cryptoasset-compliance-in-the-uk-the-story-so-far, accessed 02/06/2019.

190 Supra, note [189], Marshall (2019).

191 FCA (2019), "Global financial innovation network (GFIN)", *FCA*, 09/08/2019, www.fca.org.uk/firms/global-financial-innovation-network, accessed 10/08/2019; Strachan, D., Nair, S., Gallo, V. & Fouche, M. (2019), "A journey through the FCA regulatory sandbox", EMEA Centre for Regulatory Strategy Paper 2019, www2.deloitte.com/content/dam/Deloitte/uk/Documents/financial-services/deloitte-uk-fca-regulatory-sandbox-project-innovate-finance-journey.pdf, accessed 08/08/2019.

price volatility and inadequate understanding by retail consumers of cryptoassets the FCA consider these products as unsuitable for retail consumers.[192] This has been put out for consultation, with 3 October 2019 as the deadline for submission of comments.

It seems for now the UK government has not expanded the FCA's regulatory perimeter and has only assigned it to be the supervisor for the 5AMLD. As said earlier, the 5AMLD will introduce an anti-money laundering regime for cryptoassets. This will bring within its remit virtual currency exchange platforms and wallet providers. Thus, this will therefore help to dampen some consumer protection and market integrity fears that had emerged exposing users' identities and fund sources.

The 31 July 2019 FCA Final Guidance therefore sets out the regulatory treatment of cryptoassets within FCA's regulatory remit. This was undertaken in response to CAT's final report released in November 2018 that tasked the FCA to provide guidance pertaining to its existing regulatory perimeter. The regulatory perimeter sets the demarcation between regulated and unregulated financial services. Where entities undertake activities falling within the regulatory perimeter within the UK as part of their business, it would likely be required to be authorised by the FCA, or in some other instances by the PRA, except when exempted. Business entities are not able to issue financial promotional activities like inviting persons to partake in investment activities, such as getting them to purchase regulated cryptoassets without FCA approval or a person authorised by the FCA for approving the contents of these communications.

A person undertaking specified activities pertaining to specified investments will fall under the FCA's regulatory perimeter. The FCA in this connection has demarcated two broad kinds of unregulated tokens; utility and exchange tokens, and two broad kinds of regulated tokens, electronic money (e-money) and security tokens.

Exchange tokens are tokens not deemed as legal tender. These usually will not grant the holder any rights associated with specified investments and are decentralised with no centralised issuers obliged to honour any contractual rights. These, as exemplified by Bitcoin, Ether and XRP will fall outside of FCA's regulatory perimeter. Nevertheless, the FCA tells businesses to be aware of the country's intention to extend the requirements of the 5AMLD to include exchange services between cryptoassets, transfer of cryptoassets, cryptoasset ATMs, and new cryptoassets issued through ICOs.

Utility tokens are tokens providing consumers with access to current or prospective services or products. These are equivalent to pre-payment vouchers and will accordingly fall outside the regulatory perimeter. The FCA narrated various case examples of these.

---

192 FCA (2019), "FCA proposes ban on sale of crypto-derivatives to retail consumers", *FCA News Release*, 03/07/2019, https://www.fca.org.uk/news/press-releases/fca-proposes-ban-sale-crypto-derivatives-retail-consumers, accessed 05/07/2019.

Regulated security tokens are tokens that provide rights and obligations similar to specified investments like shares, other than e-money, will be within FCA's regulatory perimeter. The FCA cautioned that this will depend on the substance or token intention and not the form or labelling used. Regulated e-money tokens are tokens that are defined under the Electronic Money Regulations 2011 (EMRs). The EMRs define e-money as electronically stored monetary value as represented by a claim on the e-money issuer. Stablecoins referred to tokens stabilised through being backed by fiats, cryptoassets, algorithms, other tangible assets, or their combinations thereof subject to their structure and the stabilisation model and these would remain, for the moment, outside of the FCA's perimeter. Any tokens, though pegged to fiats or other assets deployed for the payments of goods and services on a network, potentially could fall within the definition of e-money and ergo within FCA's perimeter.

Mainstream cryptoassets commentators claimed that given the popularity of security token offerings there could be a blurring of the lines between these and utility tokens.[193] This is because utility tokens could be labelled as security tokens to ensure that they do not fall foul of any promotion type restrictions. This raises the question as to whether this actually alters the nature of the token itself when it comes to trading in them. The FCA though has clarified that they pay less attention to labelling than the underlying characteristics. The FCA has further clarified that further clarity between types of tokens would be forthcoming, like demarcating a specific regulated e-money token category and an unregulated category that includes utility tokens.

For this and more, the FCA would need the Treasury to bring more cryptoassets into the law, and that would require serious thinking as to the country's intention for the Fintech space. This would need to balance the benefits of innovation with the needs for investors' safety risk and financial stability considerations, but taking into considerations what other competitive hubs across the world has done thus far.

Various kinds of market participants and the activities they undertake would likely be required to comply with the Prospectus Regulation or would otherwise require authorisation for the deliver of services like the forwarding of dematerialised instructions; the safeguarding and administering of investments; the advising on investments; and dealing, arranging, or operating an OTF or an MTF.

It needs stressing that though the FCA guidance is not binding on courts, entities are generally treated to have complied with FCA rules when they act in accordance with these. The Final Guidance is, ergo, applicable to businesses that issue or generate cryptoassets, that market cryptoassets products/services, that transact on cryptoassets, that hold or store cryptoassets, financial advisers, professional advisers, investment managers, recognised investment exchanges, and consumers and consumer entities.

---

193 Allison, I. (2019), "UK finance watchdog issues guidance on regulation for Bitcoin and cryptoassets", *Coin Desk*, 31/07/2019, www.coindesk.com/uk-financial-watchdog-issues-full-guidance-on-crypto-assets, accessed 02/08/2019.

The UK through the FCA has therefore taken the initial steps in the regulatory treatment of cryptoassets in the country, but keeping in mind its mission of dealing with consumer protection harms, market integrity harms and competition harms. The FCA will strive to measure the success in achieving these outcomes via:

- evaluating feedback from Final Guidance stakeholders
- growth in the numbers and accuracies of authorisation submission from businesses undertaking regulated cryptoassets activities
- fewer referrals to its Unauthorised Business Division and Financial Promotions team showing that persons and their advisers are clearer about when they need authorisation and when FCA's financial promotion rules would set in
- fewer calls and/or requests for support via Innovate on issues pertaining to the regulatory application to cryptoassets
- evaluating feedback from consumers as to whether FCA's regulatory framework has helped consumers better understand the cryptoassets markets, by potentially measuring this through follow-up consumer surveys and analysing calls via the FCA Consumer Hub.

The Final Guidance has also informed market participants of FCA's cryptoassets regulatory works-in-progress, like as mentioned earlier, the consultation on potentially banning the sale of derivatives linked to particular kinds of unregulated cryptoassets to retail clients; Treasury's consultation on whether further regulation is required in the cryptoassets markets, especially with respect of unregulated cryptoassets mentioned earlier; and Treasury and FCA work on the transposing of the 5AMLD.

Overall, FCA's Final Guidance has contributed to enhanced understanding on how to approach the crypto industry for interested business entities. For investors and retail investors this enhances clarity of the kinds of risks involved when looking at cryptoassets as an investment class and importantly how and why they differ as well as the regulatory and hence safety implications involved. However, for many and especially those dabbling with unregulated items they might need to consult from the insights observed in other jurisdictions that have gone further on the regulatory pathways and the kind of experiences they have had thus far. This helps to explain the purpose and benefit of taking a global perspective on the laws and regulations surrounding the evolution of cryptoassets.

In any case, the sea of voices, particularly those from the primary stakeholders, not only in the UK, but out there across the other main crypto hubs in other parts of the world, could impact the regulatory agenda usually straddling between being ahead in innovations and being too loose on safety, security, and stability measures. This probably helps to explain why structures and remits are in flux as regulators and supervisors adapt their agendas and working methods to the rapidly evolving environment.[194] The trend of supervision in the sector is both widening and deepening, with supervisors needing to turn to technology or exponential techs to help them discharge their obligations more efficiently. There have been some new rule-making in some niches and in some jurisdictions, but supervisory and regulatory missions are increasingly focused on the monitoring and review of major post-crisis rules. Policymakers and regulators are yet insisting on more data and increasingly also calls from institutional investors and the industry for a rationalisation of requirements and for greater global regulatory convergence. This is not going to be easy, given today's geopolitics tempo and tantrums.

7.7 Australia's cryptoassets regulatory policy

Australia's Anti-Money Laundering and Counter-Terrorism Financing Amendment Bill 2017 (AMLCTF) was passed in December 2017, but this was further amended in 2018.[195] The initiative was aimed at imposing restrictions on digital currencies, especially Bitcoin, due to their continuous growth and adoption in the mainstream financial sector and importantly to fight the threat of financial crimes in Australia. Australian lawmakers felt the need to make this move after discovery that one of the country's major banks, the Commonwealth Bank, had violated laws pertaining to money laundering.[196] This was also the response to the Financial Task Force's report that the country's existing laws to combat money laundering have serious flaws that needed amendments to eliminate loopholes. The proposed laws empower AUSTRAC, the country's financial and intelligence agency, to monitor the activities of all cryptocurrency exchanges operating in Australia. The primary aim of the monitoring is to ensure that financial transactions are not related to money laundering or terrorism.

The AMLCTF expands the Act's object to reflect the domestic objectives of anti-money laundering and counter-terrorism financing regulations. It also expands the scope of the Act to include regulation of digital currency exchange providers, clarify due diligence obligations pertaining to correspondent banking relationships, and widen the scope of these relationships. This Act in particular would require businesses offering convertible digital currency exchange services, like exchanging money for Bitcoin or vice versa, to be registered with and subject to mandatory reporting obligations to AUSTRAC.

---

194 Brown, T. & Patterson, J. (2019), "A sea of voices: Evolving asset management regulation report", KPMG Paper June 2019, https://home.kpmg/content/dam/kpmg/nl/pdf/2019/advisory/a-sea-of-voices.pdf, accessed 08/08/2019.

195 Anti-Money Laundering and Counter-Terrorism Financing Act 2006, No. 169, 2006, Compilation No.48 Including Amendments up to Act no. 156, 2018 20 December 2018, https://www.legislation.gov.au/Details/C2019C00011, accessed 07/02/19.

196 Althauser, J. (2017), "Australian exchanges now required to register with AML regulatory body", Coin Telegraph, 09/12/2017, https://cointelegraph.com/news/australian-exchanges-now-required-to-register-with-aml-regulatory-body, accessed 02/02/2018.

If enacted in its present form, the key provisions and their implications are as follows[197]:

(i) Digital currency exchanges would be required to secure registration with AUSTRAC; undertake customer due diligence together with the usual anti-money laundering and counter-terrorism checks; provide suspicious transactions reports to AUSTRAC involving physical currencies of A$10,000 or more; and maintain particular records about transactions and customer identification for seven years.

(ii) Offering digital currency exchange services without AUSTRAC registration would be a criminal offence. For a first offence, penalties of up to two years' imprisonment and/or 500 penalty units, equivalent to A$105,000 would apply. Significantly higher penalties are applicable for repeat offences. Alternatively, offenders could be pursued through the civil penalty provisions that presently stipulates penalties of up to A$2.1 million for businesses and A$420,000 for individuals

(iii) The setting up of a Digital Currency Exchange Register gathering background information and other details on AUSTRAC-approved entities providing digital currency exchange services.

(iv) When enacted, the AMLCTF brings Australia's AML and CTF law into line with similar measures already in place in the EU, Canada and the US. In targeting the activities of Bitcoin exchange providers, the AMLCTF essentially focuses on the "entry" and "exit" points in the digital currency space. This is when a person either uses regular money to purchase digital currency or when seeking to convert digital currency back into regular money. As such, it would not impact on how digital currency could be transferred between users without thereby affecting the privacy of such transactions.

The Australian Taxation Office (ATO), in its taxation guidance for cryptocurrencies, maintains that transacting with Bitcoin is similar to a barter arrangement, with similar consequences.[198] ATO's view is that cryptocurrencies are neither money nor a foreign currency and that their supply is not a financial supply for goods and services tax (GST) purposes. It is, however, an asset for capital gains tax (CGT) purposes. As such cryptocurrency users need to keep transaction records containing the date of the transactions, the amount in Australian dollars (extractable from reputable online exchanges), what the transaction was for, and who the other party was, even if it is just their crypto address.

---

[197] Allgrove, A-M., Fair, P., Lawrence, A.J. & Patten, T. (2017), "Bitcoin to be regulated in Australia", *Baker McKenzie*, 01/12/2017, www.bakermckenzie.com/en/insights/../2017/../Bitcoin-to-be-registered-in-australia, accessed 02/02/2018.

[198] Australian Taxation Office (2019), "Tax treatment of cryptocurrencies in Australia- specifically bitcoin", *ATO*, 18/06/2019, https://www.ato.gov.au/General/Gen/Tax-treatment-of-cryptocurrencies-in-Australia---specifically-bitcoin/, accessed 07/02/2020.

When using cryptocurrencies to purchase goods and services for personal use or consumption, any gain or loss from disposal of that cryptocurrency would be disregarded as a personal use asset provided the cost is A$10,000 or less. When receiving cryptocurrency for goods and services that are provided as part of a business this would be treated as ordinary income, equivalent to the same process as receiving non-cash consideration under a barter transaction. The value in Australian dollars would be the fair market value obtainable from a reputable exchange. As from 1 July 2017, sales and purchases of cryptocurrency are no longer subject to GST, but changes might follow.

Australian regulation for cryptoassets in the capital market has advanced. The ASIC have announced in their Corporate Plan for 2018–22 that they will focus on the potential "harmful effects" in this area.[199] This means that crypto exchanges are now going to be regulated along the same lines as stock exchanges and financial market operators and will thus be required to register with the Digital Currency Exchange Register.[200] ASIC updated its regulatory guidance (INFO225) in May 2019[201] with details of legal obligations for cryptocurrency firms under Australia's Corporation Act, the ASIC Act and other applicable laws. This is far more comprehensive and now specifically refers to more business models with various examples shown to provide market participants with enhanced understanding on how ASIC would regard their use of cryptoassets. Thus, INFO225 has been relabelled to include a consideration of cryptoassets, rather than confined only to cryptocurrency. This suggests a widening of the intended guidance and due notation of the evolving nature of the cryptoassets market away from ICO offerings of cryptocurrencies towards tokenised funds and security token offerings.

Foremost, ASIC's regulatory guide will apply to cryptoassets issuers, cryptoasset intermediaries, cryptoassets exchange and trading platforms, cryptoasset payment and merchant service providers, and wallet providers and custody service providers. Second, irrespective of the labelling used, INFO225 updates previous guidance to provide further details on when ASIC will consider the features of ICOs or tokens to demonstrate that the offer is of an interest in managed investment scheme (MIS), a security, a derivative or a non-cash payment facility. INFO225 has now revised the previous guidance on MIS significantly. It has provided details pertaining to the requirements of retail and wholesale MIS offerings. It also tells why relying on an appointment as a corporate authorised representative of another Australian Financial Services Licence (AFSL) will not by itself be adequate to issue interests in an ICO or cryptoassets that has been treated as an MIS.

---

199 ASIC (2018), "18-260MR Asic's Corporate Plan 2018-2022", *ASIC*, 07/09/2018, https://asic.gov.au/about-asic/news-centre/find-a-media-release/2018-releases/18-260mr-asic-s-corporate-plan-2018-2022/, accessed 26/02/2019.

200 Suberg, W. (2018), "Australia launches new cryptocurrency exchange regulations", *Coin Telegraph*, 03/04/2018, https://cointelegraph.com/news/australia-launches-new-cryptocurrency-exchange-regulations, accessed 10/02/2020.

201 ASIC (2019), "Initial coin offerings and crypto-assets", *ASIC Information sheet INFO225*, 30/05/2019.

The INFO225 Guidance confirms that ASIC expects businesses to be able to form conclusions that their tokens or ICOs are not financial products and to know who their investors are, where the business seeks to rely on wholesale/sophisticated investor exemptions. It cautions that Australian laws cited to apply to particular tokens might not be exhaustive and responsibility will fall on the entities to ensure compliance with the laws. It has now been further clarified that to operate in Australia, exchanges listing tokens that are deemed as financial products will be required to hold an Australian market licence unless exempted. ASIC cautioned that as of now, there are no licensed or exempt exchanges in the country that could enable investors to transact in cryptoassets treated as financial products. It has also clarified that overseas token categorisations will not automatically translate to equivalent products in the country. ASIC clarified further that the country's definition of a financial products is wider than those in other jurisdictions. This means extra care on ascertaining whether an entity's token, though not treated as a financial product in other jurisdictions, could be the case. Blockchain ventures not involving the use of cryptocurrencies remain unimpacted by this guidance, even though other jurisdictions have provided clearer pathways.

This again suggests the benefits of taking a global approach when studying the nature of cryptoassets as they continue to evolve and why national regulatory and supervisory authorities need to be vigilant on the current regulatory regimes across the world to avoid being perceived as inhospitable fintech hubs, now that Switzerland, Singapore and the UK have provided relatively clear categorisation of tokens and paths forward for the issue of cryptographic tokens. Despite these, INFO225 is argued to represent one small step for man, with a giant leap to be made in regulatory treatment to accommodate blockchain initiatives such as smart contracts.[202]

7.8 Canada's cryptoassets regulatory policy

Canada, like the US, supports and advances the use of advanced technology. Again, like most advanced economies it strives to take a balanced regulatory approach that, while protecting consumer welfare, would also promote and not stand in the way of technological innovation, especially when dealing with emerging exponential industries (those using Industry 4.0 technologies that yields faster, cheaper, and higher quality outcomes relative to those using conventional technologies), such as those to do with blockchain and cryptoassets. The country has in this respect opted for timely relevant state action to leverage on the opportunities unleashed by these while being mindful of the challenges, pitfalls and risks associated with the virtual currency domain.[203]

---

[202] Bacina, M., Skevington T. (2019), "ASIC updates crypto-asset guidance-it's one small step for man ...", *Piper Alderman Paper*, 06/06/2019, www.piperalderman.com.au/publications/cryptocurrency-blockchain/article/31806, accessed 08/08/2019.

[203] Gerstein, I.R., Hervieux-Payette, C. (2015), "Digital currency. You can't flip this coin", *Senate Committee on Banking, Trade and Commerce Paper*, 30/06/2015, https://sencanada.ca/content/sen/Committee/412/banc/rep/rep12jun15-e.pdf, accessed 08/08/2019.

The country's taxation laws and rules are applicable to virtual currencies, including cryptoassets. Like the US CFTC, the Canadian Revenue Agency treats cryptoassets as commodities and not a sovereign fiat. Under general securities laws, various cryptocurrencies or tokens are categorised as securities. Thus, transactions via cryptoassets in Canada are deemed as barter transactions and gains and losses have to be reported to the tax authority.[204] Also, back in 2014, Canada amended its Proceeds of Crime (Money Laundering) and Terrorist Financing Act whereby virtual currencies are treated as money service businesses from the context of anti-money laundering law.[205]

The Canadian Securities Administrators (CSA) issued guidance on how securities law requirements could be applicable to ICOs, initial token offerings (ITOs), cryptocurrency investment funds and cryptoassets exchanges transacting in these products.[206] Canada's first DLT fund, namely Blockchain Technologies ETF was approved on 1 February 2018.[207] To enhance the understanding of how DLT could impact the wholesale payments systems, a collaborative research initiative between R3 (a DLT entity), Payments Canada and the Bank of Canada known as Project Jasper was undertaken in March 2016 along three phases. Its findings for Phase III were released in October 2018.[208] Phase I was built from an Ethereum platform, while Phase II was developed on the Corda platform. Phase III tested digital depository receipts (DDR) as a digital representation of Canadian currency in 2016 and 2017. Project Jasper tested this via CADcoin, with the Bank of Canada issuing DDR. Here, a transfer of DDR is equated with a full and irrevocable transfer of the underlying claim on central bank deposits.[209]

Cryptoassets regulation is essentially regulated under securities laws in line with the regulator's mission to protect the investing public. Securities laws are enacted and regulated under various applicable provincial laws, but these have been largely harmonised via the initiatives of the CSA that represents all provincially-mandated securities regulators in the country.

Canada used the Investment Contract Test (ICT) to determine whether a financial instrument could be categorised as a security. To fall within this categorisation, four conditions must be satisfied:[210] first, there must be an investment of money; second, there must be an intention or expectation of profit; third, there

---

204 Al-Shikarchy, M. & Gheorghiu, L. (2017), "Canadian taxation of cryptocurrency ... so far", *Gowling WSG Paper*, 14/11/2017, https://gowlingwlg.com/en/insights-resources/articles/2017/canadian-taxation-of-cryptocurrency-so-far/, accessed 08/08/2019.

205 Ahmad, T. (2014), "Regulation of cryptocurrency: Canada", *The Library of Congress*, June 2018, https://www.loc.gov/law/help/cryptocurrency/canada.php, accessed 07/02/2020.

206 Canadian Securities Administrators (CSAs) (2017), "Cryptocurrency offerings", *CSA Staff Notice 46–307*, 24/08/2017, www.osc.gov.on.ca/en/SecuritiesLaw_csa_20170824_cryptocurrencyofferings.htm, accessed 08/08/2019.

207 Milano, A. (2018), "Canadian regulators approve country's first blockchain ETF", *Coin Desk*, 02/02/2018, www.coindesk.com/canada-approves-countrys-first-blockchain-etf, accessed 08/08/2019.

208 Hendry, S., Lee, J., McCormack, A., Velissarios, J. & Webster, S. (2018), "Jasper Phase III: Securities settlement using distributed ledger technology", *Jasper III Report*, October 2018, www.payments.ca/industry-info/our-research/project-jasper, accessed 08/08/2019.

209 Supra, note [208], Hendry, Lee, McCormack, Vellissarios & Webster (2018).

210 *Pacific Coast Coin Exchange v Ontario Securities Commission*, [1978] 2 S.C.R. 112 (Pacific Coast).

must be a common enterprise; and, fourth, where the fate of the venture will be significantly impacted by the work of others, other than the investor. The courts in Canada would be guided by the substance and not the form of these contracts. The current regulatory trend in Canada involves applying and adapting existing securities laws, including the ICT to schemes involving blockchain or cryptoassets that mirrors conventional securities, without regard to the use of new technology.[211]

The CSA and the Investment Industry Regulatory Organization of Canada (IIROC) has proposed a regulatory framework for platforms that trade cryptoassets for public consultation. This potentially opens the gate for platforms transacting in cryptoassets that are securities or derivatives to operate with compliance in Canada.[212] These could include platforms doing business in security tokens or tokenised assets, decentralised prediction markets or other decentralised finance activities. This in turn could enable these platforms to establish and maintain business relationships with financial institutions, an issue now faced by many trading platforms. The benefits aside, the framework cautioned market participants of the various operational requirements intended to protect participants from the counterparty and other risks associated with platforms, as shown by QuadrigaCX's recent collapse. These would extend to requirements for market integrity, market surveillance, fair pricing, custody, clearing and settlement, conflicts of interest disclosures, and systems and business continuity planning.

All in all, Canada shows a very positive attitude towards blockchain and cryptoassets and has been in the forefront where the design of regulatory frameworks for these are concerned. This also helps to explain why many crypto miners from China have set up shop in Canada.

7.9 Switzerland's cryptoassets regulatory policy

Switzerland has sustained its reputation as the global centre for the wealth management industry, accounting for some 27% of global offshore wealth, or some US$2 trillion.[213] Switzerland's crypto and blockchain development hub in Zug city known globally as Europe's Crypto Valley[214] is ranked the fastest-growing tech community in Europe. Zug enjoys a 177% increase in meetup events in 2018 compared to 2017, followed by Novosibirsk in Russia, Ghent in Belgium, The Hague, Katowice in Poland, Dortmund in Germany, Newcastle in the UK, Sofia in Bulgaria, Essen in Germany and Cardiff in the UK.[215] Switzerland also

---

211 Druzeta, C., Grant, S. & Peters, M. (2019), "Canada", in Dewey, J. (ed.), *Blockchain and cryptocurrency regulation*, 2019 1st edn, pp. 243–253, London, Global Legal Insights.

212 Ritchies, L.E., Stein, L. & Thomas, E. (2019), "CSA and IIROC propose regulatory framework for cryptoasset trading platforms", *Osler Paper*, 15/03/2019, www.osler.com/en/resources/regulations/2019/csa-and-iiroc-propose-regulatory-framework-for-cryptoasset-trading-platforms, accessed 08/08/2019.

213 Ozelli, S. (2018), "Why Switzerland is becoming a 'Crypto Nation' with a flourishing ICO market: Expert take", *Coin Telegraph* 8/01/2018, https://cointelegraph.com/news/why-switzerland-is-becoming-a-crypto-nation-with-a-flourishing-ico-market-expert-take, accessed 08/08/2019.

214 Supra, note [213], Ozelli (2018).

215 Atomico (2018), *The state of European tech 2018*, Zurich, Atomico.

enjoys being the most blockchain friendly European country. The UK on the other hand is the leading destination for all international movers into the European tech ecosystem, followed closely by Germany, France, Netherlands, Ireland, and Switzerland.[216]

Switzerland was at risk of losing its competitive edge over rival financial markets after being pressured to giving up major aspects of its world-renowned banking secrecy laws reputation due to the aggressive moves by the US DOJ and the IRS Criminal Investigations Division. This was demonstrated by the closing down of one of its oldest private banks and billions in fines on its more prominent banks. Zug in becoming a global hub for virtual currencies seems to save the day by helping the country to acquire the reputation of being the crypto nation for the digital revolution with a flourishing ICO market.[217] Swiss-based ICOs raised about US$550 million in funding in 2017, accounting form some 14% of the global ICO market.[218] Many Swiss ICOs are designed as foundations applying for non-profit tax status with money raised in them deemed as donations that might not be returned to ICO investors.[219]

The country via the Swiss Financial Market Supervisory Authority (FINMA) is likely to deploy forward looking regulation via the tweaking of its existing laws to accommodate crypto technology and its financial applications. The regulatory journey began with a cautionary alert to investors about fake cryptocurrency in 19 September 2017. This was followed by a concise briefing on the country's ICO regulatory approach in 29 September 2017, when FINMA drew attention to market participants to comply with some potentially applicable banking, securities dealer, anti-money laundering, and prospectus laws and regulations. Towards this end, FINMA provided a detailed guidance for ICOs setting out various basic features of ICOs. These support FINMA's position that ICOs represent an approach for accessing funds digitally for entrepreneurial ventures. Here, FINMA conceded that the wide range of token and ICO start-ups virtually made it not possible to generalise legal guidance.

As such, FINMA would treat each case on its own merits and demerits, focusing on the underlying economic purpose of an ICO, especially when there are signs of efforts to circumvent existing regulations. These would include evaluating the transferability and economic function and purpose of these tokens, so as to confirm their status as payment tokens, utility tokens, asset tokens, or hybrid tokens.

As to the designation of ICOs as securities, this would depend on evaluation through the Swiss Financial Market Infrastructure Act where securities have been defined as "standardised certificated or uncertificated securities, derivatives, and intermediated securities that are eligible for mass standardised

---

216 Supra, note [215], Atomico (2018).
217 Supra, note [213], Ozelli (2018).
218 Supra, note [213], Ozelli (2018).
219 Neghaiwi, B.H. (2018), "Top Swiss cryptocurrency law questions 'stupid' ICO structure", *Reuters*, 22/01/2018, www.reuters.com/article/uk-swiss-crypto/top-swiss-cryptocurrency-lawyer-questions-stupid-ico-structure-idUSKBN1FB1TM, accessed 08/08/2019.

trading, (meaning) ... being publicly offered for sale in the same structure and denomination or are placed with more than 20 clients".[220] Guided by this, payment tokens would not be treated as securities where these are designed as a means of payments; utility tokens where their sole aim is to give digital access rights to an application or service would also not be deemed as such; while tokens designed for investment purpose at the point of issue would be treated as securities in the same way as asset tokens. Where asset tokens constitute an uncertificated security or a derivative that depends on an underlying asset for its value and these tokens are standardised suitably for mass standardised trading, they would be treated as securities under existing laws. The Swiss Federal Council on 30 November 2018 amended the Swiss Banking Act whereby effective from 1 January 2019, businesses that undertake activities beyond conventional banking features including cryptocurrency and blockchain-related entities would be able to accept public funds up to a maximum of CHF 100 million provided they are authorised or licensed and do not invest or pay interest on these funds.[221] FINMA in late 2018 issued guidance for those seeking Fintech licences.[222]

FINMA claims that they have taken a balanced approach to handling ICO ventures to enable legitimate innovators to navigate the regulatory landscape to launch projects consistent with Swiss financial services laws while simultaneously protecting investors and the integrity of the country's financial system. Switzerland is also positioning as an attractive destination for ICOs for issuers and investors owing to the country's relatively more favourable tax laws.[223] This probably tells why Facebook Libra has opted for Switzerland to be its domicile for its global cryptoasset venture, despite warnings from US authority that it would still need to adhere to applicable US rules and regulations, particularly those having to do with AML laws.[224] Switzerland would nevertheless have to take on competition from offshore financial centres like the Cayman Islands, and Malta.

7.10 The Cayman Islands' cryptoasset regulatory policy

The Cayman Islands are seeking to be the preferred global jurisdiction for the formation of investment funds by increasingly investing in cryptoassets and exploiting on its investment opportunities in this niche. This is attributed to the

---

220 FINMA Guidelines Section 1.2(b).
221 International Monetary Fund (2019), "Switzerland: Financial sector assessment programme", *IMF Country Report No.19/184*, 26/06/2019, https://www.imf.org/en/Publications/CR/Issues/2019/06/26/Switzerland-Financial-Sector-Assessment-Program-47045, accessed 08/08/2019.
222 FINMA (2018), "Fintech license: FINMA publishes guidelines", *FINMA*, 03/12/2018, www.finma.ch/en/news/2018/12/20181203-aktuell-fintech-bewilligung/, accessed 08/08/2019.
223 Bohi, R., Wenger, D. & Wandel, S.A. (2017), "Switzerland: Taxation of initial coin offerings in Switzerland", Prager Dreifuss, 27/12/2017.
224 Miller, H. (2019), "Facebook's Libra will be under U.S. money-laundering scrutiny", *Bloomberg*, 10/09/2019,www.bloomberg.com/news/articles/2019-09-10/facebook-s-libra-on-u-s-radar-terrorist-financing-chief-warns, accessed 12/09/2019.

jurisdiction's neutral tax treatment, political stability and generally respectable regulatory framework.[225] Relative to other jurisdictions, the Cayman Islands securities regime is more favourable. Accordingly, the Cayman Islands are growing as a destination of choice for many ICOs and platform development entities, including cryptocurrency exchanges. Physical presence and support personnel are easy to develop in the jurisdiction, made even more attractive with the benefits from Cayman Islands's special economic zone, known popularly as the Cayman Enterprise City (CEC) that came into being in 2012.[226] Together with this, the government has also announced that a technology neutral regulatory sandbox will be set up to foster and incubate start-ups in the digital niche.

Existing laws are relied on when dealing with the regulation of cryptoassets. These would include dealing with the Proceeds of Crime Law (PCL), the Securities Investment Business Law, the US Foreign Account Tax Complaint Act (FATCA) and OECD's CRS, the Beneficial Ownership regime, the Money Services Law, the Mutual Funds Law, and the Stock Exchange Companies Law. Section 6 of the PCL specifies that businesses undertaking relevant financial businesses (RFBs) have to comply with AML regulations. RFBs include those investing, administering, or managing funds on behalf of other persons; issuing and managing means of payment; safe custody services; and money or value transfer business. Persons in violations of AML regulations commit an offence and will be liable on summary conviction to a fine of CI$500,000, or on an indictable conviction to an unlimited fine and imprisonment for two years.

The Cayman Islands Monetary Authority (CIMA) has regulatory powers for designated kinds of funds operating in and from the jurisdictions. No taxation is, however, imposed on Cayman entities, but those implementing cryptoassets kinds of business would need to consult tax advice from their respective jurisdictions and especially with due considerations for FATCA and CRS obligations. For now, no specific laws are in play in the jurisdiction with regards to cryptoassets, but these could be launched in the future. Overall, the Cayman Islands's ambition to become a global technology hub is well-supported by a sound legal framework (reinforced by updated copyright trade mark and parent laws passed in 2016, and the 2017 Data Protection Law), modern infrastructure, state-of-the-art communication systems, a 155% mobile penetration rate and a generally stable political climate.[227]

---

225 Gobin, I. & Skotnicki, D. (2018), "Cayman Islands", The Virtual Currency Regulation Review-Edition 1st November 2018, https://thelawreviews.co.uk/edition/the-virtual-currency-regulation-review-edition-1/1176633/cayman-islands, accessed 08/08/2019.

226 Special Economic Zones (Cayman Enterprise City) Order (2019 Revision. Supplement No. 5 published with Legislation Gazette No. 4 of 21st February 2019, www.gov.ky/portal/pls/portal/docs/1/12756506.PDF, accessed 08/08/2019.

227 Colegate, P. & Thomson, A. (2019), "Technology and innovation offshore guide: Cayman Islands", *Appleby Paper*, 20/03/2019, www.applebyglobal.com/wp-content/uploads/2019/05/Appleby-FinTech-Guide-Cayman-Islands-Final-Revised-20-May-2019.pdf, accessed 08/08/2019.

7.11 Malta's cryptoasset regulatory policy

Malta's quest to be a globally competitive blockchain island that would be the magnet for entities seeking to grow their blockchain-driven enterprises led to a dedicated digital regulatory regime since the second half of 2018. This comprised the Virtual Financial Assets Act (VFAA), the Digital Innovation Authority Act (MDIA),[228] and the Innovative Technology Arrangements and Services Act (ITAS)[229], and are collectively known as the 'Digital Innovation Framework'.[230] The idea behind this is to offer a relatively high degree of legal and regulatory certainty and clarity for those engaged in the blockchain and cryptoassets. Evidently, the Maltese government has taken notice about the regulatory challenges faced by these ventures arising primarily from most other jurisdictions which are either inhospitable to such enterprises or playing a wait-and-see game, or have decided to rely on existing securities, money transmission and related regulations that might not be easy to navigate through.

The VFAA addresses virtual financial assets (VFAs) and initial virtual financial assets offerings (IVFAOs) matters and matters ancillary or incidental to them.[231] Here, cryptocurrency is categorised as a VFA, and the legislation stipulates a list of rules that assists the industry's growth while equally protecting investors' welfare. It covers those initiating cryptocurrencies and service providers including cryptocurrency exchanges, investment advisers, e-Wallet service providers, custodian and nominee services providers, portfolio managers, and brokerages. IVFAOs are the equivalent of ICOs, or a mechanism for accessing funds wherein issuers will offer VFAs in exchange for funds. The legislation sets out and clarifies the necessary licensing and other conditions that interested parties have to comply with. It also specifies the kinds of VFAs that could be issued through IVFAOs and admission to trading on a DLT exchanges via a registered whitepaper at the Malta Financial Services Authority (MFSA), or the competent authority for this business in Malta. IVFAOs are treated as DLT-enabled ways for accessing funds by a legal person registered in Malta.

The VFAA and the MDIA define a DLT as a digital or electronic database or ledger where data is stored, shared consensually, synchronised through a network of multiple nodes, is distributed/decentralised/shared/replicated, public or private, permissioned or permissionless, and immutable and protected cryptographically. A VFA is referred to as any form of digital medium or data asset that is deployed as a digital medium of exchange, store of value and unit of account; that is not a virtual token, financial instrument, or electronic money. Virtual/utility tokens are deemed as DLT assets that have no utility, value or

---

228 The Digital Innovation Authority Act 2018, http://justiceservices.gov.mt/DownloadDocument.aspx?app=lp&itemid=29080&l=1, accessed 08/08/2019.

229 Innovative Technology Arrangements and Services Act 2018, http://justiceservices.gov.mt/DownloadDocument.aspx?app=lp&itemid=29078&l=1, accessed 08/08/2019.

230 Falzon, M. & Valenzia, A. (2020), "Blockchain and cryptocurrency regulation: Malta", in J.N. Dewey (ed.), *Blockchain and cryptocurrency regulation*, London, Global Legal Insights.

231 Chapter 590: Virtual Financial Assets Act 2018, *Act XXX of 2018*, www.justiceservices.gov.mt/DownloadDocument.aspx?app=lom&itemid=12872&l=1, accessed 08/08/2019.

application outside the confines of their DLT platform and could be redeemed for funds on the platforms directly by the DLT asset issuers. VFA agents obliged to undertake designated reporting and monitoring are to be appointed by ICO issuers have to be approved by the MFSA. Entities offering VFAs, or treated as VFA services providers, have to be licensed by the MFSA. The MFSA ascertains whether a product/service falls under the financial services regulation or under the scope of the VFA legislation through the use of a financial instrument test (FIT).

This involves 12 tests, and is used primarily to determine whether the activities fall within the context of applicable EC or Maltese regulations. The first of these spotlights on virtual tokens, while the remainder covers various financial instruments such as MiFID. The MFSA, for purpose of this test, uses virtual assets definitions located in the consultation paper for the FIT. ICOs that are not financial instruments are subject to minimum disclosure requirements, like providing the necessary information to investors through a whitepaper, and further information when intending to trade the virtual currency on an exchange.

The VFAA provides the regulatory framework applicable to ICOs as well as the regulation for particular services providers engaged in ICO-related activities such as cryptocurrency exchanges. Thus, cryptocurrencies could be regulated here or in the existing financial services regulation, including but not confined to, MiFID II, the Investment Services Act and the Financial Institutions Act, depending on the assets categorisation.

Where taxation is concerned, there are no set rules for cryptoassets. This means the tax rules and principles in Malta will be applicable. The income tax legislation in the jurisdiction differentiates between income and capital receipts where the designated tax rates would apply. Money transmission laws and anti-money laundering requirements in Malta will be applicable to cryptocurrency issuers and related services providers and, as stipulated under the VFAA, will cover issuers, VFA licence holders and VFA agents.

The Malta Gaming Authority (MGA) provides guidance for the use of DLTs and the acceptance of virtual currencies in the gaming sector via its sandbox environment.[232] Both single wallet systems and multiple wallet systems are allowable under specified conditions. The Malta Stock Exchange in 2018 launched its Binance and Thomson Reuters endorsed MSX Fintech Accelerator.[233] This is offered to mentor and help start-ups in the blockchain and crypto niche by matchmaking them with global technology and well-known business players, as well as office space, state-of-the-art communications, and training facilities. Other stakeholders sharing and collaborating to advance the industry includes

---

232 Malta Gaming Authority (2018), "Guidance on the use of Distributed Ledger Technology and the acceptance of Virtual Currencies through the implementation of a Sandbox Environment", *MGA*, March 2018, www.mga.org.mt/wp-content/uploads/MGA-Public-Consultation-Guidance-on-the-use-of-Distributed-Ledger-Technology-and-the-acceptance-of-Virtual-Currencies-through-the-implementation-of-a-Sandbox-Environment.pdf, accessed 08/08/2019.

233 MSE (2018), "Binance backs Malta Stock Exchange Fintech Accelerator Programme", *MSE*, 19/06/2018, www.borzamalta.com.mt/article-pr-binance, accessed 08/08/2019.

among others, the Malta Information Technology Agency, University of Malta's Blockchain Research Group, the Blockchain Malta Association, and BitMalta. The Maltese jurisdiction is also a member of the European Blockchain Partnership[234] that seeks to foster collaboration between EU member states through the exchange of experiences and know how in this and related areas.

All in all, the cryptoassets regulatory regime in Malta supports innovation, while ensuring the effective achievements of high-level objectives set by global standard setters like the IOSCO. These being financial stability, investor protection, and market integrity, and are addressed via a predominantly principles-based approach that ensures technology neutrality without stifling innovation.[235] Thus, while the EU is pondering and reflecting on what and how to regulate virtual currencies, big individual member states like France and Germany are in final stages of cryptoassets legislation, smaller states like Luxembourg and Malta, as well as many Baltic economies have initiated legislations. Malta is said to be by far the boldest with its wide regulatory framework that seeks to enable the jurisdiction to be Europe's crypto hub as this addresses all key risks areas like risks to consumers, market integrity, financial crimes and cyber security. These came about in response to earlier investigations of several gambling firms and banks in the jurisdiction that exposed weak enforcement by local authorities. Malta uses insights from these to strengthen the quality and effectiveness of its financial services regulations and enforcements.[236]

7.12 A comparative note

The general analysis of regulatory approaches in these selected advanced economies including offshore financial centres that are protected economies of advanced economies suggest that cryptoassets can run through the full gamut of regulated financial products. The various kinds of cryptocurrencies are driven commonly by a DLT popularly referred to as blockchain with inherent encryption, but the more noticeable feature is the fluidity of the terminology deployed as they could be labelled differently in these different jurisdictions. Australia uses "digital currency", Switzerland uses "payment tokens", the UK uses "cryptoassets", while the US uses "cryptocurrency" or "virtual commodities" depending on the federal agencies involved. Also, while global cryptoassets standards setters like the FATF uses virtual currencies, the BIS uses cryptoassets. For these reasons, this book is not overly particular about the preferred terminology

---

234 Davila, E. (2019), "Standards supporting BC/DLT interoperability EU initiatives" *ITU-T ITU Workshop on Distributed Ledger Technology Scalability and Interoperability*, Geneva, 02/08/2019, www.itu.int/en/ITU-T/Workshops-and-Seminars/201908/Documents/Emilio_Davila-Gonzalez%20_Presentation.pdf, accessed 08/08/2019.
235 Buttigieg, C.P. & Efthymiopoulos, C. (2019), "The regulation of cryptoassets in Malta: The virtual financial assets act and beyond", *Law & Financial Markets Review*, 13(1), pp. 30–40.
236 Guarascio, F. (2019), "Malta leads on cryptoassets regulation while EU ponders", *Reuters*, 26/02/2019, www.reuters.com/article/us-eu-cryptoassets/malta-leads-on-cryptoassets-regulation-while-eu-ponders-idUSKCN1QF1SX, accessed 08/08/2019.

choice. To maintain the flow and clarity of discussions in this book with the formal commentaries used in different jurisdictions these various terminologies are used here interchangeably, whether they be cryptoassets, virtual assets/currencies, or cryptocurrencies as they mean almost the same thing.

A cryptoasset could be typically a consumer credit product, an insurance product, a MIS, a share, a debenture, a derivative or a payment system. Relatively less common, they could be a miscellaneous risk facility, a purchased payment facility, a foreign exchange product, a banking product, or an interest in a superannuation fund. Many of these jurisdictions look at the substance rather than the form when deciding on the regulatory treatments of these items. These selected advanced economies are not the only ones facing the problem, and as mentioned earlier most other jurisdictions are encountering a very similar set of problems as cryptoassets are cross-border financial products. This is why the OECD has called upon global regulators to collaborate quickly to provide clarity and a suitable global supervisory framework.[237] IOSCO has acknowledged the potential need for this, but thus far has only issued cautionary notices and acting as a repository of the regulatory regimes in different countries.

The advanced economies reviewed here appear to embrace certain common regulatory concerns and approaches. In general, they are all mindful of the threats and risks posed by cryptoassets to the investing community and impacts on the stability of their respective financial systems. These explain why they tend to focus on money laundering and related issues, as well as contagion effects on their financial systems. However, given the background nature of their respective economies and their legal systems, it is inevitable that variations in terms of their regulatory approaches are not unexpected in some areas. This could be problematical, as blockchain and cryptoasset impacts are not confined to national borders.

The US, the biggest economy in the world, appears to be relying on existing financial securities, and related financial services rules and regulations to police cryptoasset products and activities. This has heightened complexity, as federal regulatory agencies like the SEC, the CFTC and others, will get or not get involved depending on how each respective agency treat the various kinds of cryptoassets. The US's fragmented approach is less followed by the UK, as it relies primarily on the FCA to do the job. Though the FCA has come out with its final guidelines, it has left some gaps that it says are outside of its regulatory perimeter and this gives rise to some legal uncertainty. The EU is still reflecting and pondering on the approach to take, even as some of its bigger members states like France and Germany, and some bolder smaller member states like Malta and Luxembourg, have gone some distance. Mata deserves special mention as its comprehensive virtual assets regulatory regime is by far the boldest in Europe.

---

237 Kelly, J.L. (2019), "Do you know how your token is regulated?", *Investor Daily*, 10/09/2019, www.investordaily.com.au/analysis/45657-do-you-know-how-your-crypto-token-is-regulated, accessed 12/09/2019.

Following this in some respects are Australia and Canada. While Australia and Canada tweak their respective financial securities and banking regulations to deal with the various kinds of cryptoassets others, like the UK, have left various gaps. The potential significance of these for issues relating to innovation agility, protection of investor welfare and financial system stability remain to be seen. Various offshore financial centres have been impacted by scandals disclosed in the Panama and Paradise Papers revelations and have taken steps to improve on their reputations and regulatory system to avoid being blacklisted as financial pariahs by global regulatory financial standards setters like the FTAF, the IOSCO, and BIS, as well as multilateral development agencies like the OECD, the World Bank and the IMF.

CHAPTER 8

Cryptoasset regulatory policies in selected Asian economies

8.1 Introduction

This chapter examines regulatory initiatives in both large and small Asian economies particularly known for their active participation in cryptoasset activities. These include the large emerging economies of China and India, and the advanced economies of Japan, South Korea and Singapore in the region. They are selected as they are perceived to be cryptoassets hotspots with the resources and willingness to advance the progression of cryptoassets.

In the last three or more decades, Asia has emerged as an important global pole. Hitherto, world attention has been drawn on the US and the EU, with an occasional spotlight on Japan as it ebbs and wanes in the global economic corridors. Asia as a regional economic powerhouse of global proportion is not by accident. First, it houses five of the world's ten most populous nations; namely China, India, Indonesia, Pakistan, and Bangladesh which together account for some 45.5% of the world's total population of some 7.7 billion.[1] Asia has a good mix of advanced economies (South Korea, Taiwan, Singapore, and Hong Kong), middle-income economies (Malaysia, China, Indonesia, Philippines, Vietnam), and low-income economies (Afghanistan, Pakistan, Bangladesh, Laos, Cambodia). It includes very large economies like China, Indonesia and India. It has very fast-growth economies, like Malaysia, Philippines, Vietnam and so on. It has a good mix of economies with generally reliable and modern banking systems, like those in Singapore, South Korea and Malaysia, but also relatively less modern banking systems like those in Laos, Cambodia, Afghanistan and so on. The quality and state of physical infrastructures within the region also differs considerably, including the state of communication systems.

With regards to financial systems, the more economically aggressive and competitive economies like South Korea, Japan, and Singapore are also Fintech hotspots. These Fintech hotspots in these more advanced subsets have very aggressive and fast-moving blockchain and cryptoassets enclaves. The less well-endowed economies in the region are on the other hand looking at ways how these alluded to exponential techs can help to foster financial inclusiveness to bridge the gap between the haves and the have nots. Insights from both are important

---

[1] Worldometer (2019), "Countries in the world by population", www.worldometers.info/world-population/population-by-country/, accessed 08/08/2019.

from a global perspective. The advanced economies of the region engaged with these can potentially posed a competitive threat to those in advanced Western economies and there are telling signs that they could do with the likes of Tencent and Alibaba. Insights from crypto engagements by the less-affluent economies in the region are also useful as they could potentially show how the lower income groups in advanced economies could use the emerging techs to raise their economic welfare. How each of these selected Asian economies deal with the potentials from the crypto space will now be discussed. This commences with China, potentially the second biggest economy in the world.

8.2 China's cryptoasset regulatory policy

The People's Bank of China (PBOC) has been researching a virtual currency for some time already and this suggests the possibility of the PBOC becoming the first central bank to issue one. But, as long as it remains centralised, i.e. endorsed and controlled by the central bank, it would merely be just traditional money with a digitisation vessel that could work well for intra-bank operations but difficult for it to become widespread.[2] However, the initial plan is to issue the cryptocurrency in association with a group of Chinese banks, and named Digital Currency Electronic Payment (or DCEP for short), but only in Shenzen and Suzhou. As at the start of 2020 its precise form remains unclear, although a spokesman for the PBOC suggested that it would share some common factors with Libra. For all other purposes, cryptocurrencies are covered by the general legal ban imposed by the Chinese Government as discussed below.[3]

The Chinese Government started to advance its campaign against cryptoassets from mid-September 2017.[4] Rumours simultaneously began circulating about pending shutdowns of all local exchange platforms in the country. At the time, Jihan Wu co-founder of Bitcoin hardware firm Bitmain, claimed that the rumours were hinting of tougher regulations and temporary closure, instead of an outright ban.[5] China's National Internet Finance Association (NIFA) claimed that any cryptoassets exchange currently operating in China has no legal authorisation to engage in this kind of business.[6] There were also no clear warnings or threats that individual Bitcoin traders would be prosecuted. NIFA is a state-backed self-regulatory organisation set up by the PBOC, the country's central bank, with members comprising banks, brokerages, consumer finance

---

2 Lunn, B. (2018), "We interviewed somebody in China to find out what is happening in this critical market for blockchain, Bitcoin, and crypto", *Daily Fintech*, 03/03/2018.

3 Seth, S. (2019), "Is bitcoin banned in China?", Investopedia 25/06/19, https://www.investopedia.com/news/bitcoin-banned-china/, accessed 07/02/20.

4 Froelings, L. (2017), "China moves towards tougher Bitcoin regulation, but not to outright ban: Jian Wu", *Coin Telegraph*, 15/09/2017, https://www.cointelegraph.com/news/china-moves-towards-tougher-Bitcoin-regulation-but-not-to-outright-ban-jihan-wu, accessed 02/02/2018.

5 Supra, note [4], Froelings (2017).

6 Supra, note [4], Froelings (2017).

companies and funds. The PBOC's regulatory powers have been expanded in March 2018.

The implication of a complete ban on virtual currency trading in China would have significant outcomes, as the country is home to one of the most active cryptocurrency trading activities around the world. It has, for example been reported that a large-scale mining farm in China accounts for about one twentieth of the total daily virtual currency production worldwide.[7] Owing to the magnitude of virtual currencies in China, Liu Xiaolei, a Guanghua University professor suggests that a total ban in the country is neither feasible nor realistic.[8] Hu Bing, FINA researcher claims that a possible ICO ban may only be temporary and not permanent; and that a ban would only be temporary implemented until the Chinese authorities are able to locate effective solutions on how to regulate the new technology.[9]

In all fairness the Chinese authorities do have particular problems to deal with. There is a very strong cultural propensity towards gambling in China, often for large amounts of money and it is illegal. The population can save up and fly to the Special Administrative Region of Macau where gambling is legal and there is an assortment of very large casinos. Apart from the Jockey Club's gambling facilities in Hong Kong there is nothing else that is legal apart from the Chinese Government's official lotteries.[10] That said, one recent analysis suggests that over one trillion Chinese yuan is illegally gambled in China every year.[11]

It is in this context that the Chinese Government banned all online poker applications and adopted an extremely cautious approach to cryptocurrencies and, in addition, ICOs were banned. The PBOC demanded in its website on 5 September 2017 that all Chinese ICO activities be stopped immediately,[12] with those already using ICOs to raise funds from Chinese buyers required to make refunds.[13] The aim was to protect the legal rights of investors, to reduce financial risk and to stop people evading the country's exchange control restrictions by using cryptocurrencies as the vehicle. The PBOC statement is based on the law of the country, PBOC's laws, commercial banking and securities laws, cybersecurity and

---

7 Li, C., Marchi, G. (2017), "In China's hinterlands, workers mine Bitcoin for a digital fortune", *New York Times*, 13/09/2017, https://www.nytimes.com/2017/09/13/business/Bitcoin-mine-china.html, accessed 02/02/2018.

8 Supra, note [4], Froelings (2017).

9 Konash, M. (2017), "Chinese official: ICO ban in China is temporary", Coin Speaker, 11/09/2017, https://www.coinspeaker.com/2017/09/11/chinese-official-ico-ban-china-temporary, accessed 02/02/2018.

10 The Chinese Sports Lottery and the China Welfare Lottery.

11 Eimer, D. (9 January 2010). "China's secret gambling problem". *Daily Telegraph*. Shenyang. Retrieved 1/05/2015.

12 Technically this was in the form of Notice issued by seven government agencies of China, i.e. the PBOC, the Central Cybersecurity and Information Technology Lead Group of the Communist Party of China, the Ministry of Industry and Information Technology, the State Administration for Industry and Commerce, China Banking Regulatory Commission, China Security Regulatory Commission and China Insurance Regulatory Commission, jointly issued on 14 September 2017.

13 Zhao, W. (2017), "China's ICO ban: A full translation of regulator remark", Coin Desk, 05/09/2017, https://www.coindesk.com/chinas-ico-ban-a-full-translation-of-regulator-remarks, accessed 02/02/2018.

telecommunications law, and financing and financial activities law.[14] Other matters highlighted in the announcement included the following[15]:

(i) An ICO by its nature is an unauthorised and illegal financing activity involving financial crimes such as the illegal distribution of financial tokens, the illegal issuance of securities and illegal fundraising, financial fraud and pyramid schemes. Relevant authorities as such would closely monitor the latest market status and collaborate with the justice department and local governments.

(ii) Organisations and individuals are prohibited from starting illegal token fundraising activity. Commencing from the date of the announcement, all kinds of fundraising activity through tokens are required to cease immediately. Entities and individuals that have completed token fundraising previously would have to refund investors to protect investor rights and to deal with risks properly.

(iii) Supervision on platforms that provide exchange services for tokens issued during the fundraising would be reinforced. Henceforth, token exchange platforms should not be involved in offering exchange services between fiat currency and tokens; buying or selling tokens for cryptocurrencies; acting as a central party facilitating the trading of tokens for cryptocurrencies; or providing price bidding or middleman service for the exchange of tokens for cryptocurrency.

(iv) No financial institutions or non-banking payment institutions shall operate businesses that deal with token fundraising. As such they shall not directly or indirectly provide account opening, registration, trading, clearing and settlement services for token fundraising activities.

(v) The PBOC cautioned the public on the multiple risks posed by token fund raising, including fraudulent assets, business operational failure and speculation.

(vi) Different financial industry entities should study the regulation well. Member companies should voluntarily fight against any illegal financing activity that relates to token and cryptocurrency fund raising, keep a distance form this market chaos, improve education for investors and jointly help to maintain financial stability.

China previously banned Bitcoin by barring Chinese financial institutions from associating with Bitcoin companies in 2013,[16] followed by the shutting down of

---

14 Supra, note [13], Zhao (2017).
15 Supra, note [13], Zhao (2017).
16 Hern, A. (2013), "Bitcoin plummets as China's largest exchange blocks new deposits", *The Guardian*, 18/12/2013, www.theguardian.com/technology/2013/dec/18/bitcoin-plummets-china-payment-processors-digital-cryptocurrency, accessed 02/02/2018; Hern, A. (2013a), "Bitcoin price tumbles after warning from Chinese central bank: The People's Bank of China has issued a warning that the currency is not legally protected and has no 'real meaning'", The Guardian, 05/12/2013, https://www.theguardian.com/technology/2013/dec/05/bitcoin-price-tumbles-chinese-central-bank-warning, accessed 02/02/2018.

cryptocurrency exchanges in 2014.[17] At the time, the PBOC ordered banks to close all accounts opened by operators of websites that trade the currency by 15 April 2014, essentially forcing all Bitcoin exchanges in China to shut down. This meant that the only way out for Bitcoin websites was by moving their servers abroad and using the service of foreign banks and payment companies. This also suggests that Chinese investors would only be able to buy Bitcoins with cash. As for the other market participants, almost all of them, extending from mining, trading to storage, have moved their operations overseas because of the general ban for all Bitcoin business activities.

Back then in 2014, China enjoyed a strong competitive advantage in Bitcoin mining, accounting for around 50% of the global Bitcoin network mining power. Trading is also said to be the most important financial application of Bitcoin. There are said to be more than 100 Bitcoin trading platforms across the world, of which the top ten are based in the US, Eastern Europe, and Asia (including China, Japan and South Korea) and these accounted for more than 90% of global trading volume. Since 2015, regulatory compliance became the primary focus of BTC/USD exchanges. US based exchanges Coinbase and ItBit received relevant business licence from US authorities, but in China the relevant government departments have not enacted a licence for digital currencies thereby making compliance a major issue.[18]

Since then the Chinese Government has become increasingly alarmed at the increase in corporate, personal and government debt in the economy and have taken a number of steps to keep it under control. Ongoing controls on ICOs can also be seen in that context. Debt to GDP is rising very quickly 255% in 2016, 300% by the end of 2017 and now 329%. This is very high when compared with other countries with the same level of income per head. Household debt has risen from 40% of disposable income in 2008 to 106% in 2016. Overall debt has risen from 20% to 43% of GDP in the same time: it now exceeds 80%. A significant part of this consists of people financing buying their homes but there is considerable evidence that prices in many cities are significantly over inflated, meaning a 2008 Western style financial crisis is a real possibility.

Non-performing bank loans in the US at the start of the 2007–8 financial crisis were 6%, in China it already exceeds this. Local government debt was meant to be scaled back over recent years by using bond swaps but the reforms were used to hide increases in borrowing which then rose by 20% over two years! On top of that there is no certain way of measuring the effect on lending on the activities of the shadow market. This is such a source of concern to the Chinese Government that they have changed the system of financial regulation. Banning ICOs makes sense as part of this process.

---

17 Song, S. (2014), "The rise and fall of Bitcoin in China: Central Bank shuts down all Chinese Bitcoin exchange", *International Business Times*, 27/03/2014, https://www.ibtimes.com/rise-fall-bitcoin-china-central-bank-shuts-down-all-chinese-bitcoin-exchanges-1563826, accessed 02/02/2018.

18 Li, L. (2015), "Bitcoin in China: An insider view", Coin Desk, 22/08/2015, https://www.coindesk.com/Bitcoin-in-china-an-insiders-view, accessed 02/02/2018.

Huobi, OKCoin, and BTC China are the three Chinese Bitcoin exchanges running alongside several smaller exchanges. Some 3.6 million Bitcoin wallet service providers have emerged to enable mainstream users to send, receive and store Bitcoin easily and securely. The growth potential of Bitcoin wallets is significant in the US, but for China, due to the lack of merchants accepting Bitcoin payments and regulatory uncertainty, Chinese users tend to keep their Bitcoin funds on Bitcoin exchanges.[19] Other than Bitcoin trading, payments and international money transfers are the next most important significant applications of Bitcoin. There are more than 100,000 businesses accepting Bitcoin payments including big companies like Microsoft, Dell, Expedia, BitPay, Circle, and Newegg.

Bitcoin development could take four, though not necessarily mutually exclusive, directions. It could develop as a global financial asset; as a financial tool for improving money transfer; as a payment network; and as non-financial technology powering decentralised autonomous organisations, smart contracts, prediction markets and the internet of things. Given this, and for China to find a niche at the forefront of international finance and innovation, the country could differentiate between cryptocurrency and blockchain technology, regulate via existing laws, observe and learn from actions of others, and by supporting research and innovation.[20]

As regulations develop, China is slowly permitting Bitcoin transactions, but under certain restrictions that users need to follow.[21] Bitcoin trading is booming in China despite the official clampdown on centralised exchanges, as traders take to investing in the virtual currency through P2P exchanges. In P2P Bitcoin trade, buyers interact directly on a one-to-one basis with sellers on deals instead of in a centralised marketplace or exchange. This kind of over the counter trading is booming (according to China's National Committee of Experts on Internet Financial Security), increasing from four previously to 21 currently, while there is enhanced use of messaging platforms like WeChat and Telegram Bitcoin for users to connect.[22] Subsequent to a period of caution after the September 2014 actions, the China blockchain community appears to be back in business.

Similarly, it is expected that China's current ban on ICOs would be similarly followed through with regulation. At present the government appears to favour the Ethereum-based tokens commonly used by tech start-ups to raise funds. This suggests a direction toward niche token sales, in other words allowing the sale of tokens in a format the authorities deem safe and more measured.[23] Rumours of late are, however, saying that China will officially decide to crack down on

---

19 Supra, note [18], Li (2015).
20 Supra, note [18], Li (2015).
21 Cuen, L. (2017), "China Bans Initial Coin Offerings While Paris Hilton Promotes Lydian Coins", *International Business Times*, 09/04/2017, https://www.ibtimes.com/china-bans-initial-coin-offerings-while-paris-hilton-promotes-lydian-coins-2585985, accessed 02/02/2018.
22 Barclay, A. (2017), "China's crackdown raises cryptocurrency demands as they move to peer-to-peer platforms", *South China Morning Post*, 22/12/2017, www.scmp.com/tech/innovation/article/2125282/chinas-bitcoin-crackdown-raises-cryptocurrency-demand-they-move-peer, accessed 02/02/2018.
23 Supra, note [21], Cuen (2017).

all Bitcoin and cryptocurrency trading, not just commercial exchanges. Such a wider clampdown could include blocking mainland access to websites of foreign exchanges such as Coinbase in the US and Bitfinex in Hong Kong. Nevertheless, irrespective of China's official position on Bitcoin, the Bitcoin community in China has already reacted by transferring much of their activities to Japan where regulations are less strict,[24] and by Chinese miners relocating to Canada.[25]

It has been reported that when the terms in Chinese of Bitcoin, cryptocurrency and ICO were searched on Chinese search-engine Baidu and microblog Weibo, no obvious paid sponsored content came up alongside the expected results. Baidu and Weibo are said to have banned cryptocurrency-related advertising[26] moving in synchronisation with Facebook's[27] banned advertising of cryptocurrencies at the time. The latter justified its action citing the large number of Fintech companies on its platform not operating in good faith.

The Bitcoin community is, however, not unduly perturbed as there were plenty of other ways to reach both the mass market and virtual currency enthusiasts. Bitmain, which runs China's two largest Bitcoin mining collectives, is setting up regional headquarters in Singapore and has mining operations in the US and Canada; while Bitcoin.com, the third largest mining pool is operating a facility in Canada, and ViaBTC ranked fourth, has operations in Iceland and the US. They also promote their brand names on popular digital asset news site like Digital News Asia while Reddit and Twitter have also good been deployed as viable alternatives.[28]

When ordered to shut down in September 2017, Chinese cryptocurrency exchanges BTCC China, Huobi and OKCoin relocated their businesses to Hong Kong, rebranding respectively as BTCC, Hiobi Pro and OKEx. It is relatively easy for Chinese investors to move their funds from their Chinese bank accounts to Hong Kong Bank accounts thereby enabling them to start trading cryptocurrencies more actively and effectively bypassing China's restrictions.[29]

---

24 Buck, J. (2017), "China will heavily crack down on all Bitcoin trades", *Coin Telegraph*, 18/09/2017, https://cointelegraph.com/news/china-will-heavily-crack-down-on-all-bitcoin-trades, accessed 02/02/2018.

25 Lampert, A., Harney, A. & Goh, B. (2018), "Chinese Bitcoin miners eye sites in energy-rich Canada", *Reuters*, 12/01/2018, https://www.reuters.com/article/us-canada-bitcoin-china/chinese-bitcoin-miners-eye-sites-in-energy-rich-canada-idUSKBN1F10BU, accessed 02/02/2018.

26 Zuckerman, M.J. (2018), "With China tightening regulations, crypto-related Ads reportedly gone from local websites", *Coin Telegraph*, 04/02/2018, https://cointelegraph.com/news/with-china-tightening-regulations-crypto-related-ads-reportedly-gone-from-local-websites, accessed 18/02/2018.

27 Marshall, A. (2018), "Facebook bans cryptocurrency, ICO ads because of 'deceptive promotional practices'", *Coin Telegraph*, 30/01/2018, https://cointelegraph.com/news/facebook-bans-cryptocurrency-ico-ads-because-of-deceptive-promotional-practices, accessed 02/02/2018. Subsequently, Facebook changed this policy.

28 Lee, A. (2018), "Bitcoin ads disappear from social media in China after central bank bans cryptocurrency fundraising", *South China Morning Post*, 06/02/2018, www.scmp.com/tech/china-tech/article/2131419/bitcoin-ads-disappear-social-media-china-after-central-bank-bans, accessed 18/02/2018.

29 Young, J. (2018), "How Chinese Bitcoin buyers are getting around government ban", *Coin Telegraph*, 27/01/2018, https://cointelegraph.com/news/how-chinese-bitcoin-buyers-are-getting-around-government-ban, accessed 02/02/2018.

Hong Kong's exchanges have also integrated widely used Fintech applications in China like Alipay and Tencent's WeChatPay. The integration of these two Fintech payment networks has increased the accessibility of Hong Kong-based cryptocurrency exchanges for Chinese investors, thereby easing the process of investing in the cryptocurrency markets. The Chinese Government and the PBOC have asked local banks to disclose any suspicious transactions linked to Hong Kong-based markets, but even this move might not be able to prevent Chinese investors from accessing Hong Kong-based markets because of apps like Alipay and WeChatPay.[30]

So far China has banned ICOs, stopped local Bitcoin exchanges from trading, outlined proposals to discourage Bitcoin mining and stopped Chinese-listed companies abroad avoiding its domestic ban on ICOs. It is now said to be planning to block domestic access to online platforms and mobile apps offering exchange-like services for cryptocurrencies, targeting platforms that allow investors to trade digital assets on overseas exchange; while domestic stock exchanges are scrutinising companies that are promoting themselves as blockchain-related to boost their shares.[31] This is a concerted effort by the PBOC, the Cyberspace Administration, the Ministry of Industry and Information Technology to clampdown on cryptocurrencies and, in particular, Bitcoin. Despite this, China is not necessarily anti-cryptocurrency. The PBOC has conducted trials of its own prototype cryptocurrency, taking China a step closer to being the first major central bank to issue a virtual currency. The country's aspiration, however, seems to be based more on taking full control of such transactions in contrast to the libertarian aspirations of Bitcoin.

For the last two years, China's current government mantra focuses on cleansing risk from financial markets. Among the country's primary concerns are the booming shadow banking sector, a potential source of unregulated loans to speculators in whatever the latest financial risk happens to be. Virtual currencies provide an avenue to move money out of China, potentially adding to outflows that Chinese officials have set about aggressively stemming. According to Mark McFarland, chief economist at Union Bank Bancaire Privee SA Hong Kong, a longer-term process of tightening the scrutiny of activities that are not in the normal sort of monetary realm is under way.[32] Arising from these developments, Bitcoin is traded in over the counter markets in China, which is a relatively slower process that some say would increases credit risk.

For the cryptocurrency world at large, these moves are reshaping the Bitcoin mining industry and driving up costs. Miners initially headed to China because of its inexpensive power, local chip making factories, and cheap labour. In early 2013, China's state-run TV, CCTV (renamed CGTN) aired a short documentary

---

30 Supra, note [29], Young (2018).
31 Clark, G. & Chen, L.Y. (2018), "How China's Stifling Bitcoin and Cryptocurrencies: Quick Take", Bloomberg, 09/01/2018, www.bloomberg.com/news/articles/2018-01-09/how-china-s-stifling-bitcoin-and-cryptocurrencies-quicktake-q-a, accessed 02/02/2018.
32 Supra, note [31], Clark & Chen (2018).

of Bitcoin technology. During this period, more Bitcoin wallets were downloaded by computers in China than the rest of the world combined.[33] This was because speculating on Bitcoin constituted one of the few investment options available for retail investors in China's heavily regulated financial environment. Up to September 2017, more than two thirds of Bitcoins were mined in China, where most of the computers used for mining are manufactured.[34] Bitcoin uses a great deal of computing power, and some Chinese computer clusters used for the process enjoyed access to relatively cheap electricity especially in provinces powered by hydroelectricity, but the political environment soon began to change.

As the speculative fervour threatened to get out of hand, China became concerned about the yuan leaving the country. Though the country limits yuan outflow at $50,000 per person per year, the potential was there, as Chinese people could buy Bitcoins in yuan, sell them on an American exchange, and then withdraw the sum in dollars. In late 2013 the Chinese authorities responded by banning financial services companies from dealing with Bitcoin exchanges.[35] Following this, people could no longer withdraw yuan from their bank accounts to directly buy Bitcoins on Chinese exchanges. Now, Bitcoin miners, and other Chinese Bitcoin businesses, have to look towards Canada, the US, Australia, Switzerland and Singapore. This is because China did not just impose a limit on virtual currencies, it shut down the entire highway despite the fact that most of the 2016 Bitcoin trades were done in Chinese yuan.[36]

As mentioned earlier, Chinese people found ways around this by using cash to buy vouchers that could be traded on the exchanges, or by sending money to the personal bank account of someone who worked at an exchange. When the authorities later shut down cryptocurrency exchanges, people turned to online and offline P2P trading. Others could also buy and sell virtual currencies on the encrypted messaging app Telegram, which though blocked in China could be accessed by virtual private networks that could get around the Great Firewall. People already owning coins could also just go online, and trade them on an exchange that is based overseas, with even some trading on WeChat, China's massively popular but heavily monitored messaging app.

This capacity to avoid the restrictions arose because China did not ban Bitcoin itself, nor did it explicitly ban P2P trading and importantly has not officially banned the mining of Bitcoin. Words such as cryptocurrency, Bitcoin and ICOs now verge on being taboo words in China, but blockchain or distributed ledger technology have not. This was why and how a Chinese university professor who initially had his Bitcoin course cancelled was able to get approval when launching it under the more politically correct title of "The Smart Economy

---

33 Kapron, Z. (2014), *Chomping at the Bitcoin: The past, present and future of Bitcoin in China*, Hong Kong, Penguin Books China.
34 Parker, E. (2018), "Can China contain Bitcoin? It is trying. But the cryptocurrency is bigger than any country, even the one where it has been most popular?", MIT Technology Review, January/February 2018.
35 Supra, note [34], Parker (2018).
36 Supra, note [34], Parker (2018).

and Blockchain". This is because Chinese authorities clearly see blockchain as a technology of the future. The country counts blockchain technology as part of its 13th five-year Plan, and a useful tool for advancing its regional interest in trade. China wants to use blockchain to ensure the trustworthiness of public and administrative data, but according to Ben Kook, an engineering professor at Tsinghua University it does not want people to print their own money.[37]

Since the changes in Chinese law many exchanges launched peer-to-peer trading platforms that support direct transactions between investors without the exchange simply acting as a central counterparty. This means that the investors can buy a cryptocurrency and then pay separately by whatever payment method the exchange will accept. The key issue here is the potential long arm reach of Chinese criminal law even where the exchanges are outside China. This will only be the case if the founders or investors are Chinese citizens or operational decisions are made in the jurisdiction. At present the Chinese authorities have not been active in this regard but if they become so an exchange overseas run by people inside China would seem to be those most at risk.

China's crackdown on cryptocurrencies suggests that no one country can stop them.[38] China first banned ICOs, then exchanges and subsequently started blocking foreign currency sites from Chinese people with a firewall. In the decentralised network of cryptocurrencies, when one country bows out, another picks up the slack. Hence, when China clamped down, much of its crypto activity migrated to Japan and South Korea. Different functions seem to work in different economies. No longer able to accept cash deposits these exchanges now provide crypto to crypto exchanges along with some futures and index derivatives. Despite the tight regulation, crypto exchanges in China have managed to survive and flourish, but ICO initiatives or frauds have faced tighter regulation because of the risks they posed to the financial system. China's largest cryptocurrency exchange, Huobi, besides relocating its operations to San Francisco, Hong Kong, Korea, and Japan, has turned tighter regulation imposed into a blessing by seizing the initiative to launch user security and protections initiatives like the User Protection Funds and the Security Reserve, as well as launching the world's first autonomous token listing exchange.[39]

As for blockchain technology, in October 2016 China's Ministry of Industry and Information Technology issued a whitepaper for its development and application.[40] The Chinese Government remains extremely positive about the potential uses of blockchain itself. Hangzhou, the e-commerce city of China is the first city in the country to include blockchain in its government report. Blockchain maintain its stature alongside artificial intelligence, virtual reality, quantum technology and commercial aerospace technology. Tech giants like

---

37 Supra, note [34], Parker (2018).
38 Supra, note [34], Parker (2018).
39 Pollock, D. (2018), "Why we shouldn't pay too much attention to regulation in China, at least for now", *Coin Telegraph*, 26/02/2018, https://cointelegraph.com/news/why-we-shouldnt-pay-much-attention-for-regulation-in-china-at-least-for-now, accessed 02/03/2018.
40 Supra, note [2], Lunn (2018).

Alibaba and Ant Financials have been implementing blockchain applications since 2016 including charity platforms, mailbox verification, food production tracing, and medicals. Wanxiang Blockchain Labs, another big blockchain player, plans to invest US$30 billion over seven years to implement Smart Cities Initiative where blockchain would be the major driver.

Those seeking a technology community would do well to go to the US, while those seeking friendly laws could consider Japan and Switzerland and those seeking customers might go to South Korea. Bitcoin now presents China with the same challenge that the Internet once did. The country was initially suspicious of the Web, as letting it in would mean relinquishing some degree of control, but keeping it out would cut China off from the global economy. This time around it is too late to isolate the country from the rest of the world, as for as long as there is one cable available from the country to the outside world, Bitcoin could then survive.[41]

Bitcoin appears to have passed the China test, as it did not break after China banned it. Cryptocurrencies have delivered on the promise that they could not be defeated by any government, even one as large and powerful as China's.[42] They seem to become stronger, each time they are held down by regulations and other barriers. The famed financial adviser and cryptocurrency champion, Ronnie Moas, argues that if China bans cryptocurrencies, 190 countries around the world would not hesitate to buy them especially in a fire sale. He sees the fear and damage that regulation brings as only noise, and would worry only when China, Russia, the US, and South Korea come out with destructive policies simultaneously.[43]

In summary, the PBOC Circular 2013 and Circular 2017 constitute the primary regulatory framework for cryptoassets. Within these, cryptocurrencies are treated as virtual commodities, while ICOs are banned with resulting civil, administrative and criminal liabilities.[44] Some of these liabilities fall under existing law. The undertaking of illegal issuance and sales of tokens are, for example, mentioned under Article 20 of the Chinese Securities Law and under the said law, individuals and institutions issuing and selling tokens would be required to terminate the illegal transaction immediately and can face fines of up to 200,000 Chinese yuan. Where an ICO is treated as illegally fundraising, the issuer could be sentenced to more than ten years' imprisonment and slapped with a fine of 50,000 Chinese yuan to 500,000 Chinese yuan. Despite the prohibition of ICOs and trading platform services for cryptoassets, Chinese authorities have not forbidden the existence of cryptoassets.[45]

Being treated as a virtual commodity, there are no particular or explicit restrictions on the acquisition, ownership or trading of cryptoassets by individuals. Generally, China has been implementing further restrictions regarding

---

41 Supra, note [34], Parker (2018).
42 Supra, note [34], Parker (2018).
43 Supra, note [39], Pollock (2018).
44 Gong, L. & Yu, L. (2019), "China" in J. Dewey (ed.), *Blockchain and cryptocurrency regulation*, London, Global Legal Insights.
45 Supra, note [44], Gong & Yu (2019).

cryptoassets, extending from banning ICOs, discouraging Bitcoin miners, to a country-wide ban on Internet and mobile access to cryptoasset trading platforms. Relative to other major economies, China emerges as one of the strictest regulators with regards to private cryptoassets.

Blockchain companies on the other hand would have to follow the guidelines provided by the country's internet regulator, the Cyberspace Administration of China commencing on 19 February 2019. These include requiring companies to record and log user activity, along with maintaining backups for a minimum of six months, as well as the verification of users based on their national ID and phone number.[46] These aside, blockchain services providers are required to register with the authorities within ten days of providing the service. Those companies developing new products are required to report these to the authorities to undergo safety assessment in line with relevant regulations. Companies involved are also required to implement necessary changes so as issue warnings to users, restrict and close accounts while users violating administrative laws and regulations would have to be reported to the relevant authorities.[47]

The June 2019 Facebook Libra announcement for a global kind of cryptocurrency drew a negative response from China with the fears that this could pose a serious threat to the country's monetary sovereignty. China's electronic payment methods are already exemplary to the world, especially its popular mobile payment apps that are said to be quickly eliminating cash transactions there. There is, however, the concern that the Facebook Libra proposition, when activated, could reinforce the US dollar's outsized influence in the global financial system as Libra would be supported by a basket of sovereign currencies, with the US dollar accounting for 50% of the basket. A central bank-issued digital currency such as mooted by the PBOC, when compared to the electronic payment systems controlled by Chinese tech entities, would not face bankruptcy risk. The world is watching closely further developments from China as it would have significant implications to the international financial system.

8.3 India's cryptoasset regulatory policy

For now, there is no precise definition for cryptoassets, cryptocurrencies or virtual currencies in India. The Reserve Bank of India, the country's central bank, curtails regulated finance and banking channels from partaking in the sales and purchase of virtual currencies. This guidance circular though is being challenged by the Internet and Mobile Association of India. It appears that the Finance Ministry report pertaining to crypto regulation is awaiting formal approval.[48]

---

46 Alex, T. (2019), "China to enforce regulation for blockchain companies in February", *Yahoo Finance,* 11/01/2019, citig areport from CNN, https://finance.yahoo.com/news/china-enforce-regulation-blockchain-companies-083048347.html, accessed 07/02/2020.

47 Supra, note [46], Alex (2019).

48 Tassev, L. (2019), "Indian crypto regulations ready in July, official reveals", *Bitcoin.com*, 16/09/2019, https://news.bitcoin.com/indian-crypto-regulations-ready-in-july-official-reveals/, accessed 18/09/2019.

There are hints that the government would not allow the use of cryptoassets as currency or to allow its use in the country's payments system. It would also take steps to eliminate the illegal use of cryptoassets. Nevertheless, there could be a concession for those seeking to treat them as a financial asset class and to this end the appropriate regulations would be put in place to make these transactions transparent and legal. Cryptocurrency exchanges would likely be regulated via new regulations requiring KYC procedures and record-keeping for transactions.

Up to now, pertinent authorities in the country have been sending mixed signals pertaining to the regulatory approach for cryptoassets.[49] The Finance Ministry has been saying that cryptocurrencies are not legal tender and that it would crack down on the deployment for illegal activities. The Tax Department has issued notices to thousands of crypto investors alleging tax evasion. The Reserve Bank of India ordered all regulated institutions to stop providing services to businesses and individuals transacting in cryptoassets within three months of its notice. There have also been calls from within the corridors of powers that Bitcoin has a place in the country. Suits against these have been scheduled for court hearings, including one at the Supreme Court.

In general, stakeholders in the cryptoasset industry are up in arms against the current and soon to be the official stand of the Indian authorities to criminalise cryptoasset investment thereby putting the country as the first large democracy to ban what is viewed as an innovative technology.[50] They argued that shunning the industry would result in massive job losses and a brain drain and more importantly disrupt the country's goal to have a US$5 trillion economy, given that the crypto industry is envisaged to be a US$10 trillion industry over the next five years. They further specifically stressed that India would lose about US$12.9 billion worth of the market if cryptocurrency is eventually banned in the country. By way of example, former domestic exchange Bitbns found the inhospitable regulatory condition too troubling and is now an Estonian-based operation even though their original stand was to operate from out of India.[51]

India is globally acclaimed as a global powerhouse when it comes to IT assets and related skills. They have produced global giants. They have contributed world class talents to many Multinational Corporations across the world, especially Microsoft. Many of their talents have been helping many economies across the world especially in the Fintech space, including even the US and the UK. Bangalore in India, for example, is globally recognised as the main source for such talents. While China makes huge strides in computer hardware, India is in contrast very powerful in software engineering. While China makes impressive achievements in the Fintech space, and in particular electronic payments, India is now fast catching up. While China officially bans cryptoasset transactions,

---

49 Supra, note [48], Tassev (2019).
50 Huillet, M. (2019), "Bitcoin Ban Means Massive Brain for India, Crypto Industry Warns", *Coin Telegraph*, 16/09/2019, https://cointelegraph.com/news/indias-proposed-Bitcoin-ban-is-already-driving-a-crypto-exodus, accessed 18/09/2019.
51 Supra, note [50], Huillet (2019).

India is apparently still as yet to formalise its stand on the matter. China fears the threats of private cryptocurrencies on its authoritarian regime, while India fears their deployment in its very large informal economy thereby potentially enlarging the incidence of deployment in illicit activities rather than the risks to its democratic form of government, incidentally the world's biggest democracy.

8.4 Japan's cryptoasset regulatory policy

Cryptocurrencies are generally treated as assets in Japan, but the country's amended banking laws, via the Payment Services Act on 1 April 2017, informally dubbed as the "Virtual Currency Act", in effect launched a regulatory regime for cryptocurrency businesses, thus making Japan probably the first advanced Asian economy to do so. Subsequent to the amendment, fifteen business operators registered under this regime. This amended statute recognised that, in effect, cryptocurrencies are a legal form of payment.

These new rules stipulate that cryptocurrency exchanges seeking to operate in Japan would henceforth come under the regulatory supervision of the Japan Financial Services Agency (JFSA). As such, they would be subject to annual audits and KYC verifications so as to strengthen the country's anti-money laundering initiatives. Effectively they would operate through a system of self-regulatory bodies that would have stricter impositions on them than required by law.[52] Cryptocurrency exchange businesses all now have to be registered. Regulation in this context covers: registration, maintaining internal controls, segregation of customers' cryptocurrency from that of the exchange and publishing response policies to hacking and the retention of funds for payment.[53]

The new regulatory regime is defined as the financial value that may be employed to perform obligations in compensation for purchasing or borrowing of goods, or receiving services, against unspecified persons, which may be purchased from or sold to unspecified persons and are transferrable by an electronic data processing system, provided that such value is limited to those recorded on an electronic device in an electronic form, and does not include Japanese or foreign currencies, or assets denominated in such currencies. These as described are known as Type 1 virtual currencies.[54] In contrast, Type 2s are those that can be exchanged with Type 1s and with unspecified persons and also viewed as transferable by an electronic data processing system.

---

52 www.globallegalinsights.com/practice-areas/blockchain-laws-and-regulations/japan, accessed 08/08/2019.

53 Helms, K. (2018),"Japan Publishes Draft Report of New Crypto Regulations". *Bitcoin.com*, 17/12/2018, https://news.Bitcoin.com/japan-report-new-cryptocurrency-regulations/, accessed 24/02/2019.

54 Koinuma, M., Ohashi, K. & Sakamoto, Y. (2017), "New law and regulations on virtual currencies in Japan", *Greenberg Traurig*, 24/01/2017; Ishida, M., Mears, E. & Takeda, R. (2017), "Japanese regulatory update on virtual currency business", *DLA Piper Paper*, 29/12/2017, https://www.dlapiper.com/en/japan/insights/publications/2017/12/japan-regulatory-update-on-virtual-currency-business/, accessed 02/02/2018.

Since Bitcoin became recognised as an official form of legal payment in Japan in April 2017, more than 4,500 stores in the country began accepting cryptocurrencies, with one financial newspaper estimating that this could increase fivefold by the end of 2017.[55] The variety of stores accepting Bitcoin including electronic giant Bic Cam, as well as Bitcoin BTMs, which exchange fiat for Bitcoin and utilities has greatly increased. Despite the liquidation of Mt Gox, the then largest Bitcoin exchange in the world, the Japanese enacted regulations focusing on relevant exchanges so as protect consumers. The country's regulations on this are spelt out below[56]:

(i) Going by this classification, present major Type 1 virtual currencies are Bitcoin, Ethereum or Litecoin, while Type 2s are counterparty coins known as XCP or tokens that can be exchanged to Type 1s. Reward points granted under a particular point initiative are not deemed to be cryptocurrencies where the points could only be employed at a specified number of shops or cannot be exchanged with real currencies without any limitation posed by a point issuer. Cryptocurrencies must be convertible to fiat currencies and accepted in an open community or freely exchangeable with other virtual currencies without any limitation posed by the issuer.

(ii) Cryptocurrency exchange business refers to those entities purchasing or selling cryptocurrencies; exchanging them with other cryptos; intermediation, brokerage or acting as agent for them; acting as a defined cryptocurrency exchange; or administering customers' cash or "virtual currency" as defined.

(iii) Bitcoin users would be subject to the "know your customer" rules by Japanese cryptocurrency exchanges.

(iv) Such exchanges would be subjected to minimum capitalisation rules to avoid liquidity risks troubling some crypto exchanges across the world. Providers have to have a minimum of ¥10 million, not in possession of assets with negative values and have the necessary legal compliance to operate a cryptocurrency exchange appropriately and securely. The provider must not have had its registration in Japan as a cryptocurrency exchange service provider revoked, or registration as a similar operator based on provisions in a foreign law deemed equivalent of this Payment Services Act in the past five years. The provider must never have violated the Payment Services Act, the Law Controlling Contributions,

---

55 Sedgwick, K. (2017), "Japan teaches Western government a lesson in cryptocurrency regulation", *Bitcoin Magazine,* 13/11/2017, https://news.bitcoin.com/japan-teaches-western-governments-lesson-cryptocurrency-regulation/, accessed 02/02/2018.

56 Financial Services Authority (FSA), "Details of screening new registration application as virtual currency exchange service provider", FSA, 30/09/2017, https://www.fsa.go.jp/en/news/2017/20170930-1/02.pdf, accessed 02/02/2018; Yeoh, P. (2017), "The brave new world of Bitcoin and blockchain: From 'no-go' to 'go beyond'", Asia & The Pacific Policy Society (APPS) Policy Forum, 02/08/2017, https://www.policyforum.net/no-go-go-beyond, accessed 02/02/2018.

Money Deposits and interest or equivalent provisions of foreign laws and never have been fined in Japan or penalised under foreign laws as a result in the past five years. Other businesses operated by the provider must not harm the public interest. The provider's directors must not include disqualified individuals.

(v) The provider's organisation system must be verified that they have protective measures in place for service users. These include, for instance, whether the provider is equipped with systems to ensure that users are informed about the characteristics of cryptocurrencies such as the fact that it is not legal tender or that it carries the risk of loss due to price volatility. Providers must maintain separate management of money or cryptocurrencies deposited by users. The provider must also confirm whether they have established a risk management framework giving sufficient consideration to the possibility of risk materialisation, and whether the IT system risks management system is based on objective criteria.

(vi) Foreign currency cash service providers are allowed to operate their business in Japan, but they have to be corporations that have a representative in Japan.

(vii) Cryptocurrency trading is not subject to the 8% consumption tax in Japan. However, Japan's Tax Agency declared that profits derived from its trading are subject to income tax under miscellaneous income in contrasts dividend income, real property income, business income and employment income. The Tax Agency has not mentioned corporate taxation measures, but it is highly likely that corporate profits generated by virtual currency trading could also be subject to corporate tax.

Tokens can only be sold through a cryptocurrency exchange services provider. This also covers ICOs (discussed below) as there must already be an exchange market for the tokens.[57]

Japan's FSA cautioned investors of two risks associated with ICOs.[58] The first concerns price volatility, as a token's price may decline or become suddenly worthless. The second refers to their potential for fraud. The JFSA further cautioned that goods and services outlined in the ICOs' whitepapers might not be realised. Importantly investors should invest at their own risks after understanding the relevant risks, the content of the ICO project where the purchase of tokens are being considered and have given enough attention to the suspicious solicitation of ICOs.

---

57 Umeda, S. (2018), "Regulation of cryptocurrency: Japan", *Library of Congress*, June 2018, www.loc.gov/law/help/cryptocurrency/japan.php, accessed 07/02/2020.

58 Helms, K. (2017), "Japan's Financial Services Authority clarifies stance on initial coin offerings", *Bitcoin Magazine*, 29/10/2017, https://news.bitcoin.com/japans-financial-authority-initial-coin-offerings/, accessed 02/02/2018.

The JFSA notes that though there are no particular Japanese laws applicable to ICOs, those businesses launching ICOs should be aware that they may fall within the scope of the Payment Services Act (PSA) and/or the Financial Instruments and Exchange Act (FIEA) depending on how they are structured.[59] Where tokens fall under the virtual currency provisions of the PSA, then businesses providing virtual currency exchange services regularly must be registered with each local Finance Bureau. So far eleven such exchanges have been approved by the JFSA. Where, however, an ICO bears the characteristics of an investment, and the purchase of a token by a cryptocurrency is practically deemed as equivalent to that of legal tender, the ICO becomes subject to regulations under the FIEA. The FIEA defines an interest in collective investment schemes (CISs) as securities and would as such have to register as a financial services operator unless certain exemptions apply. Generally, an interest in a CIS would be an interest in specified legal vehicles contributed by investors that have rights to receive dividends or distribution of assets arising from businesses that use cash, securities or other specified assets.

ICOs are growing in Japan, as both small and big companies are using them to raise funds.[60] Japan's internet giant, GMO, is planning to use an ICO to sell its 7mm Bitcoin mining boards. Japan's financial services company the SBI Group has revealed plans to create a new financial ecosystem based on cryptocurrency through eight different crypto-related businesses simultaneously developed and comprising mining, hedge fund management, financing, a derivatives markets, remittance services, transaction/payments services, and an ICO and exchange platform rating information services.[61] The group's finance business promoted ICO and cryptocurrency bond issuance through entities specialised in cryptocurrency finance, as from the spring of 2018.

In August 2017, Japanese Bitcoin exchange Zaif operator Tech Bureau launched a platform known as Comsa. This is a one-stop solution that includes the creation of a multi-language whitepaper, pre-configured token sale dashboard, blockchain integration services and PR services dedicated for ICOs.[62] Singapore-based Bitcoin exchange, Quoine, with a strong presence in Japan launched a global ICO known as the Qash. Both Quoine and Zaif were among the 11 Bitcoin exchanges approved by the FSA in September 2017.[63] Japanese Bitcoin exchange Coincheck has also received hundreds of requests from Chinese start-ups and elsewhere asking it to list their tokens subsequent to the ICO ban in China.[64]

---

59 Supra, note [58], Helms (2017).
60 Supra, note [58], Helms (2017).
61 Helms, K. (2017a), "Japan's SBI Group launching eight crypto businesses including mining", *Bitcoin Magazine*, 28/10/2017, https://news.bitcoin.com/japans-sbi-crypto-businesses-mining/, accessed 02/02/2018.
62 Supra, note [58], Helms (2017).
63 Supra, note [58], Helms (2017).
64 Supra, note [58], Helms (2017).

The Japanese Blockchain Association (JBA) has 127 members, of which 15 are crypto exchange members and 35 are blockchain members. On 18 November 2017 the JBA issued a guidance for ICO token sales to Japanese residents[65]:

(i) Japan has no particular ICO regulations and does not prohibit all ICOs, but this does not mean Japan allows all ICOs. Existing financial regulations such as security and CIS regulations and virtual currency or prepaid payment instrument regulations may apply to some types of ICOs. Even when those regulations do not apply, other laws like civil law, commercial transaction law, consumer protection law and criminal law would almost always apply to ICOs.

(ii) Careful consideration is necessary when solicitation is made. When making sales via the internet, the term, "solicitation" is broadly interpreted under Japanese laws. Those ICO issuers or sellers not wanting to be regulated under Japanese laws when soliciting investors online, are advised to block all Japanese residents from transacting on their site.

(iii) The JFSA issued a warning on ICO on 27 October 2017. The JFSA stated then that even if an ICO falls within the scope of the PSA and/or the FIEA, delivering such services without registration is subject to criminal penalties. Besides the PSA and the FIEA, other applicable regulations include the Fund Regulation in the FIEA, the Specified Commercial Transaction Act, and the Consumer Protection Act.

In the wake of the recent Coincheck hack, which resulted in some ¥58 billion loss on its platform, a group of 16 Japanese crypto exchanges is reportedly seeking to form a new regulatory body to be registered with the JFSA.[66] Apparently, a plan to merge two existing groups, the Japan Cryptocurrency Business Association and the JBA, fell through. This led to the above development and came after it was announced that the JFSA would conduct on-site inspections at 15 unlicensed cryptocurrency exchanges in response to the Coincheck hack. It is unclear whether those exchanges are behind the new self-regulatory body, or whether Coincheck, which is currently awaiting licensing, is part of this founding group. It is to be noted that since September 2017, subsequent to the new legislation, the JFSA has been issuing licences to some of the country's crypto exchanges. Those which have filed but not been approved yet were allowed to keep on functioning on a provisional basis as the case of Coincheck.

---

65 Japanese Blockchain Association (2017), "Guidance for ICO token sales to Japanese residents", *JBA*, 18/11/2017, https://jba-web.jp/archives/20171118_guidance-for-ico-token-sales-to-japanese-residents, accessed 02/02/2018.

66 Palmer, D. (2018), "Report: Japanese crypto exchanges united to form self-regulatory group", *Coin Desk*, 20/02/2018, www.coindesk.com/japanese-crypto-exchanges-uniting-to-form-self-regulatory-body-report, accessed 03/03/2018.

JBA's self-regulatory standards include the maintenance of a cold wallet under the consent of its related members.[67] The JBA noted with concern that maintenance of the cold wallet was delayed causing an illegal outflow of funds. The JBA further observed that the JFSA had alerted representatives of each cryptocurrency exchange regarding their security based on the possibility of cyberattack. For the future, the JBA in order to appropriately secure the security of cryptocurrency exchange traders will establish stricter voluntary regulations and seek compliance with members.

Despite the latest Coincheck hacking and the earlier Mt. Gox scandal, Japan has not retreated when it comes to virtual currencies, and in particular Bitcoin. The country responds with stringent KYC requirements and new ICO guidelines. It tempers this with an open invitation to exchange owners, entrepreneurs, crypto pioneers and Bitcoin enthusiasts that the county is open for cryptocurrency business.[68] Japan's crypto regulatory position is therefore in sharp contrast to that in China where regulators have cracked down on the market. This enables Japan to become the powerhouse of the cryptocurrency market.[69]

Japan has also shown that it is capable of rapid response to new technological innovation. Responding to the Coincheck hack, the JFSA ordered FSHO and Bitstation exchanges based in Yokohama and Nagoya respectively to halt their operations for a month, and another five other exchanges, including Coincheck (already facing sanctions and told to submit a report by 22 March 2018), to improve on their business practices. The stolen NEM coins in Coincheck were stored in online hot wallets as against the more secure offline cold wallets generally recommended. Though Coincheck has pledged to reimburse around US$400 million (as against the US$530 million lost) to all those affected, it is unclear how and at what point in time the reimbursements would occur.

In the PSA Japan became the first country to provide a legal definition of cryptocurrencies, i.e.[70]:

(1) "property value that can be used as payment for the purchase or rental of goods or provision of services by unspecified persons, that can be purchased from or sold to unspecified persons, and that is transferable via an electronic data processing system; or

(2) property value that can be mutually exchangeable for the above property value with unspecified persons and is transferable via an electronic data processing system."[71]

---

67 Helms, K. (2018), "Japanese crypto exchanges strengthen self-regulation following Coincheck hack", *Bitcoin Magazine*, 29/01/2018, https://news.bitcoin.com/japanese-crypto-exchanges-self-regulation-coincheck-hack/, accessed 02/02/2018.

68 Supra, note [55] Sedgwick (2017).

69 Graham, K. (2017), "As China cracks down, Japan is fast becoming the powerhouse of the Bitcoin market", *CNBC*, 29/09/2017, https://www.cnbc.com/2017/09/29/bitcoin-exchanges-officially-recognized-by-japan.htmll, accessed 02/02/2018.

70 Supra, note [57], Umeda (2018).

71 Payment Services Act Article 2, para 5.

The Act also states that cryptocurrency is limited to property values that are stored electronically on electronic devices; currency and currency denominated assets are excluded.[72] Additionally, under the PSA, only business operators registered with a competent local Finance Bureau are allowed to operate cryptocurrency exchange business.[73] "Deemed dealers" must register and existing ones cannot expand until registered. Their websites must disclose their registration status.

The FSA has a draft report on the regulation of this area which is expected imminently. It is expected to show an essentially positive approach. To quote Toshihide Endo[74] "We would like to see it (cryptocurrency) grow under appropriate regulation." Additionally, for now, Japan appears to be exploring a CBDC.[75] Research has begun evaluating the options between account-based and token-based CBDCs, what other central banks such as from China are doing, and the potential of CBDC.[76]

In the meantime the Japanese House of Representatives, as noted earlier, has officially approved a new bill to amend national laws governing cryptoasset regulation. The bill would amend the two national laws currently applicable to cryptoassets. These are namely, the Act on Settlement of Funds and the FIEA. These revised legislations establish cryptoassets as the legal name for cryptocurrencies previously designated as virtual currencies are envisaged to come into force in April 2020.

Interestingly, many facets of the country's new legislation were incorporated in the IOSCO document and circulated in the G20 June 2019 meeting. The G20 leaders jointly issued a declaration on cryptoassets at the end of the June 2019 Osaka Summit reaffirming that cryptoassets do not pose a threat to global financial stability and that further work would be undertaken by standard-setting bodies. The Virtual Asset Service Providers Summit or V20, held in Osaka at the same time, announced that a group of national trade associations representing virtual assets service providers executed a MOU to establish an association to provide a global unified voice for the virtual asset industry that would assist in establishing mechanisms to engage with government agencies and the FATF to ensure that their best interests are understood and valued globally.[77]

---

72 Supra, note [71].

73 Payment Services Act Articles 63–2 & 63–3. The FSA is the regulatory agency that handles cryptocurrency transactions as a result of the Cabinet delegating its authority over most of the relevant matters under the Payment Services Act. i.e. Article 104, See also Details of Screening for New Registration Application as Virtual Currency Exchange Service Provider, FSA, http://www.fsa.go.jp/en/news/2017/20170930-1/02.pdf, accessed 24/02/2019.

74 Commissioner of the FSA.

75 Fintech News HK (2019), "Japan's central bank explores a central bank backed digital currency", *Fintech News Hong Kong*. 01/03/2019, https://www.fintechnews.hk/8652/blockchain/japan-central-bank-backed-digital-currency, accessed 05/03/2019.

76 Yanagawa, N. & Yamaoka, H. (2019), "Digital innovation, data revolution and central bank digital currency", *Bank of Japan Working Paper Series No. 19-E-2nd February 2019*.

77 Helms, K. (2019), "V20 Summit Concludes With Promises for Crypto Industry", *Bitcoin.com*, 30/06/2019, https://news.bitcoin.com/v20-summit-promises-crypto-industry/, accessed 02/07/2019.

The communique pertaining to cryptoassets evidently suggests that the G20 as a whole has not taken on board Japan's regulatory framework and opted to wait for further guidelines from the global standard setters like the FATF or the BIS. This is unsurprising. Other than the common unified stand to follow FATF's guidance for safeguards against money laundering and other related risks, most G20 members still prefer to map out their own regulatory position, despite conceding that cryptoassets are cross-border financial products requiring international cooperation to ensure effective policing.

8.5 Singapore's cryptoasset regulatory policy

Singapore's central bank, the MAS, has advised the public to act with extreme caution and understand the significant risks they take on where they so choose to invest in cryptocurrencies. This advice came in the back of recent sharp rise in Bitcoin and other virtual currencies' prices. Other pointers set out their views including[78]:

(i) A cryptocurrency is a form of digital token secured by cryptography and typically used as a medium of exchange, a unit of account or a store of value. Examples of virtual currencies include Bitcoin (by far the most dominant), Ether and Litecoin.

(ii) Cryptocurrencies are not legal tender and are not issued by any government and are not backed by any asset or issuer.

(iii) The recent strong price surge in cryptocurrencies are driven by speculation. The risk of equally sharp drop in prices is high. This implies that virtual currencies' investors run the risk of losing all their capital.

(iv) The MAS does not regulate cryptocurrencies and there is no regulatory safeguard for investments in them. MAS regulations do not extend to the safety and soundness of virtual currency intermediaries or the proper processing of their transactions.

(v) It is difficult to verify the authenticity or credibility on most operators of platforms where virtual currencies are traded as they do not have a presence in the country.

(vi) Cryptocurrency transactions are generally anonymous. This makes them vulnerable to being misemployed for unlawful activities. Where a cryptocurrency intermediary is found to have used them illegally, its operations could be shut down by law enforcement agencies. There is also the risk of loss should that intermediary be hacked, as it may not have sufficiently robust security features. For instance, in February 2014, Bitcoin exchange Mt. Gox lost 850,000 Bitcoins (valued at more than US$450 million at the time), which the exchange blamed on hackers.

---

78 Monetary Authority of Singapore (MAS) (2017), "MAS cautions against investments in cryptocurrencies", *MAS Media Release*, 19/12/2017, https://www.mas.gov.sg/news/media-releases/2017/mas-cautions-against-investments-in-cryptocurrencies, accessed 02/02/2018.

(vii) Investors who lose money from investing in cryptocurrencies would not be able to rely on any protection afforded under legislation administered by MAS. Therefore, before investing, the public should carefully consider the claims being made about the products being offered. Where the touted ease of making significant profits sounds too good to be true, it probably is. Investors should carefully evaluate whether an investment in a virtual currency is suitable for their investment objectives and risk appetite.

(viii) Investors and other members of the public suspicious of fraudulent investments involving cryptocurrencies should report such cases to the authorities.

In November 2017,[79] Singapore's largest bank, DBS, argued through Chief Information Officer David Gledhill, that Bitcoin was a Ponzi scheme. The Managing Director of the MAS CEO highlighted cryptocurrencies' potential beyond a store of value applications, such as cross-border payments.[80] He clarified though that where cross-border remittance was going through a blockchain using cryptocurrencies, it could yield benefits. He further clarified that this ought to be the question rather than whether Bitcoins or ether were rising or falling in value. He insisted that very few jurisdictions regulate cryptocurrencies, and most have taken the approach that the currency itself does not pose the risk that warrants regulation. Instead, it is the activity around it, such as Bitcoin exchanges or trading platforms that would see regulation. This is why the central bank's focus is to look at the activities surrounding virtual currencies and asking the questions on the kind of risks they pose, and which risks would require a regulatory response.

The CEO of MAS further argued that it is a known fact that cryptocurrencies are often abused for illicit financing purposes. Consequently, the MAS wants to have anti-money laundering controls and controls to counter the financing of terrorism in place. Singapore already requires cryptocurrency intermediaries such as exchange operators to comply with requirements to combat money laundering and terrorism financing. MAS will probably formalise this in the forthcoming Payment Services Regulation.[81] The MAS further mentioned that where ICOs include the promise of a dividend or other economic benefits they resemble regular securities offerings and would ergo be covered by Singapore's Securities and Futures Act, though other business models might avoid these security such as features in their digital tokens. ICOs as such would be examined

---

79 Chandran, N. (2017), "One of Asia's largest banks says Bitcoin is 'a Ponzi scheme'", *CNBC*, 15/11/2017, www.cnbc.com/video/2017/11/15/one-of-asias-largest-banks-says-bitcoin-is-a-ponzi-scheme.html, accessed 02/02/2018.

80 Chanjaroen, C., Tan, A. & Amin, H. (2017), "Singapore won't regulate cryptocurrencies, central bank chief says", *Bloomberg*, 25/10/2017, www.bloomberg.com/news/articles/2017-10-24/singapore-won-t-regulate-cryptocurrencies-remains-alert-to-risk, accessed 02/02/2018.

81 Supra, note [80], Chanjaroeh, Tan & Amin (2017).

case by case to ascertain which ones would come under regulatory ambit, and which ones could say outside.

An example of a Singapore ICO is TenX,[82] which raised S$80 million in June 2017. This Singapore-based start-up pitched its debit card as an instant converter of multiple digital currencies into fiat money including dollars, yen, and euros. MAS ICO guidelines say that offers or issues of digital tokens may be regulated by MAS where the digital tokens are capital market products under the Securities and Futures Act (SFA).[83] Capital markets products include any securities, derivatives contracts and contracts or arrangement for purposes of leverage foreign exchange trading.

Other aspects of the MAS ICO guidelines include the following[84]:

(i) The MAS will examine the structure and characteristics of, including the rights attached to, a digital token in ascertaining if that digital token is a kind of capital market product under the SFA.

(ii) A digital token for instance may constitute a share, when it confers or represents ownership interest in a corporation, represents liability of the token holder in the corporation and represents mutual covenants with other token holders in the corporation; a debenture where it constitutes or evidences the indebtedness of the issuer of the digital token in respect of any money that is, or may be lent to the issuer by a token holder; or a unit in a CIS, or an option to acquire a right or interests in a CIS. Offers of digital tokens which constitute securities or units in a CIS are subject to the same regulatory regime under Part XIII of the SFA, as offers of securities or units in a CIS respectively through traditional means.

(iii) An offer may nevertheless be exempt from the Prospectus Requirements; where the offer is a small offer of securities of an entity or units in a CIS[85] not exceeding S$5 million or its equivalent in foreign currency within any 12-month period; the offer is a private placement offer made to not more than 50 persons within any 12-month period; the offer is made to institutional investors only; or the offer is made to accredited investors. The exemptions for a small offer, a private placement offer

---

82 Ellis, J. (2017), "Singapore startup raises $80m in cryptocurrency sale; another follows suit", *Tech In Asia*, 29/06/2017, https://www.techinasia.com/tenx-crosscoin-ico, accessed 02/02/2018.

83 Sundarajan, S. (2017), "Singapore's central bank outlines when ICOs are and aren't securities", Coin Desk, 15/11/2017, https://www.coindesk.com/singapores-central-bank-outlines-icos-arent-securities, accessed 02/02/2018.

84 MAS (2017), "A Guide to Digital Token Offerings", *MAS,* 16/11/2017, https://www.mas.gov.sg/regulation/explainers/a-guide-to-digital-token-offerings, accessed 02/02/2018.

85 Collective investment schemes are defined under section 2(1) of the SFA, where "capital market products" include any securities (which include shares, debentures, and units in a business trust) units in a collective investment scheme. For the purpose of the digital token offerings guide, the securities laws refer to the SFA and the Financial Advisers Act (FAA). MAS on 1 August 2017 clarified that where a digital token constitutes a product regulated under the securities laws administered by it, the offer or issues of digital tokens must comply with the applicable securities laws.

and an offer made to accredited investors are respectively subject to certain conditions which includes advertising restrictions.

(iv) Intermediaries who facilitate offers or issues of digital tokens include a person who operates a platform on which one or more offerors of digital tokens may make primary offers or issues of digital tokens known as a primary platform; a person who provides financial advice in respect of any digital tokens; a person who operates a platform at which digital tokens are traded known as a trading platform. Persons operating a primary platform in Singapore in relation to digital tokens which constitute any kind of capital markets products may be carrying on business in one or more regulated activities under the SFA and as such must hold a capital markets services licence for that regulated activity under the SFA, unless otherwise exempted. A person who provides any financial advice in respect of any digital token must be authorised to do so in respect of that type of financial advisory service or be an exempt financial adviser under the Financial Advisers Act (Cap.110) (FAA). A person who establishes or operates a trading platform in Singapore in relation to digital tokens which constitute securities or futures contracts may be establishing or operating a market. Those establishing or operating a market or holding himself as such must be approved by MAS as an approved exchange or recognised by MAS as recognised market operators under the SFA, unless otherwise exempted.

(v) Where a person operates a primary platform, or trading platform, partly in or partly outside of Singapore, the requirements of the SFA may nevertheless apply extra-territorially to the activities of that person under Section 339 of the SFA. Where a person who is based overseas, engages in any activity or conduct that is intended to or likely to induce the public, or a section of the public in Singapore to use any financial advisory service provided by the person, the person is deemed to be acting as a financial adviser in Singapore.

(vi) MAS emphasises that the relevant MAS Notices on prevention of money laundering and countering the financing of terrorism may apply (AMT/CTF Requirements). Digital tokens performing functions which may not be within MAS's regulatory purview could be subject to other legislation for combating money laundering and terrorism financing. There are obligations to report suspicious transactions with the Suspicious Transaction Reporting Office, or the Commercial Affairs Department of the Singapore Police Force.

(vii) MAS's New Payments Framework would include rules to address money laundering and terrorism financing risks relating to the dealing or exchange of cryptocurrencies for fiat or other cryptocurrencies. Such intermediaries would be required to put in place policies, procedures and controls to address such risks. These would include requirements to conduct customer due diligence, monitor transactions, perform screening, report suspicious transactions and keeping adequate records.

(viii) Six illustrations are provided to further clarify the application of securities laws to offers or issues of digital tokens.

(ix) Entities looking to apply technology in an innovative way to provide new financial services that are, or are likely, to be regulated by MAS can apply for the regulatory sandbox. MAS would provide the appropriate regulatory support to those approved by relaxing specific legal and regulatory requirements prescribed by MAS which the applicant would otherwise be subject to for the duration of the sandbox.

MAS thus appears not to be seeking to regulate virtual currencies, except when their activities directly fall under its purview. To mitigate the challenges posed by virtual currencies being used for illicit purposes, MAS could seek to impose anti-money laundering and anti-terrorist financing requirements on intermediaries that exchange fiat for virtual currencies, such as exchanges and brokers[86] through the PSA[87] that could empower MAS to have greater jurisdiction over relevant exchanges and brokerages.

In November 2018 the MAS put forward a new regulatory framework for payment service providers. The is set out in what is now in the PSA 2019. Amongst other things it requires crypto service providers to be treated as those providing the same services for currencies.[88] The definition of e-money is being extended to e-wallets to provide greater security for the public.

Finally, as part of an ongoing attempt to create a regulatory environment that facilitates blockchain and cryptocurrency development, a regulatory sandbox has been created along the same lines as the UK. This means that those developing new products can submit details and determine the probable regulatory position in advance.

In this connection, MAS released a consultation paper on the creation of pre-defined sandboxes known as Sandbox Express to complement the existing FinTech Regulatory Sandbox launched in 2016.[89] The objective is to enable firms seeking to undertake regulated activities to embark on experiments more quickly, without having to go through existing bespoke sandbox application and approval process. Apart from cooperating with other countries similarly using regulatory sandboxes, the MAS has also joined together with 19 other countries the Global Financial Innovation Network initiated by the FCA in the UK.[90] The

---

86 Haig, S. (2018), "Singapore to extend regulatory mandate regarding cryptocurrencies", *Bitcoin Magazine*, 21/01/2018, https://news.bitcoin.com/singapore-extend-regulatory-mandate-regarding-cryptocurrencies/, accessed 02/02/2018.

87 2019, No.2. Passed 22 February 2019.

88 Fries, T. (2019), "Monetary Authority of Singapore to Introduce a Regulatory Framework for Cryptocurrency Exchanges", https://thetokenist.io/monetary-authority-of-singapore-to-introduce-a-regulatory-framekwork-for-cryptocurrency-exchanges, accessed 25/02/2019.

89 MAS (2018), "MAS Proposes New Regulatory Sandbox with Fast-Track Approvals" *MAS*, 14/11/2018, www.mas.gov.sg/news/media-releases/2018/mas-proposes-new-regulatory-sandbox-with-fasttrack-approvals, accessed 5/03/2019.

90 Trulioo (2018), "A Global Regulatory Sandbox — Collaboration, Policies and Solutions for Cross-Border Compliance" *Trulioo*, 24/10/2018, www.trulioo.com/blog/global-regulatory-sandbox, accessed 5/03/2019.

idea behind this is to help global firms interact with regulators, scale ideas and design a framework for cooperation between financial services regulators. More recently, MAS has also urged the blockchain community from Singapore and across the world to target viable use cases for blockchain technology with deep economic or social impacts and work towards bringing them to life.[91]

Singapore's tolerant approach towards cryptoassets was demonstrated when Binance, the world's largest crypto exchange announced, on 10 July 2019, the official launch of Binance Singapore in partnership with Vertes Ventures China and Vertex Ventures Southeast Asia and India. Binance concurrently mentioned that the Singapore Government exhibits an in depth understanding of cryptocurrency and is quite open towards financial innovation that would enable the city state to lead the next financial revolution. The city state has also prepared proposals that explicitly stated that it intends to remove double taxation on various major cryptoassets that include Bitcoin, Ethereum, and Litecoin[92]; and plans[93] to issue up to two full digital banking licences and three digital wholesale licences that would cater to SMEs and other non-retail segments. Singapore's carefully crafted, forward-looking regulatory approach towards financial digital assets and so on have not gone unnoticed by the world. As mentioned earlier, the founder of the World Wide Web very recently mentioned Singapore could be one jurisdiction that could contribute to the design of appropriate regulations to deal with matters in the digital world.

8.6 South Korea's cryptoasset regulatory policy

South Korea has a population of around 50 million people and a GDP of about US$1.52 trillion or GDP per capita of US$29,806 making it the thirteenth largest in the world.[94] It is estimated that the Japanese and South Korean cryptocurrency markets account for about 40% of global Bitcoin trades and ten percent of global Ethereum trade.[95] Cryptocurrency exchanges in both economies have millions of active traders. Some 80% of South Korean investors is estimated to have profited from investments in cryptocurrencies, with almost one third

---

91 Menon, R.(2019), "'Is the block chain a solution looking for a problem?' – Keynote Remarks by Ravi Menon, Managing Director, Monetary Authority of Singapore at CordaDay Singapore 2019 on 7th March 2019", *MAS,* 07/03/2019, www.mas.gov.sg/news/speeches/2019/is-the-blockchain-a-solution-looking-for-a-problem, accessed 8/03/2019.

92 Young, J. (2019), "Exclusive: Binance officially launches crypto exchange in Singapore, sees rapid growth", *Forbes,* 09/07/2019, www.forbes.com/sites/youngjoseph/2019/07/09/exclusive-binance-officially-launches-crypto-exchange-in-singapore-sees-rapid-growth/, accessed 11/07/2019.

93 Fintech News Singapore (2019), "Monetary Authority of Singapore to issues up to 5 virtual banking licenses" *FNS,* 28/06/2019, https://fintechnews.sg/31901/virtual-banking/virtual-banking-license-singapore/, accessed 02/07/2019.

94 Global Finance (2018), "South Korea GDP and economic data", *Global Finance Magazine*, 08/03/2018, www.gfmag.com/global-data/country-data/south-korea-gdp-country-report, accessed 09/03/2018.

95 Young, J. (2018), "China's largest Bitcoin exchange heads to Japan and South Korea with major bank deal", *CCN,* 02/01/2018, https://www.ccn.com/chinas-largest-Bitcoin-exchange-is-reallocating-to-japan-and-souuth-korea-with-major-bank-deal/, accessed 02/02/2018.

of salaried Koreans having an average of US$5000 in crypto, a relatively huge adoption of an untested investment vehicle based almost solely on speculation.[96]

The hype in cryptocurrency/asset investing and trading in South Korea started with the Government officially legalising Bitcoin service providers in July 2017 to facilitate payments, transfer and trade.[97] It was also envisaged at the time that the country was on the verge of providing a regulatory framework for Bitcoin trading platform and exchanges. A South Korean lawmaker proposed a bill that aims to revise the Electronic Financial Transactions Act such that traders, brokers, or other business entities involved in cryptocurrency transactions would be required to get regulatory approval from the Financial Services Commission (FSC). A key requirement includes the retention of capital of at least $436,300 and data processing facilities.

Thus, while the country's cryptocurrency industry has not been fully regulated, the Government officially legalised Bitcoin service providers to facilitate payments, transfers and trades. The Korean Herald meanwhile reported that the newly revised South Korean Foreign Exchange Transactions Act started to facilitate Fintech companies and cryptocurrency service providers to be approved by the Financial Supervisory Service, the financial regulator in South Korea.[98] The Bitcoin approved remittance method allows Fintech companies to process up to $20,000 worth of South Korean won in Bitcoin for users. This contributed to significant growth in the demand for virtual currency trading in the country as it did in neighbouring Philippines. Already according to market data sources, the South Korean Bitcoin exchange processes over 14% of global Bitcoin trades, the third largest market behind the US and Japan.[99]

News broke in August 2017 of North Korean hackers targeting South Korean cryptocurrency exchanges in retaliation to new sanctions imposed by the UN.[100] It appears that North Korea acted this way to circumvent the new sanctions so as to obtain funds to finance its nuclear and related initiatives. A security firm FireEye revealed in a threat research paper that it has found evidence to link various cryptocurrency exchange hacking attacks to North Korea, including the one that bankrupted Youbit VC Exchange.[101] By the second week of December 2017, rumours started to emerge of the South Korean Government planning to impose stricter regulations. There were then rumours that this would

---

96 Jo, H. (2017), "In a country known for its 'Bitcoin zombies', one-third of workers are crypto investors", *Quartz,* 28/12/2017, https://qz.com/1166103/a-third-of-south-korean-workers-have-invested-in-cryptocurrencies-like-bitcoin/, accessed 02/02/2018.

97 Young, J. (2017), "South Korea officially legalizes Bitcoin, huge market for traders", *Coin Telegraph,* 21/07/2017, https://cointelegraph.com/news/south-korea-officially-legalizes-bitcoin-huge-market-for-traders, accessed 02/02/2018.

98 Supra, note [97], Young (2017).

99 Supra, note [97], Young (2017).

100 Althauser, J. (2017), "North Korean Hackers reportedly attack Bitcoin exchange in South Korea", *Coin Telegraph,* 28/08/2017, https://cointelegraph.com/news/north-korean-hackers-reportedly-attack-bitcoin-exchange-in-south-korea, accessed 02/02/2018.

101 Young, J. (2017), "North Korea accused of hacking South Korean Bitcoin exchange Youbit", *Coin Telegraph,* 21/12/2017, https://cointelegraph.com/news/north-korea-accused-of-hacking-south-korean-bitcoin-exchange-youbit, accessed 02/02/2018.

escalate into an outright ban on cryptocurrency exchanges as a way to cool down the digital currency craze, especially after the Prime Minister's warning that it might corrupt the nations' youth and that crypto is a gateway to pyramid schemes and speculative investment when left unchecked.[102] However, by this time, South Korea had already surpassed its neighbour China in cryptocurrency trading.[103] The Government groups represented in the Virtual Currency Task Force and the FCS were apparently divided on the matter, with some fearing the stifling of cryptoassets and Fintech innovation. However, the FCS Chairman confirmed that any decision to prohibit transactions must have a legal basis.[104] Investors welcome the idea of regulation as they expect this to help the government process what is happening while simultaneously making it more legitimate for bigger financial institutions to put funds into cryptocurrencies. The country presently bans financial institutions from dealing with them.

As far as ICOs are concerned it is clear that their ban remains. In the meantime, six safeguards are being pushed forth for operating exchanges. Such conditions include confirming the user's real name, submitting proof of income, face to face interviews for compliance with KYC requirements, as well as providing cryptographic keys to set up anti-money laundering systems, including separating fiat currency accounts and supplying sufficient investment warnings.[105] These are expected to weed out criminal participants and may thus assist in making cryptocurrencies part of the market place. The country demonstrated considerable crypto enthusiasm compared to other south east Asian states as Bitcoin was trading at a $3,500 premium in South Korean exchanges compared to the rest of the world. This could partly be due to the limited liquidity or supply of Bitcoin coupled with strong demand from the finance sector.[106]

The news of a complete cryptocurrency ban surfaced again after a statement from the Ministry of Justice that the Government was preparing a bill to ban trading of cryptocurrency on domestic exchanges.[107] Responding to the market's sharp reaction to the announcement, the Presidential office said hours later that a ban on the country's cryptocurrency exchanges had not yet been finalised, though it was one of the measures being considered.[108] Subsequently, the Finance Ministry clarified that discussions were proceeding on how the Government could reasonably regulate cryptocurrency trading. It clarified further that a

---

102 Ambler, P. (2017), "South Korea Is Not Banning Bitcoin Trade, Financial Regulators Clarify", *Forbes*, 12/12/2017, https://www.forbes.com/sites/pamelaambler/2017/12/12/south-korea-is-not-banning-bitcoin-trade-financial-regulators-clarify/#628f1e3a1427, accessed 02/02/2018.
103 Pauw, C. (2018), "South Korea and crypto regulations, explained", *Coin Telegraph*, 06/02/2018, https://cointelegraph.com/explained/south-korea-and-crypto-regulations-explained, accessed 10/02/2018.
104 Supra, note [102], Ambler (2017).
105 Supra, note [102], Ambler (2017).
106 Supra, note [102], Ambler (2017).
107 Kim, C. & Kim, D. (2018), "South Korea plans to ban cryptocurrency trading, rattles market", *Reuters*, 11/01/2018, https://www.reuters.com/article/us-southkorea-bitcoin/south-korea-plans-to-ban-cryptocurrency-trading-rattles-market-idUSKBN1F002B, 02/02/2018.
108 Supra, note [107], Kim & Kim (2018).

balanced perspective is necessary as blockchain technology has high relevance to many industries, including security and logistics. Even were there to be an agreement to move forward with a draft bill to ban cryptocurrency trading, this would require a majority vote in the country's National Assembly before it could be enacted into law and such a process could take a considerable time.

South Korea is the third largest Bitcoin trading market in the world after Japan and the US. There is a particular concern in that cryptocurrency trading in South Korea is highly speculative and their prices are significantly higher than elsewhere in the world. South Korean authorities have taken steps to limit speculation in the market including prohibiting cryptocurrency exchanges from issuing new trading accounts, as well as talk of taxing capital gains arising from trading.[109]

The South Korean Government later announced that they would be taxing cryptocurrency exchanges at 24.2% in line with the South Korean tax code for all corporations that made an annual income of over 20 billion Korean won. Apart from banning anonymous trading, there would also be a ban on foreigners and minors from opening new accounts.

It is worth mentioning in this respect that major South Korean banks provide local cryptocurrency exchanges with virtual bank accounts that traders and investors could use to deposit or withdraw large amounts of Korean won without having to use actual bank accounts that are costly and time consuming. This was one of the factors that fuelled the crypto craze in the country. The Government has frozen the opening of new virtual accounts and virtual currency traders will not be allowed to make deposits into their cryptocurrency exchange wallets, unless the name of their virtual currency exchange matches that of their bank accounts.[110] The financial authorities have also requested relevant exchanges to overhaul their KYC and AML systems.[111]

Meanwhile, South Korea's FSC confirmed that new measures to tackle cryptocurrency speculation has been implemented in 23 January 2018 via a newly released document that amongst others include the following[112]:

(i) The guideline requires financial institutions to conduct enhanced due diligence (EDD) in transaction with cryptocurrency exchanges to ensure users' money are in safe hands. The EDD requires banks to verify additional information for cryptocurrency exchanges; the purpose of financial transactions and the source of money; details about services that the exchanges provided; whether the exchanges are using real-name accounts; and whether the exchanges verify their users' identifications.

(ii) The guidelines identify types of financial transactions deemed money laundering using virtual currencies. For example, a user makes deposits

---

109 Supra, note [107], Kim & Kim (2018).
110 Supra, note [103], Pauw (2018).
111 Supra, note [103], Pauw (2018).
112 Financial Services Commission (FSC) (2018), "Financial measures to curb speculation in cryptocurrency trading", *FSC Press Release*, 23/01/2018, https://www.fsc.go.kr/eng/new_press/releases.jsp?menu=01&bbsid=BBS0048, accessed 02/02/2018.

or withdrawals of more than KRW10 million or KRW20 million per week, a company or organisation deposits or withdraws their money from bank accounts to trade virtual currencies. These all constitute a kind of suspicious transactions for money laundering, which prompt banks to submit a Suspicious Transaction Report to the Korea Financial Intelligence Unit.

(iii) The guidelines mandate banks to refuse to offer accounts to cryptocurrency exchanges if they do not provide their users' ID information. Banks can also reject any transaction if they deemed to be having a high risk of money laundering.

(iv) The guidelines require financial institutions to strengthen their internal controls relating to cryptocurrency and share information regarding cryptocurrency exchanges with each other.

(v) The FSC expects the measures as announced to reduce room for cryptocurrency transactions to be exploited for illegal activities like crime, money laundering and tax evasion. These measures are expected to have the effects of forcing out those exchanges with high risk of money laundering and prevent speculative money or illegal funds from flowing into cryptocurrency trading through bank accounts.

(vi) The FSC stresses that the guidelines are not intended to formally institutionalise cryptocurrency exchanges or facilitate virtual currency trading through the exchanges.

After initially drifting towards strict cryptocurrency regulation, South Korea now appears to be tilting towards normalisation, as if in response to recent US regulators' comments that they are some distance from developing a complete regulatory framework for cryptocurrencies and the view of EU lawmakers' that a holistic cryptocurrency regulation is fairly low priority. In almost all parts of the world its regulation as a general asset class has still not evolved. This is mainly because they do not fit neatly into any one category, with some crypto issues appearing to be currencies, some debt paper, some equities, some commodities, some derivatives and others not fitting easily into pre-existing legal categories.

Participants in the cryptocurrency space in South Korea said the steps taken by the authorities were positive. Julian Hosp, co-founder and president of VC start-up TenX, stated that this could be the start of a crackdown on anonymity and the illegal use cases that some cryptocurrencies have faced.[113] John Sarson, the managing partner at Blockchain Momentum[114] is of the view that protocols to protect investors have been what the cryptocurrency markets have been missing and this is what the South Korean legislation seeks to implement.

---

113 Cheang, M. (2018), "New cryptocurrency rules just came into effect in South Korea", *CNBC*, 30/01/2018, https://www.cnbc.com/2018/01/29/south-korea-cryptocurrency-regulations-come-into-effect.html, accessed 02/02/2018.
114 A firm investing in cryptocurrencies and blockchain based businesses.

REGULATION IN SELECT ASIAN ECONOMIES

There seems to be a dichotomy between the extremely cautious view of the Government so far and that of the population. In January 2018 200,000 people signed a petition asking that the Government's crypto regulatory approach be ended. Matters relaxed on 30 October 2018 when the FSC cleared banks to work with crypto exchanges by providing virtual bank accounts. Banks were only permitted to reject exchanges if they failed to satisfy the money laundering laws. In early 2019 seven of the 21 cryptocurrency exchanges who applied has their security policies approved.[115] The exchanges themselves are heavily used, thus:

	Bithumb	Upbit	Coinone	Korbit
BTI rank	5	7	18	–
CMC rank	4	15	63	80
Web users / 24 hours	15.5K	8.4K	3.5K	1.5K
Mobile users / 24 hours	32.9K	22.9K	8.9K	0
% API trading	60%	60%	65%	93%
Total active users	48.6K	31.2K	12.4K	1.5K
Trading volume / 24 hours	$408.1M	$259M	$27.2M	$1M
API trading volume / 24 hours	$244.9M	$155.4M	$17.7M	$4.2M
Volume / visitor	$3,358	$3,323	$771	$224

Figure 8.1 Largest Crypto Exchanges in South Korea by Daily Volume
Source: Young, J. (2018), "Binance remains biggest crypto platform, volume of exchanges in Korea surge", CCN 7/11/18, https://www.ccn.com/binance-remains-biggest-crypto-platform-volume-of-exchanges-in-korea-surge/, accessed 07/02/20

---

115 Tomasicchio, A. (2019), "South Korea: 7 crypto exchanges and their security policies have been approved", *The Cryptonomist*, 11/01/2019, https://en.cryptonomist.ch/2019/01/11/south-korea-crypto-exchanges-security-policies/, accessed 07/02/2020.

There has already been one legal dispute. In *Coinis Exchange v. Nongyup Bank* (2018)[116] the bank had unilaterally terminated the banking facilities of the exchange, claiming that in so doing they had followed FSC guidelines. The court disagreed and determined that the banking facilities had to be continued. The same bank also had a legal dispute with a crypto exchange, Bithumb, withdrawing facilities after the exchange suffered two hacking attacks. This was amicably resolved after the exchange overhauled its security and internal management systems.

Therefore, as shown in the regulatory shift in South Korea, a tilt towards a light touch regulatory approach or the use of self-regulatory initiatives in other situations could be the way forward. That said, there is still a blanket ban on ICOs though, in what may be a sign that the wind is starting to change direction, Min Byung-du, Chairman of Korea's National Policy Committee called for their adoption "with practical, positive and efficient regulatory frameworks." Rumours have emerged that this approach may be adopted by the end of 2019.[117]

In December 2018, the Ministry of Finance announced plans to tax ICOs and digital currencies, which seems indicative of a government seeking to work with, rather than against, the new cryptocurrencies. There are now six crypto bills before the National Assembly, although none of them have emanated from the FSC. Matters are likely to see considerable progress during 2019. In the meantime, there is presently no law or clear guidance from regulatory authorities in the country providing clarity on legal matters pertaining to cryptoassets and how they would be handled under Korean laws. More effective monitoring and enforcements could be achieved when regulators across economies co-operate as cryptocurrencies are cross-border financial products. In this context, South Korea's suggestion of working with China in this area may prove a constructive step.

8.7 A comparative note

This chapter's review of cryptocurrency regulations in these large highly competitive Asian economies suggests varied responses. These extend from the hard stance taken by China that includes the outlawing of cryptocurrency exchanges, to the more hospitable Japanese stance that allows cryptocurrency activities subject to various regulatory rules that are not overly restrictive, to the more rigid stance taken in India where they are expected to fall under very strict regulatory rules or even subject to some kind of ban. It appears that such varied responses might be linked to each respective economies' state of health, the financial system in place, the cultural traditions of regulation in those states and the level of risks they see from cryptocurrency activities.

---

116 Central District Court's 50th Civil Affairs Division, South Korea.

117 Young, J. (2018) "State of Regulation in South Korea: Banks Required to Provide Fair Services to Crypto Exchanges" *Coin Telegraph*, 14/11/2018,https://cointelegraph.com/news/state-of-regulation-in-south-korea-banks-required-to-provide-fair-services-to-crypto-exchanges, accessed 25/02/2019

It has been argued that the evolution of cryptocurrencies resonates with insights arising from the 1997 Asian Financial Crisis. This as well as the subsequent 2008 GFC stressed the importance of early warning systems to detect risks and vulnerabilities arising from large and volatile capital flows brought about by excessive speculation. Indeed, the prudence and financial reforms built up by the Asian economies after the 2008 GFC insulated most of them from exposures to toxic subprime loans and related financial instruments that induce the 2008 GFC. These provided them with the resilience that enabled them to escape almost unscathed at the commencement of the crisis. The prudence that has in general serve them well appears to be replicated in their treatment of cryptocurrencies. This could be gleaned from the table below[118]:

Status	Economy
Banned	Indonesia; Macau, China; People's Republic of China; Vietnam
Regulated	Democratic People's Republic of Korea; Japan; Myanmar; Philippines; Republic of Korea; Taipei, China; Thailand
Fully liberalised	Brunei Darussalam; Cambodia; Hong Kong, China; Lao People's Democratic Republic; Malaysia; Mongolia; Singapore; Timor-Leste

Thus, the potential benefits together with the macroeconomic risks of cryptoassets raise various questions as to what could be determining the aversion or policy openness. Recent research suggests that a certain level of institutional quality might be necessary before opening up new kinds of financial technology,[119] such as the blockchain now underpinning the evolution of cryptocurrency.

There is the further need to take cognizance of the different pace in development of institutions and the financial market. The latter tends to outpace the former. It was only three years after the inception of Bitcoin that other cryptoassets made the scene. Thereafter, other market participants joined the fray to exploit the opportunities unfolding. Several legal and security problems then came along. Meanwhile, the pace of strengthening institutions by enhancing bureaucratic effectiveness, or the credibility of legal systems have not matched up to the demands of financialisation. While some jurisdictions conceded the gap in institutional capacity to regulate and intervene, and ergo advocating for non-intervention to market development or innovation, others out of great fear of potential risks to the stability of financial systems and deployment in illicit

---

118 Bernadette, J. & Shirakawa, R. & Korwatanmasakul, U. (2019), "Cryptocurrency in emerging Asia", *Asia Pathways ADB Institute Paper*, 25/07/2019, https://www.asiapathways-adbi.org/2019/07/cryptocurrency-in-emerging-asia/, accessed 08/08/2019.

119 Shirakawa, J.B.R. & Korwatanasakul, U. (2019), "Cryptocurrencies regulations: Institutions and Financial Openness", *ADB Working Paper 978*, Tokyo, ADB.

activities opted for the ban option. However, it is the quality of governance that would give policymakers the credibility in enforcing their policy choice, irrespective of the decision to intervene, regulate, or let markets be. This is because it is the trust in the system that could facilitate financial development. This suggests that improving institutions could be justifiable moving forward, even if it is outrun by financial development.[120]

Also, the decentralised and global nature of the cryptoassets industry suggests further the need for global cooperation.[121] This is generally recognised across the world, among nations, multilateral developmental agencies and global standards-setters as discussed previously. Outstanding issues include avoiding potential circumvention of regulation and supervision in the international transactions of cryptoassets, especially for preventing terrorism financing or money laundering. Cryptoassets stakeholders but especially policymakers need to be vigilant of potential spill over effects of volatility in the cryptoassets market. Growingly, macro-financial linkages could render the real sector vulnerable to amplified adverse impacts flowing from new exponential financial technology, more so when cryptoassets become a more significant part of mainstream finance.[122]

Insights drawn from these and the previous chapter covering selected advanced economies suggest that while some regulatory authorities are pondering whether to regulate crypto, some have responded with bans that they now start to review in view of the impact of regulatory arbitrage that result in business and talents migration. For those contemplating how to regulate crypto they are hesitating or unsure about the use of direct centralised regulation for various reasons including the lack of adequate skills and knowledge when dealing with the emerging technology. The "how to" approach could instead rely on the market-based regulation of the activities involved in the business. This formed the basis of the regulatory framework found in some jurisdictions that are relatively more enthusiastic about the potential of the industry. Both these chapters show the difficulties in arriving at a global solution, as national sovereignty issues, cultural issues, legacy issues, economic competition issues, legal system issues and different perspective of the nature of market risks stand in the way. The closest to one comes from the FATF, but this focused mainly on money laundering and related issues. Many regulators from across the world would continue to grapple with this crypto dilemma, but hopefully as the search goes on for a more global solution, policymakers and other stakeholders would continue to work together to solve the problem.

---

120 Supra, note [119], Shirakawa & Korwatanasakul (2019).
121 Supra, note [119], Shirakawa & Korwatansaskul (2019).
122 Circle/FireEye/Marsh & McLennan (2019), "Crypto-assets and blockchain technology: On the brink of technology?", Circle/FireEye/Marsh & McLennan Paper January 2019, https://www.mmc.com/content/dam/mmc-web/Files/On%20the%20Brink%20of%20Legitimacy%20-%20MMC%20Report%20-%20January%202019.pdf; FSB (2018), "Crypto-asset markets: Potential channels for future financial stability implications", *FSB*, 10/10/2018, https://www.fsb.org/wp-content/uploads/P101018.pdf, accessed 08/08/2019.

As the nature and form of cryptoassets are still evolving, the question of treating the phenomenon as a category of financial asset class, form of global payment mechanism, or global virtual/digital currency is still under debate now that big banking institutions like Goldman Sachs and JP Morgan and big tech platforms like Facebook and Amazon could be getting potentially more involved in the business. The issues are complicated by the possible plans of big economies like China and small economies like the Marshal Islands to issue central bank digital currencies. Yes, the crypto world is still evolving despite a decade of market presence, and yes regulators are still struggling to deal with the opportunities and threats posed by it. This is where researchers, users and activists can contribute by interacting with key stakeholders to exchange views and experiences across the world, from small to large economies and from more social to more capitalist economies. In other words, a global perspective is called for.

CHAPTER 9

Distributed ledger technology

9.1 Introduction

While this text has focused on cryptocurrencies it is already clear that blockchain has a much wider potential application.[1] Its generic name "distributed ledger technology" gives a more accurate idea of what the concept is. Essentially, there is a ledger which is distributed on the Internet on a peer-to-peer network and runs on the users' computers, not on a central data base. It is:

> ... a purely distributed peer to peer system of ledgers that utilises a software unit that consists of an algorithm, which negotiates the international content of ordered and connected blocks of data together with cryptographic and security technologies in order to achieve and maintain its integrity.[2]

Or as Vitalik Buterin, the creator of Ethereum put it, it is:

> a ... computer that anyone can upload programs to and leave the programs to self-execute, where the current and all the previous states of every program are always publicly visible, and which carries a very strong cryptoeconomically secured guarantee that the programs running on the chain will continue to execute in exactly the way that the blockchain protocol specifies.[3]

The essential concept is not new, it having a history dating back to the start of the 1990s when Haber and Stornetta created a system of documented time stamps that could not be retrospectively interfered with. Together with Bayer they then incorporated "Merkle trees" into the design to facilitate this by the successive elements being constructed into a continuing block.[4]

---

1 This is not universally accepted. See for example, Danielson Jon "Cryptocurrencies: Poliy, economics and fairness." *Systemic Risk Centre Discussion Paper 86*, London Scool of Economcs at p. 14.
2 Drescher, D. (2017) *Blockchain Basics*, Apress, Frankfurt am Mein, 2017, p. 35.
3 Buterin, Vitalik "Visions part 1. The Value of Blockchain Technology.", *Ethereum Blog*, 13/05/2015, https://ethereum.github.io/blog/2015/04/13/visions-part-1-the-value-of-blockchain-technology/. See also Borg, J.F. & Schembri, T. (2019), "The regulation of blockchain technology" in J. Dewey (ed.), *Blockchain and cryptocurrency regulation*, London, Global Legal Insights.
4 Narayanan, A., Bonneau, J., Felten, E., Miller, A., Goldfeder, S. (2016), *Bitcoin and Cryptocurrency Technologies: a Comprehensive Introduction*, Princeton University Press, 2016. Haber, S., Stornetta, W. S. (1991), "How toTime Stamp a Digital Document." *Journal of Cryptology*, Jan 1991, **3** (2), pp. 99–111. Bayer, D., Haber, S., Stornetta, W. S. (1992), "Improving the Efficiency and Reliability of Digital Time Stamping." *Sequences*, **2**. pp. 329–334, March 1992.

All blockchains are not the same, indeed the variety is extensive and they can be public and permissionless or private and permissioned and there are also hybrid versions. In the case of the former anyone can download and use the relevant software and create a new cryptocurrency or asset. This was the original form in which they were created. The latter on the other hand are, as their name suggests, run on a private network or intranet. They have normally already been created to carry out a specific function and may operate inside a company or syndicate. By their nature those using the system are known and permission must be granted before someone can join. Hybrid blockchains, as their name suggest combine the two, and as Herian put it: "data from a closed network can be shielded by a registry layer and moved or released to permissionless blockchains for the purpose of allowing public scrutiny of or prescribed or specified data at a given point in time. The hybrid distinction also includes the option of using ledgers, most likely in permissioned form as an access control medium for other, additional registries or databases in off-chain or offline servers and storage infrastructures."[5]

Almost anything could be collected and progressed on DLT, for example a business transaction can develop from the initial contact, through the negotiations, up to the final contract. If the parties later agree to amend the contract, then this can be added. All set out in a system that allows for no retrospective amendment without the parties' agreement, so the risk of a party seeking to renege by arguing over what had been previously agreed is removed. It thus has great potential for storing government records. Indeed, the claims being made for its potential verge on the surrealistic: as significant for British Society as the creation of the Magna Carta, was one suggestion.[6] Others have proposed that it could radically change the manner in which society operates[7] and a solution to virtually every human problem in existence[8] was another. Even allowing for over enthusiasm there seem reasonable grounds to suppose that blockchain has a potentially important future.

9.2 Encryption

The DLT is open to access by third parties but is also encrypted utilising both public and private keys. Every ten minutes[9] in the case of Bitcoin the transactions are checked, transacted, cleared and locked into the ledger on a time-stamped

---

5 Herian, R. (2019), *Regulating Blockchain. Critical Perspectives in Law ND Technology*, Routledge, 2019, p. 16.

6 Mulligan, C. (2016), "Applications in Government" in Government Office for Science, *Distributed Ledger Technology: Beyond Blockchain*. A report by the Chief Government Scientific Adviser. (n 1) p. 65.

7 Wright, A., De Phillipi, P. (2015), "Decentralised Blockchain Technology and the Rise of Lex Cryptographica" 2015. https://papers.ssrn.com/sol3/papers.cfm?abstract_id=2580664.

8 Walch, A. (2016), "The Fiduciaries of Public Blockchains" http://blockchain.cs.ucl.ac.uk/wp-content/uploads/2016/11/paper_20.pdf.

9 Though in some cases, eg, Etherium, it is more frequent and can be carried out in a few seconds.

basis in a link with the preceding transaction. For anyone to interfere with the process they would need to access and alter the blockchain history which would be almost impossible at the current level of software development and computer capacity.[10]

This can also operate just as easily on a multi-lateral basis. For example, most of the population own credit and debit cards which facilitate paying for goods and services. However, the data which develops in such a system is owned by the company issuing the card. They also charge an annual fee and a percentage of the outstanding amount on the card. It is normally the case that the holders of these cards have a credit line enabling them to spend in excess of their current cash value. A blockchain-based payment system would involve the payor and payee dealing directly with each other on the blockchain with the system showing the payment being made within ten minutes and the confirmation of transfer of title being returned at the same speed. Credit facilities could still be obtained by users from third parties, but the credit provider would not need to become involved with the process and would no longer own the overall arrangement.

9.3 Overheads

The key point is that there are virtually no overheads in utilising a blockchain-based system for such payments although, as discussed earlier, costs may start to arise with Bitcoin once no further new coins are issued to miners and it becomes necessary to pay for payments to be verified. All the financial transactions carried out by banks through the SWIFT system or cheque clearing can be carried out directly and at lower cost by the parties to the transaction dealing directly with each other. In addition, a significant part of the world's population, especially in the less developed parts of the world, do not live near a bank branch. The capacity to use mobile access through iPhones and the like opens them up to a much wider range of financial facilities than are currently available to them. That said the size of the hard drive needed to operate blockchain means that such an iPhone would need to be linked to a powerful base unit, which at present may limit its use in the poorer parts of the world.

The fundamental development that this involves is that digital assets can be controlled and their availability restricted, thus maximising their potential sale price. Music and films, for example, were originally purchased but the availability of digital, online versions quickly meant that they could be enjoyed free of charge by the users. New business models evolved which utilised advertising as the income stream but for product producers in, for example, the music and film industries, the financial loss has been enormous. Blockchain enables the product to be made available again on a controlled basis, meaning that the product itself can be sold, potentially increasing profits. That said the old digital online system

---

10 Tapscott, A., Tapscott, A. (2018), *Blockchain Revolution*, Penguin Random House, London, 2018, pp. 6–7.

has not gone away so there will continue to be competition from this source, especially in the form of pirated online material for the foreseeable future.

Fund managers can also operate DLT systems and reduce costs to the investors through reducing administration costs, fewer intermediaries and significantly less administration. In addition, the automated real time process whereby the trades both self clear and settle will reduce them further.[11]

Trade finance is an area where many see great potential[12] and this was apparent from the feedback to HM Treasury's Cryptocurrency Task Force. The current arrangements involve letters of credit and/or bills of exchange to facilitate payment. There are also time delays with the majority of letters of credit being initially rejected by banks for failure to be precisely accurate, often on quite trivial points of detail because of the operation of the relevant law in this area.[13] That said, the vast majority are settled within 48 hours, albeit at some inconvenience to the payee. However, were the payment system for a letter of credit and/or bill of exchange to be constructed on a DLT basis the money could be released to the vendor at the moment of the delivery of the goods, with the process being self-checking and self-recording. Recent steps taken by the Monetary Authorities of Hong Kong and Singapore have picked up on this possibility and provide what may be the first of many such steps in creating an international information highway to facilitate trade finance.

The initial design of the respective DLTs is still at a fairly early stage and questions have been raised[14] regarding the trade off between performance, resilience and privacy. Performance is still slow at the moment in the context of cryptocurrencies. Transactions can take anything from ten minutes to an hour to go through. In comparison with payment by cash or credit card this is a significant timeframe and reduces the attractiveness of cryptocurrencies as medium of exchange. Transaction costs for Bitcoin have been assessed at varying between US$0.45 to US$55.[15] The platform being used may also involve extra fees. This compares with no cost for using cash and a nominal, indirect one for using credit or debit cards. That said, for international transactions the picture changes. The normal banking tool is SWIFT, which in comparison with cryptocurrencies is slow and more expensive. There are other cash transfer systems but the average cost of transferring US$200 is 7.1%, rising to 9.4% in sub-Saharan Africa.[16]

---

11 "The Investment Management Strategy II." HM Treasury 2017.

12 Hong Kong Monetary Authority (2017), "Press release – Hong Kong and Singapore launch a joint project on cross-border trade and trade finance platform", *Hong Kong Monetary Authority*, 15/12/2017, https://www.hkma.gov.hk/eng/news-and-media/press-releases/2017/11/20171115-6/.

13 *United City Merchants v Royal Bank of Canada* [1983] 1 A.C. 168 (HL); *Kvaerner John Brown Ltd v Lear Siegler Services Ltd* [2006] EWCA Civ 1130 and *Balfour Beatty Civil Engineering Ltd v Technical and General Guarantee Co Ltd* [2000] 68 Con. L.R. 108. See also Haynes, A. (2018), *The Law Relating to International Banking*, Professional Publishing, 2018 at pp. 260–265.

14 See for example Cyproassets Taskforce, final report, October 2018, p. 26.

15 Danielsson J. (2018), "Cryptocurrencies: Policy, economics and fairness" *Systemic Risk Centre*, London School of Economics, Version 1.2, November 2018, p. 20.

16 Supra, note [15], Danielsson (2018).

9.4 Security offerings

Companies also raise finance by selling shares which provide a degree of equity in their business to those who will buy them. Now security token offerings can be made on blockchain and can potentially provide a far cheaper way for shares to be issued publicly. This raises the possibility of more smaller companies going to market to sell shares than at present, thus hugely increasing the size of the share market. Legal issues still arise as share sales normally have to be accompanied by a prospectus, a legal document setting out the finances of the issuing company, the details of the share issue and what the funds will be used for. These are time consuming and expensive to produce, requiring extreme care and accuracy because of the criminal and civil legal consequences that can be attracted if they are not. Many security token offerings currently seem to be issued on the assumption that these rules do not apply if the share issue is carried out on an ICO basis but steps are currently being taken be regulators to disabuse issuers of this fact.[17] Once those in the marketplace understand this the costs will rise, but it will still be potentially much cheaper than a standard share issue. Very significant cost savings will still be made though from the reduction in investment bank fees, stockbrokers and sales agents as the online sales process will hugely reduce the expense of the share issue.

Likewise, a multi-party system such as a bond issue,[18] or ICO as they are called if the bond exists in the form of an e-currency offering, can all sit on blockchain. Over US$3 billion was raised in this way in 2017. That said, the same legal requirements regarding prospectuses crop up here and it is clear that market participants have also been cavalier in this context. The company wishing to raise finance therefore has to list any prospectus[19] on the blockchain. The lenders can submit payment and receive their title to the debt on the system, and, in due course, if they wish to sell title to the debt on to another person, which frequently happens, this will also take place and sit on the blockchain record. Repayment by the borrowing company can also then take place on the same system. In addition, the automated process is much cheaper to operate than the current process and reconciliation, settlement and record keeping are all automated with all parties sharing identical data.

Shares,[20] bonds and derivatives can all be traded on such a system and probably will be on a large scale within the next few years.

---

17 SEC (2017), "Investor bulletin: Initial coin offerings", *Investor Alerts and Bulletins*, 25/07/2017, www.sec.gov/oiea/investor-alerts-and-bulletins/ib_coinofferings, accessed 01/03/2019.

18 The issue of debt paper, normally by a corporate or government to raised finance at a stated interest rate for a set period.

19 The legal document advertising the details of the bond issue and the company issuing it. Alternately, if the bond is issued in high enough denominations to remove the risk of ordinary members of the public being able to afford them, a simpler and cheaper to produce document, called an "information memorandum", will be issued.

20 Recent tests in the UK by the FCA Sandbox have shown that DLT based share transfer systems can be set up so that changes of ownership are automatically registered at Companies House.

However, for banks there is one downside as the existing system requires clearing houses for shares and derivatives. These can take three days to clear trades even though the trades themselves will usually clear in seconds. This should not be a problem once blockchain-based systems take over as the trades will self clear. The current system does allow participants to engage in multi-lateral netting. This consists of the parties and the clearing house netting all trades off against each other by each trade being constructed of a sale by the seller to the exchange or clearing house and an immediate sale by the exchange or clearing house to the buyer. As a result the exchange is a counterparty to each deal and in the event of a participant becoming insolvent all the trades that remain outstanding will be offset against each other thus hugely reducing the amount of money at risk to the other parties involved.[21] The relative ease with which LCH Clearnet was able to cope with the financial consequence of Lehman Bros collapse is a good example. There were some issues with identifying the clients to whom certain uncleared trades related and some delays in getting margin payments back to those who required it, but essentially the multi-lateral netting approach worked well in reducing the total amount of money at risk.

What multi-lateral netting offers the banks is the opportunity to greatly reduce the amount of capital they have to hold in reserve against the trades they enter into, which is required by the Basel III banking capital requirements which are being applied in all the world's more advanced economies. In addition, reconciliation processes that can be both time consuming and slow can be avoided.[22] No doubt in due course amendments to the banking capital rules are likely to be made to move it in line with the financial risk that are left with the banks under a blockchain-based system.

This process would not be without risk though. While it would significantly reduce costs in that the trading process would no longer need intermediaries the market could end up in a decentralised financial world where trades were no longer centrally cleared and such a state of affairs "will simply be a collection of interwoven smart contracts that facilitate the buying and selling of blockchain based assets."[23] This will not offer the same facility as the present exchanges in holding capital against the risk of a participant becoming insolvent and thus the risk of a market failure, or at least a localised one based on one collection of interwoven blockchain-based contracts, will be much higher.

9.5 Criminal factors

Crucially blockchain also makes it much more difficult for fraudsters to operate as they cannot go back later and hide the fraud. Any activity is recorded and

---

21 Supra, note [13], Haynes (2018), p. 291.
22 Press Release. "ESMA assesses DLT's potential and interactions with EU rules", *European Securities and Markets Authority*, 2017. www.esma.europa.eu/press-news/esma-news/esma-assesses-dlt%E2%80%99s-potential-and-interactions-eu-rules.
23 De Philippi, P., Wright A. (2018), *Blockchain and the Law: The Rule of Code*, Harvard University Press, 2018, p. 102.

clears itself removing the need for traditional audit to verify it. Indeed, given the limited requirements placed on auditors to be "a watchdog not a bloodhound"[24] in comparison with the inability of the blockchain system to do anything other than record accurately, the future system should be much safer, automatic and not require audit fees. "If the (blockchain) ledger says something is true then it is true."[25] That said, to have a checking and regulatory capacity that works properly both auditors and regulators will need to be granted access rights to the DLT to check.

This makes blockchain and currencies based on it less attractive to criminals. With criminal funds, money laundering and terrorist finance there are a multiplicity of ways in which the criminals can hide their identity and the overall transaction. Blockchain records all the details of the trading and thus the capacity to hide what is going on becomes much more difficult, though there will remain the capacity for the person using the system to do so from behind a false identity. Even so police, tax authorities and intelligence services will be able to trace money flows back to their source. That said, some cryptocurrencies such as Monero and Zcash are more difficult to police. Monero has an obfuscated public ledger which makes it extremely difficult to trace back. It hides the recipient of the deal and creates a new electronic address and a secret key for them.[26] Zcash[27] has a cryptography-based system to guarantee privacy but with a selective disclosure capacity built in. Its accounts cannot necessarily be traced and its blockchain does not store information concerning the source and destination of the "money". Thus, for money laundering and disclosure rules the owner can elect to release information or not.

The other criminal issue is that although criminals may find interfering with the blockchcain process to be prohibitively complicated there is still the possibility that with cryptocurrencies or other items of value based on blockchain those parties will engage in market manipulation. The other possible way of illegally obtaining money through the new system is to hack people's computers to access their codes as was discussed earlier.

The regulatory approach has been discussed earlier in the book. What is already apparent is that blockchain-based systems do not fit neatly into existing regulatory structures. Some states have categorised cryptocurrencies differently from each other and in the US money transmission is regulated at state level, while the impact of the new developments will have an impact both nationally and internationally. The regulators are facing a situation where the two parties to a trade or transaction will be in possession of potentially large amounts

---

24 Lopes CJ in *Re Kingston Cotton Mills (No.2)* (1896) 1 Ch. 331.
25 Interview between Austin Hill, Don Tapscott and Alex Tapscott, 22 July 2015. Recorded in Tapscott, A. and Tapscott, A. (2018) *Blockchain Revolution*, Penguin Random House, London 2018, p. 76.
26 Fink, M. (2019), *Blockchain Regulation and Governance in Europe*, Cambridge University Press, 2019, p. 97.
27 A joint development between Israeli and US cryptographers. See supra, note [23], De Philippi, P. and Wright, A. (2019), p. 67.

of information, while the regulators themselves will have access to very little. They are also operating against a background of very rapidly changing circumstances, which historically they have not always adapted well to.

Across all these potential activities, and the others that will be created, the new distributed systems will be more resilient than the current centralised systems.[28] This is because having separate copies of data accessible to multiple participants greatly reduces the potential risk of data loss. As the blockchain is developed with an ever increasing number of participants this becomes more and more the case. A web attacker would need to take control of multiple participants to attack the system and the longer a distributed ledger has been in use the greater this number is likely to be: it could be vast. Thus, the system is capable of continuing to perform even if part of it successfully comes under attack as virtually all the participants will still be able to get direct access to their own data, which will be identical. That said the Bank of England's testing of a multi-node Etherium protocol-based project warranted further investigation of "scalability, security, privacy, interoperability and sustainability."[29] Even so most observers see DLT-based systems as stronger in these regards than the systems they are starting to replace.

However, now decentralised organisations with illegal intent have been created. Daemon for example, will enable its anonymous shareholders to manage a market on the dark web. Its aims, amongst other things, are to evade government interference.[30]

There is a further problem in that behaviour that any objective observer would regard as criminal may technically not be so because the wording of the law lags behind the technological developments. For example, the DAO hack arose when US$150 million was invested in Ether by around 11,000 people. The idea was to create a start-up fund which would be operated on a democratic basis by the votes of the contributors. Due to a bug in the code a hacker was able to remove a third of the fund without breaching the criminal law.[31] There was then a democratic vote of the contributors and 87% of the relatively small number that voted agreed to create a hard fork reversing the effect of the hack.[32] Perhaps surprisingly some opposed this on what seem to be philosophical grounds, i.e. that on principle the blockchain should not be reversed.

---

28 Cyproassets Taskforce, *final report*, October 2018, p. 22.

29 "FinTech Accelerator Proof of Concept." *Bank of England*, 2016 www.bankofengland.co.uk/research/fintech/-/media/boe/files/fintech/pwc.pdf.

30 Supra, note [23], De Filippi, P. and Wright, A. (2018), p.145. Butnix, J.P. "Daemon Wants to Become a Decentralized Etherium-Based Smart Darknet Market." *The Merkle*, 04/04/2016. https://themerkle.com/daemon-wants-to-become-a-decentralized-ethereum-based-smart-darknet-marketplace/.

31 Supra, note [26], Fink, M. (2019), p.187, Raskin, M. (2017) "The Law and Legality of Smart Contracts", *(2017) Georgetown Law and Technology Review*, 305, 335, Werbach, K. and Cornell, N. "Contracts *Ex Machina*", *(2017) Duke Law Journal*, 313, 365.

32 Technically there were two votes, the first on the procedure to be adopted and the second to reverse the blockchain.

9.6 Downsides

What then are the downsides? Energy consumption needs to be considered. The process of running transactions through the secure algorithm[33] consumes a significant amount of energy. That said there seems to be a huge variation in the estimates that "experts" calculate is utilised.[34] That needs to be offset though against the quantity of electricity that would otherwise be consumed by whatever alternative method had been adopted to carry out the transaction.

The greater the resilience built into a system the more limited the capacity will tend to be and some of the systems will be designed to cater for huge numbers of users. To maintain privacy encryptions are used but there are suggestions that this can reduce performance. That said, in many situations the use of encryption is a necessary factor to maintain sufficient security, so from the vantage point of the user this is not going to be a negotiable element. Finally, the resilience of a system can be strengthened by limiting the distribution of data. Unfortunately, this is often not an option as the common distributed ledger will be a key element of making the system attractive to potential users.

There may prove to be overheads related to coordination once the systems are in widespread use, though this should probably prove considerably less than current systems where parties other than those dealing directly with each other are concerned.[35] As years go by the complexity of some of the programs may become greater to handle all the data and security will become a greater concern, especially once computers that can handle mega data become operative.

In addition, there is as yet no standard form of platform for participants to use although IOSCO are looking into this.[36] It will be simpler to operate a system where there is an international standard, but there is no guarantee that one will emerge. Indeed, some participants may seek a competitive advantage through developing newer systems which have advantages over pre-existing ones.

9.7 The current situation

At the time of writing the US leads DLT start-ups, with the UK in second place,[37] with London having the second highest number of such projects listed, close behind San Francisco. However, the scale of the Internet capacity and that of the computers most people use on the system is not capable

---

33 Algorithm 256 (SHA-256).
34 Schneider, N. (2015), "After the Bitcoin Gold Rush", *The New Republic*, 24/02/2015. Kaminska, I. (2014), "Bitcoin's Wasted Power", *Financial Times*, 05/09/2014 and CIA (2012), "The World Factbook".
35 Supra, note [2], Drescher, D. (2017), p.13. Stead, C. (2018), *What is cryptocurrency: Your complete guide to blockchain, Bitcoin and beyond*, Sydney, Finder, 09/11/2018. Ganne, E. (2018), *Can blockchain revolutionize international trade?* Geneva, WTO, pp. 90–110.
36 "ISO/TC 307 Blockchain and Distributed Ledger Technologies", *International Standards Organisation*, 2016. www.iso.org/committee/6266604.html.
37 "State of Blockchain 2018 Q2 Report", *Coindesk*, 2018. www.coindesk.com/research/state-of-blockchain-q2-2018.

of carrying a multiplicity of large scale blockchain transactions: the transactional capacity is not there. It will not be many years before it is and until then DLT is likely to develop progressively. Some aspects relevant to its development, such as law and regulation, can be developed fairly quickly. Some areas such as money laundering, market manipulation and theft will always be with us but the security DLT provides should render them safer than other methods of financial transfer.

Strictly speaking, the World Trade Organisation (WTO) maintains that blockchain represents only one type of DLT, but the term now is commonly employed to refer to them in general. Many would agree that blockchain goes beyond the cryptocurrency hype. Its potential trade-related applications are numerous and could probably significantly transform international trade. Some possible deployments of cryptocurrency could include trade finance, customs and certification processes, transportation and logistics, insurance, distribution, intellectual property, and government procurement.[38] Even as the technology unfolds, interesting opportunities appear to enhance efficiencies of numerous processes so trimming costs in these areas. The technology though is not a solution to everything and this requires carefully weighing the costs and benefits involved. Interestingly, blockchain could help implement the WTO Trade Facilitation Agreement, as well as facilitating business to government and government to government processes at the national level.

The World Economic Forum has predicted that 10% of global GDP could be stored on blockchain systems.[39] It sees it as akin to the invention of the Internet, a system that functions as a general purpose technology. Unfortunatley, it remains held back by the limitations of the size of the distributed computer system.

There remain issues to be fully resolved if blockchain is to fulfil its potential: the issues of privacy, security, scalability, costs, hidden centrality, lack of flexibility and critical mass.[40] Privacy arises because the nature of the blockchain is open so that users can verify ownership and transactions. However, it is possible to limit this, as has been seen with the obfuscated ledger technology used in Monero and the cryptography-based system used for Zcash.

Security is a potential worry with any software system. In the case of blockchain systems the accounts are cryptographic keys that are accessed through the system. It is safe as long as only the relevant person has access to the cryptographic key. If a third party can access its details then they can access the system as though they were the other person. The security in the system is so strong that a third party is only likely to access it if they are given it or access records the owner has kept outside the blockchain system. Related to this is the possibility that governments may require computer codes to have trapdoors built into them facilitating analysis,

---

38 Ganne, E. (2018), *Can blockchain revolutionize international trade?*, Geneva, WTO, 2018.
39 www3.weforum.org/docs/WEF_GAC15_Technological_Tipping_Points_report_2015.pdf, *World Economic Forum*, 2015, p. 7.
40 Supra, note [2], Drescher, D. (2017), p. 206.

suspension or disabling.[41] That said, the users cannot be stopped from running the system without it, though this would presumably be illegal. Such an approach by governments would almost certainly lead to a kind of regulatory arbitrage where systems were based in jurisdictions that did not do so.

The scalability element arises as a result of the security that is built into the system. To stop later users altering earlier records the system is constructed of the history of the transactions so far with each having a hash puzzle added each time a block is added into the system. To retrospectively change this at the current level of software development would be prohibitively time consuming and expensive. The consequence of this is that processing speed and the maximum scale that the systems can currently operate on are limiting factors. This overlaps with the issue of cost, though that needs to be offset against the cost of any alternative system that would have been used by the parties instead. As that would often currently involve the use of third parties, those costs could be considerably higher.

The weak link may be the 51% rule discussed earlier. In a smaller system it may be possible for someone with considerable software power to achieve 51% control of relevant nodes. The larger a blockchain system becomes, the safer it is from such attacks.

As is apparent elsewhere in this book, the current state of legal and regulatory clarity is extremely low. Where there is any, that in one part of the world often contradicts that in another. It is an area where it is reasonable to expect rapid development. It would appear that the blockchain ecosystem is positive towards effective regulations that would deter nefarious deployment of the technology.

Despite present limitations, blockchain enthusiasts have to be mindful of the potential liability. This raises questions concerning how DLT should be structured, owned and ultimately regulated. In this respect, consideration should be given as to whether the system is permissioned or permissionless, whether the legal structure is specified in the pertinent agreements, the system's express or implied purpose, the system's consensus mechanism, and the matter of pre-existing relationships between the parties.[42] These features could be treated in law to be one of several legal entities: from a joint venture, or a multi-party contract to a partnership. For instance, the group that designs the code that governs the ledger could be deemed a joint venture and that this could extend to nodes or even simple users of the ledger depending on the extent of their participation. Conversely, the distributed ledger system could be treated as a multi-party contract where the group that sets up the code design and nodes is under a contractual obligation to maintain the system's security and operations. These potential legal structures could also differ across disparate jurisdictions.

The challenge hinges on the ability of law makers to strike a balance between the need for governance and the avoidance of strong state intervention that could

---

41 Supra, note [23], De Phillipi, P. and Wright, A. (2018), p. 181. It could be argued that this would merely be an extension of the current arrangements whereby some governments impose obligations on those creating codes, e.g. the Digital Millennium Copyright Act in the US.

42 Zetzsche, D. A., Buckley, R. P. & Arner, D. W. (2018), "Blockchain distribute ledgers and liability", *Journal of Digital Banking*, 2 (4), pp. 298–310.

terminate the innovation.[43] There is therefore the need to carefully analyse the functional features of various concepts under evaluation and their implications and risks to enable the delivery of appropriate and sufficient response to regulatory concerns without over regulation. This is not easy as blockchain is at an early stage of development and it is not clear what forms it will evolve into. Technologically blockchains are also rather limited in that every full node must process each transaction and keep a full copy. This inevitably slows down its utilisation: a problem that will increase as the size of a blockchain grows. Security for users will potentially be at the price of growing inefficiency. That said, there are developments such as off-chain payment channels, arranging for different nodes to store and process only part of the process, carrying out calculations outside the chain and directed acrylic graphs (DAGs) which do not use a linear blockchain approach.[44] Directed acrylic graphs or DAGs allow multiple chains of blocks to co-exist and interconnect. This enables a whole new menu of possible confirmation options thereby eliminating the need for block times leading to the unprecedented potential for highly scalable and fast information flow on a completely decentralized network. DAGs are, however, relatively less secure as the classic blockchain, but experts are working hard to transform this concept into a usable, secure and highly scalable solution.[45] Other approaches will also no doubt emerge.

Accordingly, regulatory intervention should be functional, technology neutral, and premised against regulatory goals and principles.[46] Indeed, like the Internet before it, DLT would be subject to regulation from governments around the world.[47]

Finally, blockchain provide potential benefits in terms of improved transparency and reduced transaction costs by the more effective managing of data and streamlining of processes, improving supply chains, enabling tracking and management of intellectual property, improving the reliability and traceability of records, reducing the speed and cost of settlement, facilitating copyright and patent protection, as well as improving efficiency through automated reporting and smart contracts. Its broader applications are facing various significant challenges. These include amongst others, the following[48]:

(i) Transaction capacity and scalability issues relative to conventional banking payments system.
(ii) Rising concerns over privacy and security matters. In particular, blockchain design choices frequently lead to inevitable tradeoffs needed

---

43 Borg, J. & Schembri, T. (2019), "Blockchain & cryptocurrency regulation 2019: The regulation of blockchain technology", in J. Dewey (ed.), *Blockchain & cryptocurrency regulation*, London, Global Legal Insights (GLI); Yeoh, P. (2017), "Regulatory issues in blockchain technology", *Journal of Financial Regulation and Compliance*, 25 (2), pp. 196–208.

44 Supra, note [26], Finck, M. (2019), p. 31.

45 Fantom Foundation (2018), "DAG- How they differ from blockchain", Medium 21/06/18, https://medium.com/fantomfoundation/an-introduction-to-dags-and-how-they-differ-from-blockchains-a6f703462090, accessed 07/02/20

46 Supra, note [43], Borg & Schembri (2019).

47 Rodrigues, U. R. (2019), "Law and the blockchain", *Iowa Law Review* 104 (2), pp. 679–730.

48 Madir, J. (2019), "Introduction – what is FinTech?", in J. Madir (ed.), *FinTech: Law and Regulation (Elgar Financial Law and Practice series)*, London, Edward Elgar, 02/09/2019.

between performance, privacy and the degree of decentralisation. Future technical progress, hopefully could potentially resolve these.
(iii) Interoperability challenges between different blockchains, between applications built on the same blockchain, and between blockchain and legacy systems.
(iv) Rising fears over the theft or loss of private keys. This is best exemplified by the Bitcoin theft of around US$500 from Mt. Gox in 2014.
(v) Tradeoffs in relation to the governance of blockchains.
(vi) To achieve wider deployment, the technology needs to be fully accommodated within public policy and legal frameworks and this suggests the need for clear rules.
(vii) Competition issues may need attention. This is because as permissioned blockchain network advanced to become essential infrastructure say in clearing and settlement, competition issues may surface around access.

In 2016, though still in the early days, France installed rules allowing the holding and transfer of non-listed securities via blockchain. Japan also enacted rules requiring the registration of virtual currency exchange business operators. In 2018, the 26 member states in the EU signed a Declaration to create the European Blockchain Partnership, as well as cooperating in the setting up of a European Blockchain Services Infrastructure to support the delivery of cross-border digital public services marked by the highest standards of security and privacy.[49]

The advent of blockchain is viewed by some as a revolutionary event moving through the five stages of denial, anger, negotiation, depression, and eventually, acceptance.[50] At its commencement, Bitcoin was largely ignored as an Internet-based "geek" money without mainstream interest or a future. Then anger came as a result of it being used for transactions by terrorists, money launderers and drug dealers. Next, even though Bitcoin was deemed unsavoury, the blockchain technology (DLT) underpinning it is viewed positively, and hence the negotiation phase. The technology went into a depression phase in 2017, but beliefs and passion for this returned strongly in 2018, with many quarters rallying behind its wider applications in financial services and beyond. Indeed, DLT along with other exponential technologies,[51] like the Internet of Things (IoT), 3D, edge computing, robotics, and artificial intelligence have become the symbols of the Fourth Industrial Revolution,[52] as they transform business and public processes to be many times faster, better, and cheaper.

---

49 Digibyte (2018), European countries join blockchain partnership, *Europa*, 10/04/2018, https://ec.europa.eu/digital-single-market/en/news/european-countries-join-blockchain-partnership, accessed 12/11/2019.

50 Mignon, V. (2019), "Blockchain-perspectives and challenges", in Kraus, D., Obrist, T. & Hari, O. (eds.), *Blockchains, smart contracts, decentralized autonomous organizations and the law*, London, Edward Elgar, 2019.

51 Ismail, S., Malone, M. S. & Van Geest, Y. (2019), *Exponential organizations*, New York, Diversion Books.

52 World Economic Forum (2019), *Globalization 4.0: Shaping a global architecture in the Age of the Fourth Industrial Revolution*, WEF Annual Meeting 22–25 January 2019. Overview, www3.weforum.org/docs/WEF_AM19_Meeting_Overview.pdf, accessed 12/11/2019.

CHAPTER 10

Conclusions

10.1 Introduction

Overall, international economic and financial regulators appear to perceive that there are no significant systemic risks posed by cryptocurrencies as the transactions involved are small relative to mainstream financial products and services. While the BIS stresses the need for regulatory intervention to pre-empt systemic risks from building up until it is too late to avoid the crisis, as with that in 2008, others called for more in depth analysis of the pertinent issues first. They believe that for now continuous monitoring of the cryptocurrency space will suffice, together with the exchange of information between global agencies and national authorities.

Different legal systems have responded to the regulatory enigma posed by cryptocurrencies through four different approaches.[1] There are economies where no action has been undertaken to regulate cryptocurrencies, and they form the majority. These include Argentina, Australia, Belgium, Canada, Chile, Croatia, Cyprus, Denmark, Estonia, the EU, France, Germany, Hong Kong, India, Indonesia, Iceland, Italy, the Netherlands, New Zealand and Taiwan. Some of these require those entities that interface with cryptocurrency transactions to comply with reporting obligations attached to their existing AML/CTF rules and these are increasing in numbers because of growing concerns that cryptocurrencies could be used for illegal activities. There are those regulating cryptocurrency merely for tax purposes, such as the UK, Norway, Spain and Finland where they are subject to VAT or capital gains tax. Then there are those prohibiting or curtailing the use of cryptocurrency, led by China (though they are taking steps to establish a state run system), Thailand, and Iceland. In the case of Iceland though there is a bit of uncertainty or tentativeness here, as some researchers have argued that Iceland regulates virtual currencies as electronic money via the Icelandic Exchange Act that effectively prohibits entities from partaking in the exchange of virtual currency.[2] Others cautioned about legal tentativeness in Iceland, wherein separate aspects of cryptocurrencies are both banned and

---

[1] Borroni, A. (2016), "Bitcoins: Regulatory patterns", *Banking and Finance Law Review*, 32(1), pp. 47–68.

[2] Cvetkova, I. (2018), "Cryptocurrencies legal regulation", *BRICS Law Journal*, Vol. V(2018), pp. 128–153.

encouraged.[3] Only a few economies recognise cryptocurrencies such as Bitcoin as a form of currency. By doing so, these jurisdictions appear to be leveraging concepts from traditional financial regulation and adapting them for use with cryptocurrencies.[4] In Brazil for example, Law No.2 12,865 of 9 October 2013, Article 6-VI allows for the creation of electronic currencies.

Germany, Japan and Sweden exemplify economies regulating cryptocurrencies, Germany considers their exchanges as financial service companies that must fulfil strict standards of operation including meeting initial capital requirements, maintaining certain professional qualifications and reporting transactions to BaFin, the country's financial regulator. Japan is also closely following this approach.

This short review suggests that thus far there has been no uniform regulation of cryptocurrencies, which explains the call for direction towards this by the BIS and the IMF. In particular various regulatory entities have acted independently to provide guidance as to the treatment of cryptocurrencies under the laws within their purview as exemplified by the CFTC in the US. This contributed to some clarity but, it also resulted in fragmented and incoherent regulatory frameworks, difficulties in developing frameworks tailored to the unique characteristics of virtual currencies and failures to give sufficient consideration to the full menu of regulatory issues raised by decentralised cryptocurrencies to result in regulatory frameworks suffering from an unintended lack of oversight in scope.[5]

10.2 Cryptocurrency regulatory issues

Relative to other digital means of exchange that have preceded it, cryptocurrencies face unique challenges. Owing to their decentralised nature they evade the traditional forms of state regulation, lack a provider or issuer that could be held accountable, or a central database. Instead of these, there is a community of users existing operating only in cyberspace. Three potential regulatory regimes could be evaluated for their efficiencies in terms of both cryptocurrency users and national governments. These refer to prohibition, self regulation and intermediary regulation.[6]

Regulators are going to take prohibitive measures against cryptocurrencies when used for unlawful purposes, but such might not be the case, as many

---

3 Frebowitz, R.L. (2018), "Cryptocurrency and state sovereignty", Masters Thesis Naval Postgraduate School Monterey California June 2018; Tatar, J. (2019), "Iceland- Time to free Bitcoin", The Balance 25/06/19, https://www.thebalance.com/iceland-time-to-free-bitcoin-4030896, accessed 07/02/20.

4 De Filippi, P. (2014), "Bitcoin: A regulatory nightmare to a libertarian dream", *Internet Policy Review*, 3(2). DOI: 10.14763/2014.2.286, www.policyreview.info/articles/analysis/Bitcoin-regulatory-nightmare-libertarian-dream, accessed 02/02/18.

5 Tu, K. & Meredith, M. (2015), "Rethinking virtual currency regulation in the Bitcoin age", *Washington Law Review*, 90 (2015), pp. 271–347.

6 Supra, note [1], Borroni (2016).

regulators take care of the integrity aspects by mandating AML/CTF reporting obligations.[7] In any case cryprocurrencies would be outlawed where they actually posed a threat to an existing fiat currency especially with respect of the seignorage income of governments. Further arguments against prohibition include the consideration that they are not yet a major element in mainstream finance and too insignificant to pose systemic risk.

Besides, a stern regulatory stance against cryptocurrencies could stunt their natural development and growth. This may well drive exchanges to migrate to jurisdictions with low compliance costs as already seen in some far flung offshore financial centres and also contribute to a surge in transaction costs in a process of regulatory arbitrage. It could be counterclaimed that appropriate regulations could boost market and investor confidence, while the possible increase in transaction costs would be minimal compared to the costs of losing cryptocurrencies and assets from the absence of consumer protection.[8]

When faced with the threat of regulation, market participants respond with self regulation, though, this is not something novel. Market participants have consistently argued that the relationships among users within cyberspace should be governed by social norms and market mechanisms without the need for state intervention.[9] However, as over the decades the Internet has evolved to become an important medium for commercial exchanges, self regulation may no longer be the best solution because of the inequities that are bound to arise.

In addition, cryptocurrency transactions are virtually irreversible owing to the computer power which secures them. This ends up benefiting merchants and retailers who are safeguarded against fraudulent practices undertaken by dishonest buyers, but it is concurrently unable to protect buyers from dishonest merchants or retailers. It is generally ineffective to rely on the reputation systems and escrow services available. Cryptocurrency software provides no way to punish its users if they engage in criminal activity, thereby making state intervention necessary. Self regulation therefore appears to have a limited impact and is sustainable only within small groups which appears to make this solution generally ineffective. The enforcement of existing laws to thwart fraud attempts as shown in the US FBI shutting down of Silk Road appears to support this contention.[10]

Given the difficulties of using the above two suggestions, a third intermediary regulation could be reflected upon as cryptocurrency use becomes more widespread. For the most part, operations involving cryptocurrencies are accomplished through virtual currency exchanges. This makes exchanges a good starting point for the implementation of anti-criminal mechanisms concurrently with the use of relevant existing laws. The US, for example, classifies

---

7 Supra, note [1], Borroni (2016).
8 Supra, note [1], Borroni (2016).
9 Doguet, J.(2013), "The nature of the form: Legal and regulatory issues surrounding the Bitcoin digital currency system", *Louisiana Law Review*, 73 (4), pp. 1119–1153.
10 Supra, note [1], Borroni (2016).

CONCLUSIONS

cryptocurrency exchanges as money transmitters, thereby compelling them to comply with various requirements including registration with FinCEN; the compilation of reports or records pertaining to criminal, tax, or regulatory investigations; and the implementation of anti-money laundering programmes, along with the need to follow KYC rules.[11] The evident advantage of using pre-existing rules is that no additional undertaking is necessary to design a new and ad hoc regulation of Bitcoins as existing provisions could have achieved the desired aims with a minimal need for amendments.[12] This is, however, unsuitable to address all issues of private international law that may arise with respect to cryptocurrencies as they are a cross-border phenomenon.[13]

This shortcoming could, however, be solved partially by the legal interoperability approach.[14] This is a regulatory mechanism that does not require regulation via direct state intervention. It focuses on working together among legal norms, either within the legal system of a nation state or across jurisdictions or nations. Within the context of digitised economies and digitisation, policymakers might have to make initiatives to increase the interoperability of policies and rules as the world heads toward a multilevel governance system, within which co-operation and interconnection of the various layers are unavoidable elements. The approach's advantages include costs reductions associated with cross jurisdictional business transactions; the further promotion of innovation, competition, trade and economic growth; and incentives for the global recognition of fundamental values and rights like information privacy and freedom of expression.[15] This suggestion is premised on the notion that increasing number of legal institutes fall outside the scope of states' regulation, and hence have to be regulated at the supranational level.

10.3 General regulatory issues

Even as regulation is necessary for the cryptocurrency phenomenon to deter fraud and harm to the global economy and to national currencies, regulators might have to be careful by adopting a delicate approach.[16] This is because excessively restrictive laws might induce innovation to circumvent these

---

11 Middlebrook, S. & Hughes, S. (2013), "Virtual uncertainty: Developments in the law of electronic payments and financial services", *The Business Lawyer*, 69 (2013), pp. 263–273.

12 Supra, note [1], Borroni (2016).

13 Brito, J., Shadab, H. & Castillo, A. (2014), "Bitcoin financial regulation: Securities, derivatives, prediction markets, and gambling", *Columbia Science and Technology Law Review*, XVI (Fall 2014), pp. 144–221.

14 Gasser, U. & Palfrey Jr., J. (2011), "Fostering innovation and trade in the global informational society: The different facts and roles of interoperability", *Swiss National Centre of Competence in Research Working Paper No. 2011/39,* June 2011.

15 Trautman, L. (2014), "Virtual currencies Bitcoin & what now after Liberty Reserve, Silk Road, and Mt. Gox", *Richmond Journal of Law & Technology*, 20(4), pp. 1–108.

16 Howden, E. (2015), "The cryptocurrency conundrum: Regulating an uncertain future", *Emory International Law Review*, 29(2015), pp. 741–798.

controls to foster the development of new virtual currencies, reduce demand for established virtual currencies to harm the global economy.[17]

Further, softer laws are also being advocated whereby regulators would not create new rules but instead adapt existing frameworks to render transactions safer and more transparent by promoting enhanced public–private co-operation doing tougher enforcement on non-compliant Bitcoin exchanges and advocating for more active filings of suspicious activity reports (SARs),[18] but not just simply burdening the reporting authorities with massive volumes of SARs.[19]

Yet others, rather than directly regulating cryptocurrencies, opt to facilitate the creation of self-regulatory organisations, non-governmental organisations that formulate and enforce best practices to protect consumers or other kinds of self regulation. This is because they claim that there is something special about the cryptocurrency that makes it inherently resistant to state control.[20] Bitcoin is uniquely predicated on an open source protocol that could be modified and regulated by those who use it. Specifically, system changes have to be accepted by the system users is evidence of the network's self-regulating capability.[21]

Such a display of lack of consensus by regulators over cryptocurrency regulation is muddied further by the widely differing approaches taken recently by national parliaments as well as by ambivalent positions taken by supranational entities. This might not be sustainable in the longer term. A collective of Bitcoin miners have mustered control over forty two percent of the computer processing power of the Bitcoin network.[22] This is uncomfortably close to the fifty percent that gives a group of people the power to assume control over the Bitcoin system. Concurrently though, hundreds of new and competing cryptocurrencies have emerged, such as exemplified by NXT, that relies on a system that is impossible for anyone to assert control over most of the processing power within the system.[23] Although these are unlikely to quickly replace Bitcoins owing to the network effect, namely the capital investment already incurred by the system's participants, which comprises miners, merchants, and simple users.[24] That said, despite these difficulties, some entity needs to protect consumers and the global economy.

---

17 Sonderegger, D. (2015), "A regulatory and economic perplexity: Bitcoin just needs a bit of regulation", *Washington University Journal of Law & Policy*, 47 (2015), pp. 175–216.

18 Kirby, P. (2014), "Virtually possible: How to strengthen Bitcoin regulation within the current regulatory framework", *North Carolina Law Review*, 93 (1), pp. 189–221.

19 Haynes, A. (2017), "The Fourth Anti Laundering Directive: More of the same?", *Company Lawyer,* 38 (4), pp. 120–122.

20 Papp, J. (2014), "A medium of exchange for an Internet Age: How to regulate Bitcoin for the growth of E-Commerce", *Journal of Technology Law & Policy*, XV (Fall 2014), DOI 10.5195/tlp.2014.155, pp. 33–56.

21 Supra, note [15], Sonderegger (2015).

22 Supra, note [14], Howden (2015).

23 Ziskina, J. (2015), "The other side of the coin: The FECS move to approve cryptocurrency use and deny its viability", *Washington Journal of Law Technology & Arts*, 10 (4), pp. 306–327.

24 Supra, note [21], Ziskina (2015).

CONCLUSIONS

The Internet's facilitation of people to communicate and transact with each other across different sectors and across jurisdictions imply that uniform legislation of cryptocurrencies could be more viable. Short of this, cryptocurrencies could well go the way of autonomous vehicles where the need to conform to separate domestic legislation could slow down the implementation of an otherwise beneficial technology.[25] Supranational authorities such as the EU are deemed too regional and have too limited a regulatory scope, while cryptocurrency activities too fall outside the ambit of the WTO. This leaves the IMF as the better equipped to engage with them since the IMF's primary purpose is to ensure the financial stability of the international monetary system.[26] Moreover the IMF's mandate was updated in 2012 to cover all macroeconomic and financial sector issues that potentially impact on global stability. Also, among IMF's original aims was the promotion of exchange stability and importantly the establishment of a multilateral system of payments.

However, to put cryptocurrencies under IMF purview would require the necessary amending of IMF's separate currency provisions, but no cryptocurrency is as yet deemed an official currency by any economy. This would then have to involve empowering the IMF with the competence to amend its charter, something that it is extremely difficult to do.[27] The alternative is to respond to the IMF's current call for regulators and others to get together under its banner to carve out a uniform supranational regulation, something previously undertaken before on other complicated issues.[28]

10.4 Public opinion

Where the general stand is to view cryptocurrencies positively, a clean up of their present image would help given that they are tarnished by illicit activities[29] and this should be undertaken together with its endorsement by large businesses, including financial services, accepting Bitcoin as alternative means of payments, including by the IMF itself.[30] These concurrent measures could mitigate the impact of Bitcoin on foreign currency markets by bringing Bitcoin within its reach under the categorisation of separate currencies.[31]

Then again, the matter is far more complicated than this. Opposition to Bitcoin is still very strong within the mainstream economic and financial communities.

---

25 Jeans, E. (2015), "Funny Money or the fall of fiat: Bitcoin and the forward-facing virtual currency regulation", *Colorado Technology Law Journal*, 13 (1), pp. 99–128.

26 Supra, note [1], Borroni (2016).

27 Supra, note [1], Borroni (2016).

28 Hagan, S. & Mayeda, A. (2018), "IMF calls for global talks on cryptocurrencies" *Bloomberg*, 19/01/18, https://www.bloomberg.com/news/articles/2018-01-18/imf-calls-for-global-talks-on-digital-fx-as-bitcoin-whipsaws, accessed 02/02/18.

29 Sirila, D. (2014), *The pleasures and perils of new money in old pockets: M-PESA and Bitcoin in Kenya*, Boston, Harvard University Press.

30 Supra, note [1], Borroni (2016).

31 Plassaras, N. (2013), "Regulating digital currencies: Bringing Bitcoin within the reach of the IMF", *Chicago Journal of International Law,* 14 (1), pp. 377–407.

Loud voices have been voiced against cryptocurrencies, calling them a scam, a fraud or a Ponzi scheme.[32] This has turned them into a regulator's nightmare as whether to prohibit them outright, wait and see, or to regulate them and if so how and by whom. This is because in cyberspace[33] the world is not identified by geographic features and as such might be classified under different legal institutions and governed by specific provisions. This strengthens the case for regulation by supranational organisations or alternatively through international instruments.

Novel innovations such as blockchain technology are often accompanied by legal inertia prompted by the initial disorientation pervading the legal domain dealing with them. However, any regulation once adopted could quickly become obsolete because of the capacity for high speed evolution amongst the technologies involved.[34] Care and prudence would have to be exercised. Where governments and international organisations over regulate the cryptocurrency space, the benefits and potential benefits attached to it could dissipate quickly. This is why experts have urged regulators to be prudent and adopt well calibrated policies designed to encouraging resilience and adaptation by existing institutions.[35]

10.5 Regulation – historical issues

As the world reflects on this it could be useful to take a brief historical snapshot of the general principles behind financial regulation, which is the modern state's approach for guiding markets.[36] In its narrow definition,[37] regulation refers to sustained and focused control exercise by a public agency over activities valued by the community and in its broader definition[38] refers to all initiatives of the state by whatever means to control and guide the economy and society. Regardless of the width of definition, regulation projects the perception that the state controls private actions through various mechanisms. Regulation is complex as it binds powers of state agencies from the field of public law with rights of private entities from the field of private law, thereby requiring a balance between values and interests that could clash with one another.[39]

---

32 Roubini, N. (2018), "The blockchain pipe dream", Project Syndicate, 05/03/18, https://www.project-syndicate.org/commentary/blockchain-technology-limited-applications-by-nouriel-roubini-and-preston-byrne-2018-03, accessed 06/03/18; Kharpal, A. (2018), "Blockhchain is 'one of the most overhyped technologies ever,' Nouriel Roubini says", *CNBC*, 06/03/18, https://www.cnbc.com/2018/03/06/blockchain-nouriel-roubini-one-of-the-most-overhyped-technologies-ever.html, accessed 08/03/18.

33 Supra, note [1], Borroni (2016).

34 Supra, note [1], Borroni (2016).

35 Supra, note [11] Brito, Shadab & Castillo (2014).

36 Majone, G. (1997), "From the positive to the regulatory state: Causes and consequences of changes in the mode of governance", *Journal of Public Policy*, 17(2), pp. 139–167.

37 Selznick, P. (1985), "Focusing organization research on regulation", in G.N. Noll (ed.), *Regulatory policy and the social sciences,* Berkley, University of California Press, pp. 363–367.

38 Levi-Faur, D. (2011), "Regulation and regulatory governance", in D. Levi-Faur (ed.), *Handbook of the politics of regulation,* Cheltenham, Edward Elgar, pp. 3–21.

39 Plato-Shinar, R. (2018), "Principles of financial regulation", *Journal of International Banking Law and Regulation*, 33(3), pp. 108–110.

CONCLUSIONS

The most prominent model for supervising private sector activities applied in many economies is that of the Regulatory State.[40] This is premised on the use of regulation as a means of governance and on professional regulatory agencies supervising the activities of the private sector. The uniqueness of these agencies pertains to the high degree of independence they enjoy compared to governmental ministries that report to ministers and to parliament.[41] Over time, the Regulatory State became gradually more dependent on regulatory tools and policies so as to achieve their objectives. This culminated in a significant expansion of administrative legislations, proliferation of independent regulatory agencies, expansion of their powers and improvements in the means of supervision.[42]

The Regulatory State notion raises the question as to the extent of state involvement that is desirable in the relationship between individuals in society. The solution lies, not merely on the worldview embraced, but also on the particular issues under scrutiny. In general, there seems to be a general consensus that in democratic societies there is little space for public supervision of private entities, unless required to entertain a public need. Sometimes, supervision is required to address market failures, or to ensure suitable conditions of the supply of essential services. All such circumstances and matters do not concern only the imposition of supervision, but also the extent or intensity of supervision deemed to be appropriate.[43]

10.6 Global co-operation

The 2008 global financial crisis displayed how globalisation served as a catalyst for systemic risk, undermining both the capacity and incentives of national regulators to respond to the relevant risks.[44] Among the many insights that arose from the crisis was the necessity for effective global co-operation and from the application of both soft and hard laws to achieve such co-operation.

While such initiatives are unlikely to change the fundamental nature of the international monetary and financial system, it remains important to design it in a manner that reduces global and domestic imbalances over time, while preserving international stability to support global growth and development. This calls for global co-operation including a greater legitimacy and hence more authority for supranational entities and to protect global stability. It also calls for incentives for market participants and national authorities to align themselves with the promotion of systemic stability. This in turn requires policymakers

---

40 Scott, C. (2017), "The regulatory state and beyond", in P. Drahos (ed.), *Regulatory theory: Foundations and applications*, Canberra, ANU Press.
41 Supra, note [37], Plato-Shinar (2018).
42 Majone, G. (2010), "The transformation of the regulatory state", *Osservatorio sull'Analisis di Impatto della Regolazione*, http://www.osservatorioair.it/wp-content/uploads/2010/10/Paper_Majone_RegulatoryState_sept2010.pdf, accessed 02/02/18.
43 Supra, note [37], Plato-Shinar (2018).
44 Stiglitz, J.E. (2017), *Globalization and its discontent revisited: Anti-globalization in the era of Trump*, New York, WW Norton & Company.

to embrace a systemic perspective and to be ready to implement policies that, while serving national interests, also support a stable international monetary and financial system to contribute to a thriving global economy.[45]

Discourse on financial regulation typically focuses on the issue of the quantity of regulation and the hard choice between regulation and deregulation, best now seen in play in the US with the ascendancy of the Trump administration in 2017.[46] Other insights from the 2008 global financial crisis suggest that regulation could be necessary, but this does not rule out the fact that regulation could be counterproductive. Good regulation serves the public interest through supporting ongoing confidence in the processes as exemplified by the market process where the public participates in activities such as auditing. Regulation is therefore necessary to support confidence in the markets and trust in the reliability of financial reporting and financial services generally.[47] Good financial regulation could then be said to be any regulation that protects consumers and users, and reduces the extent of fraud and corruption in financial services without imposing excessively high costs on the community.[48]

10.7 The essentials of good regulation

Proposals have also been advanced for the art of designing good regulations that bear the minimum core characteristics of addressing market failures that generate greater benefits than costs and that do not treat businesses differently from one another.[49] Good regulation extending from these needs appear to exhibit the following charateristics[50]:

(i) It must actually do good, meaning it must have a sound rationale and be shown to bring net benefit to society, necessitating costs as well as benefits to be accounted for.

(ii) It must be better than any alternative regulation or policy tool. In this regard it is not sufficient to compare a regulation to a counterfactual

---

45 European Central Bank (ECB) (2011), "The financial crisis and the strengthening of global policy co-operation", *ECB Monthly Bulletin January 2011*, pp. 87–97.

46 Zarroli, J. (2017), "Fed Chief Yellen warns against dismantling bank regulations", *NPR*, 25/08/17, https://www.npr.org/2017/08/25/546076064/janet-yellen-warns-against-dismantling-bank-regulations, accessed 02/02/18; Shapiro, S. (2017), "What Trump means for regulation", *Scholar Strategy Network*, https://scholars.org/sites/scholars/files/ssn_regulation_fact_sheet.pdf, accessed 02/02/18.

47 Thomadakis, S.B. (2007), "What makes a good regulation?", *Paper Presented by Stavros B. Thomadakis, Chairman Public Interest Oversight Board at the IFAC Council Seminar Mexico City, 14/11/2007.*

48 Moosa, I.A. (2018), "Good regulation versus bad regulation", *Journal of Banking Regulation*, 19(1), pp. 55–63.

49 Furchgott-Roth, H.W. (2000), "The art of writing good regulations", *Federal Communications Law Journal*, 53(1), pp. 1–4.

50 Banks, G. (2003), "The good, the bad and the ugly: Economic perspectives on regulation in Australia", *Paper Delivered by Gary Banks Chairman Productivity Commission at the Conference of Economists, Business Symposium,* Hyatt Hotel, Canberra, 02/10/2003.

of no regulation, but to compare outcomes across all feasible policy alternatives.
(iii) The regulatory evaluation process should take into account the likely outcomes, including a rapid capability for correcting mistakes.
(iv) It should contain the seeds of its own destruction. Good regulations are not necessarily equated with the presumption of their own immortality, but allow for the ongoing appraisal of their risks and continued effectiveness. Where a regulation endures, that should be because it continues to pass stringent tests.
(v) It should state (ex-ante) what it is going to do and, as far as possible, set up verifiable performance criteria. This evaluates a regulation for precision and relevance and provides a basis for assessment of ex-post effectiveness.
(vi) It should be clear and concise. This implies that it should also be communicated effectively and be readily accessible to those impacted on by it. Not only should market participants be able to find out what regulations apply to them, the regulations themselves must be capable of being readily understood.
(vii) It should be consistent with other laws, agreement and international obligations. Inconsistency could create division, confusion, and waste.
(viii) It must be enforceable. However, it should involve incentives or disciplines no greater than are needed for reasonable enforcement and involve sufficient resources for the purpose.
(ix) Finally, it needs to be administered by accountable bodies in a fair and consistent manner. This means having good governance arrangements in place. Aside from clear reporting responsibilities and the scope for judicial or administrative review, important features of good governance include clear statutory guidance, transparency of both process and judgement, and public accessibility.

A major failing of previous regulatory approaches was the assumption that where there was a market failure, the appropriate instrument for addressing this was through a non-market approach, usually a command and control mechanism that is often highly prescriptive. The general acknowledged aim now is to achieve the desired regulatory outcomes at least cost. This led to a wider menu of regulatory approaches, including recognition of the flexibility and information-laden characteristic of market-based mechanisms that could assume the following forms[51]:

(i) incentive-compatible mechanisms like taxes and competitive tendering;
(ii) mandatory information disclosure with the threat of more heavy handed regulation and public disapproval; and,

---

51 Supra, note [50], Banks (2003).

(iii) self regulation, where an industry must devise a workable regulatory approach to achieve accepted performance standards with minimal prescription by regulators.

Markets therefore offer the potential for achieving regulatory objectives more efficiently than prescriptive regulations. For instance, it is possible to make a reduction in some undesirable outcomes a market good in itself, thereby bringing to bear the inventiveness and cost consciousness that characterises market competition. Regulations of this nature, can allow for the fact that the costs and benefits of regulation vary across businesses and over time can allow businesses the freedom to determine what technology is used to achieve a given performance target, and as a consequence is informationally efficient, meaning not requiring the regulator to know a lot about the technologies or costs of regulated businesses. A well designed market generates incentives for individual businesses to act on the information they have. Overall, carefully designed and prudently applied economic instruments offer great potential for achieving better regulatory outcomes at lower cost.[52]

Self regulation has the benefit of allowing much greater freedom by an industry regarding the detail of regulation, including dispute resolution. It economises on administration costs to governments and uses specialist industry information more efficiently than command and control kinds. Self regulation is used widely in financial services, telecommunications and elsewhere. It is inappropriate where performance standards cannot be readily verified, or if penalties are too weak relative to the costs of poor performance or dispute resolution poor. Self regulation is argued to be a cost-effective alternative to government intervention where these criteria are met.[53] It merits noting that some apparent self regulation is actually co-regulation in that the government still acts as a monitor and enforcer of some transparent performance criteria.

The reality of regulatory fallibility suggests that there should be appropriate checks and balances, and clear statutory guidance for regulators. Regulators also need to consult more widely about the potential impacts of regulations especially on compliance costs and ensure that regulations are regularly tested for continued relevance and cost effectiveness. Regulatory norms further need confronting. The risks and failures linked to regulatory initiatives should be highlighted so as to avoid having an automatic culture of apparent regulatory fix for every problem coming across. Regulatory forbearance could be an apt option for circumstances involving market outcomes that are only a little imperfect.[54]

Finally, it is worth noting the political economy of financial regulation.[55] Research suggests that regulators and policymakers do not always strive to promote the public interest, but instead could be motivated by a wide menu

---

52 Supra, note [50], Banks (2003).
53 Supra, note [50], Banks (2003).
54 Supra, note [50], Banks (2003).
55 Supra, note [37] Plato-Shinar (2018).

of extraneous factors including self interest. This in turn could lead to various regulatory failures such as regulatory capture, regulatory inaction and regulatory competition prompting regulatory arbitrage, and so on. Mechanisms such as transparency requirements, independent oversight, constraints on regulators' discretionary powers and impositions of institutional and personal liability are fortunately available to hold regulators and policymakers to account.[56]

Given the already difficult agenda and mission of national financial regulators, the advent of Bitcoin and other crypytocurrency equivalents have presented them with a regulatory dilemma as it has for supranational regulators across the world. Cryptocurrencies could be issued privately or by central banks. It could be a cryptocurrency, randomised, or tethered. Its scheme might be centralised or decentralised and its value might be self anchored or of a specified fiat currency. When facilitating electronic transmission of payment media between distant parties, cryptocurrency currency schemes, as the equivalent to hand to hand physical cash delivery might irreversibly transform the global payments landscape and necessitate novel solutions.[57] Some important aspects of these have been highlighted and discussed.

Ultimately however, cryptocurrencies will most probably depend on various factors, of which the most significant appears to be whether central banks and governments will regulate it out of existence.[58] Were enough countries to follow the decision of Vietnam, the cryptocurrency story potentially ends.

However, if they can work in harmony with traditional fiat currencies offering alternative transaction completion methods and investment opportunities, both are likely to be viable. Further, in the absence of intermediation, new solutions would be needed to resolve conflicts of law and other challenges. Legal theorists would need to locate an approach that would avoid fragmentation of internationally issued securities portfolios by identifying a single jurisdiction to which there is sufficient connection to make it reasonable that the law of that jurisdiction should govern an entire portfolio of interests recorded in a distributed ledger.[59] International co-operation for this is crucial and this means the call by the IMF for co-operation in the treatment of cryptocurrencies merits support.

Blockchain is now increasingly looked upon as foundational and not disruptive. Bitcoin is the first application of this technology, but unlikely to be the last, as major players in just about every sector from finance to health, and utilities to retail announced they too are getting involved, thereby signalling its potential

---

56 Armour, J., Awrey, D., Davies, P., Enriques, L., Gordon, J.N., Mayer, C. & Payne, J. (2016), *Principles of financial regulation,* Oxford, OUP.

57 Geva, B. (2016), "Disintermediating electronic payments: Digital cash and virtual currencies", *Journal of International Banking Law and Regulation,* 31(12), pp. 661–674.

58 Anderson, T. A. (2014), "Bitcoin-is it just a fad? History, current status and the future of the cyber-currency revolution", *Journal of International Banking Law and Regulation,* 29(7), pp. 428–435.

59 Kalderon, M., Snagg, F. & Harrop, C. (2016), "Distributed ledgers: A future in financial services?", *Journal of International Banking Law and Regulation,* 31(5), pp. 243–248.

shift to the mainstream.[60] Interestingly, a blockchain is now available that not only matches daters based on compatibility like a Match.com or mutual interest like Tinder, but also safety via pre-date video chats, sobriety checks, and "safe" words that the Loly app would listen for. Where the app hears the safe word, it can initiate a call enabling the concerned partner to extricate from the date. This security feature in Loly is claimed to account for those edge use cases where bad participants slip through the cracks onto the platform.[61] Meanwhile, in the shorter term, it looks as though cryptocurrencies and assets are here to stay, but the longer term it remains a matter of speculation.

Cryptocurrencies and assets offer a wider potential change for the future. A limitless series of peer-to-peer networks will be created that will disseminate power and control to those using systems. Suggestions that this will also provide a fairer distribution of wealth[62] remain to be seen, but it is certainly the case that many Internet-based facilities, including finance will be far more readily available to those in parts of the world where direct access to mainstream institutions is inconvenient or impossible. How well law and regulation can keep on top of this remains to be seen. Vitalik Buterin suggested that "there is a large chance that we will never come up with a blockchain governance process that is sufficiently robust that it will be capable of regularly doing things like adjusting fundamental economic parameters."[63] As to the extent to which this will work, time will tell. It may or may not prove to be El Dorado, but regulators of various types will certainly face a dilemma.

---

60 Butter, J. (2018), "In Focus: Blockchain, Foundational Not Disruptive", *Sustainability RADAR*, https://radar.sustainability.com/issue-16/in-focus-blockchain-foundational-not-disruptive/, accessed 18/03/18; Iansiti, M. & Lakhani, K.R. (2017), "The truth about blockchain", *Harvard Business Review*, 01/03/17, https://hbr.org/2017/01/the-truth-about-blockchain, 18/03/18.

61 Koetsier, J. (2018), "Sex is now on the blockchain. Cue end of western civilization: Men's top fear when going on a blind date is that the woman is fatter than her photo, Women's No.1 fear? Being murdered", *Inc.*, 03/03/18, https://www.inc.com/john-koetsier/this-augmented-reality-dating-startup-uses-blockchain-to-verify-consent.html, accessed 08/03/18.

62 Tapscott, D. and Tapscott, A. (2018) "Blockchain Revolution", 2nd Edn, Penguin, p. 14.

63 Fink, M. (2019), *Blockchain Regulation and Governance in Europe*, Cambridge University Press, p. 209.

INDEX

AADHAR 89
ABN Ambro 77
Abu Dhabi Global Market Sandbox 64
Accenture 73
acceptance as payment for goods/
 services: China 205; EU 163; evolution
 of Bitcoin 29; Facebook Libra 129;
 Finland 78; IMF concerns 106;
 Japan 214; Netherlands 77–78; OECD
 concerns 101, 102; offshore financial
 centres 91; UK 72, 74; US 146, 156
Action Fraud 23
activity-based regulatory approaches 63
ACX 75
advertising 179, 206
Africa 29, 54, 67, 68, 238
agency, law of 25
agile business 77
airdrops 20
airline miles 40, 51, 105
algorithms 7, 11–12, 41, 50, 120, 243
Alibaba 201, 210
Alipay 207
Alliance Global 36
altcoins 3–4, 36, 41
Amazon 37, 234
American Association of Retired
 Persons 150
AML/CTF (anti-money laundering/
 counter-terrorism financing): Australia
 186, 187; automation of compliance
 125; and the BIS 45; Canada 190;
 Cayman Islands 194; due diligence
 103; EU regulation 166–167, 168,
 173, 174, 183; evolution of Bitcoin 34;
 and the FATF 64; Financial Crimes
 Enforcement Network (FinCEN) 156;
 G20 97; general regulatory issues 64,
 103; and ICOs 104; IMF 108, 109, 110;
 Japan 213; Malta 196; mandatory 250;
 multilateral regulatory approaches
 132, 133; OECD 99; offshore financial
 centres 91; regulation of virtual asset
 service providers 128; risk continuum
 108; security risk 21; Singapore 86,
 221, 223, 224; South Korea 227,
 228; standardised regulation of 103;
 Switzerland 192–193; UK 176, 180; US
 139, 142, 145, 251
Amsterdam 69
anonymity: and criminal activity 242;
 EU regulation 163, 166, 171; general
 regulatory issues 49, 50; history of
 cryptoasset regulation 136; IMF 106,
 110; OECD 98, 101; offshore financial
 centres 93; Singapore 220; UK 180; US
 144, 162
Ant Financials 210
arbitrage 16n62, 17, 105, 126, 174, 233,
 245, 250
Argentina 68, 69
Arizona 140
Armstrong, Brian 18, 71
Arnhem 77
artificial intelligence (AI) 72, 114, 115,
 118, 197
Asian Financial Crisis 1997 232
asset, cryptocurrencies as an 60, 61, 136,
 187, 212, 213
asset freezes 110, 146
asset seizures 110
asset transfer systems 50
asset-based tokens 41–42
ATM machines 139
ATMs, cryptocurrency 68, 74, 78, 80, 121
audit 100, 213, 241
Augur 45
AUSTRAC 186, 187
Australia: Bitcoin-friendly economies
 74–76; due diligence 103; merchant

numbers 68; OECD concerns 102; regulatory policy 59, 60, 186–189, 199
Australia Post 75
Australian Financial Services Licence (AFSL) 76, 188
Australian Securities and Investments Commission (ASIC) 75, 79, 188, 189
Australian Securities Exchange (ASX) 75
Australian Taxation Office (ATO) 187
authorisation regimes 63–64, 76, 99

background checks 157
BaFin 249
Bagehot, Walter 29
Bahamas 92
Bahrain 92
Baidu 206
bailment 25
Baltic states 197
Bangalore 212
Bangladesh 84
bank bailouts 39
bank deposits, monetary nature of 135–136
Bank of Canada 190
Bank of England 30, 42, 72, 132, 175, 177, 178, 181, 242
Bank of Japan 84
banking access 29, 35, 38, 53, 54, 69, 129
banking systems 50, 67, 85, 94, 121, 155
barter systems 37–38, 39, 158, 187, 188, 190
Base Erosion and Profit Shifting (BEPS) 92
Basel 51
Basel Process 121
Bata 75
bear markets 15
Belgium 191
Berkeley 36
Bermuda 92
Berners-Lee, Tim 87
bespoke regulations 62, 63–64
best practice standards 63, 92–93, 99, 113, 252
Bic Cam 214
big data analytics 117
billionaires (in cryptoassets) 15–16, 69
bills of credit 158
Binance 196, 225
Binance Coin 14, 18, 44
biometrics 89, 114
BIS (Bank for International Settlements) 45–46, 66, 82, 93, 105, 119–123, 126, 132, 199, 220, 248, 249

Bit Trade Australia 75
Bitbns 212
Bitcoin: Australia 186, 187; Bitcoin-friendly economies 70–95; blockchain 11, 125; blockchain native tokens 42; and the CFTC 140; China 56–57, 201, 203–204, 205, 206, 207–208, 210; as commodity 32, 148; cryptoasset hubs 67; as dominant example of cryptocurrency 7; economic opportunities 13; electronic funds transfer 157–158; employment statistics 13; evolution of 29–35; focus of book on 9; forks 120; futures products 61, 140, 148, 149; and the G20 96; geographical distribution of 68, 69; history of 9, 10–11; imitators of 10; India 212; inflationary risks 112; insurance 22; Japan 214, 218; legal status 30; market capitalisation 13, 15, 36, 52, 147; market share 4, 13, 15, 23; medium of exchange 33; as money transmission service 156; offshore financial centres 54; open source 41, 252; overheads 237; as peer-to-peer system 8; price crash (2018) 1, 4, 36, 52, 69–70, 96; price volatility 3, 4, 9, 14–15, 16, 24, 27–28, 52, 69; public opinion 253–254; as pure cryptocurrency 45; as revolutionary event 197; Singapore 220, 226; South Korea 225, 227; speculative nature of 29; status as virtual currency 40; transaction costs 238; UK 183; uniqueness of 259; US 139, 142; variants of 41; and VAT 30
Bitcoin Australia 75
Bitcoin BTMs 214
Bitcoin Cash (BCH) 8, 14, 120
Bitcoin Core (BTC) 8
Bitcoin diamond 120
Bitcoin ETFs 61
Bitcoin Foundation 100
Bitcoin gold 120
Bitcoin SV 14
Bitfinex 206
Bitfinex LEO 44
Bithumb 230, 231
BitKRX 84
BitLicense concept 29, 157
Bitmain 201, 206
BitPay 77–78, 205
Bitstation 218
Bittiraha 78
black market transactions 16, 21, 120
black money 89
blacklisting 132
Black-Scholes formula 16, 17–18

block rewards 122–123, 172
blockchain: advertising 146; Australia 75, 189; Bitcoin 11, 42, 125; blockchain native tokens 42; Canada 74, 189, 190, 191; Cayman Islands 90–91; CFTC 151; China 90, 205, 208–210, 211; for citizenship 80; criminal factors 241; and cryptocurrencies 10–16; cryptographic risk 111; and cryptography 7; dApp tokens 43; digital barter economy 39; distributed ledger technology (DLT) 235–236, 239–240, 244; Estonia 80; as evidence 140; foundational nature of 259; and the global financial system 9–10; and government intervention 7; and ICOs 104; IMF 115; India 90; internal tokens 44; interoperability between blockchains 247; Japan 217; *lex cryptographica* 132–133; Libra (Facebook) 129; likelihood of adoption of 30, 94; loyalty programmes 51; Malta 195, 197; multilateral regulatory approaches 132; Netherlands 77; OECD 98–99, 102; proprietary blockchain 37; registration of shares 140; Securities Exchange Commission (SEC) 139, 153; share prospectuses 239; Singapore 86, 87, 221, 224, 225; South Korea 228; standardised systems 72; structural shifts in finance industry 107; Switzerland 191, 192, 193; transaction speeds 246; UK 72; and unbanked populations 54; as the underlying technology 2, 3; US 71, 145; user analysis 114
Blockchain Momentum 229
Blockchain Technologies ETF 190
Blockstack 44, 45, 56, 139, 143
Blumer, Brendan 18
Boesing, Ronny 79
bond issues 239
borderless nature of cryptocurrencies 49, 92, 102, 114, 162
Brazil 67, 68, 249
bright line tests 138
British Virgin Islands 92
Brito, Jerry 139
Brunei Darussalam 232
BTC China 205, 206
BTCC 206
BTM/Bytom 72
bubbles 10, 36, 39, 53, 69–70, 171
Buenos Aires 69

Bulgaria 191
business taxes 81, 93, 215, 228
business to business (B2B) use 10, 35
Buterin, Vitalik 18, 71, 235, 260

CADcoin 190
Calibra 129
California 56, 71
Cambodia 232
Canada: AML/CTF 110; Bitcoin-friendly economies 74; cryptoasset regulatory policy 189–191, 199, 206; digital currencies in 42–43; global cryptoasset hubs 67, 88; innovation friendliness 29; Investment Industry Regulatory Organisation of Canada (IIROC) 63; private wealth 92
Canadian Revenue Agency 190
Canadian Securities Administrators (CSA) 190
capacity issues 26, 28
capital controls 135
capital gains taxation 60, 73, 111, 140, 172, 187, 228, 248
carbon trading 42
Cardano 36
Cardiff 191
Carney, Mark 30, 65, 72, 132
cashless societies 79, 82, 89, 211
Castillo, Andrea 139
Catalonia 34
Cayman Enterprise City (CEC) 91, 194
Cayman Islands 54–55, 90–91, 92, 193–194
Cayman Islands Monetary Authority (CIMA) 194
CCEDK 79
CENT 43
Central Bank Digital Currency (CBDC) 42, 45–46, 132, 219
central banks: and the BIS 119–120, 132; cooperative regulation 121; cryptocurrency payments 45, 89; and distributed ledger technology 109; and fiat money 28, 60; and the global financial system 50; historical background 136; independence 49–50; issuing currencies 30, 34, 38–43, 57, 72–73, 88, 90, 114–115, 123, 137, 190, 201, 211, 234; lending of last resort 29; and money supply 52; multi-coin world 38; and new technology 122; and public trust 122; regulation of cryptocurrencies 102; *see also specific countries' banks*

INDEX

Chainlink token 44
change in possession 175
charities 151
Chicago Board Options Exchange (CBOE) 3, 32, 61, 140, 149
Chicago Board Options Exchange (CBOE) Futures Exchange (CFE) 32–33
Chicago Mercantile Exchange Inc. (CME) 3, 32, 140, 149
Chile 67
China: attitudes to cryptoassets 87–88, 94, 110, 132; Bitcoin mining 81–82; circumvention of exchange and capital requirements 111; crackdowns 161, 171, 209; cryptoasset regulatory policy 201–211, 231, 232; environmental concerns 61; miners and mining 13, 88, 202, 204, 206, 207–208; new payments technologies 122; private wealth 92; prohibitions on cryptocurrencies 47, 84, 88, 102, 202, 203–204, 205–206, 208; regulation of cryptocurrencies 21, 40, 56–57; self-regulation 103; state-backed cryptocurrency 34, 40, 47; using cryptoasset hubs 67; volume growth in cryptoassets 67
China Banking and Insurance Regulatory Commission (CBIRC) 57
chose in action/chose in possession 25
Chou, Juthica 71
Chubb 22
Circle 205
citizenship 80, 89
city-based digital currencies 36
civil enforcement actions 148, 149, 150, 153
Clayton, Jay 138
clearing systems 34, 76, 99, 240
closed system cryptoassets 106, 108, 163
cloud-based financial services 36
CME Group 61, 71
Coin Drop Markets 149
Coinbase 33, 204, 206
Coincheck 22, 82, 216, 217, 218
Coinflip 139
CoinList 71
Coinmap 68, 71
Coinone 230
Coinplug 84
cold calling 179
cold wallets 22, 218
collective investment schemes (CISs) 216, 217, 222

Colombia 67
Committee on Payments and Market Infrastructures (CPMI) 109
commodities, cryptocurrencies as 61, 78, 102, 136, 148, 152, 159, 160, 190, 210
Commodities Futures Trading Commission (CFTC) 32, 97, 102, 139–140, 141, 142–143, 147–151, 152, 153–154, 159–160, 162, 249
commodity tokens 42
commodity-based assets 51–52
Common Reporting Standard (CRS) 92, 194
Commonwealth Bank 186
Commonwealth Secretariat 109
community currencies 158
competition 51, 76, 99, 102, 247
complementary currencies 51–52, 55
Comsa 216
consensus valuation frameworks 14
consumer education 150
Consumer Finance Protection Bureau (CFPB) 23, 150
consumer protection: Australia 76, 187; BIS 121; Canada 189; EU regulation 168, 170, 183; FSB 118; IMF 109, 110; Libra (Facebook) 130; OECD 98, 99, 100; Singapore 223; South Korea 228; UK 73, 178, 179, 185; US 139, 157
consumption taxes 215
continuously revised delta hedging 17n66
convertible cryptocurrencies 106
cooperative approaches: BIS 119–120; EU regulation 162; FATF 128; FSB 117; global co-operation 255–256; IMF 112, 113; IOSCO 126; Japan 219; OECD 104–105; reasons for regulation 64, 66, 254; South Korea 231; UK 175, 182
Corda 190
Corporate Tax Haven Index 92
corporate taxation 215, 228
corruption 87, 89
counterfeiting 122, 158, 192
counterparty risk 36
counter-terrorism financing (CTF) *see* AML/CTF (anti-money laundering/counter-terrorism financing)
crackdowns 161, 171, 209
credibility of the issuer 134, 135
credit cards 237
credit risk 111
criminal law 142, 179, 187, 209, 210, 212
cross-border nature of cryptoassets: EU regulation 162, 163; FSB 117;

264

general regulatory issues 61, 63, 198, 231; global cryptoasset hubs 84, 94; historical background 136; IMF 109–110, 111–112; and international law 251; IOSCO 126; OECD 104–105; Singapore 221; UK 182; US regulation 143–144
crowdfunding 68–69, 71, 94, 162
crypto addresses 7
crypto hubs 61, 67–95
Crypto Valley 191
cryptoassets: practical issues with 49–53; and risk 65; types of 41–46; valuations 18–21
Cryptoassets Taskforce (CAT) 73, 177–181, 183
cryptoassets working group (US) 97
cryptocurrencies definition 7–10
Cryptocurrency Task Force 238
cryptocurrency to cryptocurrency payments 13
crypto-dollar 43
cryptography 7, 8, 11–13, 43, 106, 111, 114, 136, 227, 235, 241, 244
crypto-ruble 42
currency controls 49–50, 57, 60
currency equity 35
currency vaults 129
custodianship 25, 76
custom of the market place 25
Cyber Unit (SEC) 146
cyber-attacks 120; *see also* hacking; malware
cybersecurity 86, 115, 117
Cyberspace Administration of China 207, 211
Cyprus 54, 92, 111

Daemon 242
DAO 32
DAO tokens 145, 242
dApp tokens 43
dark web 110, 171, 242
Dash 3
data protection 67, 175
dating apps 260
Davos 171
DBS 221
De Filippi, P. 7, 20
debentures 222
debt controls 204
debt registries 36
Decentral 74
Decentralised Oracle Protocol 45

deflation 38–39, 112
Delaware 140
democracy 54, 55, 58, 89, 94, 213
demonetisation 89
Denmark 78–79
deposit insurance schemes 111
depository authorisations 76
derivatives: as cryptoassets 19; distributed ledger technology (DLT) 239; evolution of Bitcoin 32; IOSCO 125; Switzerland 192–193; UK 177, 180, 185; US 139, 140, 147, 148, 152, 154
devaluations 34
Devcoin 41
Di Iorio, Anthony 18
diamonds 146
differences contracts 177
digital bailment 25
digital barter economy 38, 39
Digital Currency Electronic Payment (DCEP) 201
Digital Currency Exchange Register Australia 187, 188
Digital Currency Group 71
digital depository receipts (DDR) 190
digital dollars 34
digital fiat currencies 38–41, 42
digital identities 75, 80, 130
digital learning technologies 113
Digital News Asia 206
digital ownership tokens 37, 125
digital signatures 114
digital symbols (versus actual digital currencies) 57
Digix gold 44
DigixDAO 44
directed acrylic graphs (DAGs) 246
directory of cryptoassets regulators 119
disclosure requirements 104, 117
discounts 20
Disney 37
disruptive innovation 101
distributed ledger technology (DLT) 235–247; accountability 66; Canada 190; CFTC (Commodities Futures Trading Commission) 150–151; changing business models 113; charitable uses 151; China 208; costs of running 120, 237–238; criminal factors 240–242; derivatives 239; encryption 236–237; growth in 124–125; history of 235–236; India 90; initial coin offerings (ICOs) 169; IOSCO 124; Malta 195–196; node

operator responsibilities 182; OECD concerns 98, 104; overheads 237–238; practical issues with cryptoassets 48, 49; regulation of 64, 109; scalability 245–246; Securities Exchange Commission (SEC) 146; securities markets 125–126; security offerings 239–240; structural shifts in finance industry 107; UK 177–178, 182; US 142, 145; values of 72
Distributed Ledger Technology Working Group 146
"do no harm" 151
Dogecoin 3
Dombrovskis, Valdis 170–171
Dorsey, Jack 71
Dortmund 191
dotcom boom 2, 14, 114
double spend problem 8, 11, 59, 122
double taxation 75
Draper, Tim 18
drug dealing 34–35, 48, 171
Dubai 34, 92
due diligence 103, 128, 187, 223, 228
Duffy, Terry 71

Earn.com 71
ECB Crypto-Assets Task Force (ECBCTF) 164–165
e-commerce 107, 129, 163, 164, 209
electricity consumption 61, 74, 120, 208, 243
electronic funds transfer 157–158
e-money 40, 42, 76, 106, 174, 183, 184, 224, 248
Endo, Toshihide 219
enhanced due diligence 228
Entrepreneurs Headquarters Limited 149
environmental concerns 61, 120
EOS 14, 19, 36
equity tokens 44
e-Residents 80, 89
Espinoza case 31
Essen 191
Estonia 60, 62, 80–81, 212
Ether 4, 42, 44, 45, 183, 220, 242
Ethereum 3, 14, 16n62, 17, 32n25, 35–36, 44; Canada 190; China 57, 205; encryption 236; Germany 77; insurance 22; Japan 214; security 242; Singapore 225; South Korea 225; US 71, 143
Ethereum Classic 3
Ethereum Cloud Mining 41
Etherparty 74

EU (European Union): Bitcoin-friendly economies 76–77; e-money 40; European Blockchain Partnership 178, 197, 247; European System of Accounts 103; and offshore financial centres 90; regulatory policy 49, 66, 162–175
Euro crisis 135
Europe: European trading styles 17; and the G20 96; growth in cryptocurrency 68; price relative to other geographic areas 16; *see also* EU (European Union); *specific countries*
European Banking Authority (EBA) 105, 109, 165, 167, 169, 170, 174
European Blockchain Partnership 178, 197, 247
European Central Bank (ECB) 96, 101, 105, 122, 135, 163, 164
European Commission 96, 173, 174
European Court of Justice 172
European Insurance and Occupational Pensions Authority (EIOPA) 169, 174
European Parliament 166, 167
European Securities and Markets Authority (ESMA) 18, 105, 125–126, 167, 168–170, 173–174
Europol 180
e-voting 80
exchange rates 107, 129, 135
exchange solvency 99
exchanges: anti-money laundering (AML) 183; Australia 76, 187, 188; blockchain 13; China 201, 203, 205, 207, 208–209; digital-fiat currency exchange 136, 156, 204, 208; distributed ledger technology (DLT) 240; electronic funds transfer 157; Estonia 80; EU regulation 166, 168, 170, 173; as financial institutions 99; general regulatory issues 18, 54, 61, 63, 65, 108–109; geographical distribution of 68; hacking 85; Hong Kong 206; India 212; Japan 81–82, 213–214; Korea 83; Malta 196; mandatory capital holdings 100; OECD concerns 101; risk of breach 102; Singapore 87, 221, 224; South Korea 228, 229–230; and trust 120; UK 178; US 97; virtual currency exchanges 108
exit scams 59

Facebook: credits 40, 136; cryptoassets generally 234; Libra 35, 48, 57, 88, 97, 123, 128–130, 131, 132, 193, 201, 211;

266

INDEX

marketing restrictions 206; security measures 146; US concerns over move into finance 137
FACTA 194
fake cryptocurrencies 192; *see also* counterfeiting
false coins 23
false information 146
FBI (Federal Bureau of Investigation) 104, 150, 250
fear of missing out (FOMO) 2, 14, 37, 143
Federal Deposit Insurance Corporation 22
Federal Reserve 33–34, 47, 48, 50, 130, 141, 154, 155
Federal Reserve Bank 43
Federal Reserve Bank of Chicago 150
fees 8, 50, 51–52, 172; *see also* transaction fees/costs
fiat currencies: converting cryptocurrencies to 108; countries with weak 54; crypto fiat currencies 38–41, 42; cryptocurrencies as a threat to 60, 101–102, 130, 152, 250; cryptocurrencies as substitutes for 36, 106; cryptocurrencies working alongside 35, 77–78, 79, 91, 141, 158, 259; digital currencies as representations of 136; and e-money 184; fear of citizen desertion of 59–60; government control of money 47–48, 49; hierarchical nature of 134–136; history of 28, 135–136; price variations of cryptocurrencies relative to 17, 27–28; promise to pay 134
Final Guidance on Cryptoassets (FCA) 176, 183, 184–185
Financial Action Task Force (FATF) 64, 66, 94, 97, 105, 109, 110, 128, 131, 132, 133, 163, 174, 186, 199, 220, 233
financial advice services 76
Financial Conduct Authority (FCA) 18, 64, 73, 175, 176, 177, 178–179, 181, 182–184, 185, 198, 224
Financial Crimes Enforcement Network (FinCEN) 34, 139, 150, 156–157, 251
financial inclusion 118, 130; *see also* banking access
Financial Industry Regulatory Authority (FINRA) 126
financial instrument, Bitcoin as 76
financial instrument, cryptoassets as 173
financial instrument test (FIT) 196
financial integrity 109–110
Financial Intelligence Units 173

Financial Market Supervisory Authority (FINMA) 192, 193
Financial Ombudsmen Scheme 180
Financial Secrecy Index 92
Financial Sector Assessment Programmes (FSAPs) 124
financial service, cryptocurrencies as 78
Financial Services Compensation Scheme 180
Financial Stability Board (FSB) 61, 66, 72, 97, 115–119, 124, 126, 131–132, 174
Financial Stability Oversight Council 150
financial stability risks 21–26, 65, 111, 115–119, 121, 122, 128, 131, 164, 203, 219
financialisation of economies 93, 94
FinCCX 78
FinHub 162
FinHub (Strategic Hub for Innovation and Financial technology) 162
Fink, M. 11
Finland 78
FINMA (Swiss Financial Market Supervisory Authority) 55, 61
Fintech: and the 2008 global financial crisis 94; and central banks 122; CFTC (Commodities Futures Trading Commission) 151; China 87, 207, 212; EU regulation 173; Facebook 206; Financial Stability Board (FSB) 116–118; general regulatory issues 53, 55, 56, 62, 64; global cryptoasset hubs 67, 71; global nature of 126; Hong Kong 207; India 58, 87, 212; IOSCO 124; Japan 82, 200; Malta 196; regulatory sandboxes (RSs) 182, 224; risk 20; Singapore 85, 87, 200; South Korea 200, 226, 227; spillover effects 233; UK 71–72, 134, 178, 184
FinTech Regulatory Sandbox 224
firewalls 208, 209
fiscal policy 49, 60
Florida 31
foreign currency, cryptocurrencies' status as 30, 73, 76, 79, 107, 111, 140, 159–160
forks 12, 41, 120
France: blockchain 247; and the G20 96; Libra (Facebook) 123; offshore financial centres 92; regulation of cryptocurrencies 63–64; repudiation of cryptocurrencies 102; securities law 125–126; tech communities 192
fraud: CFTC 140, 147, 149, 154; China 88; distributed ledger technology

267

(DLT) 240–241; fraud risk 23, 53, 59; initial coin offerings (ICOs) 61, 138, 153, 180–181; investor protection 19; IOSCO concerns about 127; Japan 215–216; regulation of cryptocurrencies 66; Securities Exchange Commission (SEC) 146; Singapore 221; South Korea 84; US 142, 143, 146, 161
free market economics 38
freeriding 122
frequent flyer miles 40, 51, 105
FSHO 218
funds, definition of 31
futures products 3, 32–33, 36, 42, 61; China 209; UK 177; US 140, 142, 147, 149, 159, 162

G7 97
G8 131
G20 41, 83, 96–97, 115, 116, 119, 124, 127, 131, 172, 219–220; Osaka Summit 63, 97, 128, 131, 174, 219; Virtual Asset Service Providers Summit (V20) 97, 219
gambling, Bitcoin trading as 74
gambling laws 91, 139, 202
game only schemes 40
gaming 44, 136, 196
Garlinghouse, Brad 18, 115
gatekeeper regulation 109, 138, 146, 153
General Data Protection Regulation (GDPR) 175
Germany: AML/CTF 110; attitudes to cryptoassets 161, 171–172; Bitcoin-friendly economies 76–77; Bundesbank 172; Federal Financial Supervisory Authority (BaFin) 172; and the G20 96; government control of money 48; private wealth 92; repudiation of cryptocurrencies 102; tech communities 191, 192
Ghent 191
Gibraltar 54
Gledhill, David 221
Global Digital Finance 181–182
global financial crisis (2007/8) 8, 15, 28, 29, 38, 48, 50, 92, 94, 131, 204, 232, 248, 255–256
Global Financial Innovation Network 224
Global Innovation Index 55
Global Policy Council, Bitcoin Foundation 100
Global Stability Report (IMF, 2018) 115

GMO 216
Gnosis 44
gold 28, 41, 47, 51, 54, 60, 100, 105, 135
gold standard 112, 135
Goldman Sachs 234
GoldMint 42
goods and services taxation 75, 187, 188
GovTech Catalyst Fund 178
Greece 111, 135
greed 94
Guardian Vaults 22
Guernsey 92
guidance, regulatory 62, 63, 73, 113

hacking: blockchain 241; distributed ledger technology (DLT) 242; general regulatory issues 58; IMF 114; Japan 82, 213, 217; North Korea 85; risks 2, 21–22; Singapore 220; South Korea 226; US 141, 144, 146
Hague, The 191
Hangzhou 209
hard forks 12
hash functions 7, 11–13, 41, 245
Hayek, Friedrich August von 76, 100
hedging 16n59, 17, 18, 216
Herian, R. 236
Hiobi Pro 206
hodlers 18
Hofrichter, Stefan 36
Hong Kong: Chinese crypto activity in 209; distributed ledger technology (DLT) 238; exchanges 206; gambling laws 202; global cryptoasset hubs 67, 85, 87, 88; private wealth 92; regulatory policy 40, 55, 59, 64, 232; regulatory sandboxes (RSs) 64; tax havens 92
Hoskinson, Charles 18
Hosp, Julian 229
Howey test 32, 159
Hu Bing 202
human rights 102
humanitarian applications 151
Huobi 205, 206, 209
hybrid blockchains 236
hybrid models of cryptoassets 106, 140
hybrid tokens 44
hydroelectricity 208

IBM 37
Iceland 206, 248–249
identity verification: China 211; EU regulation 173; IMF 106, 110–111; IOSCO

INDEX

125; OECD 99, 101; South Korea 227, 228, 229; *see also* know your customer (KYC)

illegal transactions 210

illicit purposes: BIS 120, 121; China 203; cryptoassets generally 41; digital fiat currencies 39; EU regulation 171; evolution of Bitcoin 34; general regulatory issues 48, 49, 50, 60; IMF 110; India 212; OECD 101; offshore financial centres 91, 94; Singapore 220; South Korea 227; UK 179; US 144, 160–161; *see also* AML/CTF; tax evasion

Impak Coin 74

income tax 215

India: attitudes to cryptoassets 89–90; competing agendas 58–59; prohibitions on cryptocurrencies 47, 84, 90; regulatory policy 29, 63, 211–213; using cryptoasset hubs 67; volume growth in cryptoassets 67

indirect exposure to cryptocurrency risk 19

Indonesia 29, 84, 232

inequality 94, 102, 250

inflationary risks 39, 112

information memorandum document 21

ING bank 77

initial coin offerings (ICOs): Australia 75, 76, 188–189; calls for global regulation 103; Canada 190; Cayman Islands 194; China 202, 203, 204, 205–209, 216; distributed ledger technology (DLT) 239; EU regulation 168–169, 173; evolution of Bitcoin 32, 36; fraud 144, 146, 153, 169; geographical distribution of 68–69; "get rich quick" 70; IOSCO concerns about 126; Isle of Man 91; Japan 82, 215–216, 217; Malta 195, 196; OECD concerns 104; profits from 101; regulation 61; regulation of 18–21, 41, 44, 47, 103–104; risks 23; Securities Exchange Commission (SEC) 137–139, 142, 152–153; Singapore 86, 221, 222; South Korea 231; Switzerland 55, 192; UK 180–181; US 56, 137–138, 145

innovation friendliness: BIS 121; Canada 189; countries with tendencies towards 55–56; Estonia 80; Finland 78; IMF 108; Japan 218; Malta 197; practical issues with cryptoassets 53; Singapore 224, 225; UK 178; US 157

Innovation Hub and Regulatory Sandbox (UK FCA) 178

insider trading 32

insurance 22

intangibility of cryptoassets 175

inter-agency cooperation 61

interest payments 14

interest rates 38

International Monetary Fund (IMF) 41, 43, 45, 53, 67, 88, 93, 105–115, 124, 132, 199, 253, 259

international money transfers 205

international multilateral supervisory organisations 64, 96–133

Internet and Mobile Association of India (IAMAI) 89, 211

internet development 151, 161

Internet of Things 197

interoperability, legal 251

interoperability between blockchains 247

interoperability between digital currencies 73

investment: bubbles 69–70; cryptoassets 18–21; futures markets 32–33; ICOs as 56; investment contracts 159, 190–191; investment risks 21–26, 83, 113, 126, 151, 168, 176, 180, 215–216, 221; investment stimulus 49; investor education 127; investor protection 19, 118, 121, 127, 138, 141, 143–144, 150, 203, 229; investors' alert notices 18, 20, 138, 144, 169, 227

Investment Contract Test (ICT) 190–191

Investment Industry Regulatory Organisation of Canada (IIROC) 63, 191

IOSCO (International Organization of Securities Commissions) 18–19, 20, 123–127, 150, 197, 198, 199, 219, 243

IOUs 41–42, 105

Iran 60

Ireland 42–43, 92, 192

IRS (Inland Revenue Service) 33, 102, 140, 154, 192

Isle of Man 54, 91–92

Israel 64, 68, 241n27

ItBit 204

Ithaca HOURS 158

Japan: attitudes to cryptoassets 55–56, 161; Bitcoin-friendly economies 75, 81–83; blockchain 247; Chinese crypto activity in 209, 216; Financial Services

269

Agency 126; hacking 144; merchant numbers 68; price relative to other geographic areas 16; private wealth 92; regulatory policy 21, 64, 206, 213–220, 231, 232; tech communities 210; thefts of Bitcoin 22; Working Group of the Financial System Council 126
Japan Financial Services Agency (JFSA) 213, 216, 217
Japanese Blockchain Association (JBA) 217
Japanese Virtual Currency Exchange Association (JVCEA) 63
Jaxx 74
Jersey 92
Jihan Wu 201
JP Morgan 44, 234

K Star 136
Kansas 157
Katowice 191
Kenya 68, 122
Kickstarter 19
Kirgizstan 84
Klayman, Joshua Ashley 138
KnCMiner 79
know your customer (KYC): India 212; IOSCO 125; Japan 213, 214, 218; OECD 102, 103; offshore financial centres 91; regulatory policy 60; risk management 21; South Korea 227, 228; US 139, 145, 251
know your transaction (KYT) 60
KodakCoins 36
Komono 43
Kook, Ben 209
Korbit 84, 230
Krugman, Paul 10

Lagarde, Christine 113, 114
Lao 232
Larimer, Dan 18
Larsen, Chris 18
Latin America 67–68
LAToken 42
LCH Clearnet 240
Le Maire, Bruno 170–171
Lebanon 92
Ledger X 71, 140
Lee, Charlie 71
legal interoperability 251
legal ownership 25
legal risks 25

legal tender status: exchange tokens 183; India 212; Japan 215, 216; OECD 100; regulation of cryptocurrencies 33, 34, 55; Singapore 220; US 137, 141, 158
legal title 25
Lehman Bros 240
lender of last resort 28, 29, 112, 113
lex cryptographica 20, 132
LG 84
liberalism 67, 81, 232
Liberty Dollars 158
Libra (Facebook) 35, 48, 57, 88, 97, 123, 128–130, 131, 132, 193, 201, 211
Libra Association 129, 130
Library of Congress 61
licences: Australia 76, 188; China 204; EU regulation 167; Financial Action Task Force (FATF) 128; government licences 13; Japan 217; regulation of cryptocurrencies 64; Singapore 225; UK 179; US 146, 151, 157
Lietaer, Bernard 51
Lightning Labs 71
Lightning Network 3, 37, 123
light-touch regulation 154, 231
LiquidApps 43
liquidity risk 111, 122–123, 135, 214
Litecoin 3, 14, 41, 45, 71, 214, 220, 225
Liu Xiaolei 202
Ljubljana 69
loans 155
local alternative currencies 47, 158, 160
local area networks 44
Local Exchange Trading System (LETS) 51
LocalBitcoins 78, 80
location-based data 67
logistics 37
London 69, 71–72, 243
London Stock Exchange 181
Long Island Iced Tea 36
LongFin 2
lost cryptocurrency 1, 18
loyalty programmes 40, 44, 51
Lubin, Joseph 18
Luxembourg 92, 182, 197
Lyfft 129

Macau 92, 202, 232
Maker 44, 45
Maker DAO 45
Malaysia 67, 84, 232
Malta 54, 92, 182, 193, 195–197, 198

INDEX

Malta Financial Services Authority (MFSA) 195–196
Malta Gaming Authority (MGA) 196
Malta Stock Exchange 196
malware 21–22, 69
managed investment scheme (MIS) 188
Mann, Thomas 9
Marcus, David 130
market manipulation 148, 241, 244
market risks 23
marketing restrictions 153, 179, 180, 206
Marshall Islands 234
MAS (Monetary Authority of Singapore) 86, 220–221, 223, 225, 238
Mastercard 129
Mazzant, Amos L 160
McFarland, Mark 207
media 15–16, 122, 206
medical records 37
medium of exchange: cryptoassets as 136; and the definition of money 4, 9; Denmark 79; digital currencies 28, 30, 31; EU regulation 165; IMF (International Monetary Fund) 107; IRS definition 33; local alternative currencies 158; multi-coin world 38; regulation of 49, 109; and taxation 111; UK 72, 175–176, 179; US 160
Mellon, Matthew 18
memoranda of understanding (MOUs) 97, 126, 219
MetaStable 71
Mexico 67
Microsoft 212
Middle East 67, 68
middle parties (lack of) 8, 27, 36, 49, 50, 237
Min Byung-du 231
miners and mining: Bitcoin processing power 252; Canada 74; China 13, 88, 202, 204, 206, 207–208; costs of 153; creation of cryptocurrencies 11, 12, 13, 18; electricity consumption 120; EU regulation 172; geographical distribution of 68; income generation 122; Japan 216; North Korea 85; profit-making 156; regulation of cryptocurrencies 48, 50; Sweden 79; tax 73, 111, 172
Mining-Max 84
Mitsui Sumitomo Insurance 22
Moas, Ronnie 210
mobile payments 111, 211, 237

Monero 241, 244
monetary policy 108, 109, 112, 114, 130, 137, 164
money: debate over cryptocurrencies' status as 9, 28, 29, 30; definition 9, 31, 39–40, 72, 106, 107, 122; and faith/trust 29, 49, 100, 122; monetary value 31
Money Laundering Reporting Office Switzerland (MROS) 61
money transmission laws 48, 121, 144, 155, 156, 196, 251
money-laundering: Australia 186; BIS concerns about 120, 121, 123; blockchain 241; Canada regulation 190; digital global currency 34, 35, 43; distributed ledger technology (DLT) 244; EU regulation 166, 171, 173; Financial Crimes Enforcement Network (FinCEN) 139, 156, 157; G20 concerns 97; investment risks 113; Japan 83, 220; Libra (Facebook) 130; OECD concerns 98, 101; offshore financial centres 54; regulation of cryptocurrencies 49, 59, 60; risks 2, 21, 108; South Korea 228–229; UK 102, 176, 180; UN Office on Drugs and Crime (UNODC) 109; *see also* AML/CTF
Mongolia 232
Montreal 74
Moscovici, Pierre 170
Mt. Gox 22, 49, 59, 69, 214, 218, 220, 247
multi-coin world 37–38
multi-currency countries 55
multilateral clearing 76
multi-lateral netting 240
multilateral regulatory approaches 64, 96–133, 150, 154, 199
multinational corporations 92, 212
multi-party contracts 245
multi-signature (Multi-sig) transactions 100
multi-stakeholder working 102, 196–197
Munchee enforcement action 153
mutual credit systems 51
My Big Coin Pay Inc. 149
Myanmar 232

Nakamoto, Satoshi 9, 10–11, 27, 35
Namecoin 41
NASDAQ 14, 80
National Association of Software and Services Companies (Nasscom) 59

National Attorneys General Training and Research Institute 150
National Committee of Experts on Internet Financial Security 205
national competent authorities (NCAs) 173
National Conference of Commissioners on Uniform State Laws 140–141
National Internet Finance Association (NIFA) 201
national-to-cryptocurrency payments 13
nefarious users 171
negotiability 30
Neo 36
Nepal 84
net neutrality 172
Netherlands 77–78, 92, 191, 192
network tokens 44
network value tokens 44
Neufund Equity Tokens 44
New York 29, 40, 56, 69, 71, 160
New York State Department of Financial Services (NYSDFS) 157
Newcastle, UK 191
Newegg 205
Nigeria 68
Nokia 78
Nomura 2
non-banks 107, 122, 203
non-governmental organisations 252
non-native protocol tokens 44–45
non-profits 129, 192
North American Securities Administrators Association (NASAA) 150
North Korea 16, 58, 60, 85, 111, 226, 232
Norway 43
Novacoin 41
Novogratz, Michale 18
Novosibirsk 191
NXT 252

obliged entities 173
OECD (Organisation for Economic Co-operation and Development) 53, 90, 92, 98–105, 109, 131, 198, 199
OECD 2019 Global Blockchain Policy Forum (OECD GBPF) 102–103
off-chain payments 246
offline cold wallets 218
offshore financial centres (OFCs) 35, 54–55, 62, 76, 88, 90–93, 141, 157, 162, 199
oil 51
OKCoin 205, 206
OKEx 206
OmiseGo 3

online credit exchange 40
open identity standards 130
open source 41, 160, 252
open system cryptoassets 106
operational failures 21–22
operational risk 111
opt-in authorisation regimes 63–64, 99
options contracts 16n60, 17–18, 177
OTC (over the counter) trading 205, 207
OTC derivatives 125
over-regulation 103, 154, 162
oversight and monitoring 61, 119, 125, 142, 148, 149, 151, 164, 173
ownership history 101
ownership representation 125
ownership tokens 176

PACTE (Action Plan for Business Growth and Transformation) 64
Pakistan 87
Panama 92
Panama Papers 62, 90, 91–92, 171, 199
Paradise Papers 62, 90, 91–92, 171, 199
patents 124, 246
Paxful 80
payment finality risks 122
payment instruments 31
payment networks 13, 78, 205
payment provider rules 62
payment system risks 111, 121, 129, 163, 178
Payments Canada 190
PayPal wallets 136
peer review of software coding 66
Peercoin 41
peer-to-peer systems: Bitcoin 8, 27, 47; China 205, 209; and cryptocurrencies 7; distributed ledger technology (DLT) 235; Libra (Facebook) 129; open source 160; regulation 20, 49, 109, 132; UK 180; virtual currencies 39
People's Bank of China (PBOC) 56–57, 88, 201–202, 203, 204, 207, 210
permissioned DLT 124, 236, 245
permissionless DLT 124, 236, 245
Petro 36, 42
Philippines 226, 232
Pierce, Brock 18
piggybacking 122
Pokecoins 136
Poland 191
politically exposed persons (PEPs) 167
Ponzi schemes 10, 23, 35, 84, 149, 221, 254

INDEX

Porter, Michael 85
Powell, Jerome 137
predictions markets 139
pre-payment vouchers 183; *see also* utility tokens
Price, John 76
price crash (2018) 1, 4, 36, 52, 69–70, 96
price surges 1–2, 3, 9
price variations: relative to fiat currencies 17, 27–28; relative to other geographic areas 16–17
price volatility: and Bitcoin as means of payment 120; China 88; cryptocurrencies 3, 14, 23, 24, 27–28, 33; and cryptocurrencies as means of payment 122; different types of cryptoassets 41, 50, 52; EU regulation 169, 170; IMF (International Monetary Fund) 107; investment risks 114; Libra (Facebook) 129; OECD concerns 98; Senate Hearings 154; spillover effects 233; UK regulation 176
Primecoin 41
privacy 89, 130, 137, 238, 243, 246
private currencies 47–48, 51, 57, 100, 106
private digital money 136
private digital tokens 122
private keys 13n34, 23, 25, 182, 236, 244, 247
private money 73, 76
private wealth 244
profit-based taxation 77
prohibitions on cryptocurrencies: BIS 121; China 47, 84, 88, 102, 202, 203–204, 205–206, 208; different types of cryptoassets 41; general regulatory issues 47, 54, 59, 62, 63, 232–233, 249–250; India 90; OECD 99, 101; South Korea 84; UK 47; US 160–161
Project Jasper 190
promise to pay 135, 136
promises registries 36
proof of work 122, 123
proofs of concepts 125
property 33, 40, 111, 140, 160, 175
property transaction rules 33, 36
proxies 36
Prudential Regulation Authority (PRA) 175, 177n169
pseudo-anonymity 106, 180
pseudo-bank accounts 155
public awareness campaigns 127
public keys 236

public ledger technology: and blockchain 8, 11–13; regulation of cryptocurrencies 48; as the underlying technology 3; *see also* distributed ledger technology (DLT)
public versus private provisions of currency 106–107
pubs/bars 72
pump and dump 146
purchase tokens 45
pure cryptocurrencies 45
pyramid financial fraud 49, 88, 203, 227

Qantas 51
Qash 216
Qtum 36
QuadrigaCX 191
quantitative easing 39
quantum encrypted global transactions 114
Quark 41
Quarles, Randal 119
Quoine 216

R3 190
ransomware attacks 2, 69
Ravikant, Naval 71
Realcoin 36
real-time processes 35, 125, 179, 238
Reddit 206
refugees 151
registration schemes 128, 157, 167, 187, 219, 247; *see also* licences
regulatory loopholes 64
regulatory risk 21
regulatory sandboxes (RSs) 64, 102, 182, 194, 196, 224, 239n20
Regulatory State model 255
re-hypothecation 125
Reputation 45
Reserve Bank of India 59, 63, 84, 89, 211–212
retail acceptance *see* acceptance as payment for goods/services
retail financial system 43
retail investors 19, 104, 127, 143
retail stores as places to buy Bitcoin 84
retrofitted regulations 62, 63–64, 181–182
reward tokens 214; *see also* frequent flyer miles
Rice, Gerry 113
Riksbank 79, 88
Ripple 3, 4, 16n62, 18, 35, 42
risk profiles 14–15, 21–26

273

risk-based approaches 128
robotics 80
Rochester, Jordan 2
Rossiello, Elizabeth 71
Roszak, Matthew 18
Russia 34, 36, 42, 68, 92, 191, 210

SAFE Network 43
Safecoin 43
Safello Bitcoin exchange 79
safety deposit technology 22
sales tax 111
Samsung 84
San Francisco 69, 209, 243
sanction powers 168
sanctions-dodging 16, 60, 85, 226
Sandbox Express 224
Sarson, John 229
Saudi Arabia 68
SBI Group 216
scale risk 26, 37
scalping 146
scarcity limits 39, 41, 45, 106, 237; see also miners and mining
Scott, Hugh B 160
script algorithms 41
secrecy 92–93, 192; see also anonymity
Secretariat for International Finance (SIF) 61
Securecoin 41
Securities Exchange Commission (SEC) 18, 23, 32, 56, 97, 137–139, 141–146, 150, 151, 152, 154, 162
Securities Investor Protection Corporation 22
securities law: Canada 190–191; China 203, 210; general regulatory issues 21, 32, 62; IOSCO 123–124; Singapore 86; Switzerland 192–193; US 152–155, 159
security risks 21–22
security token offerings (STOs) 44, 183–184, 188, 191, 239–240
self-certification regimes 33, 149
self-regulation 32, 103, 217–218, 231, 250, 252, 258
semi-autonomous payments 45
Senate Hearings 97
Shadab, Houman 139
shadow banking 118
shared learning 118
shares, digital tokens as 222
shares and bonds issuance regimes 153
short term debt trading 125
sign-up bonuses 20

Silbert, Barry 18, 71
Silk Road 49, 59, 110, 250
silver 28, 47, 51, 135
Singapore: Bitcoin-friendly economies 84, 85–87; cryptoasset hub 67; distributed ledger technology (DLT) 238; evolution of Bitcoin 29; private wealth 92; Quoine 216; regulatory policy 59, 64, 220–225, 232; regulatory sandboxes (RSs) 64
Singapore International Airlines 51
Skype 80
Slovenia 69
Smart Cities Initiative 210
smart contracts 37, 45, 59, 74, 117, 125, 133, 236
smart proprietary notion 37
social media 129, 206; see also Facebook
Sofia 191
soft forks 12
software as commodity 78
solicitations 215, 217
Song Chi-Hyung 18
South Africa 68
South Korea: Bitcoin-friendly economies 75, 83–85; Chinese crypto activity in 209; competing agendas 58–59; merchant numbers 68; price relative to other geographic areas 16; regulatory policy 17, 48, 64, 102, 210, 225–231, 232; self-regulation 103; tech communities 210
sovereign states: and legal tender 100; and money supply 47, 135; price variations between 16–17; and the right to regulate money 9; and taxation 100
speculative nature of cryptocurrencies: China 208; digital global currency 28, 29, 33–34; EU regulation 168; general regulatory issues 49; IOSCO 126; Singapore 220; South Korea 84, 227, 228; US 137
spillover effects 46, 233
spot markets 32, 142, 148–149, 150, 154, 178
spot platforms 141
Square 71
Srinivasan, Balaji 71
stablecoin 35, 104, 131, 164, 184
Stacks 44, 45
Standard & Poor 14
Standing Committee on the Assessment of Vulnerabilities (SCAV) 119
Stark, Elizabeth 71

INDEX

start-ups: Australia 75; Canada 74; China 205; EU regulation 169; Financial Stability Board (FSB) 116; financing 18, 55, 56; Sweden 79–80; UK 71–74
state-backed cryptocurrency 34, 36, 40, 47, 72, 74, 90
Steem 42, 44, 45
Stellar 4, 35
Stockholm 79
store of value 27–29, 30, 39, 72, 90, 101, 107, 111, 122, 159
Strategic Hub for Innovation and Financial technology (FinHub) 162
subpoenas 155, 160
suicides 2
Sun, Justine 88
superpowers 56–58
supply chain diligence 103
supply chains 37
supply limits 38–39, 41, 45, 106, 237; *see also* miners and mining
suspicious transaction reporting 128, 207, 223, 229, 252
sustainable development 102
swap execution facilities 140
swaps markets 147
Sweden 79–80, 88
Swedish Financial Supervisory Authority 79
SWIFT 237, 238
Swiss Financial Market Supervisory Authority (FINMA) 55, 61
Switzerland: attitudes to cryptoassets 161; Bitcoin presence 29, 69; digital currencies in 43; Libra Association 129; private wealth 92; regulatory policy 51, 55, 58, 61, 191–193; tax evasion 93; tax havens 92; tech communities 210
synthetic hegemonic money 72
systemic risk 63, 65, 111, 124, 147, 248
systemically important financial institutions (SIFIs) 118

tail risks scenarios 111
Taipei 232
Taiwan 85, 92
Tallinn Stock Exchange 80
Tampa 69
Tanzania 68
tax: Australia 74–75, 187, 188; business taxes 81, 93; Canada 190; capital gains taxation 60, 73, 111, 140, 172, 187, 228, 248; Cayman Islands 194; consumption taxes 215; corporate taxation 215, 228; and cryptocurrencies' status as foreign currency 30; Denmark 79; Estonia 81; EU regulation 172; Germany 76, 77; goods and services taxation 75, 187, 188; IMF (International Monetary Fund) 111; income tax 215; India 89, 212; Japan 215; Malta 196; payment in cryptocurrency 52, 60, 140; payment in legal tender 102; profit-based taxation 77; sales tax 111; South Korea 228; Switzerland 193; tax havens 91–92; UK position on Bitcoin as private money 73; VAT (value added tax) 30, 73, 78, 102, 111, 172, 248; virtual currency as property 33
tax avoidance 16, 171
tax evasion: BIS 120, 121; evolution of Bitcoin 33, 34, 35; general regulatory issues 49, 54, 60; IMF 110–111, 114; India 212; OECD 98; offshore financial centres 93; risks 21, 108; South Korea 229; UK 176
tax havens 54, 91–92, 93, 94
tax risks 24–25
Tech Bureau 216
Tech City 55
Techfin 122; *see also* Fintech
Tel Aviv 69
Telegram 205, 208
Tencent 201, 207
TenX 222, 229
Terra 51–52
Terracoin 41
terrorism financing: Australia regulation 186; blockchain 241; EU regulation 167, 171, 174; Financial Crimes Enforcement Network (FinCEN) 139; investment risks 110, 113; UK regulation 176, 180; *see also* AML/CTF
Tesla 78
Tether 14, 42
Texas 157
Tezos 14
Thailand 67, 92, 102, 232, 248
theft 2, 11, 22, 69, 98, 161, 218, 244, 247
third parties 27, 33, 39, 57, 117, 244
Thomson Reuters 196
Time Dollars 158
time stamps 12, 236
token creation activities regulation 63; *see also* miners and mining
Token Day (Singapore) 86

275

token fundraising activity 203, 210; *see also* initial coin offerings (ICOs)
token listing exchange, autonomous 209
token sales 19, 36, 168
tokenomics 104
tokens versus coins 42
Toronto 74
tourism 82
trading platforms: Australia 76; Canada 191; China 204; IOSCO 127; Japan 82; OECD 101; Singapore 220, 223; US 141, 142–143, 151
transaction confirmations 35
transaction fees/costs 8, 108, 122, 125, 161, 237, 238, 250
transaction speeds 26, 29, 37, 108, 114, 123, 125, 129, 236, 237, 238
transaction verification 50
transparency 36–37, 83, 86, 106, 110, 136, 141, 142, 147, 167, 179, 252
trapdoors 244
trial and error computations 11
Tron 4, 88
Trump, Donald 48, 50, 52, 256
trust 99, 102, 106, 120, 121, 122, 130, 164
trusted agencies 106, 132
trust-less transactions 99
trusts law 25
TRX 88
Turkey 68
Twitter 206

Uber 129
UK: Action Fraud 23; AML/CTF 110; attitudes to cryptoassets 171; Bitcoin-friendly economies 71–74; Brexit 134; capital gains taxation 60; cryptoasset hub 94; digital currencies in 30; distributed ledger technology (DLT) 243–244; Financial Conduct Authority (FCA) 18, 64; financial services 93; Fintech 71–72, 134, 178, 184; innovation friendliness 29; mercantile usage 30; private wealth 92; prohibitions on cryptocurrencies 47; regulatory policy 40, 49, 58, 59, 64, 175–186, 198, 239n20; Select Committee Hearings 97; tax 24, 102; tech communities 191, 192; Treasury 175, 177, 181, 184, 185, 238
Ukraine 68
UN Office on Drugs and Crime (UNODC) 109
under-reporting 33, 34

Uniform Law Commission (ULC) 140–141
United Arab Emirates 92
units of account 30, 76, 106, 107, 120, 122, 147, 171, 172
unlimited issues 106
unofficial private currencies 51
Upbit 230
Uphold 36
US: AML/CTF 110; arbitrage 17; Bitcoin 69, 71; concerns over cryptoassets 97; Congress 32; Constitution 135; cryptoasset hub 94; cryptoassets working group (US) 97; currency controls 50; distributed ledger technology (DLT) 243–244; ending of net neutrality 172; Federal regulators 31–32; Federal Reserve 43, 137; federal versus state regulation 140–142, 154–155; Financial Crimes Enforcement Network (FinCEN) 34; Financial Industry Regulatory Authority (FINRA) 126; financial services 93; FinTech 134; global reserve currency 56; government control of money 48; growth in cryptocurrency 68; innovation friendliness 29; insurance 22; IRS 33; legal status 31; Libra (Facebook) 123, 130; potential cryptoasset regulation 152–162; price relative to other geographic areas 16–17; private wealth 92; privately issued currency 47; prohibitions on cryptocurrencies 47, 160–161; regulatory policy 32, 40, 48, 56, 64, 66, 137–152, 198, 250–251; regulatory sandboxes (RSs) 182; Securities Exchange Commission (SEC) 18, 23, 32, 56, 137; Securities Investor Protection Corporation 22; Senate Banking Committee 147, 154; Senate Hearings 143, 152, 154; Supreme Court 32, 159, 160; and Switzerland 192; tax 24, 93, 102; tech communities 210; Treasury 97, 139, 154, 156; Trump on cryptocurrencies 48; Virtual Commodities Association Working Group 63
usage tokens 45
User Protection Funds 209
utility tokens 45, 145, 176, 183, 193

value: acceptance by purchasers 101; digital representations of value 105–106, 175; EU regulation 163, 165; inherent

INDEX

value of Bitcoin 8; intrinsic value 29, 36, 47, 90; Japan 218; versus medium of exchange 4, 23, 28, 30; store of value 27–29, 30, 39, 72, 90, 101, 107, 111, 122, 159; unbacked nature of 106; volatility in 29
Vanbex Group 74
Vancouver 51, 69, 74
Vancouver LETS scheme 51
VAT (value added tax) 30, 73, 78, 102, 111, 172, 248
Vavilov, Valery 18
Venezuela 34, 36, 42, 47, 54, 60, 67, 111
venture capital 19, 124, 157
Venus 48
Vermont 140
ViaBTC 206
Vietnam 47, 84, 232, 259
Virtual Asset Service Providers Summit (V20) 97, 219
virtual asset service providers (VASP) 128
virtual commodities 57
Virtual Commodities Association Working Group 63
virtual communities 163
virtual currencies: CFTC (Commodities Futures Trading Commission) 149; definition 40, 175; historical background 136; IMF 105, 108, 110; and private issuers' credibility 106; as securities 139; virtual currency exchanges 250–251
Virtual Currencies Report (ECB) 164
virtual financial assets (VFAs) 195–196
virtual private networks 88, 94, 208
Visa 129
volatility rates 14, 15, 33; *see also* price volatility

Wall Street Blockchain Alliance's Legal Working Group 138
Wall Street regulated futures trading 3
wallets: after death 18; anti-money laundering (AML) 183; Australia 76; characteristics of 13; China 205, 208; deposit insurance schemes 111; EU regulation 168, 173; geographical distribution of 68; India 89; Japan 218; legal risks 25; Libra (Facebook) 129; and location-based data 67; Malta 196; offline cold wallets 22, 218; PayPal wallets 136; regulation of 62; Singapore 224; statistics on active 13; as storage 155
WannaCry 2, 69
Wanxiang Blockchain Labs 210
wash trading 148
weak currencies, countries with 54
WeChat 205, 208
WeChatPay 207
Weibo 206
Weinberg, Joseph 103
WhatsApp 129
whitelist approaches 64
wholesale payments 118, 190
wills 36
Winklevoss, Tyler 18
WIR 51, 55
work tokens 45–46
World Bank 105, 124, 199
World Economic Forum 244
world reserve currency status 34–35
World Trade Organisation (WTO) 244, 253
Worldcoin 41
Wright, A. 7, 20
WTO Trade Facilitation Agreement 244
Wuermeling, Joachim 171

Xapo 55
XCP 214
XL Catlin 22
XRP 14, 18, 183

Yellen, Janet 137
Youbit 85, 226
Yuko Kawai 82

Zaif 216
Zcash 43, 45, 241, 244
Zhao, Changpeng 18
Ziddu.com 2
Zimbabwe 54
Zug city 191–192
Zurich 69